Preface to Peasantry

SOUTHERN CLASSICS SERIES
John G. Sproat and Mark M. Smith, Series Editors

THE BLACK BELT'S RIDDLE—TO WHOM DOES THIS COTTON BELONG: TO THE TENANT
FARMER WHO GREW IT, TO THE LANDLORD WHO FURNISHED THE TENANT, OR TO
THE BANKER WHO FINANCED THE LANDLORD?

AN EX-SLAVE—HE WASHED HIS HANDS AND HIS FACE FOR HIS FIRST PICTURE

AN EX-SLAVE—SHE OWNS A SMALL FARM WEST OF THE RIVER IN MACON COUNTY

Preface to Peasantry

A TALE OF TWO BLACK BELT COUNTIES

Arthur F. Raper

New Introduction by Louis Mazzari

University of South Carolina Press

Published in cooperation with the Institute for Southern Studies
of the University of South Carolina

New introduction © 2005 University of South Carolina

Cloth edition published by the University of North Carolina Press, 1936

This paperback edition published in Columbia, South Carolina,
by the University of South Carolina Press, 2005

Manufactured in the United States of America

09 08 07 06 05   5 4 3 2 1

Library of Congress Cataloging-in-Publication Data

Raper, Arthur Franklin, 1899–
  Preface to peasantry : a tale of two black belt counties / Arthur F.
Raper ; new introduction by Louis Mazzari.
    p. cm. — (Southern classics series)
  Published in cooperation with the Institute for Southern Studies of the
University of South Carolina.
  Originally published: Chapel Hill : University of North Carolina Press,
1936.
  Includes index.
  ISBN 1-57003-603-9 (pbk. : alk. paper)
    1. Land tenure—Southern States. 2. Macon County (Ga.)—Rural
conditions. 3. Greene County (Ga.)—Rural conditions. 4. United States
—Economic policy—1933–1945. I. Title. II. Series.
  HD207.R3 2005
  333.3'09758'513—dc22   2005006859

Publication of the Southern Classics series is made possible in part by the
generous support of the Watson-Brown Foundation.

CONTENTS

PART SIX
INSTITUTIONS

SERIES EDITORS' PREFACE

As PASSIONATE about exposing racial and social injustices in the South in the 1920s and 1930s as he was relentless in systematically investigating and documenting them, Arthur Raper ranked among the leading white southern social scientists of his day. *Preface to Peasantry* charts the impact of the Great Migration on the rural South in depressing if compelling detail. Louis Mazzari's elegant new introduction echoes the very best in Raper's work and explains why this classic study remains of enduring value to sociologists, anthropologists, and historians.

Southern Classics returns to general circulation books of importance dealing with the history and culture of the American South. Sponsored by the Institute for Southern Studies and the South Caroliniana Society of the University of South Carolina, the series is advised by a board of distinguished scholars who suggest titles and editors of individual volumes to the series editors and help establish priorities in publication.

Chronological age alone does not determine a title's designation as a Southern Classic. The criteria also include significance in contributing to a broad understanding of the region, timeliness in relation to events and moments of peculiar interest to the American South, usefulness in the classroom, and suitability for inclusion in personal and institutional collections on the region.

MARK M. SMITH
JOHN G. SPROAT
Series Editors

[ix]

NEW INTRODUCTION

A YOUNG HOBO in dusty bib overalls with a bundle in a red bandana tied to a stick and a hungry look on his sunburned face stood by the side of a dirt road and pointed a thick thumb at the Ford that slowed as it passed by, then circled back, and stopped. The passenger door flung open.

"Well, I'm going to Atlanta," Arthur Raper called out over the running motor of his Model T. "If you want to go, why, jump in." Raper, himself a white southerner, was a sociologist traveling the backwaters of the South in the fall of 1930, investigating the scenes of recent lynchings, poking at a rural populace that still often practiced a vigilante justice. He had just left the small downtown of Ocilla, Georgia, where several days of buttonholing people at the town hall and the barbershop, the filling station and the luncheonette had left him with nothing on a race murder that had sparked the town a couple of weeks earlier. He was tired and frustrated, ready for home. And yet, who knew? This young fellow might know something about the lynching.

Turned out, this fellow knew a great deal about the lynching. In fact, in hearty response to Raper's questions and encouragement, he rooted around in his deep pants pockets and held out in his huge, calloused palm a shriveled, black toe.

He was on the road to Texas to look for work, the fellow said, and he planned to have it ossified when he got there. Turn it into a stone to use for a type-end or a paperweight. Or maybe he could sell it. His friends had many different plans for what they would do with their own souvenirs. Raper tried to remember the names he mentioned—Jim Stokes and Lon Ripple and all the rest—all the information Raper had not been able to gather from the folks in town.

All of a sudden, though, the fellow realized he had been talking a lot. "Hey," he stopped himself and demanded, "who are you anyhow?"

"I'm an ethnologist."

"Oh." The fellow paused. "They deal with the Okefenokee Swamp, don't they?"

"Yes," Raper agreed, "and a lot of other things, too."

He saw that the fellow had noticed how low they were getting on gas. *I'm not about to fill this thing up for that guy to knock me on the head and drive off in,* Raper thought. His heart was racing, and he knew he needed some help. Raper never carried a gun.

He found a well-lighted filling station, pulled in, and raised a commotion. He shouted to the attendant to fill it up, catching the attention of the station's several loafers. He pulled out his wallet and handed the tramp a few bills. "Well, this is as far as I can take you," he told him loudly and cheerfully. In a few seconds, through a spray of gravel, Raper had aimed his headlights at the dust of the road, as though he were stabbing with two small knives against the big, dark night.[1]

Raper knew how lucky he had been to have escaped Ocilla unharmed. The young tramp was hitching the country road of an old South whose white folks would swap stories of all sorts with a friendly stranger who shared an accent and a style of speech. Even though in terms of money and power the North called the tune the South sang, its ideas still seemed far away. But now, in part through Raper's work, the North's opprobrium and control seemed to come dressed in southern clothes. Far from playing the role of a dispassionate social scientist—or a benign ethnologist—Raper's documentary sociology, of which *Preface to Peasantry* is the best example, made him witness to an emotionally charged cultural transformation. A community's racial practices—whether concerning mob murder or public education, police protection or health care or sharecropping—were no longer a community's own closely held business. By the middle of the 1930s, when *Preface to Peasantry* was published, Raper had become instrumental in making such practices the stuff of wire services, press releases, and scientific investigation.

Arthur Raper was an unlikely hero for the civil rights movement. A white, southern farm boy, son of a Carolina tobacco planter, born just at the start of the twentieth century in a land where the codification of racial inequality was an element of progressive legislation, he nevertheless would be among the first southerners, white or black, to look scientifically and systematically at the racial caste system of the South. Raper's is the story of a social and political radical grown from conservative roots during the time of transition from agrarian to industrialized America—a radical who began his career traveling the woods and fields of the rural South and ended it advocating Jeffersonian democracy throughout Asia and Africa. In *Preface to Peasantry* and the other books he wrote during the 1930s, Raper claimed the South's longstanding reliance on the sharecropping system and cheap factory labor was implicated in its social and racial problems. Raper was a strong advocate of New Deal federal planning and a severe critic of the hoary, but persistent, doctrine of states' rights. To be sure, these were not the most popular positions to take among the southern demagogues and the farm folk of the rural South. He was a social scientist and a public intellectual, a white southerner who took up the issues of race and class to advocate change in a part of the world where adherence to the past was almost pathological. "When I look back," he concluded from the vantage point of the 1970s, "I find I have nearly always worked at matters that were but barely tolerated."[2]

Raper was at the forefront of white civil rights advocates who recognized the value of pragmatic social science and the mass media in countering racial and social injustice. The television coverage of the marches on Selma and Birmingham that had so much impact in the 1960s had its roots in Raper's work in the 1930s.

As an activist intensely concerned with race relations and rural poverty, Raper became a progressive and controversial voice throughout the South. His particular lens was rural sociology, and he studied what he saw as the feudal nature of southern race relations during the time that Memphis, Atlanta, Chattanooga, Chicago, and Detroit were drawing impoverished blacks from all across the southern countryside. He not only studied the way the agrarian South was industrializing, by fits and starts, but also opened to public view the people who were being forced into the modern era, the refugees pushed from their farms and pulled to the cities of the South and North. To Raper, giving more people—blacks and poor whites as well—a greater stake in their own communities was a rational response to the onset of industrialization. The South's social, economic, and legal caste system was irrational and anachronistic. As long as the system survived, the nation would have trouble facing up to the demands of a mechanized, urbanized environment. A more democratic South with a rational distribution of the new agricultural technologies and machines would mean an opportunity finally to fulfill the Jeffersonian ideal of the self-sufficient family farm as well as a better chance of managing the industrializing future.

Raper saw himself as a pragmatic realist. It was realistic for the people who worked the land to have a say in both what happened to that land and who benefited from its use. His homeland, the South, however, had obscured reality with its concocted past. He thought conservatives were recalcitrants, who in a time of rapid change were trying to stave off the inevitable collapse of obsolete racial customs, social conduct, and economic practices. They were clinging in a raging river to a branch about to break from the bank.

Right through the Depression, Raper's research, writing, and social advocacy carried him into the last remnants of the Old South. To Raper, as a politically minded modernist, race was a test of how realistic the South was in its approach to the twentieth century. *Preface to Peasantry* was the report card of that test, a documentary study from the roots up of the way the Great Migration was draining the Black Belt farms of the South and creating America's newly forming ghettos.

Because the South was undergoing such rapid change in the 1920s and 1930s, it was a tremendous place to ask some crucial questions: How will the nation respond to a dramatic shift from rural to urban life? What will be the impact of new technologies on folk cultures and political ideologies? What roles will women play in the newly industrialized nation? Raper talked about these questions in cotton fields and on shop floors, in legislative hearings and in church groups, in newspapers, in magazines, over radio broadcasts, and in his own books. In so doing, Raper himself moved from the absolute periphery of modernity to its very point of incursion into the heart of the vanishing past.

THE CROSSROADS OF COMMUNITY AND ENTERPRISE

In *Preface to Peasantry,* Raper mined the ordinary in the life of the South, in part, because he knew southern folkways from the inside out. Raper's father was a yeoman farmer, a Scot, who sacrificed his family cropland, acre by acre, to put his eight children through college. Raper's German mother was a Moravian, a member of a close-knit religious community founded in Central Europe on radical egalitarian values, which moved as a self-sustaining community, first to Pennsylvania, then to Winston-Salem. Raper was raised to respect both the individual yeoman farmer and the importance of a cooperative-minded community.

Born in 1899, Raper grew up thinking about society, politics, and government during the years when the telephone, the automobile, and a decline of church influence in civic affairs were changing Davidson County, North Carolina. Raper's father, Mr. Frank, as everyone called him, farmed tobacco, and he and Julia Crouse Raper raised their family outside the hamlet of Arcadia, a few miles south of Winston-Salem, in the Carolina piedmont. Mr. Frank was among the progressive voices in town and one of the county's most civic-minded benefactors. He gave the county five of his best acres in the mid-1910s, for example, then helped build a consolidated schoolhouse on the land—and then the road that led to it. In many ways the symbolism of Raper's childhood and homelife sounds like a mythic tale of progressivism. The Raper family farmhouse was built near the intersection of Community and Enterprise roads.

In the 1910s Davidson County's most pressing questions revolved around education and community planning, and Raper's own family exemplified the change from isolated farming village to progressive community. To raise one tuition after another, as each of the Raper children went off to the University of North Carolina or North Carolina State and, eventually, Harvard and Columbia, Mr. Frank and his boys cut down their trees, chopped them into wheel spokes, loaded their wagon, and rode the muddy roads to sell them in Winston-Salem. Raper wrote that September after September, as each son and daughter left for college, the farm's tall trees seemed to gather closer and closer around the old house.

Mr. Frank's racial views, unorthodox as they were in rural Carolina, were consistent with his concern for community improvement. "He always said that if the Negroes had a chance to own their own land, they would be good citizens," Arthur explained. Raper's own work in race relations stems from the conviction that, in his homeland, the racial caste system was the most obvious breach of, and obstacle to, participatory democracy. He never underwent any conversion experience, so to speak, in regard to his views on racial equality. In fact, he remembered his mother chiding him as a child for the way he always liked to play with neighboring black children. He grew up in a southern farm family that exemplified what he came to identify as the values of Jeffersonian agrarianism, including equal rights and responsibilities for everyone, regardless of race or class.

At Chapel Hill in the early 1920s, Raper was greatly influenced by the history he studied with Frank Porter Graham, who as president of UNC became one of the South's foremost progressive voices. In 1924 Raper went on to Vanderbilt for a master's degree in sociology, then returned to Chapel Hill two years later to work on his doctorate with Howard Odum, the voice of regionalism and the don of southern sociology, becoming involved in race activism and working on related projects, including studies of chain gangs and opportunities for black workers in Tampa's cigar factories.

Sociology, as practiced at Chapel Hill, was broad enough to include community studies, agricultural practices, and folktales. As a sociologist, Raper concerned himself with everything from the legal impediments African Americans faced to the way blacks and whites arranged themselves around the hot stove in a small-town general store. He was among the first generation of southern public intellectuals, an engaged academic in a region where anti-intellectualism had a long and healthy tradition, where change was considered a repudiation of principles, and where the topic of race was explosive. Raper's sociology was a secular, scientific activism, shorn of Christianity and moralism, but also of positivism. He agreed with John Dewey that social science could produce the kinds of knowledge needed for rational action in a society undergoing rapid transformation, and he adapted Dewey's pragmatism to the peculiar conditions of the South.

Raper's work was also influenced by the Chicago school of sociology, which developed a research protocol in the 1910s that employed a variety of previously ignored sources—from workers' diaries and newspapers to handbills and club minutes—integrated into a big-picture framework. John Shelton Reed makes the case that by the 1950s much of the kind of work produced in Chicago and Chapel Hill in the 1920s and 1930s would have been considered too broad for academic social science.[3]

Howard Odum was bustling Will Alexander around Chapel Hill one spring day in 1926 when Alexander asked him to recommend a researcher who would like to leave the old brick buildings in Chapel Hill and get out and work among the people, as he put it. Alexander was a former Methodist minister, who founded the Commission on Interracial Cooperation (CIC) in 1919 as a way to curb the racial violence that accompanied the return of black soldiers after the Great War. The CIC began by providing African Americans quiet assistance offered in Christian charity. But once Raper jumped at the chance to get out among the people and joined the staff, the CIC moved from faintly Victorian good works to modern sociology, and from a conciliatory attitude toward white supremacy to a strategy of using public-relations tactics against the South's most egregious race laws and social crimes. While the CIC was never as liberal as the NAACP or many local black activist organizations and it never denounced segregation, Raper helped Alexander push the interracial commission toward a more aggressive stance, armed with the modern weapons of social science and a documentary approach to questions of racial equality. To black activists— W. E. B. DuBois and Charles S. Johnson in particular—Raper's first book, *The Tragedy of Lynching,* a study of mob violence published in 1933, was the first crack they saw in white, southern racism, the first indisputable sign that they had dependable allies within the scientific community and within the white South.

Through the first half of the 1930s, at the height of its efforts, during the depth of the Depression, the CIC created the nation's first mass-media, public-relations campaign to promote racial justice, first by investigating lynching, then through studies (including *Preface to Peasantry*) that looked at the specifics of how Jim Crow repudiated democracy and shaped the South, from the intimate details of the racial dances played out in general stores and county courthouses to the way it controlled the agriculture and economy of the region and was retarding the South's ability to modernize.

THE BELLWETHER OF DEMOCRACY

In 1927 Raper had asked Alexander to support a study to consider why were black tenants and sharecroppers still moving to

the cities and northward by the thousands, years after the soldiers had returned from the Great War? To study the question
closely, Raper went to a place where he could watch and measure as the Old South disappeared beneath the tide of gasoline
and electricity, mass media, and a national, free-market economy. Raper found that a large number of the refugees who
had landed in Atlanta were from Greene County, southeast of
Atlanta, in Georgia's piedmont region. In fact, during the course
of the 1920s, Greene's population had dropped by a third. Raper
and Alexander decided to contrast Greene with a county from
which few had left, hoping to throw into clearer relief the reasons for Greene County's staggering out-migration. Very few
had left nearby Macon County, so they had their test. Was it
because race relations were better in Macon County? Economic
conditions? Political opportunities? Farming practices?[4]

Preface to Peasantry was to be a look at the whole of a society, at all the dynamics—social, racial, political, economic, and
legal—swirling around the transformation of the rural South on
the cusp of the modern age, where the death of the plantation
system had coincided with the plague of the boll weevil, from
which a vast, landless underclass was being driven off the land
and into the new cities of the industrial age. Beyond its masses
of statistics and its controlled, detached tone, *Preface to Peasantry* was a wholesale critique of the system of beliefs at the core
of white southern society.

Published in 1936, *Preface to Peasantry* is a comprehensive
picture of farming life—in all its homely virtues and awful sins
—by the last generation of Americans for whom the small
farmer was still seen as the bellwether of democracy. The way
people lived in farming towns was important to Raper—as it
was to DuBois and Alexander, to Franklin Roosevelt, Walter
White, Henry Wallace, Margaret Mead, John Dollard, and many
others—because rural life was still at the center of the nation's
sense of itself. While Raper was writing, many around him
believed that if they could make small-town America more

equitable, democracy might have a chance in the metastasiz-
ing cities of the industrial future. *Preface to Peasantry* was re-
searched and written with the breath of the ghetto on Raper's
neck.

Preface to Peasantry expresses Raper's belief that in southern
culture and society, race, politics, and economics were inextrica-
bly bound together. It was the South's rigid race and class lines
that created both its economic feudalism and those elements—
the one-party system, the white primary, and the poll tax—that
sapped the democratic process. He was aware of the South's
position as an economic colony, but he viewed the region's own
racial and social barriers as its primary limitation.

Raper and Alexander wanted to study how life in the Black
Belt had changed under the social and economic dislocation of
the Great Depression. In the late 1920s, Raper had visited all the
black and white farms in both counties, and he had visited all
the schools. In the fall of 1934, after finishing his work on *The
Tragedy of Lynching,* Raper returned to Greene and Macon
counties to assess the Depression's damage and to examine the
effects of the New Deal on the lives of small farmers and sharecroppers. The result, *Preface to Peasantry,* gave scientific backing to the liberal view that racial injustice injures both black and
white. Raper focused on the debilitating effects of racial inequalities, particularly in education, that resulted in an evermore
dependent population of blacks and whites, both. He visited
every family of black owners, tenants, and croppers in both
counties to gather information about them and about family
members who had moved to the city. And he spent a great deal
of time hanging around and talking with blacks and whites
in Greensboro and Montezuma, the two county seats, and be-
friending people, eccentrics and local leaders. During the winter
of 1935, Raper tramped through one cold Negro schoolhouse
after another in Montezuma and Macon City and Friar's Point,
Georgia, where the condition of walls and ceilings offered a ready

opportunity, as he would write, for the study of geography, mete-orology, and astronomy.

Raper's research convinced him that the source of Greene's poverty was the continuing hold of the traditions of the planta-tion economy, from its poor soil conservation practices to the social and economic inequalities it had fostered. Both counties were deep in the Black Belt, but Greene had been settled in the late eighteenth century and was a region of Old South planta-tions, while Macon became a solid cotton producer only after the Civil War. Raper concluded that Greene County's older planta-tions had more cleanly stripped the soil of its fecundity than had Macon's, thereby forcing sharecroppers off the land. Greene County had suffered longer under a decaying plantation system. Where smaller, more diversified farms were the norm—in Macon County and certain parts of Greene—farm families had survived.

In the late 1910s, the boll weevil had hit Greene County harder than it had Macon, and Raper examined in detail how this had happened. "It seems clear," he concluded, "that Macon's cotton output is the most important reason why her popula-tion remained relatively stable between 1920 and 1930, while Greene's decreased so much." Macon's soil, Raper found, had a larger gravel content, which meant it reflected the sun's heat and killed more of the weevil larvae. Beyond that Macon County had fewer acres covered in the sedge, brambles, and pine where the weevils hibernated.[5]

Although the boll weevil was the immediate cause of the exo-dus, Raper wrote, the fundamental problem was the plantation system itself, with its reliance on cotton and its lack of diversi-fied and self-sustaining practices. Instead of drawing out the implications of boll weevil infestation, Raper focused on the sociology of the dying plantation. He used the question of migra-tion as a wedge to begin an assessment of the racial inequalities that existed in both counties. He tucked away the weevil in a chapter on population movements, in the book's midsection, and seldom mentioned it again. The facts surrounding soil content and weevil larvae were not something that he could fix. He chose instead to see Greene County as Macon's cautionary tale, a malignant case further advanced. The obsolete plantation system—with its agriculturally destructive overreliance on cotton and with the social injustices that adhered to it—was unable to handle a blow such as the weevil. A more democratic-minded system, using diversified agriculture, would not have thrown families off the land they worked. Raper saw the boll weevil as the straw—"a heavy one, 'tis true"—that broke Greene County's back, but he believed the county's longstanding social, political, and environmental practices weighed even more heavily in its crash.

Raper was fascinated by the dynamic between a people's culture and the way they used their land, in what he called "man-land" relations. In the context of Greene County, he concluded that the culture and economy of slavery continued its sway into the twentieth century. He found that plantation agriculture, holding out against modern democracy, was ruining the South's chance to manage a change that would soon be sweeping across the land. The plantation system relied on a workforce that was not only amenable to instruction, but under complete control. Its workers lived in housing provided by the landowner, accepted the landlords' and merchants' accounting, and remained landless. Raper saw that the shiftlessness and irresponsibility of both black and white hands—about which owners so often complained—were actually required by the plantation system. The viability of the system was threatened when tenants accumulated property or exhibited any independence.

"A CHANCE TO BECOME MORE INDEPENDENT?"

When Raper examined the effects of the New Deal in the second half of the book, the criterion he used to judge federal programs was this: "Is the New Deal going to make farm tenants more

dependent or more independent? Will it result in a wider ownership of land, or a further concentration of it? Will it aid in the
transformation of the old plantation or will it merely extend its
life past the time of its natural and otherwise inevitable death?"[6]
His answers to these questions were mixed and ambiguous.

He found that wide racial differences characterized the administration of most New Deal programs in Greene and Macon
counties. Whites on relief fared much better than blacks. Ana-
lyzing Greene's Civil Works Administration (CWA) and Federal
Emergency Relief Administration (FERA) expenditures, for
example, Raper concluded that rural black schools, which were
in greatest need of improvement, received few federal resources.
The benefits of the Civilian Conservation Corps (CCC) were virtually limited to whites. The National Recovery Act (NRA)
unintentionally pushed employers to cut jobs from their payrolls,
rather than raise the wages for them.[7]

Raper saw New Deal programs, by and large, as administered
too timidly to assist those who most needed help. The Agricultural Adjustment Act (AAA), for one example, favored the Black
Belt's wealthy: planters, businessmen, and cotton factors received the lion's share of agency disbursements. The Bankhead
Allotment Bill, for another, was a backward-looking response at
a time that required systemic change. In an attempt to cap farmers' taxes, the bill fixed the number of cotton bales that would be
tax-free. Because that number was based on the crop production
of the most recent—poor—years rather than pegged at the years
of highest yield, during the 1910s, Raper saw the bill making
permanent the depression from which Greene County was just
emerging.[8]

He described the powerful fear of change in the southern
power structure, that is, until the planters and landlords discov-
ered that they could take advantage of the New Deal programs
themselves. In the past landlords had found it useless to press
their tenants for payments of their debts; they knew their tenants

had virtually no access to cash. But now, Raper observed, tenants with relief checks in hand could be pursued more profitably.[9]

After scores of interviews, talks, asides, conversations, and jokes, in dozens of courthouses, swamps, dance joints, and cotton fields, Raper found little consensus among rural Georgians about the New Deal programs in general or in particular. Many farmers who favored the cotton-reduction program, for example, resented the relief aid, and vice versa. "At almost any place in these counties where people come together," Raper observed, "various reactions to the New Deal and particularly to the relief program will be heard. Some will say that it is ruining labor, others that it is all wrong, or that it is doing some good, or that it is indispensable."[10]

Still and all, *Preface to Peasantry* struck a tone of hopefulness about both the usefulness of federal programs and the willingness of rural southerners to work cooperatively. Raper wrote with confidence, for example, about a Greene County immunization project that saved many poor children from diphtheria. "It was really a county-wide service, for even though a fee of twenty-five cents was asked, any person who could not pay it was served without cost," he explained. "This project seems to demonstrate that a rural county can cooperate with the federal government in serving all the people."[11]

Beyond hopefulness Raper's on-the-ground study reported that the New Deal did much real good, in spite of its deficiencies. Raper heard time and again, from all kinds of people, that without the New Deal their suffering would have been much greater. Black and white farmers and workers told Raper that federal money kept them from hunger and homelessness and bankruptcy in the fall of 1934 and all through 1935.

It was clear to Raper that Greene and Macon counties, along with the rural South as a whole, reaped definite benefits from the New Deal. Even though the South insisted on wage differentials based on race and had the lowest wages under the NRA and

CWA, the AAA programs approximated the national standard. Compared with wealthy whites, black and poor white southerners were faring badly at the hands of New Deal programs; but because they had been so devastated, the little that the dispossessed received had made a big difference on their tables, and by the mid-1930s the South appeared to be moving toward recovery.[12]

The dispassionate approach and tone Raper maintains throughout *Preface to Peasantry* feels tentative, perhaps, in its criticism of the obvious injustices he is reporting. The incredible inequalities of the educational systems he describes make a twenty-first-century reader want to push Raper into finger-pointing denunciation. Instead he gives us statistics, and we may even feel that he is disinclined to push his fellow white southerners too far—that he may not have been so liberal after all. And yet the measured tone reflected a confident belief that science and objectivity were the ways to win the future. For instance Raper starts his consideration of the New Deal effects on Greene and Macon counties, with a bland and unpromising opening sentence: "The program of the Georgia state executive has not always paralleled the efforts of the national administration."[13]

In truth Gov. Eugene Talmadge was a prototypical demagogue, a race-baiting, pseudo-populist, a southern lawyer whose homespun drawl drew in the white farm folk and belied his fealty to big industry and finance. For Raper to write that Talmadge "has not always paralleled the efforts" of the New Deal was so understated as to be silly. Talmadge may, in fact, have been Roosevelt's most bitter enemy, a political hack who attacked the New Deal and dragged his feet at every reform for the sake of lower taxes for the wealthy and against higher wages in factories and on shop floors. But that is not the language in which modern science spoke. Instead Raper offered the most general observation about Talmadge, then spent the next pages showing what Talmadge's positions were on a range of social and agricultural issues, vis-à-vis the New Deal, through a marshaling of facts and statistics. The mode of argument in *Preface to Peasantry* is not of claims but of demonstration. Raper wants to persuade not with rhetoric, but as an equation "persuades," not with heat, but inexorably.

Of course, beneath the statistics and dispassionate descriptions, it is clear that Raper's is an egalitarian's agenda. But, like many modern artists, writers, and scientists, his palette was an "objectivity" that believed passionately in manipulating the reader to his own conclusions. For Raper, as for modernists in many fields, the ability to keep from pointing a finger—in a time of so much deadly finger-pointing—was an act of courage. The faith in social science his prose wears is principled, and from the perspective of the next century, it becomes poignant.

"HIS HEAD ALWAYS LOOKS NICE"

Preface to Peasantry delivered the facts of everyday life without either Old South ideals or a muckraker's zeal—but with an eye toward the telling detail and a sense of narrative. The book is subtitled "A Tale of Two Counties." Beyond its wink at Dickens, the title promises a story, rather than a study or an investigation, implying a sensibility attracted to narrative, even in what is purported to be a treatise on the economics of rural agriculture.

Raper's goal was similar to that of Walker Evans, Dorothea Lange, William Carlos Williams, and John Steinbeck—modernists whose realism aimed to see clearly the gritty stuff of life. They hoped to depict actual conditions, while offering a sense of their subjects' inner lives, aspiring to what Edward Steichen called "human documents." Raper's presentation of sociological and economic data incorporated a subjectivity intended to elicit empathy and a sense of immediacy. Raper was among those who spoke and wrote from the American hinterlands, but who were well equipped to approach social questions from a scientific and secular mind-set rather than a religious and moralist perspective. He joined William Faulkner, Richard Wright, Wilbur

Cash, Eudora Welty, C. Vann Woodward, and Lillian Smith in rejecting southern exceptionalism and writing about their society with an ironic, twentieth-century sensibility.[14]

Raper's imagination was always sparked by the intricate distinctions within the South's complex racial codes. He was keenly aware of the range of burdens the Depression hoisted onto the backs of southern blacks, of how occupations that had for decades been reserved for black men—jobs as bellhops, porters, and trolley conductors among them—were increasingly commandeered by out-of-work whites. At the time he was researching *Preface to Peasantry,* Raper was particularly attuned to the race bonding that grew in response to economic collapse and watched how it played out in day-to-day settings. In the hamlets and small towns of the South, for instance, the barbershop was the point through which all the village news traveled.

All the time he was researching Greene and Macon counties for *Preface to Peasantry,* Raper was looking at carnivals and county fairs, general stores, tobacconists, garages, and lunch spots with an eye for some detail or an offhand comment that opened a window onto the way racial etiquette entwined with economics. At Chapel Hill he had cut his fellow students' hair while sampling their views on birth control and religion and race. Over and over throughout his career, the barber's chair offered Raper a view of the southern caste system in all its breadth and subtlety of play.

The first thing Raper would do when he needed data on a town was to get a haircut. Time and again Raper walked into a "Dry September" barbershop, smelled the talcum powder and the sour hair tonic in the sweet, hot air, made some small talk, and started asking questions. It was not until after he had his trim, spent half an hour at the town's filling station, and struck up a conversation or two at the Main Street luncheonette that he would visit the police station, the town hall, and the courthouse.

Throughout the mid-1930s, he was shuttling among Greene and Macon counties and the CIC offices in downtown Atlanta. One day he stopped in at the shop near his office for a cut, climbed into the chair, and fell to talking with his usual barber about the weather, about politics and soup lines, and about the large numbers of farm folk who were passing by more and more frequently on the sidewalk in front of the shop. Just then, a friend of Raper's walked past and waved to them both. In studied casualness, the barber asked Raper, "Who cuts Mr. Brown's hair?"

Raper knew that his friend patronized a black shop on Peachtree Street, but he parried. "Well, somebody does better by him than I give you the chance to do by me. Why, he gets a haircut every week or ten days."

"Well, he must have a good barber."

"Yes, his head always looks nice."

The barber's tone was appreciative, admiring, almost deferential. "I've noticed how well his head looks all the time," he told Raper, "and I said to myself, 'Now, that man has a good barber, and he stays with him.'"

"He tells me," Raper confided, "he has been using the same barber since he came to Atlanta ten years ago."

"Well, I surely don't blame him."

Raper finally answered the question. "I think that Mr. Brown has his barber work done in Herndon's shop."

The clippers flitted methodically behind Raper's head while the barber mused over the news. He began a story, a parable, really. "Some years ago," he told Raper, "I had a customer who came to me for shaves, massages, and shampoos. I shaved him every day, and massaged and shampooed him every week, but I never cut his hair. Finally one day I said, 'Mr. Smith, I don't want to pry into your business at all, but I notice that you always have a good haircut.'"

"'Yes,' Mr. Smith replied. 'I have been going to a Negro barber at Herndon's for twenty-three years.'"

"And I said, 'Well you always have a good haircut.'"

Another Saturday afternoon, Mr. Smith stepped up in the chair, and the barber told him, admiringly, "Well, you have had another one of these good haircuts. It surely is a good one." The barber continued, "And I went on about massaging him, and told him about a friend of mine who liked steaks. I told him there were places all over town where you could buy and eat steaks, good steaks—places on Peachtree run by white people, and that people who bought steaks there helped these white people maintain a decent standard of living."

By this time the barber was dusting Raper's neck. He chuckled, "You know, I've been cutting Mr. Smith's hair ever since. That was three years ago. He never had realized before that a white man ought to trade with white people."

Raper walked out of the shop into the sunlight of the downtown sidewalk, realizing the barber hoped he might someday pass along the story to Mr. Brown. But the kind of moral Raper had found, the moral that would fill the pages of *Preface to Peasantry,* revealed the hypocrisy of the barber and his brethren. Just a few years before, practically all the barbers in Atlanta had been black. Through the years of the Depression, they had lost their trade to white barbers. In some cases, as Raper knew firsthand, black workers lost their jobs through organized threats and violence. Other jobs just went away. And some lost their jobs, as Raper later wrote, through the play of friendship and pressure, subtle as a spider web, "by methods similar to that utilized by the white barber who used to cut my hair every month."[15]

THE LONG ROAD FROM WALL STREET

Once he had finished *Preface to Peasantry* and during the rest of the 1930s, Raper broadened his influence on the lecture circuit, by continuing to speak to agricultural organizations about, for example, the economic benefits of soil conservation. As a graduate student he had taught Sunday school in the new slums of Nashville, and throughout the Depression he spoke to church groups about Christian values and racial equality. He taught sociology part-time at Agnes Scott College and brought his affluent, white students to Atlanta's ghetto. He pledged support to African American fraternal organizations and business groups. He hectored white businessmen on the radio and at Elks Club meetings for their support of a separate wage system for whites and blacks. He supported the Mississippi Delta Farm Cooperative. He conducted workshops on labor organizing. He helped organize the Southern Conference on Human Welfare. In spite of the intransigence of some segments of the white South, Raper's experience nevertheless indicates that, by the time of the Depression, a sizeable number of small-town southerners were ready at least to hear a call for a change in the region's racial and economic practices.

In 1938, after Will Alexander had left the CIC and the commission had begun to drift, Raper took his leave as well and signed on to research and write for Gunnar Myrdal, whose *An American Dilemma* would become the most influential study ever published on race in the United States. Raper's notes on the conditions that African Americans faced in the court system and with the police are fascinating and vivid snapshots of the legal caste system. Then he coauthored with Ira De A. Reid, an African American sociologist, another broad study, *Sharecroppers All*. Published in 1941, it was an indictment of industrial capitalism, updating an old populist idea with Raper's trope of Wall Street being the other end of the long road that led to the sharecropper's cabin.

Raper and Reid began their investigation of southern society by considering the sharecropper's bargain with his landlord and traced the inequalities of industrial capitalism. Bank clerks, stenographers, and elevator operators—all were sharecroppers, so to speak, whose labor was largely usurped by the capitalist. It says a lot about the Roosevelt administration that Raper was offered a position as social science analyst with the federal

government immediately after publishing *Sharecroppers All.* As
an outspoken advocate of civil rights who spent all of the Depression working on the ground for social justice and who had voted
the socialist ticket as a young man, Raper turned enthusiastically
to the New Deal. Although he taught part-time at Agnes Scott
College for a few years, before his politics got him into trouble, his
views were too controversial for any southern institution (except
the University of North Carolina, where he turned down an offer
from Odum). Nor did he ever hold a job in private industry or in
state government. By the late 1930s only Roosevelt's New Deal
was liberal enough to hire him.

In 1940 Raper returned to Greene County to evaluate the
impact of New Deal programs on the lives and farms of its black
and white tenants and sharecroppers. He had expected to spend
only a few months back in Greene, but he was so encouraged by
what he was seeing, in terms of effective coordination among the
individual farmers and the various levels of government, that he
and his family stayed for two years. He wrote about the changes
he saw in *Tenants of the Almighty,* a book so filled with both
history and personal detail that it can hardly be called a sociological study. *Tenants of the Almighty* is another in the line of
1930s documentary books, complete with photography by Farm
Security Administration (FSA) photographers Jack Delano and
Dorothea Lange. Raper was surprised at how much the racial
attitudes of both blacks and whites had changed since he had
last studied the county for *Preface to Peasantry* five and more
years earlier. He ended *Tenants of the Almighty* with a story that
would have been impossible at the time of *Preface to Peasantry*
—a black boycott of Greensboro's first movie theater over an old
racial joke uttered from the stage on opening night, when the
whole black balcony trooped out of the packed house.

During the war years, Raper traveled throughout the United
States for the Department of Agriculture, as a sort of sociological ear-to-the-ground, reporting back to Washington the view from

the hinterlands, assessing the farming practices and cultural attitudes of rural communities. As the war rolled on, however, conservatives in Congress were seeing their chance to roll back New
Deal programs under the name of patriotic belt-tightening. The
cultural aspects of Raper's studies were eliminated in favor of a
more strictly quantitative approach to documenting agriculture
in a way that was more useful to the military, industry, and private enterprise. Raper had wanted to help save the family farm,
which he saw as the social and economic template of Jeffersonian agrarianism. By the end of World War II, however, it was
clear that further industrialization had permanently altered the
nation's rural communities and the business of agriculture was
ascendant.

The problems and conditions that *Preface to Peasantry* described and analyzed in such detail were soon made obsolete by
the transformation of the South from an agrarian to an urbanized, industrialized consumer society. The Depression South had
been the last vestige of preindustrial America. By World War II,
the agrarian world in which Raper had worked to promote racial
and economic justice was evaporating, and with it the import
of Raper's work. Twenty years later any talk of an American
peasantry was ridiculous. Now, though, when we look back at
the twentieth century, Raper helps us understand the distance
between the Depression and cold war worlds in terms of America's liberal politics and its shifting race relations. Using social
science and the mass media, Raper injected scientific modernism
directly into the mainstream of a Victorian, agrarian society.
His experience shows that the white South's response to a situation of drastic change was at once both deeply entrenched and
extraordinarily adaptable.

After his work on sharecropping, Raper was approached by
Hollywood agents in 1940 about a movie designed to draw on
the popularity of *The Grapes of Wrath*. The next year, impressed
with the changes the New Deal was making in the rural South,

Life magazine sent a camera crew to visit Raper in Greene County, Georgia, and prepared a several-page layout for a mid-December issue—Pearl Harbor struck it from *Life*'s pages. All of a sudden, the nation lost interest in its sharecroppers and tenant farmers. As much as he had helped lay the groundwork for the civil rights movement, Raper had been surveying the South at the moment of the plantation's final collapse. By the 1950s that moment had quickly lost relevance in regard to race, and agrarian America, with its traditional communities of family farms, had passed from center stage.

World War II marked the turning point in Raper's career. Within two years of Hiroshima, Raper was assisting the Allied occupation forces in the rural reconstruction of Japan. He worked as part of a spectacularly successful reconstruction conducted through policy that constituted the fullest expression of New Deal liberalism.[16] By going to Japan, Raper was pursuing twin goals of scientific planning and individual self-determination throughout the world. After working at the request of Douglas MacArthur on a massive redistribution of Japanese farmlands, Raper traveled throughout the 1950s, working for various U.S. agencies in Taiwan, the Philippines, Afghanistan, Iran, India, Pakistan, and North Africa and advising on rural development projects to replace feudal farming systems with more democratic and scientifically oriented agricultural practices. In Raper's mind this goal required corresponding social change, but his work to redistribute land and resources often ran up against State Department policies promising stability to regimes friendly to U.S. interests and directives that attempted to use social-science advisers as cold war operatives.

From the late 1940s through the early 1960s, at just the time when the leadership of the civil rights movement in the South was shifting from white liberals—who prompted dialogue on questions of justice—to black activists—who had begun turning to civil disobedience and talked about ending segregation—

Raper was working throughout the Third World. During the heyday of the American civil rights movement, Raper continued to work in Asia, the Middle East, and Africa. He sent money, offered time, and wrote letters back home, but he never picked up a bullhorn. In the 1930s he had been saying that American cities would inevitably explode from unplanned growth and racial prejudice. In the late 1960s, when the ghettos of Washington, Detroit, and Los Angeles were in flames, he, and his wife, Martha, had settled on Slope Oaks—say it fast to get the joke— a farm in the rolling hills of Vienna, in the Virginia piedmont, twenty miles outside Washington, among flower growers, gray-flannel commuters, and a band of hippies squatting in an old farmhouse down the road. By the late 1970s Arthur and Martha had lived into a different world.

In his old age Raper grew his white hair long, like Walt Whitman, and he wore a long beard, part southern gentleman, part aging radical. He made it a matter of principle to mix hard work and pleasure.[17] He was fascinated by the medusalike phenomena that had sprung from industrialization, but he found it hard to engage with the post-sixties, corporate, consumerist America, a nation inconceivable to the decade of *Preface to Peasantry*. He and Martha were elder statesman and stateswoman to the hippies, whose roots were sunk in the Depression but whose sensibilities and viewpoints flowered in the mass-market counterculture of the 1960s. Not that this counterculture left him at ease. He shared the views of the organic farming movement, for example, but he found its rhetoric a bit too precious for his taste.

He had expected the attention of history. The impulse of Depression America to document itself, to show life at the dawn of the modern age to the people of the future, reached its apogee in Raper. In retirement he worked assiduously on his files— boxes and boxes of all sorts of materials compiled with the same scrupulous intent that marked all his sociological studies. He created a documentary of the southerner as New Deal liberal.

Knowing how unusual his career had been, he proved, through accurate documentation and intimate detail, the existence of white southerners at the cutting edge of modern social theory, who also worked on the ground for racial justice. When historian Walter Jackson interviewed him, skeptical about Raper's claim that he had learned racial equality in the cradle, Raper could open his files and find the diaries and remembrances of his brothers as well as his own school essays on fair treatment for all.

Raper lived to see how wrong he had been to believe that mechanization would bolster the fortunes of the family farm. Before the war, he reflected, technology seemed a solution to problems of social inequality, as well as of lagging production. He had been wary about opening the Pandora's box of industrialization, but traditional agricultural societies had limited the opportunities for social change. Still, by the mid-1970s, he felt let down. "How far from adequate in our estimates we were," he acknowledged, "is now being proclaimed on TV, radio, and in our morning papers."[18]

The old, liberal, New Deal sociologist also felt blindsided by Vietnam. The war was a massive government initiative, directed by well-informed and scientifically aided government officials and given a wealth of resources and expertise, that had spun slowly but surely off its course into disaster. The conditions under which the United States sank into a quagmire of mistakes were those of an enlightened, modern democracy. It did not seem reasonable to Raper that such circumstances would lead into a nightmare.

Science itself had helped despoil the land and exacerbate inequality. And yet, in spite of everything, science was still also the only means of making things right. "I am still an optimist," Raper concluded, "but not an easy one." He never despaired of his liberal sociologist's belief that actions have demonstrable causes, however difficult they may be to uncover. To the end he believed the problems of modernity lay not with technology, per se, but with the masters of science who had dictated the pre-eminence of the profit motive.[19]

First Arthur, then Martha, died in 1979, coincident with the rise of the New Right, the exhaustion of America's faith in large-scale federal programs, and the country's cynicism about the results that social planning could provide. Raper had distrusted the ability of private industry to answer social questions expeditiously and judiciously. He gave only cursory attention to the role that business and industry would play in the nation's future and was puzzled by the increasing control that corporate America had begun to exert over social and governmental institutions. Raper offers a chance to see where the Old Left succeeded and where it so underestimated the allure and power of American capitalism.

Soon after their deaths, the symbolism that began at the intersection of Community and Enterprise roads ended with the transformation of Raper's rolling farmland and meticulously cultivated fields into a rolling development of high-priced, neo-colonial McMansions. Through Slope Oaks, Lincoln Navigators now roll along quiet streets called Whippoorwill and Windbrook, past houses where gold chandeliers shine through bay windows across ultragreen lawns shorn of their oaks.

Preface to Peasantry was first reprinted in 1967, and sociologist Gilbert Osofsky wrote an introduction that was characteristic of the sixties' bent toward the dramatic. He set Raper against James Agee, whose own portrait of the rural South, *Let Us Now Praise Famous Men*—with its brooding, blood-eyed world of sublimity and homespun surrealism, cosmic and quotidian— was being rediscovered by many of the decade's romantics. Osofsky claimed that Agee would not have understood Arthur Raper, with his steady columns of figures and dutiful paragraphs of straight facts. In one way he is right. Agee began *Let Us Now Praise Famous Men* by telling us to turn up the volume on

Beethoven and sit on the floor with an ear to the speaker. Raper was quite a musician himself, he often played the violin, and he loved his RCA Red Seal records. And if Agee had turned up the volume on *Preface to Peasantry,* he would have heard the intensity of Raper's rural South—its injustice and misery, its mystery and doom and bonhomie and grit, and Raper's faith in science and progress writ large, but also his outrage and love, all sotto voce. If Agee had sat down on the floor and placed an ear to Raper's quiet recitations of Greene and Macon counties' facts, he would have heard, too, the faint tolling of distant bells, the soft end of a grand opera, the long, slow rustle of a curtain falling on the Old South.

NOTES

1. Arthur Raper, videotape interview by Sue Thrasher, Peter Wood, and Larry Goodwyn, Vienna, Virginia, April 24–28, 1978, University of North Carolina, Southern Historical Collection (SHC), Arthur F. Raper file, folder 3966/2.

2. Raper, family letter, November 22, 1974, SHC, Raper file, folder 482.

3. John Shelton Reed, "On Narrative and Sociology," in *Surveying the South: Studies in Regional Sociology* (Columbia: University of Missouri Press, 1993).

4. Morton Sosna, "Personal interview with Arthur Raper," April 23, 1971, SHC, Raper file, folder 370.

5. Raper, *Preface to Peasantry: A Tale of Two Counties* (Chapel Hill: University of North Carolina Press, 1936; Columbia: University of South Carolina Press, 2005), 209, 210. Citations are to the 2005 edition.

6. Ibid., 179–80.

7. Ibid., 259, 311, 263.

8. Ibid., 245–53.

9. Ibid., 256–57.

10. Ibid., 267.

11. Ibid.

12. Ibid., 272.

13. Ibid., 225.

xxxviii   NEW INTRODUCTION

14. Carl Fleischhauer and Beverly Brannan, eds. *Documenting America, 1935–1943* (Berkeley: University of California Press, 1988), 9.

15. Arthur Raper, "Buy 'White,'" *Far Horizons* (May 1936): 197. SHC, Raper file, folder 47.

16. John W. Dower, "A Warning from History," *Boston Review* 28, no. 1 (2003): 6.

17. Raper, "I Like to Live at Slope Oaks," SHC, Raper file, folder 560.

18. Raper, "On the Crests of Forming Waves," unpublished manuscript, SHC, Raper file, folder 548.

19. Raper, "Our Hope Still Lies in Science and Technology," unpublished manuscript, SHC, Raper file, folder 629.

PREFACE TO THE FIRST EDITION

THIS STUDY of Greene and Macon counties, Georgia, has been made over a period of seven years. It was begun in the summer of 1927 under the auspices of the Georgia Committee on Interracial Cooperation, when Will W. Alexander, Director of the Commission on Interracial Cooperation, and T. J. Woofter, Jr., research professor at the University of North Carolina, suggested that a comparison of conditions in a Black Belt county which had suffered a great population decrease since 1920 with conditions in one which had retained its population should throw into relief the fundamental causes of the movement of Negroes from the Black Belt to cities of the South and North. After two years of field work and nearly two more devoted to the classification and interpretation of data, a report was written and is now on file among the doctors' dissertations of 1931 at the University of North Carolina Library under the title of "Two Rural Black Belt Counties"

Early in 1934 Will W. Alexander, Charles S. Johnson of Fisk University, and Edwin R. Embree of the Rosenwald Fund began a study of the Negro in industry and agriculture with the view of collecting information which might be of assistance to the government in its various activities affecting the Negro. This committee determined that a study should be made of the Negro's status in three selected industries: iron and steel, railroads, and meat packing. George S. Mitchell of Columbia University was in charge of this study. A second study, dealing with agriculture, was divided between Rupert B. Vance of the University of North Carolina, who assumed the responsibility for the collection of statistical data, and Charles S. Johnson who with a staff of field workers began the systematic collection of current materials from eight counties in four states.

[xxxix]

While the plans for these studies were still in their formative state, it was decided that a comprehensive study should be made of one or two representative counties in the rural Black Belt to determine the meaning of the various New Deal activities to the population groups there. Largely because of the work which I had already done in Greene and Macon counties, I was asked to prepare this report. The statistical facts were brought up to date in the summer of 1934, and from early fall until after Christmas I again spent considerable time in the counties.

The collection of the data for this book has been made easy and pleasant by the wholehearted cooperation of farmers of both races, of religious and civic leaders, and especially of the public ofcials in both counties—superintendents of schools, sheriffs, tax collectors and assessors, clerks of court, county commissioners and boards of education, relief administrators, farm agents, and school teachers. The Exchange Club at Greensboro and the Kiwanis Club at Montezuma appointed advisory committees to the study. I am particularly indebted to Floyd Corry, Hart Sibley, T. B. Rice, Richard Weil, J. B. Dolvin, Mrs. W. O. Mitchell, Wade West, Robert Lewis, and Iverson Ward in Greene County and to Felder Frederick, John B. Guerry, J. Frank Murph, C. T. Harden, Mrs. W. A. Thomas, Ed M. McKenzie, Edward Richardson,* and John West* in Macon County.

For filling in the detailed blanks of 323 Negro farm families in 1927 and 319 Negro and white farm families in 1934, the basis of the data presented in Chapters III, IV, and V, I acknowledge grateful appreciation to J. W. Dobbs, Jr.,* V. A. Edwards, and Alton Glasure.

I am under no little obligation to Howard W. Odum, Eugene Cunningham Branson,* Ada Woolfolk, John Hope,* Forrester B. Washington, and others who have expressed a keen interest in the work and have made helpful suggestions from time to time; and to T. J. Woofter, Jr., Benjamin F. Hubert, H. A. Hunt, and P. H.

* Deceased.

Stone for having read and criticized all or parts of the earlier manuscript. I am especially indebted to Will W. Alexander, Charles S. Johnson, R. B. Eleazer, and Martha Jarrell Raper for their encouragement and advice, and to Carolyn Blue for her patience and skill in preparing the manuscript for publication.

It has been a real privilege to live in each county for months at a time, and to become personally acquainted with a large number of people representing all elements of the population. I have spent considerable time securing data from the tax digests, court records, and other public documents on file in the court-houses and in the relief offices; I have interviewed all the Negro landowners at their homes, many white landowners, and scores upon scores of wage hands and tenants of both races; I have gone to church on Sunday, hung around the store at night, sat through the picture show and attended the carnival over the week end; now and then I have had the privilege of tramping after the hounds, or scrambling through the thickets along the Oconee and Flint rivers with farmers turned huntsmen and fishermen. Besides being a lot of fun, these various contacts have provided a basis for an understanding of attitudes and outlooks.

ARTHUR RAPER

Atlanta, Georgia
March 1936

FOREWORD

WITH MINOR VARIATIONS, the conditions of the farm people pictured in these two Georgia counties are typical of the cotton-growing sections of the old South.

The decadence of this civilization is far advanced. The fertility of much of the soil has been mined away. Most of the fine old houses have fallen into disrepair. Many of the resourceful descendants of the more influential families have abandoned these rural areas, as have many of the more alert farm tenants. Poverty, illiteracy, undernourishment handicap most of those who remain. The decadence of this once prosperous and influential section was not inevitable. Much of the soil was originally highly fertile. The climate and rainfall always have been adequate for successful agriculture and a desirable life for the people.

Most of the conditions detailed by Dr. Raper are not the result of the depression or of the collapse of agriculture throughout the nation. Like a deadly disease, the factors undermining the Black Belt plantation economy have been working for years—agriculture here has been crumbling for decades.

The situation is due in part to the misuse of the land. What has happened in these Georgia counties is typical of the nation as a whole. The land-hungry settlers of this country took for granted that land was everlasting and that ownership of it insured security. Tools would wear out and men die, but the land would remain and support whoever was resourceful enough to acquire it or fortunate enough to inherit it. This was assumed to be true of all land. Hence there was no limitation as to the land which should be put into cultivation. The forests were ruthlessly stripped from the hillsides to make way for fields. Erosion set in and lands which would have yielded a perpetual harvest of timber were soon turned into valueless wastes.

[xliii]

The more desirable lands in this area of Georgia were capable of producing a variety of crops with which to sustain life. Many of these crops, with intelligent use, would have maintained the fertility of the soil. But from the early days of settlement, cotton had cast a spell over the farmers of this area. Cotton was a money crop. Year after year these good soils were planted to cotton; they were robbed of their fertility and left bare and unprotected from erosion. Through the constant shipping away of the fertility of the soil in the form of lint cotton, much of the best land is now worn and sterile and, even by heavy applications of expensive fertilizer, will not produce cotton at a profit. The old Southeast can no longer compete with the newer cotton regions of the world in the production of this staple. A few years ago the boll weevil came to these depleted fields. There was not sufficient fertility in the soil or resourcefulness in the people to resist the onslaught. This was the final episode in the collapse of the regnant cotton culture of the old Southeast. Cotton farming in this area is doomed.

Cotton culture not only has destroyed the soil, but also has resulted in the neglect of a large portion of the population. Most of the neglected people were black, or one of the many shades found among the colored people of the South. Whatever the shade of color, in the eyes of the ruling class they were Negroes and fit only for cotton and servitude. They were to be "kept in their place"—a place assumed to be fixed by Holy Writ as forever that of an inferior. For such people, education was not considered important. Schools adequate to make them allies in maintaining a civilization or even an adequate food supply were never provided. These colored people were left in ignorance and poverty.

But there were also white people who lived on the fringes of this economic system. Today in these Black Belt counties are to be found many white people who are as illiterate and poor as their colored neighbors. No way has ever been found to keep a man in a ditch without some one's staying down there with him. So Negroes and poor whites live out the unenlightened years in the half stupor induced by malnutrition and neglect.

The exhausted lands of the Black Belt can be restored to productiveness. Such a restoration, however, must be accompanied by the rehabilitation of the people. To restore the land and rehabilitate the people will require a new leadership with intelligence enough to understand that the maintenance of a decent civilization in the South depends more upon the constructive use of the soil than upon the "maintenance of white supremacy"—the imaginary task that has preoccupied so much of the political leadership of this section.

The breaking up of the old plantation system offers a new beginning for the land and for the people who remain on it. The new land policy must be one of restoration and rehabilitation. It must retire from cultivation those lands which never should have been put under the plow, and must restore them to timber and other natural uses. It must change fundamentally the relation of the majority of the people to the land, by affording an opportunity for ownership of the land by the man *who works it*. It must substitute for cotton production a program of general farming, which will emphasize the improvement of soil and the production of food. These things accomplished, many of the rural South's disinherited people may be rehabilitated into useful and intelligent citizens—an end which never can be attained under the cotton tenancy system that has prevailed in the past.

WILL W. ALEXANDER

Atlanta, Georgia
April 1936

PART ONE

Introduction

CHAPTER I
PLANTERS AND TENANTS

THE BLACK BELT

IN THE heart of the South there are approximately two hundred counties in which over half the population is Negro. These counties lie in a crescent from Virginia to Texas and constitute the "Black Belt." They contain the big plantation area of today and coincide with the location of the slave plantations of a few decades ago.

The Richest Soil and the Poorest People.—The Black Belt includes the most fertile soil of the South, and contains a disproportionate number of its poorest people. The ownership of the best land is in the hands of a comparatively small group of white families; landlessness and chronic dependence is the lot of over half the white families and nearly nine-tenths of the colored. The Black Belt is the home of a few planters and many tenants. Thousands of families have no cow, no hog, not even chickens, and own no workstock or farm equipment, not even a hoe. Rickets and pellagra are common among those who till the most productive soils of the South.

A Preface to Peasantry.—When the plantation is flourishing, one finds a few large, well-built dwellings where the owners live, and a great number of small, twisted, unpainted cabins which house the landless agricultural workers—usually wage hands and croppers. As the plantation deteriorates, the big houses go without paint, the roofs leak, the porches tumble down, one field and then another is abandoned to brambles and gullies, and the tenants either migrate to the cities or remain as renters to eke out what existence they may. The collapse of the plantation system, rendered inevitable by its exploitation of land and labor, leaves in its wake depleted soil, shoddy livestock, inadequate farm equipment, crude agricultural practices, crippled institutions, a defeated and impoverished people. Such

[3]

is already the picture in a considerable part of the older Black Belt.

The Black Belt plantation economy, whether regnant or declining, prepares the land and the man for the emergence of a peasant rather than for the appearance of the traditional independent American farmer. Before the plantation structure crumbles, the owners dominate the economic and cultural life of the entire community, and a few of them may be relatively wealthy; but even then the majority of the plantation folk are subpeasants—no property, no self-direction, no hope of either. As the plantation crumbles, most of the erstwhile owners and some of the more alert tenants abandon the scene, leaving in the decadent area plantation families schooled in dependency, unaccustomed to responsibility, without experience in community leadership. These remaining families tend to become independent renters or small owners, and are characterized by very low but relatively secure planes of living. Such are the beginnings of peasantry in the New World—the collapse of the Black Belt plantation system is a preface to American peasantry.

North European peasantry has its background in feudalism; the emerging American type, in the plantation system. The European peasant had been a subpeasant, a feudal serf; the emerging American peasant, too, is a subpeasant, but it does not necessarily follow that his plane of living will also be improved. For, in addition to stifling racial factors which penalized Black Belt whites along with Negroes, the plantation economy in America had rested upon a reckless exploitation of natural resources unknown to European feudalism. The primary differences are two: the European feudal lord had stationary headquarters and looked upon his serfs as permanent fixtures; the traditional Black Belt planter often moved his seat of operations from exhausted land to virgin soil, and regularly discarded the least satisfactory workers in his search for more desirable ones, always enforcing upon them economic and cultural dependency.

The Most Solid Part of the "Solid South."—The Black Belt sketches the section of the nation where the smallest proportion of the adults exercise the franchise and it defines the most solid part of the Solid South. White supremacy and its instrument, the white primary, are more sacred than any other political tenets. Though the Democratic Party in the South is normally Protestant, Ku-Klux Klannish, and dry, the Black Belt counties in 1928 gave an overwhelming majority to the Democratic presidential candidate, Catholic and wet; at the same time many urban communities in the same states gave a majority to the Republican candidate.

This most Democratic part of the nation is perhaps the least democratic part of the nation: from six to sixty times as much public money is spent for the education of the white as for the Negro school child; Negro officeholders are unknown; scarcely any Negroes register and vote in national presidential elections, almost none participate in local politics.

More than elsewhere in the South one finds in the Black Belt "unreconstructed rebels." Sherman's march to the sea is referred to daily; openly justified are the terroristic methods used to disfranchise the Negro, and revered is the white primary which legalizes this disfranchisement. With the financial, educational, and religious institutions maintaining the status quo and keeping the Negro "in his place," the threat of violence always hangs over his head and violence itself frequently is used upon slight provocation.

The Plantation Dominates the Region.—To no small degree the Black Belt is the seed-bed of the South's people and her culture. Human relations in Atlanta, Birmingham, Montgomery, Memphis, New Orleans, and Dallas are determined largely by the attitudes of the people of the Black Belt plantations from which many of their inhabitants, white and Negro, came. The standard of living in these cities does not escape the influence of this area of deterioration. No real relief can come to the region so long as the planter, who wants dependent workers, can confound the situation by setting the white worker over against the black worker, and so long as the industrialist, who wants cheap labor, can achieve his end by pitting urban labor against rural labor. There are literally millions of farm laborers in the Black Belt who are eagerly awaiting an opportunity to work for wages even smaller than are now being paid textile and steel workers in southern cities.

The South can hope to be nothing but the Orient of this nation so long as its wages and working conditions are determined by the competition of plantation workers accustomed to practically no money and a minimum diet. The imminence of a mechanized cotton picker only complicates the picture.

The Rural Handicap.—The city's working family has advantages unknown to the farm tenant, such as public hospitalization, public outdoor nurse service, public clinics, and public school facilities infinitely superior to those provided in the rural section where many of the white and practically all the Negro children attend one-teacher schools. In many respects the city family without employment is actually better off than the rural landless family with employment, for city relief often provides a better fare than a tenant farm.

The depression which reached the cities of the United States in the fall of 1929 had settled upon the rural South a half-dozen years earlier. Many banks had closed, millions of acres had been lost to creditors and sold for taxes, seventy-five thousand farms had been abandoned; hundreds of rural dwellers had been disillusioned and great numbers were drifting off to the cities and towns in hope of finding work. During this period the price of farm products had dropped faster than the price of other goods, and by the winter of 1932 the region was virtually bankrupt.

The New Deal Reaches the Black Belt.—The New Deal with its cotton restriction program, its relief expenditures, and its loan services, has temporarily revitalized the Black Belt, has rejuvenated the decaying plantation economy. Those who control the plantations are now experiencing relative prosperity. On the other hand the landless farmers, though able for the

most part because of the New Deal to pay their rents and settle
their accounts, are not only failing to escape their chronic dependence but are actually losing status.   Many tenants are being
pushed off the land while many others are being pushed down
the tenure ladder, especially from cropper to wage hand status.

The various federal resources which come into this region
tend to be spent in conformity with the plantation, the philosophy and practices of which root back into slavery.   New techniques of exploitation have been evolved.   Many of the benefits
meant for landless farmers have been appropriated by the planters and merchants, upon whom the landless farmers have been
continuously dependent, to whom they have been continuously
in debt.

PERTINENT QUESTIONS

The center of the Black Belt lies in Georgia, and includes
nearly fifty of its counties.   Two of these counties, Greene and
Macon, have been studied intensively, and concerning them
many questions arise:

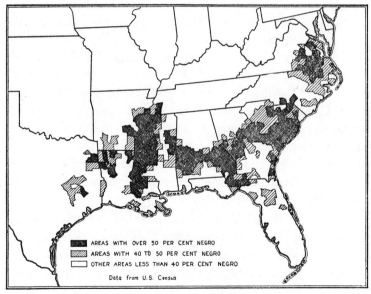

THE BLACK BELT, 1930

Are Greene and Macon counties representative of the Black Belt?

Farm Incomes and Man-Land Relations.—What is the annual income of farm families? Do the Negroes live as well as the whites in the same tenure class? Who owns the land? Do white and Negro tenants compete for the same farms? What are the basic assumptions of the landlord, of the tenant? Is the plantation a civilizing force for its workers? Why did Greene County's population decrease nearly 34 per cent between 1920 and 1930? Who migrated in the greatest numbers, the whites or the Negroes, the illiterate or the educated? Where did the migrants go?

State and Federal Recovery Programs.—Why do the farmers like the cheap automobile tag? Who benefited by the reduction of utility rates and state taxes? Is the "prevailing wage" of farm labor in these counties a living wage?

How much land had been sold for taxes when the New Deal was launched? How many plantations had been forfeited to loan companies? Has the New Deal reached all elements of the Black Belt? Why did the whites not object to the Negroes' voting in the Bankhead Allotment Bill election in the fall of 1934?

Who borrowed money from the Federal Land Bank, the Land Bank Commission, and the Home Owners Loan Corporation? What did the planters think of the free distribution of Red Cross flour and cloth? How much money was spent in Greene and Macon counties by the Federal Emergency Relief Administration, and for what projects? Was the differential between the white and Negro schools increased or decreased by the use of FERA funds for educational purposes? What is the meaning of "on the county"?

Institutions and Attitudes.—Do Negroes and whites sit together around the stove at the Black Belt store? Why is court week so popular? Are whites or Negroes more likely to be arrested, to get on the chain gang, to receive the longer sentence? How much more public money is spent for the education of the white child than of the Negro child? What are the differences between white and Negro schools in monthly salaries, in length of terms, in equipment? Are the white and Negro teachers and preachers acquainted? What lodges and societies have the rural dwellers? What are their pastimes? What are the prospects for the future?

CHAPTER II

GREENE AND MACON COUNTIES

The conditions in Greene and Macon counties in Georgia, besides affording an interesting contrast, are illustrative of the Black Belt as a whole.

Geographic, Historic, and Social Factors

Greene and Macon counties represent, respectively, the older and newer Black Belt of Georgia. They have parallels throughout the plantation area of the South, with the pattern modified in Virginia and North Carolina by the production of both cotton and tobacco there, and in the Southwest by the late development of plantation farming.

Location and Topography.—Greene County, with an area of 416 square miles and a population density of 30.3 per square mile, is in the lower part of the Piedmont Plateau about midway between Augusta and Atlanta. Macon County has an area of 332 square miles, a population density of 50.1, is in the upper edge of the Upper Coastal Plain midway between the cities of Macon and Albany. Greene has an average altitude of nearly 600 feet, Macon approximately 350 feet. Their climate is much the same, except that Macon has a slightly longer growing season and the winters are a little milder. Rivers which must be crossed by bridges run the entire length of both counties from north to south; the Oconee flows through the northwestern part of Greene and along its western boundary in the southern half, while the Flint bisects Macon County.

The topography of Greene is generally rolling with short steep hills near the larger streams in the western portions of the county. According to the soil survey of the United States Department of Agriculture the topography of Greene County is "typical of the Piedmont region, the upland being cut by the larger streams into major divides, which are in turn subdivided

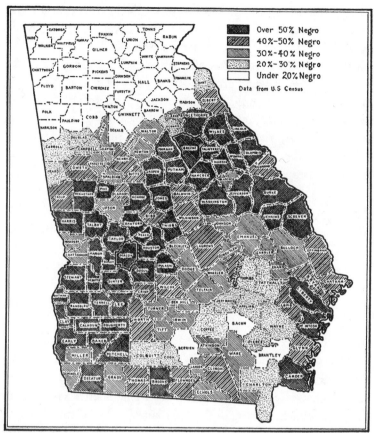

DISTRIBUTION OF NEGRO POPULATION IN GEORGIA IN 1930

by the smaller streams, until the whole region is a series of
ridges, the surface varying from undulating to gently rolling,
rolling, and hilly. . . . The topography of the southeastern part,
the region of gray lands, is very smooth for the Piedmont
region. . . . A characteristic of this section of the county is the
frequent occurrence of series of low, rounded knolls."[1]

Macon County, too, is generally rolling, but the knolls and
ridges are not so high as those in Greene, the slopes are longer
and more gradual, the streams are farther apart, have more

[1] *Soil Survey of Oconee, Morgan, Greene, and Putnam Counties, Georgia*
(Bureau of Soils, United States Department of Agriculture, 1922), pp. 7-8.

swamp land along them, and are more likely to dry up during summer droughts. East of the Flint River there are wide expanses of generally level upland which usually drop abruptly within a few hundred yards of a stream. Extending westward from the Flint River there is a strip of low, level land varying in width from four miles in the northern part of the county to less than two miles in the southern. Back of this level area, which gradually rises as the river is left behind, there are low knolls and then higher ones until the southern edge of the Sand Hills region is reached.

With the exception of considerable outcroppings of granite in southwestern Greene and bauxite deposits near the Sumter County line in Macon, there are no minerals of known commercial value.

Soils and Farm Economy.—Within each county the soil types vary widely. The most obvious difference is that in wet weather certain portions are characterized by very muddy roads, while in other portions the roads are sandy. This was forcefully brought to the writer's attention one gray afternoon several years ago when the Greene County School Superintendent advised: "If it is not raining in the morning we will visit the other schools above Penfield; if it is raining we had better visit schools down around Siloam and White Plains." In Macon County, the areas which the school superintendent visits in dry weather are in the eastern half of the county and along the river in the western half.

The muddy-road portions of both counties describe the areas of the large landholdings of today and of the large slave plantations of the past. Then as now the small white landowners have occupied the sandy-road parts of both counties. Soils which do not get muddy in wet weather have a high gravel content and are poorly suited to general agricultural purposes.

The whole of the southeastern portion of Greene County, generally called the "white land section" by reason of the color of its soil, has been occupied from the outset by small white

THE OLD PLANTATIONS IN GREENE COUNTY ARE ON RED LAND

THE LIVE-AT-HOME SMALL WHITE FARMERS ARE ON WHITE LAND

THE BIG PLANTATIONS IN MACON COUNTY ARE EAST OF THE RIVER; THE LAR
PLANTERS LIVE IN MONTEZUMA AND MARSHALLVILLE. SMALL LIVE-AT-H
OWNERS ARE COMMON WEST OF THE RIVER.

MACON COUNTY—OGLETHORPE'S OLD EAGLE AND PHOENIX HOTEL HAS BEE
TRANSFORMED INTO A NEGRO CHURCH

owners who cultivate most of or all their acreage. In this section the surface soil is characterized by pea-sized gravels and the subsoil is very compact, making seepage slow. The seeds of early plantings often rot from wetness. The white land has the further disadvantage of deteriorating more rapidly than the red land. These conditions made the section unattractive to the planter class. Slave plantations were scattered over the remainder of Greene County, with the greatest concentration of large owners in the Greshamville and Oakland communities in the northwest, the Bethesda Baptist Church community in the northeast, and two smaller centers at Salem in the southwest and Bethany in the extreme southeast.

In Macon County, as in Greene, soil types vary widely and account for the distribution of landholdings by size. The large plantations are located east of the Flint River and in the strip of low level land immediately west of it. West of that is the rolling and hilly section, throughout the county's history the home of small white landowners. In both counties the poorest lands have been farmed by resident owners while the richest lands have been the site of the plantations.

Greene County—An Early Cultural Center.[2]—That there were relatively fewer large slave plantations in Macon than in Greene in 1860 was due to the earlier settlement and earlier development of Greene, which in 1786 was formed from a part of Wilkes County and "was settled soon after the Revolutionary War by pioneers from Virginia and the Carolinas."[3] Macon County, formed in 1837, was settled principally by the overflow population from the lower Piedmont counties of central Georgia

[2] George White, *Historical Collections of Georgia* (New York, 1854), and George Gilman Smith, *The Story of Georgia and the Georgia People, 1732 to 1860* (Macon, Ga., 1900) are valuable for this period. A great mass of material, to be published in book form in the near future, has been collected by T. B. Rice, official historian of Greene County. Over a period of months he has had double-column articles in the Greensboro *Herald-Journal* (county weekly) under the title, "The Checkered Career of Greene County from 1786 to 1934."

[3] *Soil Survey of Oconee, Morgan, Greene, and Putnam Counties, Georgia* (Bureau of Soils, U. S. D. A., 1922), p. 8.

and by a group of South Carolina slave-owning families who were pushing to the frontier to secure new lands.

Greensboro, the county seat of Greene since it was formed, early became a cultural and business center. The Greensboro Female College, founded by the Synod of Georgia, and opened in 1852, was housed in a building which cost $13,000. Just a few miles north of Greensboro, at Penfield, was Mercer Institute which in 1838 received a charter from the Georgia Legislature with the title of Mercer University. Besides smaller contributions from many sources, $138,200 was given to this Baptist institution prior to 1860 by the Reverend Jesse Mercer, who came into considerable money by his marriage to a wealthy Jewish woman.

Some of Georgia's leading citizens prior to 1860 lived in Greene County: "Near here [Greensboro] the great Georgia bishop, George Foster Pierce, was born, and here he spent his childhood, and from Greensboro he went to college at Athens." "Bishop Asbury preached at Little Britain, and at Bush's, now known as Liberty, and the South Georgia Conference was held at this church in 1808. Asbury and McKendree were both present." Dr. Francis Cummings,[4] "one of the oldest and most respected Presbyterian ministers of the Southern States" died in Greene County. United States Senator, William C. Dawson, was a native of this county. The "eccentric but sterling" Peter Early, Governor of Georgia, "lived in this county and is buried on what was his manor." The governor's father, Joel Early, coming to Greene County from Virginia, bought a large tract of land on the Oconee River and "kept up the style of an English baron."

It is reported that Dr. Sanders, of Mercer University, fell sick and diagnosed himself as suffering from what is now called

---

[4] About five miles east of Siloam stands old Bethany Presbyterian Church, first church organized in what is now Greene County: "Dr. Cummings, Dr. Francis Goulding, and other great ministers preached here . . . and here the first 'Monkey Trial' on record was held when Dr. Woodrow (ancestor of Woodrow Wilson) was tried for heresy in 1886."—T. B. Rice, article in *Herald-Journal*, March 8, 1935.

appendicitis. He is said to have died while begging his colleagues at the University to make an incision and remove his appendix.[5]

Both of the Georgians who have won places in the National Hall of Fame were born and lived within twenty miles of Greene County soil: Dr. Crawford W. Long was a resident of Washington, Wilkes County; Alexander H. Stephens lived in Crawfordville, Taliaferro County.

Greene's Early Manufactories.—White mentions three manufacturing centers in Greene County in 1854: "Greensboro Manufacturing Company—situated at Greensborough; motive power, steam; cost, $70,000; spindles, 4,000." "Scull Shoals Manufacturing Company—situated at Scull Shoals, on the Oconee River; cost $50,000. Spindles and looms, 2,000. Annual consumption of cotton, 4,000 bales. Annual value of goods produced at present price, $200,000." "Curtwright Manufacturing Company . . . situated at Long Shoals, on the Oconee River. Cost of property, $140,000; spindles and looms, 4,000. The company owns an elegant stone bridge across the Oconee, with flour and sawmills, and a large tract of land."[6]

Hardly a trace of the manufacturing establishments at Scull Shoals and Long Shoals can be found. At the former, in the northern part of the county, one trudges through a narrow and deep-rutted road to a dilapidated house of pretentious dimensions; in the cow pasture between it and the Oconee River, a hundred yards away, one sees the foundations of the Scull Shoal Manufacturing Company being gradually buried beneath the silt and mud which is left when the river overflows; just beyond the disappearing foundations in a clump of willows may be seen a pier of the old bridge. In the southern part of the

[5] Other noteworthy Greene County people included: Augustus Baldwin Longstreet, judge, minister, and author; Thomas Stocks, planter, president of Georgia's first State Fair Association, and the "father" of Georgia's Department of Agriculture; Shelton P. Sanford, mathematician and author of textbooks; James H. Kilpatrick, minister; the Widow Greenwood, owner of the slaves who were factors in the unfrocking of Bishop Andrews, her husband, and in the formation of the Methodist Episcopal Church, South.

[6] *Op. cit.,* pp. 478-79.

county, also at the end of a one-way, dry-weather road, is the site of the Curtwright Manufacturing Company at Long Shoals; here amid the rank undergrowth of the river bottom are some half-decayed beams of enormous size almost buried in the mud; they would have been washed down the river except for the remaining portions of the stone bridge against which they are lodged.

Dead and Dying Towns.—Dead towns, such as Scull Shoals and Long Shoals, are not limited to Greene County, however, for Lanier, eight miles up the Flint River from Oglethorpe in Macon County, and once the "seat of justice," has disappeared so thoroughly that the county historian in her official history quotes the following comments from Walter Paschall:

> It was just a country town with rambling, spacious houses, wide, sun-burned streets, and smiling darkies. It had its parsons and its drunkards and its hound dogs yawning in the noonday. And no one can ever complain that it has grown too big and lost its character, nor can anyone feel sad because it looks run-down and impoverished. The people who built it came and settled, talked politics and slavery, and cotton, drank their scuppernong wine, "Stump Molly," lived graciously and gracefully as only such people could, and when they decided to depart they took their houses with them and left the land to settle back into peaceful cultivation. . . . So by 1870, the site of Lanier was as empty and vacant as it had been in 1820, and the little patch of land along the right bank of the Flint had had its interlude of glory and had melted back into itself, quite like a lovely dryad who, having ventured from her dwelling to dabble her toes in the river, became suddenly frightened by the whistle of a locomotive and scampered back, dissolving herself forever into a myrtle tree. . . .
>
> Lucky Lanier—to have existed only at that most beautiful period when young men bowed gravely with tall hats at their breasts and young ladies curtsied sweetly from trailing fortresses! No town should ask a lovelier fate.

But this romancing writer is further quoted:

> It took strong men to build a town, and strong men liked to engage in physical contests, so "wrestling" matches were a common diversion. Such matches were most remarkable for their ferocity and the complete lack of rules. They consisted, actually, of plain,

downright fighting. The spectators stood around in a ring, taking sides noisily, and the contestants fought until they were exhausted or until one cried defeat. No holds were barred and a yanked-off ear or a gouged-out eye were greeted with yells. This somewhat brutal entertainment was doubtless avoided by gentlemen.[7]

Travelers' Rest is the name of a second dead town in Macon County; it was located about a mile south of present-day Montezuma. "A giant corporation made its appearance along the north bank of Beaver Creek, and on across Flint River, and the exodus from Travelers' Rest set in to Montezuma and Oglethorpe, two towns just freshly born on the line of the railroad. Travelers' Rest (like Lanier) was dead, the victim of a corporation."[8]

Oglethorpe, located at the terminus of the railroad built in 1851, was made the county seat in 1854.

In 1855, Oglethorpe enjoyed its heydey . . . a population of twenty thousand people . . . one of the largest cities in Georgia . . . An effort was made to move the Capitol of Georgia to Oglethorpe . . . the state legislature put the matter in the hands of the people . . . defeated by only one vote . . . eighty business houses, ten large cotton warehouses, eight livery stables, and four or more spacious hotels. . . . The largest and most beautiful hotel in the city was the Eagle and Phoenix . . . a four-story brick building, together with wings and annexes . . . near the hotel was Oliver Hall, built by Oliver Cox, a Negro speculator, who brought slaves to Oglethorpe and sold them. He got rich. . . . Oglethorpe already noted for its aristocracy, now became a city of culture . . . the pendulum of prosperity began to swing backwards . . . a serious blow to Oglethorpe was the extension of the railroad to Americus . . . a hundred houses were moved to Americus. . . . But alas! . . . a far greater disaster . . . an epidemic of smallpox . . . virulent . . . hundreds died each day, and whole families were buried in one night . . . in the "silent cemetery" (formerly burying ground of the Indians), since known as Smallpox Cemetery. . . . The town was ruined, desolation. . . . Hundreds of people made a quick exodus and were never heard of again . . . until in later years their heirs began writing back from all parts of the country to settle claims on property . . . This state of affairs became

[7] Walter Paschall, quoted in Louise Frederick Hays, *History of Macon County* (Atlanta, 1933), pp. 169-74.
[8] W. R. Harrison, quoted in *ibid.*, p. 134.

so bad that the town council was forced to issue a proclamation granting a clear title to the present owners of the property around Oglethorpe. . . . Beautiful suburbs laid off in streets and crowded with homes extended through what is now cotton patches, corn fields, pecan groves. . . .[9]

Oglethorpe now has a population of less than a thousand, and except for the location of the county courthouse there the population would probably be even smaller.[10]

Until a half-dozen years ago, there was every indication that Penfield, the site of Mercer University until 1860 when it was moved to the city of Macon, would be numbered among Greene County's dead towns. The transportation to Penfield of children from near-by white schools has slowed down its deterioration for the time being.

Towns and Transportation Facilities.—The largest towns in Greene are Greensboro with a population in 1930 of 2,125; Union Point, 1,627; White Plains, 406; Woodville, 332; Siloam, 269; and Penfield, 184. In Macon are Montezuma with a population of 2,284; Oglethorpe, 953; Marshallville, 931; and Ideal, 285. Except for minor manufactories in Greensboro and Union Point, and in Montezuma and Oglethorpe, these towns are only trading centers for outlying farm communities.

No point in either county is more than twelve miles from a railroad. The Georgia Railroad, with its Atlanta and Athens branches converging at Union Point, roughly divides Greene into three parts, while the Central of Georgia Railroad and the Atlanta, Birmingham, and Coast Railroad quarter Macon. Each county is quartered by state highways. There are two bridges across the Oconee River in Greene and one across the Flint River in Macon. Neither county had a hard-surfaced road across it in 1928, and no town in either county, with the exception of Montezuma, had paved streets. A hard-surfaced road now extends across Macon, and half-way across Greene.

[9] Mary Belle Powers, quoted in *ibid.*, pp. 174-83.
[10] See *ibid.*, pp. 171-72 for statement of Montezuma's unsucccessful effort to move the courthouse.

Both Greensboro and Marshallville have paved their main streets.

Present-day Manufactories and Agriculture.—There are small cotton textile factories at Greensboro and Union Point in Greene and at Montezuma in Macon County. Both Greensboro and Montezuma have cotton oil mills, and there is a planing mill at Woodville, in Greene, and one at Oglethorpe, in Macon. Between Oglethorpe and Montezuma there is a small fertilizer factory; Montezuma has a meat-curing plant, and an establishment for packing frozen fruits. To date, this latter industry has proved very expensive to its investors, for the equipment has remained idle except for a few weeks in the summer of 1931 when it was erected. Though most of the capital came from the outside, Macon County citizens invested several thousand dollars in the venture.[11]

The 1930 census report showed 802 people engaged in fourteen manufacturing plants in Greene and 246 in fifteen in Macon. The total value of Greene's manufactured products of that year was $1,938,094, an average of $2,417 per worker; Macon's total was $1,208,653, or $4,913 per worker. During this same year 2,588 Greene County people were engaged in agricultural pursuits, producing crops valued at $1,080,867, an average of $418 per worker; in Macon 5,056 agricultural workers produced crops valued at $2,673,834, or $528 per person.[12]

The major agricultural products of Greene County are cotton and corn, with minor dairy and poultry enterprises supplementing the home production of part of the meat and other foods consumed by the county's farm families. In addition to cotton and corn Macon County's agricultural products include peaches,[13] asparagus, melons, pecans, and peanuts in marketable quantities. The major portion of the county's farmers, however,

[11] In the summer of 1935 the plant was being used to extract peach juice for wine.

[12] United States Census.

[13] The Elberta Peach was originated by Samuel H. Rumph of Marshallville, Macon County, about 1875.

are limited, as in Greene, to the production of cotton and corn and a part of the meat and other foods consumed.

Rank of the Counties.—The per capita value of all agricultural and manufactured products in 1929 was $239 in Greene, $233 in Macon, $327 in Georgia.[14] The per capita value of taxable property in 1930 was $246.59 in Greene, $221.53 in Macon, $348.03 in Georgia.[15] In 1925 there was one income tax return in Greene to every 154 persons, one in Macon to every 158, one in Georgia to every 46 persons; in 1932, in Greene one income tax return to every 350 persons, in Macon one to every 361, in Georgia one to every 87.[16] The bank deposits per capita in 1925 were $43 in Greene, $50 in Macon, $116 in Georgia; in 1934, $27 in Greene, $41 in Macon, $91 in Georgia.[17] The per capita retail trade in 1929 was $104 in Greene, $99 in Macon, $219 in Georgia.[18]

In 1925 the population per automobile was 24.9 in Greene, 16.5 in Macon, 14.2 in Georgia; in 1934 the population per automobile was 10.4 in Greene, 15.0 in Macon, 7.3 in Georgia.[19] In 1934 the population per telephone was 41.5 in Greene, 46.9 in Macon, 18 in Georgia.[20] In March 1933, the population per residential electricity subscriber was 28.9 in Greene, 40.4 in Macon, 23.1 in Georgia.[21]

The number of persons per medical doctor in 1930 were 1,577 in Greene, 1,492 in Macon, 1,034 in Georgia.[22] The infant mortality rate per thousand live births in 1933 was 80.0 in Greene, 75.7 in Macon, 67.2 in Georgia.[23]

There is little need to present further data to establish the fact that Greene and Macon counties rank below the state av-

[14] United States Census.
[15] Tax Digests of Greene and Macon counties, and of Georgia.
[16] Rand McNally Commercial Atlas (1935).
[17] Data from the Federal Reserve Bank in Atlanta.
[18] United States Census.
[19] Compiled from Georgia state records.
[20] Compiled from data furnished by the Atlanta office of the American Telephone and Telegraph Company.
[21] Compiled from data obtained from the Georgia Power Company.
[22] Compiled from data obtained from the Georgia Department of Health.
[23] Compiled from data obtained from the Georgia Department of Health.

erage, as do most rural Black Belt counties. Black Belt states in turn rank at the bottom when the forty-eight states are rated on over fifty per capita measures, including those listed above.[24]

Population Elements.—In 1930, 99.9 per cent of all the people of both counties were native born whites and Negroes, the latter constituting 52.2 per cent of Greene's and 67.2 per cent of Macon's total population. Greene had but thirty-four persons of foreign or mixed parentage, Macon but thirty-two.

The whites are descended in main from the English, Scotch, Irish, and German stocks, although Norwegian, French, Italian, and Semitic strains are not altogether lacking. The Negroes are descended from various African peoples, including the Sudan and Bantu stocks, with a considerable admixture of other groups, particularly the Arabs, the American Indians, and the American whites. Despite the mixed heredity of the members of both races, there are almost no strangers in either county. From these rural families young men and women have migrated to cities in the South and North.

Man-Land Relations.—The agricultural ladder has four rungs: landowners at the top, renters next, then croppers, and wage hands at the bottom. Only one out of every ten Negro farmers owns any land, and scarcely half of these have enough to make a living on. Of the nine-tenths who own no land, about half are croppers, owning no work animals or plows or other farm equipment; nearly a fourth are farm wage hands, the poorest people in the community; the other fourth are renters, who own some work stock and farm equipment, and occupy a place midway between the owners and the croppers.

Although the whites own more than ninety-five out of every hundred acres, a little over half the rural white families are landless. They live as renters and croppers and wage hands in competition with the Negroes in these same tenure classes. About two-thirds of the resident whites who own land cultivate

[24] See R. B. Vance, *Human Geography of the South* (Chapel Hill, N. C., 1932), S. H. Hobbs, *North Carolina: Economic and Social* (Chapel Hill, N. C., 1930), and H. W. Odum, *Southern Regions* (Chapel Hill, N. C., 1936).

their own acreage. The remaining white families, about one-sixth of the total, are plantation owners on whose lands live most of the landless agricultural workers of both races. Here, as in other southern rural communities, the wage hands and croppers, the poorest people, live on the richest soil.

Until recently, the Negroes have moved slowly toward ownership in the face of heavy odds; it is very difficult for dependent agricultural workers to accumulate any cash; moreover, many local white people still feel that the Negro should remain a tenant, and that he is getting out of "his place" when he attempts to become independent through the ownership of land. This attitude explains why the Negro seldom buys land on the open market, why he must have the personal assistance of some landed white man to become an owner, why he usually purchases the less desirable land.

The Negro owner tends to become the leader and center of a new Negro community. He is the permanent resident of an otherwise shifting Negro farm population. He provides leadership and much of the support for the local institutions of his race. With an abiding interest in the land he cultivates, in the stock he raises, in the trees he plants, and in the community where he lives, the Negro owner, like the white owner, stands in sharp contrast with the landless farmers who move every two or three years from one barren farm cabin to another.

LOCAL COLOR

Man-land relations, landlord-tenant patterns, the white primary, the expenditures for public schools, the location of the churches, the everyday doings of whites and Negroes all foster the sentiments and differentials which define and maintain the Black Belt's way of life. From the local point of view there are few problems: the tenant is improvident, dependent, and childlike and the planter furnishes him food and supervises his labor; mortal violence sometimes overtakes the Negro—two were lynched in Macon in 1910, accused of murder, and one was lynched in Greene in 1920, accused of sheltering a Negro who had wounded a local white planter; several threatened lynchings have been prevented in recent years by vigilance of local officers and transference of the accused persons to distant jails for safe keeping. Lynching is resorted to only when the implied threat of it appears to be losing its efficacy.

The general peaceful relations between the two races in these counties rest, to no small degree, upon the Negro's acceptance of a rôle in which he is neither moral nor immoral—just nonmoral; neither saint nor sinner—just a rowdy; neither deceitful nor trustworthy, just lazy and easy-going; neither slave man nor free man—just an inferior man, just a "nigger."

Hospitality, Masters, Slaves.—These counties have their own stories of southern hospitality, masters, slaves, the Civil War, Reconstruction, Ku Klux Klan, disfranchisement of the Negroes, and on and on. According to an old diary, a resident of Lanier on March 20, 1856, dined with Colonel George W. Fish at Oglethorpe, Macon County, and enjoyed true southern hospitality: "Directly after entering the house, we were invited to the dining-room in the basement story, to drink wine or brandy. I took wine. Back in the parlor, we examined plats of Shakespeare, two volumes costing $140. Then to dinner. There were three glasses at each plate, one for wine, one for champagne, and the other for hot water. Soup constituted the first course, then wine; we were helped to meats, turkey, rice, ham and so forth. This course through, champagne."[25]

From the same diary in 1855 comes a record of master-slave relations: "Bill awakened me about 2 this morning saying that Lucy Long was dead. Perturbed in spirit, arose, dressed and read until day. This death falls heavily upon us—pecuniarily $900, as a cook and house servant she served as one of the family—her loss is therefore felt in a social way. Lucy Long was a good Negro, honest and true. Bill made her coffin, June and Nelse dug her grave at the churchyard. All the negroes went

[25] Quoted from the diary of James D. Frederick in Hays, *op. cit.*, p. 178 n.

to her burial."[26]   Another Macon County planter, standing over the open grave of a slave child, sobbed: "I would rather have lost a thousand dollars than that little nigger!"

War and Reconstruction.—In March, 1859, seven months before the election of Abraham Lincoln to the presidency, the general presentments of the Macon County grand jury included the following:

We should regard the election of a Black Republican professing "higher law" and "irrepressible conflict" doctrines to the Presidency as a declaration of war against the Constitution and against the rights and social institutions of the South to be resisted at the very threshold by every means which God and nature have placed in our power, even to a disruption of every tie which binds us to the so called "labor state."

And we further recommend to our fellow citizens not to support for political office any man or party who is not prepared to enforce rigidly all the guaranties of the Constitution and especially those relating to the rendition of "fugitives from justice and labor," those guarantying to each and every State the protection of the government of the United States against invasion and that, too, whether that invasion be by a foreign nation, an Indian tribe, or by another State of the Confederacy, and we insist that the government of the United States should be held to a strict performance of its duty in protecting our rights of property, including property in slaves, wherever that government has jurisdiction, whether on land or sea.

And we recommend to the next Legislature to have an act passed taxing all property manufactured in any of those states that have passed any hostile acts against the institution of slavery, that does virtually annul the Constitution of the United States or the laws of Congress passed in accordance with the same; and we request the Senator and Representative from this county to introduce and have passed such a law.[27]

The presentments of the Macon County Grand Jury of March, 1862 pointed out that

it behoove[s] us all to avert the evil that might befall our young Confederacy in the way of provisions by planting three or four times as much corn, peas, potatoes, rice, sugar cane, all sorts of vegetables,

[26] *Ibid.,* p. 170 n.
[27] *Ibid.,* pp. 289-90.

as we have ever before planted. In short, that we plant no cotton, except what we want to spin and weave at home, that we pay more attention to stock of all kinds and have them fat and fine, especially the pigs, calves and lambs, that we make our own clothes at home, tan our own leather and make our own shoes—make our own hats, and weave our own blankets. Those and many other things we can and must do for ourselves, thereby encouraging our Brothers and Sons in the field who are bearing the hardships of the war— having sent off six full companies into the service, we are willing to send yet another,[28] should it be called for.[29]

The Grand Jury in September of this same year petitioned the Senator and Representatives from Macon County to procure a law "prohibiting the manufacture and vending of ardent spirits in the county of Macon.[30] . . . Every bushel of grain converted into spirits diminishes the support of the soldier and his family, and contributes to the gratification and swells the profit of the extortioners who now afflict the land, and who are worse enemies to the cause of freedom than the hordes now arrayed with arms in their hands against our rights and liberties."[31]

The Justices of the Inferior Court of Macon County in July, 1864, following the Battle of Atlanta, set aside a day for prayer:

Whereas, it has pleased the Almighty to vouchsafe to us his Signal protection during the fearful Struggle we have been making for liberty and independence, and has blessed us in a thousand ways, far beyond what we have deserved; and especially has this portion of our beloved State been favored by his Providence in the fact that we have been blessed with good crops and with the absence of the vandal[32] foe from our midst.

We, therefore, the undersigned Justices of the Inferior Court of said County, impressed with the deep sense of the obligation of our people for the Merciful Providence of God to us, we hereby

[28] Four more companies were sent.

[29] Hays, op. cit., pp. 290-91.

[30] In 1876 Macon County passed a law restricting the sale of liquor: "Marshallville was not satisfied with a bare restriction, so . . . voted itself dry, and ranks as one of the first towns, if not the very first to take such action." Ibid., p. 215.

[31] Ibid., pp. 291-92.

[32] Greene County did not escape the "vandal," for Sherman's troops burned Parks Mill and did other damage in the county.—T. B. Rice, county historian.

request that the people of Macon County meet at their Several places of public worship on Friday, the 15th inst., and observe that day in fasting, humiliation and prayer to God for his blessing.

B. A. Hudson, J.I.C.,

Benja. Harris, J.I.C.,

W. W. Hill, J.I.C.,

R. Williams, J.I.C.[33]

A young Greene County father volunteered for service in the Confederate Army, leaving to the care of the family slaves his wife and a young daughter named Secessia in honor of the southern cause. Three years later he was home on a furlough to secure additional men and supplies.[34] In preparing to return, he and his slaves were on the front porch repacking some gunpowder. A spark from the father's pipe fired the cotton about the powder, which he quickly brushed off the porch. The burning cotton fell upon little Secessia, who was playing among the boxwood in the yard. She died. The heartbroken father returned to the army on schedule time with men and supplies.

Greene and Macon counties furnished more than a score of companies to the armies of the Confederacy; their casualties ran into the hundreds; the Confederate monument is conspicuous in each county. At the southwestern corner of Macon County is Andersonville, site of the Andersonville Prison for captured federal troops; near by is the National Cemetery where the 13,000 casualties of this prison lie buried.

At the close of the War came the "carpetbag" rule, after which white men, many under legal age, voted again and again in their own and adjoining counties, or took the tax receipts of Negro registrants to keep them from voting, or stood with a leveled gun at the courthouse to keep the Negroes from disturbing "the count" when a minority white vote was determining the election.[35]

Present-Day Relationships.—The Emancipation Proclama-

[33] Hays, *op. cit.*, pp. 293-94.

[34] There was a Confederate pistol factory at Greensboro, according to T. B. Rice.

[35] These and numerous other similar instances have been reported to the writer by elderly inhabitants of Greene and Macon counties.

tion by no means eradicated distinctions felt by both Negroes and whites, nor did it change the paradoxical feelings of affection and devotion which have always existed between many members of both races, as is shown in the following incidents.

"Stand up! Stand up! Can't you see it's a white man?" stormed a stout Negro woman to her pupils when she answered a knock at the schoolhouse door and saw a white man there. Bewildered, the visitor asked the children to sit down—he little expected such obsequiousness, even in Greene County.

A Negro tenant went to his landlord's store to complain of the white overseer's treatment; the landlord was attentive and sympathetic, but when the enraged overseer rushed in with a mattock handle, the landlord and the other whites looked on while the defenseless Negro was sworn to absolute silence: "You don't need to be running to Mr. John about me! Now, d— you, do you hear?" "Ya-as sir, but—" "But what? Now none of your mouth, or I'll maul your brains out!" And that was the end of the matter that day; but when the year was ended the white overseer, no longer needed on this plantation, found employment elsewhere, while the Negro tenant remained.

It was Saturday afternoon in Marshallville, and many Negroes were standing about the store. A white planter entered and upon spying his old Negro Mammy said, "Why hey there, Mammy." His reminiscing with her about old times proved so entertaining to the Negroes and scattered whites that he found himself suggesting: "How about lulling me to sleep, Mammy?" "No-o! you'se done too big now, Mr. Bud," was her reply. Not to be outdone, the planter sat down in her lap anyway. Everybody shouted, "Just Mr. Bud and his old Mammy a-playin'."

At Montezuma, an elderly mother, head of a prominent family, petitioned the city council to allow her family servant, a Negro, to be buried in the cemetery along with the members of the family. The petition was granted.

In Greene County, the direct descendant of an early planter was scrambling about in a thicket to find the tombstones of her illustrious forbears, Virginians who had moved to Georgia. "Now, who was this? Why I don't remember him," she mused by one tombstone. After some time she realized that it marked the burial place of a slave. The fence around the white graves had rotted down—time is careless of distinctions marked off by fences.

Human Pictures.—The Black Belt's way of life is best felt through the little everyday human incidents which may be observed anywhere. Pride is here, and wariness, good-natured humor, hard work, and protracted loafing.

A storekeeper, seeing a white tenant spit upon his floor, tactfully suggested that he would find a sand-box to the right of the stove; the tenant turned and walked out of the front door and down the sidewalk. "Oh well," sighed the storekeeper, "if he doesn't feel at home here let him go where he will."

Another storekeeper, at Siloam, had been bothered for several weeks by thieves' breaking his oil pump and stealing small quantities of crankcase oil. Padlocks failed to stop them. He decided to mix discarded oil with molasses and pour it into the drum. Some mornings later a most unusual report went about town: an old Ford had been dragged in from down around White Plains; it had got hot and the cylinder had locked; the mechanic found molasses in the crankcase. It was not until nearly noon that the white boys, sons of tenant farmers in the lower part of the county, learned that everybody in town had been laughing at their stealing molasses for an automobile.

A Negro wage hand bought a plug of Taylor's Special tobacco and a plug of Brown Mule. He put the latter in his pocket with no wrapping on it. "There is more chewers than buyers," he said, "so I always has some cheap backer loose in my pocket—it takes less when it's been sweated on."

James, eighteen, dresses every afternoon at three and walks down to the store; on Saturdays he arrives at ten. His father works in the railroad shops of a distant city to earn a livelihood for the family and to pay taxes on the old plantation. Without any particular reason for doing so, James is following the schedule of his planter grandfather.

A mother left her tenant cabin with a baby in her arms, broke a sapling, carried it to the middle of the field, stuck it in the ground and tied her crawling child fast to it to keep him in the shade while she hoed. In another field there was a thirteen-year-old boy with a hoe; he had been hoeing seven years.

In 1928, before the depression had reached the cities, a new-comer to Greene or Macon counties might well have said: "If somebody has something he needs laborers to do, here would be a good place to start a business. These people will work and work hard for just a little more than the little which they are now making." In the succeeding pages we shall follow the fortunes of the rural dwellers under the ravages of the boll weevil, under the general depression, under the New Deal.

PART TWO

Planes of Living

CHAPTER III

INCOMES AND EXPENDITURES

THAT THE income of southern families is low is generally known. To obtain accurate information for Greene and Macon counties, a visit was made to each of over 300 farm families in 1927 and again in 1934. Careful questioning determined: first, the total cash income of each family; second, the expenditures for food, tobacco, clothing, and so on; third, the gross income, including the value of all home-grown provisions consumed by the family.

The distribution by race and tenure class of the families studied is shown in the table below. It will be observed that families of both races were studied in 1934, Negroes only in 1927. The Negro families are representative of all Negro farm

TABLE I

DISTRIBUTION BY RACE AND TENURE CLASS OF FAMILIES STUDIED
INTENSIVELY IN GREENE AND MACON COUNTIES, GEORGIA[1]

| | 1927 | | | 1934 | | | | | | |
| | NEGROES | | | WHITE | | | NEGRO | | | BOTH RACES |
TENURE	Greene	Macon	Total	Greene	Macon	Total	Greene	Macon	Total	Total
Owners.........	19	13	32	16	21	37	14	11	25	62
Renters.........	58	19	77	13	14	27	45	11	56	83
Croppers........	57	91	148	6	6	12	30	43	73	85
Wage hands, etc. .	14	52	66	5	3*	8	27	54	81	89
Total...........	148	175	323	40	44	84	116	119	235	319

*Farm managers and overseers.

families. The white families, too, are representative except of the largest planters who are comparatively few in number and usually live in the towns.

The composition of the Negro families studied in 1927 was briefly as follows: the average number of persons per household was 5.2 in each county; in both counties the renter and cropper

[1] A detailed questionnaire was filled in for each of these families, and all tables in this chapter not credited to other sources were compiled from these questionnaires.

households were above that average, owners slightly below, and wage hands about 40 per cent below the average. Because of the great migration from Greene during the twenties, resulting in the movement of a disproportionate number of the young and middle-aged adults, more of the households there than in Macon County are made up of elderly people and young children, frequently left behind by migrating parents. The composition of the white households, though slightly smaller than the Negro, follows the same general pattern, both parents being present in a slightly larger proportion of the cases.

The tenure distribution of the Negro families in 1927 and in 1934 shows that the number of families in the owner and renter groups remained about constant during the period, while the croppers decreased and the wage hands and laborers increased, making this lowest tenure class the largest, with 34.5 per cent of all families in both counties in it. The fact that the same Negro families were studied in 1934 as in 1927, except

TABLE II

PERCENTAGE DISTRIBUTION BY TENURE CLASS OF NEGRO FARM FAMILIES STUDIED IN GREENE AND MACON COUNTIES, GEORGIA, IN 1927 AND 1934

TENURE	GREENE		MACON		TOTAL	
	1927	1934	1927	1934	1927	1934
Owners...................	12.8	12.1	7.4	9.2	9.9	10.6
Renters...................	39.2	38.8	10.9	9.2	23.8	23.8
Croppers.................	38.5	25.8	52.0	36.2	45.8	31.1
Wage hands and laborers...	9.5	23.3	29.7	45.4	20.5	34.5
Total...................	100.0	100.0	100.0	100.0	100.0	100.0

for the eighty-eight which could not be located in the latter year, makes the increase of the lowest tenure class even more significant, for quite naturally a much larger proportion of the more stable families than of the less stable ones were still in the county in 1934. Here again we have evidence of the cotton farmer's recent downward shift on the agricultural ladder, with its four rungs—wage hands on the bottom, croppers on the next rung, renters on the third, and owners at the top.

ANNUAL CASH INCOME PER FAMILY

The cash income of the families, varying by race and tenure class, averages less than a dollar a day per family, less than twenty cents a day per person.

Three Hundred Dollars a Year.—It will be observed from the following table that in 1934 in Greene the average cash income was $301.26 per rural white family and $150.74 per rural Negro family; in Macon, $872.21 for the white and $299.56 for the Negro. The relatively high cash incomes of the white families in Macon are due to the operation of large

TABLE III

ANNUAL CASH INCOMES OF THE FARM FAMILIES STUDIED IN 1927 AND IN 1934, GREENE AND MACON COUNTIES, GEORGIA

| | NEGROES | | | | WHITES | |
| | Greene | | Macon | | Greene | Macon |
	1927	1934	1927	1934	1934	1934
AVERAGE INCOME.........	$302.06	$150.74	$ 380.79	$299.56	$301.26	$872.21
OWNERS:						
Cotton...............	359.68	183.36	914.03	750.14	123.44	706.29
Other Crops..........	109.20	23.83	44.09	3.75	100.56	117.19
Wages...............	26.04	28.77	20.91	40.64	96.38	119.17
Relief.................	......	.89	......	......	*75.31	....
Total.............	494.92	236.85	979.03	794.53	395.69	942.65
RENTERS:						
Cotton...............	242.59	132.91	353.76	345.05	180.05	715.91
Other Crops..........	32.07	14.02	21.96	5.04	9.50	9.50
Wages...............	15.59	22.12	36.76	30.78	55.77	145.00
Relief.................	......	3.41	......	.14	*47.23	......
Total.............	290.25	172.46	412.48	381.01	292.55	870.41
CROPPERS:						
Cotton...............	156.59	109.30	363.63	315.93	50.00	638.08
Other crops...........	20.50	3.66	33.41	7.65	4.83	13.17
Wages...............	100.02	21.00	61.67	15.11	**126.67	66.67
Relief.................	......	1.69	......	.43	15.00	......
Total.............	277.11	135.65	458.71	339.12	196.50	717.92
WAGE HANDS, ETC.:						
Wages...............	130.99	71.92	280.23	142.65	121.50	580.66
Relief.................	......	14.74	......	7.99	25.90	......
Total.............	130.99	86.66	280.23	150.64	147.40	***580.66

*Includes pensions and supervisory jobs with Federal relief.
**Though listed as croppers, they are in a transitional stage and approximate wage hands.
***Farm managers and overseers.

acreages by subletting to other tenants or by using wage hand labor, the expenses of which come out of the cash incomes here reported. With but one exception, the Negro renters in Macon in 1927, it will be observed that the owners of each race in each county had the largest cash income, the renters next, croppers next, and wage hands least, and that within each county by tenure class the cash incomes of white families were higher than of Negro families.

Though the cash incomes of the Negroes in each tenure class in each county were below those of the whites in that county, it will be noted that in 1934 the Macon County Negro owners, renters, croppers, and wage hands, respectively, had higher cash incomes than the Greene County whites in the same tenure classes. The slightly higher average income for all Greene whites than for all Macon Negroes is caused by the larger proportion of owners and renters in the white group.

Cash Income in 1927 and in 1934.—In 1927 the Negro families had low annual cash incomes, averaging $302.06 in Greene and $380.79 in Macon; by 1934 the average had dropped to $150.74 in Greene and $299.56 in Macon. The 1934 incomes of Negro wage hands in Macon and of all Negro tenure classes in Greene were under $250.00 for each group. The annual cash income of wage hands in Macon fell from $280.23 to $150.64—a 46.0 per cent shrinkage—and in Greene from $130.99 to $86.66—a 34.0 per cent shrinkage. This does not represent the whole story, for while his dollars were fewer in 1934, each one of them would buy less than in 1927. Nor is this all, for the proportion of rural families in the wage hand group, as stated above, is much larger now than in 1927, which means that while the fourteen Greene families which were wage hands in 1927 and 1934 received a cash income shrinkage of 34.0 per cent, the thirteen other families which dropped from the cropper group of 1927, with an average cash income of $277.11, suffered a shrinkage of nearly 70.0 per cent. For the Macon family that slipped from the status of cropper in 1927 to wage hand in 1934, there was a drop from $458.71 to $150.64, a shrinkage of 67.0 per cent.

But low incomes are by no means limited to wage hands, for their plight of receiving fewer and cheaper dollars is common to all tenure classes. Other farm families with cash incomes in 1934 of less than $100.00, including relief, involved, in Greene one-fourth of the Negro owners, nearly one-third of the Negro renters, a little more than one-third of the Negro croppers, and about one-fifth of all white farmers, some of whom were small owners. In Macon, except for the Negro wage hands, one-fifth of whom received less than $100.00, scarcely one-thirtieth of the Negro farm families and none of the whites fell in this lowest income bracket.

In 1927 only one-tenth of Greene's Negro families, including wage hands, had received annual incomes of less than $100.00, while only one-fortieth of Macon's families had received incomes so low. Excluding wage hands, the five lowest cash incomes in Greene for 1934 were: $10.00, $22.90, $30.00, $30.45, and $31.80; for 1927 the lowest were: $25.00, $31.27, $44.34, $59.09, and $73.21.

Cash from Cotton.—Except in the case of wage hands, cotton is the principal source of cash income of practically all the rural families. By referring to the table above, showing cash incomes, it will be observed that in every instance, except white owners in Greene, all tenure classes with an average cash income of over $350.00 received three-fourths or more of it from cotton alone. But many tenure classes with an average cash income of less than $350.00 also received more than three-fourths of it from cotton, namely the Negro owners, renters, and croppers of Greene in 1934. Clearly enough, only the white farmers in Greene have even attempted to escape the dominance of cotton, and their cash incomes by tenure classes, as mentioned above, are uniformly lower than those of the Macon County Negro farmers of the same tenure classes, almost exclusively cotton producers.

Other Sources of Cash.—Among the white owners, partic-

TABLE IV

PER CENT OF ALL CASH INCOME FROM COTTON ALONE,
GREENE AND MACON COUNTIES, GEORGIA[2]

| TENURE | NEGROES | | | | WHITES | |
| | Greene | | Macon | | Greene | Macon |
	1926	1934	1927	1934	1934	1934
Owners..................	72.7	77.4	69.2	94.4	31.2	74.9
Renters..................	62.4	77.1	85.8	90.5	61.5	82.2
Croppers................	56.5	80.6	79.3	93.2	25.4*	88.8

*These croppers are approximating wage hand status.

ularly of Greene, a considerable proportion of the cash income
is secured from the sale of such miscellaneous farm products as
milk, butter, chickens, eggs, dry beans, potatoes, and other
vegetables. The cotton mills at Greensboro and Union Point
provide some market for Greene County farm products, while
Athens, Madison, and even Atlanta and Augusta are not wholly
inaccessible.

In Macon some of the largest planters, particularly east of
the river, produce peaches, watermelons, asparagus, and other
crops for shipment. The peach and watermelon crops are large,
but less important than a decade ago, as are also peanuts, and
cowpeas. There is in each county some development of beef
herds, and poultry yards, with little indication that they will become popular. Cotton is still king. In 1929, as reported by
the census, Macon County's cotton sold for nearly $1,400,000;
peaches and pecans for $541,000; asparagus for $128,778; watermelons for $47,568. Moreover, since diversification is limited
almost entirely to the big plantations around Montezuma and
Marshallville, the typical farmer still secures practically all his
cash income from cotton. Of Greene's $1,080,692 value of all
farm crops in 1929, cotton alone accounted for over $750,000.

Cash incomes from livestock, though important to a few
farmers, are quite small for the average farmer. In 1929, the
total value of all the cattle and chickens in Greene County was
less than $190,000, in Macon less than $125,000, with cash

[2] Computed from Table III.

CHOPPING COTTON—THIRTY TO FIFTY CENTS A DAY

POTATO HILLS, IF ENOUGH OF THEM, MEAN POTATOES ALL WINTER

MACON COUNTY—THE ANGELUS OF THE BLACK BELT

AND THE GLEANERS, PLANTING CABBAGES

incomes from these sources certainly not more than $75,000 in Greene and $50,000 in Macon.

The two remaining sources of cash income are wages and relief, and there is little room for hope from either, for there are more laborers than there are jobs, and relief as now administered in these counties offers a means of subsistence, where it is available, rather than an opportunity to secure an adequate cash income. Except for the whites in Greene County, the rural families studied had secured but little help through relief, including pensions. Details about the administration of relief appear in a later chapter.

The Wages of Wage Hands.—Irregular employment is but half the explanation of the wage hands' low cash income; the daily wage for the last two years has ranged between forty and sixty cents for men and thirty and fifty cents for women, in some instances even lower and in others a bit higher.

Listed here are the figures from one plantation for four weeks in May 1933, and four weeks in April 1934. The daily wage, it will be noted, was for men forty cents and for women thirty cents in 1933, though one or two received more. In 1934 the wages were ten cents a day higher. The seven or eight families represented here secure scarcely any income from other sources. It will be observed that wages are by the day rather than by the week or month, meaning that rainy days and slack work seasons are periods of little or no income.

Eight to ten dollars a month for the head of the house, that much more for the labor of his wife and children during the busy months, and half as much monthly during the other eight months—$128 to $160 cash income a year—is a very liberal estimate for the typical wage hand family for 1933 and 1934. Even if half the wage hands' money is spent for food products from the plantation commissary, where in one instance at least they are sold at about half-price, the value of the wage hand family's cash income is even then scarcely $200 at the most.

By Way of Summary.—In this discussion of cash incomes, six facts are important: first, the low cash incomes of rural fam-

TABLE V

NUMBER OF DAYS WORKED AND WEEKLY WAGES RECEIVED BY WAGE HANDS
ON A MACON COUNTY PLANTATION, MAY, 1933[3]

NAME OF WORKER	FIRST WEEK		SECOND WEEK		THIRD WEEK		FOURTH WEEK		TOTAL FOR FOUR WEEKS	
	Days	Wages	Days	Wages	Days	Wages	Days	Wages	Days	Wages
Doc	5½	$ 2.20	5½	$ 2.20	5½	$ 2.20	6	$ 2.40	22½	$ 9.00
Gus	5½	2.20	5½	2.20	5	2.00	6	2.40	22	8.80
Major	5½	3.30	5½	3.30	5½	3.30	5½	3.30	22	13.20
Little Joe	3½	1.40	5½	2.20	1	.40	....	.....	10	4.00
Old Joe	....	.....	5	5.50	5	2.00	5½	2.40	15½	9.90
Wolf	....	1.50	....	1.50	....	1.50	....	1.50	....	6.00
John Henry	2	.80	4	1.60	1	.60	5½	2.20	12½	5.20
Rosa	3½	1.05	4¼	1.30	1¾	.52	....	.....	9½	2.87
Sam	3½	1.05	4¼	1.30	1¾	.52	½	.15	10	3.02
Mary	3	.90	4	1.20	....	.....	....	.....	7	2.10
Fannie	3	.90	3¼	1.00	1½	.45	....	.....	7¾	2.35
Mary	2	.60	....	.....	....	.....	....	.....	2	.60
Lissie	3½	1.05	4¼	1.30	1¾	.52	½	.15	10	3.02
Speed	....	.....	3	3.00	....	.....	....	.....	3	3.00
Pete	....	.....	....	.....	2½	1.00	....	.....	2½	1.00
George Cook	....	.....	....	.....	1½	.60	....	.....	1½	.60
Guy	....	.....	....	.....	....	.....	½	.20	½	.20
Tom	....	.....	....	.....	....	.....	2½	1.00	2½	1.00
Big Boy	....	.....	....	.....	....	.....	½	.20	½	.20
Total	40½	$16.95	54	$27.60	33¾	$15.61	33	$15.90	161¼	$ 76.06

ilies; second, the close relationship of incomes in each county to race and tenure status; third, the uniform decrease of incomes between 1927 and 1934; fourth, the increase of the proportion of all farm families in the wage hand groups in 1934 as compared with 1927; fifth, the uniformly lower incomes of Negroes within each tenure group in each county; sixth, the uniformly lower incomes by race and tenure class in Greene as compared with Macon.

A partial explanation of the distribution of cash incomes by tenure classes, races, and counties lies in the number of acres in the farms of the various groups. As will be noted by comparing the accompanying table with the one above on incomes, the lower incomes and the smaller acreages go together—the Negro family is uniformly below the white in each county by tenure class,

[3] Data copied from day book of a Macon County plantation.

TABLE VI

NUMBER OF DAYS WORKED AND WEEKLY WAGES RECEIVED BY WAGE HANDS ON A MACON COUNTY PLANTATION, APRIL, 1934[4]

NAME OF WORKER	FIRST WEEK		SECOND WEEK		THIRD WEEK		FOURTH WEEK		TOTAL FOR FOUR WEEKS	
	Days	Wages	Days	Wages	Days	Wages	Days	Wages	Days	Wages
Doc............	5½	$ 2.75	5½	$ 2.75	4¾	$ 2.35	5½	$ 2.75	21¼	$ 10.60
Major...........	5½	3.85	5½	3.85	4	2.80	5½	3.85	20½	14.35
Jim............	5½	2.75	5½	2.75	4	2.00	5½	2.75	20½	10.25
Daniel..........	5½	2.75	5½	2.75	3¾	1.90	5½	2.75	20¼	10.15
Asbury..........	5¼	2.60	5½	2.75	4	2.00	2¾	1.35	17½	8.70
Mack...........	5½	2.75	5½	2.75	1½	.75	5½	2.75	18	9.00
Joe Cook........	5	2.50	5½	2.75	3¼	1.60	4¾	2.35	18½	9.20
Pete...........	5½	2.75	5½	2.75	3¼	1.60	5½	2.75	19¾	9.85
Al.............	5½	2.75	½	.35	½	.25	1½	.75	8	4.10
Harry..........	½	.25	5	2.00	3¼	1.60	5½	2.75	14¼	6.60
Jerry...........	....	.....	....	.....	....	.....	4	2.00	4	2.00
Lissie..........	1½	.60	....	.....	1¾	.70	....	.....	3¼	1.30
Wolf...........	....	2.00	....	2.00	....	2.00	....	2.00	....	8.00
Sam............	1½	.60	....	.....	1¾	.70	....	.....	3¼	1.30
Reub...........	....	.....	4½	2.25	....	.....	5¼	2.00	9¾	4.25
Sambo..........	....	.....	4½	2.25	4¼	1.75	5½	2.75	14½	6.75
Malinda........	....	.....	....	.....	1¼	.50	....	.....	1¼	.50
Zinie..........	....	.....	....	.....	1¼	.50	....	.....	1¼	.50
Sally..........	....	.....	....	.....	¾	.30	....	.....	¾	.30
Lizzie.........	....	.....	....	.....	¾	.30	....	.....	¾	.30
Fannie May......	....	.....	....	.....	¾	.30	....	.....	¾	.30
Lil............	....	.....	....	.....	....	.30	....	.....	....	.30
Grace..........	....	.....	....	.....	....	.10	....	.....	....	.10
Boots..........	....	.....	....	.....	....	.10	....	.....	....	.10
Total......	52¼	$28.90	58½	$31.95	44¾	$24.40	62¼	$33.55	218	$118.80

and the Greene family is uniformly below the Macon family by tenure class, so much, in fact, that by tenure class the Macon Negro families rank above the Greene white families in acreage as they did in cash incomes. The fact that the larger incomes coincide with the larger acreages has but one exception, that of the Negro owners who, as shown in this and other chapters, often increase their cash incomes by working for wages and by the weekly sale of animal products and miscellaneous crops from their relatively small farms.

[4] Data copied from day book of a Macon County plantation.

TABLE VII

AVERAGE NUMBER OF ACRES IN FARMS BY RACE AND BY TENURE CLASS, GREENE AND MACON COUNTIES, GEORGIA, 1929[5]

TENURE	NEGROES		WHITES	
	Greene	Macon	Greene	Macon
Owners......................	20.3	42.3	33.8	67.6
Renters......................	23.8	45.8	26.9	61.4
Croppers....................	21.7	40.9	26.5	57.9

FAMILY EXPENDITURES

The principal expenditures of these rural families are for food, clothing, and tobacco.

Food from the Store.—In both counties the wage hand families spend more than half their cash income for food, the exact amounts for 1934 averaging $43.48 in Greene and $80.13 in Macon. Croppers and renters in Greene spent ten dollars more than did wage hands; in Macon, the food costs of the three lower tenure groups were all in the eighties. The Negro owners, as might be expected from their live-at-home habits, spend slightly less for food than the wage hands. The variation among white families follows the same pattern, the amounts being 10 to 20 per cent higher.

In 1927 Negro families in Greene had spent nearly twice as much for food as in 1934, but in Macon only one-eighth more. The principal foods bought were meat, lard, meal, flour, sugar, and such items as coffee, baking powder, salt, pepper, and soap. More than one-third of all the money spent for food by Macon's Negro wage hands, croppers, and renters went for meat; the Negroes in Greene spent about one-fifth for meat, the whites in each county approximately one-tenth. The families with the most home-grown meat bought little or none.

Some owners without meat, and now and then a successful tenant family may buy a quarter of beef, half a veal, or a smoked ham. The typical cropper and wage hand family, except for an occasional can of salmon, and once or twice during the winter a "mess" of fresh pork, buys only slabs of western fat meat,

[5] United States Census.

called "fatback" and "sow belly" by those who eat most of it. The smoke which rises three times a day during the work season from the landless farmer's cabin attests to the fact that he eats fried fat meat for every meal, and usually with it corn bread and molasses, and when times are good coffee with sugar.

Dippin', Chewin', and Smokin'.—Tobacco is prized by many rural dwellers. Whether because they had more money or for other reasons, the Macon white families spent most for tobacco, averaging $33.82 per year; the Greene whites spent $15.91; the Macon Negroes, $14.90; and the Greene Negroes $9.57. But, by tenure class and by race the landless farmers—croppers and renters—regularly spent more than the owners and wage hands. In short, tobacco is consumed in greatest quantities by the families "furnished" by landlords.

The amount spent for tobacco in 1927 by Negro families was nearly 25 per cent above the 1934 expenditure. For the landless farmer's family tobacco is usually included in "the provisions." If the landlord provides trade, tobacco is a legitimate item; if the head of the family is given a check by the landlord once a month during the growing season, a practice less common now than in 1927, the members of his family impress upon him the necessity of "bringin' de snuff and chewin' backer." Many tenants maintain that they cannot "turn off" work unless they have an ample supply. What the tenant has to do is to convince his landlord that a little more tobacco in his mouth will mean a lot more cotton in the warehouse.

Dipping snuff, though common among the women, is by no means limited to them. With brushes and without, a considerable proportion of the men, women, and children of both races use snuff. Chewing, too, is limited to neither race nor sex. Smoking—the old clay pipe of the stooped Negro woman on the back of the plantation is a reminder of the Black Belt's yesterday; the cheap rolled cigarette in the mouth of her cotton-picking granddaughter is evidence that the Black Belt of today shares in the national culture. Generally speaking, however, smoking is a man's pastime, and he rolls his own from the

TABLE VIII

ANNUAL EXPENDITURES FOR FOOD, TOBACCO, AND CLOTHING OF RURAL
FAMILIES AND CASH REMAINING FOR ALL OTHER PURPOSES, BY RACE
AND TENURE CLASS, IN GREENE AND MACON COUNTIES,
GEORGIA, 1927 AND 1934

| | NEGROES | | | | WHITES | |
| | Greene | | Macon | | Greene | Macon |
	1927	1934	1927	1934	1934	1934
EXPENDITURES FOR:						
ALL FAMILIES:						
Food.................	$104.46	$ 51.50	$103.38	$ 81.78	$ 68.19	$ 73.61
Tobacco..............	16.62	9.57	19.84	14.90	15.91	33.82
Clothing.............	......	19.96	......	32.42	55.46	137.59
Total..............	......	81.03	......	129.10	139.56	245.02
OWNERS:						
Food*...............	94.13	37.54	67.89	65.90	65.02	56.76
Tobacco..............	12.21	7.00	9.30	12.48	15.12	30.86
Clothing.............	......	32.30	......	42.78	60.37	139.14
Total..............	......	76.84	......	121.16	140.51	226.76
RENTERS:						
Food.................	104.30	56.73	95.65	85.16	76.12	81.71
Tobacco..............	15.39	11.32	18.23	14.46	20.35	44.36
Clothing.............	......	24.28	......	41.48	65.31	147.64
Total..............	......	92.33	......	141.10	161.78	273.71
CROPPERS:						
Food.................	120.09	57.55	113.57	87.05	62.19	95.00
Tobacco..............	19.03	9.85	22.68	16.65	11.17	21.50
Clothing.............	......	17.09	......	39.45	36.92	142.50
Total..............	......	84.49	......	143.15	110.28	259.00
WAGE HANDS, ETC.:						
Food.................	59.03	43.48	96.64	80.13	65.00	125.67
Tobacco..............	11.42	7.68	18.09	14.09	12.60	30.00
Clothing.............	......	9.54	......	22.89	36.39	70.00
Total..............	......	60.70	......	117.11	113.99	225.67
REMAINING CASH:						
All Families...........	......	67.91	......	170.46	161.70	626.19
Owners...............	......	160.01	......	673.37	255.18	715.90
Renters..............	......	80.13	......	239.91	130.77	596.70
Croppers.............	......	51.16	......	195.97	86.22	454.92
Wage Hands..........	......	25.96	......	33.53	33.41	354.99

*The smaller expenditures for food by the owners than by other tenure classes reflect the production
of more foodstuffs on their farms.

cheapest of bagged tobacco. Prominent on the shelves of the stores are a half-dozen brands of snuff in small tin cans, a three-foot row of plug tobacco in broken boxes, neat stacks of smoking tobacco in extravagantly painted tins or little sacks, with plenty of cigarette paper free. There are cigars and cigarettes, too, but less prominently displayed, for calls are fewer.

Clothing the Family.—The expenditures for clothing are closely related to total cash incomes, the owners of each race spending most, renters next, then croppers, and wage hands least. The Negroes used a smaller proportion of their cash incomes for clothing than the whites, in Greene 13.2 per cent in contrast with 18.4 per cent by whites, in Macon 10.8 per cent against 15.8 per cent. The average annual clothing bill for white families was $55.46 in Greene and $137.59 in Macon, for Negroes $19.96 in Greene and $32.42 in Macon.

With their small cash incomes, it is little wonder that most of the farm Negroes and many of the poorer whites literally live in overalls, in winter wearing one or more pairs of old pants under them, in summer wearing them "agin de skin." It is easy to believe the common report of Negro teachers that some of the children cannot come to school because of inadequate clothing. The writer has seen a few Negro children in school in January barefooted. New dresses for the farm mother and her daughters are few and cheap, and although many are made at home on sewing machines or by hand, the poorest people of both races frequently buy ready-made dresses, and shoes with shiny qualities rather than lasting ones, in their effort to dress up in Sunday clothes for a few dollars.

People accustomed to being poor and wearing the same clothes for weeks and months at a time—literally everyday clothes, these are—get a real thrill out of a cheap, gay outfit which costs no more than one good pair of boots and lasts hardly one-fourth as long. For a few days the farm peasant escapes his lot—he wears clothes not made to work in. Even this empty relief is outside the reach of many families who spend less than fifteen dollars a year for clothes; the Negro wage hands and croppers in Greene and the wage hands in Macon averaged but $9.54, $17.09, and $22.87 respectively. The tenant farmer, often with debts to his landlord absorbing all his cash income, pleads for a little money—at least enough to buy his wife a new dress. Each year in the Black Belt thousands of farm mothers chop cotton and pick cotton and then fail to get one new cotton dress at the end of the year. The clothes for the children in many of the families are strikingly inadequate; thousands of babies have only two or three dresses and a half-dozen napkins each, and most of these are made from feed and salt sacks.

"Ten Per Cent Interest" on Tenant Advances.—The bills for food, tobacco, and clothing, which the tenants repay when they sell their cotton in the fall, include the interest charged, usually "10 per cent," sometimes even higher, in some instances lower. This 10 per cent interest must be analyzed to be understood. Suppose, for example, a cropper operating two plows accumulates an indebtedness of $100 during the six-months' period, March 15 to September 15. On October 15 the cropper sells his cotton and the landlord secures $110, the $10 being the 10 per cent interest. Actually, the cropper's interest is 35 per cent per annum, for he has had the money on an average of but three and one-half months. Raising the real interest rate still higher is the not uncommon practice of charging credit prices against the purchases of tenants—interest rates of 40 per cent and above thus occur where 10 per cent interest is charged, meaning that the tenant's dollar is only one-half to two-thirds as productive as the dollar of the pay-as-you-go farmer.

The Remaining Cash, Demands Upon It.—After expenditures for food, tobacco, and clothing were deducted from the annual income, the cash left for the family to spend for all other purposes[6] averaged $67.91 per Negro family and $161.70 per

---

[6] It should be borne in mind that the landless farm family has no cash outlay for house rent and seldom for fuel. The house is used without direct cost to the family, and wood is usually taken from a woodlot near by. Farm houses, however, are by no means "free," for their use is limited to families whom the landlord wishes to employ. Only in the tumble-down shacks on abandoned plantations can a rural family live without contracting his labor

white family in Greene, $170.46 per Negro family and $626.19 per white family in Macon. It will be observed from the table above that the average wage hand in Greene had but $25.96, and that five other tenure groups, including the white wage hands and white croppers in Greene, had less than $90 left.

From his cash surplus the owner must buy his land, and equipment, his fertilizer and, usually, feed; he must pay his taxes. Will he be able to pay his doctor, his lodge dues, contribute to his church, keep his children in school, help his sick neighbor, or buy an automobile? The renter from his surplus must settle his accounts for seed, feed, and fertilizer, and maintain his work stock and farm implements. If he has any money left, he can pay a doctor's bill, buy schoolbooks, get a tooth crowned, contribute to the local church, join a lodge, buy a second-hand car. The cropper from his cash balance must repay his half of the fertilizer bill; if he has anything left he may then buy a cook stove, a new bed, schoolbooks; he may subscribe to a newspaper or surprise his children with a little red wagon; he may get drunk and gamble away the family's small cash resources; he may use his money to help a kinsman get out of jail; he may devote the year's cash to the purchase of a cheap mule in the hope of becoming a renter.

The tenant's fertilizer bills, like his expenditures for food, tobacco, and clothing, may carry just the "ten per cent interest" or they may be on the basis of credit prices. In some cases where the landlord pays cash for fertilizer the tenant shares the benefits of this earlier settlement; in others he does not, the landlord holding that there is no reason why he should pass on to the tenant the advantage secured by arranging the cash payment. In another chapter are discussed the services of federal agencies to farmers, and their effects upon interest rates.

Doctors, Drugs, Nurses.—In Greene, half the white and nearly half the Negro farmers had doctor bills in 1934, all white families averaging $11.46, Negroes $5.57; in Macon over

and that of the other members of his family to the owner of the house he lives in.

three-fourths of the whites had had the services of a doctor, averaging $47.58, and nearly one-half of the Negroes, averaging $11.15. For drugs the Greene whites averaged $2.26, with two-fifths of them making purchases; the Negroes averaged $2.71, with nine-tenths of them making purchases. In Macon, nine-tenths of each race spent money for medicine, the whites averaging $13.13, the Negroes $2.54. Of all the families studied intensively, but one had the services of a trained nurse during the year.

Midwives and Patent Medicines.—When a family goes a whole year without the services of a physician, as did nearly one-half of them in 1934, it means much unnecessary suffering and death. With the paucity of physicians on the one hand and low incomes on the other, the mass of farm tenants have no choice but midwives and patent medicines. The services of midwives are cheap, usually five dollars or less; patent medicines can often be bought on credit. In Greene there is one physician to every 1,577 people, in Macon one to every 1,492, in Georgia one to every 1,034 people. One of Greene's eight physicians is a Negro, respected by both races and with a large practice, not all Negro. Macon's nine physicians are white.

Greene has thirty-two midwives, Macon twenty-six, all Negroes, and they deliver half the babies in these counties. In Georgia, according to the State Department of Health, there are 3,344 midwives, most of them Negroes. Approximately 42 per cent of Georgia's children are delivered by them.[7]

The same families who employ midwives rely almost wholly on patent medicines in case of sickness. The Black Belt storekeeper sells medicines he knows little or nothing about, for sick people whose conditions he is wholly unable either to diag-

[7] The State Department of Health, through its licensing of midwives, has rendered a double service: first, by conducting short schools for them; second, by refusing to license those who fail to meet the minimum requirements. In 1934 licenses were refused to 3,402 in Georgia, fifteen in Greene, and forty in Macon. Even though there are now very few "bootleg deliveries" by these unlicensed midwives, the few days' training leaves the licensed midwives about where they were before, except for the packets of silver nitrate for the infants' eyes and the contents of their maternity kits.

nose or to prescribe for. The writer has seen a tenant father enter the store, explain to the storekeeper the ailings of his wife, and walk out with medicine. In one instance the man behind the counter asked whether the last bottle seemed to have helped; upon being told, "Why, not much, at any rate," he turned to another shelf with, "Well, John, you try this kind this time."

While medical service is provided by the planters for the workers on a few of the largest plantations, and doctors and druggists do a considerable amount of charity and near-charity work, the mass of poorest people of both races rely largely upon the midwives and the tonics and heart, liver, and kidney remedies sold from the shelves of the general store. There is no public hospitalization provided in either county. Greene has no hospital. Macon has only the new hospital at Montezuma which is a private enterprise manned by three white physicians, four white nurses, and one Negro nurse. The plant is modern in design, and when fully equipped will have a capacity of about fifty beds, ten or twelve of which are on a separate floor and will be for Negroes. Some of the county officials have expressed the desire to try to work out arrangements for the care of the indigent poor.

Where vitality is high and nature is kind, midwives and patent medicines may prove potent, but in other situations only physicians, nurses, and prescribed medicines can conserve life. Accustomed to taking care of their sickness without a physician, many families call the doctor only in cases of desperate illness, meaning, of course, that too frequently the doctor arrives only in time to see the patient die.

Supporting the Rural Church.—The church, next to the family, is the rural dweller's most cherished institution. But small as are the expenses for physicians and nurses, the money contributed to the church is even less. In Greene with scarcely half the white farmers making a contribution, the average per family was $6.70, five-sixths of the Negro families made some contribution, averaging $3.79 per family per year. In Macon the average for whites was $16.11, with seven-eighths making some contribution, for Negroes $4.11 with nine-tenths contributing. In each race the owners and renters made the largest contributions. In some instances there were church members, particularly croppers and wage hands, who did not—perchance could not—make a contribution during the year.

Magazines and Newspapers.—Approximately half the white families and one-eighth of the Negro families studied spent money for newspapers and magazines. The expenditures in Negro families averaged but twenty-three cents per year in each county; the whites in Greene averaged $1.01 per year, in Macon, $2.77.

When cash incomes are so low, clothing is scanty, books and magazines are rare, health is neglected, recreation is meager, and institutions are poorly supported. People with small cash incomes do little buying; merchants dependent upon them do little selling.

But, says a certain type of agrarian, it is best that rural dwellers buy little. And so it is, if they have what they need at home. The remainder of this chapter and the two which follow set forth just what these rural families have and do not have at home. First discussed is home-grown provisions, next household furnishings, and then livestock and farm implements.

The Value of Home-Grown Provisions

The value of home-grown provisions consumed by the rural families in Greene and Macon counties was generally low.[8] While some few families, usually owners, produced practically all their food at home, many families had no garden and the gardens of others were poor.

[8] The value of home-grown provisions consumed by the family was arrived at by ascribing to the products consumed the prevailing local price in the fall of 1927 and in the fall of 1934. The exact figures used for the latter year were: chickens @ 30c each, eggs @ 20c per dozen, meat @ 10c per lb., butter @ 20c per lb., milk @ 10c per gal., canned fruit @ 15c per qt., canned meat @ 20c per qt., syrup @ 50c per gal., potatoes @ 75c per bu., dry beans and peas @ 10c per qt., wheat @ $1.50 per bu., corn @ $1.00 per bu., turnips @ 75c per bu., figs @ $2.00 per bu., peaches @ $1.00 per bu., onions @ $1.00 per bu., snap beans @ $1.00 per bu., tomatoes @ $1.25 per

An Increase of Home-Grown Provisions.—Since 1927, there has been a marked increase in the value of home-grown provisions among the Negro families of both counties. In the latter year, it will be observed in the accompanying table, the values were over twice those of 1927 for each tenure class in each county. A part of this increase is accounted for by the higher prices of 1934—about 30 per cent over 1927—and the larger part by the low price of cotton in the early thirties, which made it necessary to grow more food in order to get along with reduced cash incomes.

Many of the smaller owners in 1927 were more or less live-at-home farmers. The croppers and renters, in accordance with the expressed wishes of their landlords and the traditional practices of their own groups, though often having pigs, or cows, or vegetables, "bothered" little with them. These things required attention when all hands were needed to chop or pick cotton; the landlords were interested in crops from which cash could be secured, and the tenants were not zealous to cultivate gardens for themselves after having worked all day for their landlords.

TABLE IX

AVERAGE VALUE OF HOME-GROWN PROVISIONS CONSUMED BY FARM FAMILIES BY RACE AND TENURE CLASS IN GREENE AND MACON COUNTIES, GEORGIA, 1927 AND 1934

TENURE	NEGROES				WHITES	
	Greene		Macon		Greene	Macon
	1927	1934	1927	1934	1934	1934
Owners.................	$125.38	$264.71	$137.99	$338.01	$251.81	$256.18
Renters................	111.92	244.51	142.60	263.48	258.20	279.33
Croppers...............	64.62	145.93	77.41	180.81	188.35	293.33
Wage hands, etc..........	14.67	25.00	10.44	33.02	96.29	179.53
All Families.............	$ 87.82	$170.41	$ 67.88	$135.92	$221.55	$263.38

With the boll weevil, and later with five- and six-cent cotton, the planters first encouraged and then instructed their tenants

bu., okra @ $1.00 per bu., squash @ $1.00 per bu., cabbage @ 1c per lb., peanuts @ $1.00 per bu., pumpkins @ 10c each, dried fruit @ 50c per gal., rabbits @ 15c each, o'possum @ 15c each, blackberries and muscadines @ 15c per qt., fish @ 5c per lb., and turtles @ 25c each.

to raise foodstuffs; garden plots were set aside, wire and paling fences were put up; pig pens and cows on chains were more in evidence. The same cotton system which had robbed the southern tenant farmer of adequate home-grown foodstuffs was now demanding that he produce them. Before home-grown provisions can assume their rightful place in the diet of the farm family, their production will be on the basis of the welfare of the family rather than upon the needs of the cotton system. Despite the exigencies of recent years, not every farmer has a garden.

Of all rural families with children in school, in Greene one-thirtieth of the whites and one-fourth of the Negroes still have no fenced gardens; in Macon one-fiftieth of the whites and one-seventeenth of the Negroes have none. Most of the Greene families without gardens are in the areas depopulated a decade ago.

The Three M's, and Baked "Taters."—Fresh garden foods, such as carrots, beets, okra, spinach, squash, parsnips, English peas, and lettuce, while affording a considerable proportion of the food of a few, constitute probably less than one-tenth of the food consumed by the mass of rural families. Their diet, rich in fats and low in vitamine content, is one of the main factors accounting for the low vitality, frequent ill health, high susceptibility to contagious diseases, and high death rate among farm tenant families. Dorothy Dickens'[9] data on the food habits of Negro families in the Mississippi Delta parallel rather closely those of Greene and Macon counties.

It was noted above that the principal foods bought were meat, meal, flour, and molasses. The chief foods produced at home are hog meat, molasses, and sweet potatoes or yams. The three "M's"—meat, meal, and molasses—and baked potatoes, called "taters" by those who eat them most, still constitute the main table fare of the poorer rural families of both races, who

[9] *A Nutritive Investigation of Negro Tenants in the Yazoo Mississippi Delta* (Bulletin No. 254, August, 1928, Mississippi Agricultural Experiment Station, A. & M. College, Mississippi), especially pp. 29-32, 42 and 46-47.

are accustomed to little else, unless it be dried peas or beans and an occasional dish of greens.

It is highly probable that a wide range of garden dishes will be relished by rural families only when farm women devote more time and more butter and eggs to their preparation. Pumpkin pie, sweet potato puddings, cole slaw, Irish potato salad, stewed corn, corn on the cob, baked potatoes, and other vegetable dishes might be prepared and served without eggs, milk or butter, but they would seldom be popular. While no vegetables may be more cherished by the farm family than string beans cooked with side meat and potatoes fried in lard, the very names of others, such as buttered beets and creamed potatoes and candied yams, attest the importance of eggs and milk and butter in the preparation of tasty vegetable dishes.

Traditional rural cooking was well described by the Negro woman who answered, when asked if she could cook for fifteen men, "Yas, suh, jest gimme de grease!" Other types of seasoning are strikingly absent from the premises of the poorer families of both races. Of the Negro families studied intensively in 1927, as will be evident in the next chapter, one-third had no cow, and one-fifth had either no chickens or less than four.

Now chicken is the "company dish" of country hospitality and the choice viand for the sick room. But one-seventh of the families went a whole year without eating a chicken or an egg. A third of the families raised no meat, one-fourth no potatoes, two-fifths had no canned goods. The families who neither grow nor buy chickens are the same families who have least of other types of food. When a rural tenant family cannot serve fresh chicken to the visitor and to the sick member of the family, "sow belly," sweet potatoes, and molasses are the bill of fare. The families with most chickens usually have a cow or two, pigs, a garden, and canned goods, and a good meal can be spread upon short notice.

"*Living at Home.*"—In contrast with the inadequate diet of the majority of rural families, the tables of some literally groan beneath the weight of their home-produced foods—chicken, pork, ham, veal, beef, potatoes, asparagus, nuts, melons, fruits, and on and on. Of the families who eat well, some have local reputations for their roast hams, others for their grilled steaks, for their vegetables, or salads, or pies, or cakes, or drinks.

While canned fruits, vegetables, and meats appear in quantities in some tenant families, and on a few plantations each tenant will have potato hills and fattening hogs, the majority of the live-at-home families are landowners. The smaller owners of each race often pay particular attention to livestock and small crops. About three-fourths of the white owners raised practically all their meat, as did also half the Negro owners, in contrast with scarcely one-fifth of the Negro tenants studied. Meat has been mentioned often, and correctly, for lean or fat it is a most common dish upon the tables of the rural families, whether best fed or poorest fed.

Gross Incomes of Rural Families

The annual gross income of the farm family is the aggregate of the cash income from all sources and the value of all home-grown provisions consumed by the family during the year.

Decrease in Cash; Increase in Home-Grown Provisions.— Between 1927 and 1934 the cash income per Negro family dwindled, while the value of home-grown provisions increased. The exact figures are presented in the table on the following page. Even though the value of home-grown provisions has practically doubled in the seven years, a great proportion of families, as shown above, are still without meat and milk and vegetables from their own farms.

In 1934 over half the total gross income of the Negro families in Greene was from home-grown provisions; the home-grown provisions of the whites in Greene and of the farmers of both races in Macon, though more valuable, in no instance equalled their cash income. The low gross income of the Negro farmer in Greene is not the result of a bad ratio between cash income and food produced at home, but of both a low cash income and a low production of foods.

Intra-County and Intra-Racial Comparisons.—Within each tenure class and within each race there are marked differences between the red land and white land sections of Greene and between the eastern and western halves of Macon County. For the same race and tenure class, the incomes in the white land section of Greene were uniformly above those in the red land section. To illustrate, white land Negro renters had a gross income of $592.03 and red land renters of $390.05, white land croppers $417.65 and red land croppers $266.45. The same sort of differences were noted in 1927, with the cash incomes

TABLE X

GROSS INCOME PER FARM FAMILY, FROM CASH AND FROM VALUE OF HOME-GROWN PROVISIONS CONSUMED BY RACE AND TENURE CLASS IN GREENE AND MACON COUNTIES, GEORGIA

TENURE	NEGROES								WHITES			
	Greene				Macon				Greene		Macon	
	1927		1934		1927		1934		1934		1934	
	Amount	Per Cent	Amount	Per Cent	Amount	Per Cent	Amount	Per Cent	Amount	Per Cent	Amount	Per Cent
OWNERS:												
Cash Income.........	$494.92	79.8	$236.85	47.2	$979.03	87.6	$794.53	70.2	$395.69	61.1	$942.65	78.6
Value of H. G. Prov....	125.38	20.2	264.71	52.8	137.99	12.4	338.01	29.8	251.81	38.9	256.18	21.4
Total.............	620.30	100.0	501.56	100.0	1117.02	100.0	1132.54	100.0	647.50	100.0	1198.83	100.0
RENTERS:												
Cash Income.........	$290.25	72.3	$172.46	41.4	$412.48	73.0	$381.01	59.1	$292.55	53.1	$870.41	75.7
Value of H. G. Prov....	111.92	27.7	244.51	58.6	142.60	27.0	263.48	40.9	258.20	46.9	279.33	24.3
Total.............	402.17	100.0	416.97	100.0	555.08	100.0	644.49	100.0	550.75	100.0	1149.74	100.0
CROPPERS:												
Cash Income.........	$277.11	81.1	$135.65	48.2	$458.71	85.5	$339.12	65.2	$196.50	51.1	$713.92	71.2
Value of H. G. Prov....	64.62	18.9	145.93	51.8	77.41	14.5	180.81	34.8	188.35	48.9	293.33	28.8
Total.............	341.73	100.0	281.58	100.0	536.12	100.0	519.93	100.0	384.85	100.0	1007.25	100.0
OTHERS: Wage Hands, etc.												
Cash Income.........	$130.99	89.9	$ 86.66	77.5	$280.23	96.4	$150.64	82.2	$147.40	68.0	$580.66	76.4
Value of H. G. Prov....	14.67	10.1	25.20	22.5	10.44	3.6	33.02	17.8	69.29	32.0	179.53	23.6
Total.............	145.66	100.0	111.86	100.0	290.67	100.0	183.66	100.0	216.69	100.0	760.19	100.0
ALL FAMILIES												
Cash Income.........	$302.06	75.4	$150.74	46.9	$498.36	85.7	$299.56	68.7	$301.26	57.6	$872.21	76.8
Value of H. G. Prov....	87.82	24.6	170.41	53.1	67.98	14.3	135.92	31.3	221.55	42.4	263.38	23.2
Total.............	389.88	100.0	321.15	100.0	566.24	100.0	435.48	100.0	522.81	100.0	1135.59	100.0

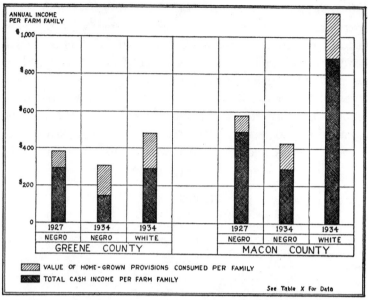

AVERAGE ANNUAL INCOME PER FARM FAMILY BY RACE IN 1927
AND 1934 IN GREENE AND MACON COUNTIES, GEORGIA

and value of home-grown provisions regularly larger for the white land farmers.

In Macon the incomes in the eastern half of the county are higher than those in the western half. In 1934 the white owners in the eastern half had an average gross income of $1,198.83, in the west $463.56. White renters and croppers showed similar differences. The Negro incomes, too, were higher in the eastern half—croppers $522.46 against $478.83, wage hands $195.76 against $141.29. In 1927 the eastern Negro cropper's average gross income was $608.17, while the westerner's average was $402.86. The reasons why the incomes are largest in the plantation areas of Macon and smallest in the plantation areas of Greene will be developed in succeeding chapters.

Savings Against Hard Times.—With the small cash and gross incomes noted in this chapter, it is almost self-evident that the general plane of living is low. Though lodges and societies are discussed at another place, it is well to inquire here what means the families have of meeting the expenses of sickness and death. While the owner families, except the poorest ones, can arrange with neighbors or merchants for the money required, the great mass of tenants and wage hands are almost wholly without resources other than an occasional life insurance policy and the sick benefits and death claims which they carry in connection with their lodge memberships.

The proportions of rural families with some member having either lodge insurance or commercial insurance were as follows: In Greene, one-fifth of the white families had commercial insurance policies, and almost half the Negroes had either commercial or lodge insurance; in Macon, half the whites and two-fifths of the Negroes had some type of insurance.

Practically all the life insurance policies held by farmers in these counties have bi-weekly or monthly premiums. There are but few Negro policyholders with as much as $1,000 insurance. The lodge policies feature small death claims and weekly benefits in case of sickness. Most of them have death claims of less than $500, and a large percentage are for $100 and below. On the whole the premiums are high, particularly for Negroes; the usual policy is something like this: $200 death claim and $2.25 benefit per week during illness for a premium of $1.50 per month; $500 death claim, no sick benefit, for $1.00 per month; $50 death claim, $3.00 sick benefit per week, for $1.00 per month.

Within each county and for each race the owners had insurance most often; the wage hands and laborers had insurance more frequently than the tenants. At first surprising, too, is the fact that Negro wage hands in Macon have insurance more often than the owners in Greene. This doubtless is accounted for mainly by the fact that the Macon wage hands and laborers have been relatively more prosperous during the last ten years than the farmers higher up the tenure scale in Greene. Moreover, the wage hand or laborer, when working, has some cash at intervals throughout the year. The wage hand, in fact, is on a daily or weekly or monthly budget, while the renter or cropper is on a yearly budget.

The prevalence in Macon County of Primitive Baptists who do not believe in lodges or other organizations restricts the number of insured persons there. Another reason the number of policyholders is no larger is that several families have let their insurance lapse. This happened because the crop was poor, because there was a conflict between the policyholder and the agent, or because the family thought that the insurance was not worth what it cost. Hundreds of policies have lapsed in these two counties, and in practically every case the policyholder lost everything he had put into it. Here are some of the comments made by Negro landowners about policies which they had once carried: "Jest let 'er drap—too high." "Los' out." "Weren't no good." "Got in bad shape and come out o' it." "Dropped my policy in 'hard times'." "Drapt it, didn't stand to promise." "Dee weevil took me outa dat, too."

Many of the poorer rural families are without either cash, credit, or insurance. When sickness and death come, they secure any help they can—a little food from a relative, some medicine from a friend, a cheap coffin from the landlord or a former landlord. In a later chapter we shall see what assistance this element of the rural community has received from the New Deal.

CHAPTER IV

HOUSING AND HOUSEHOLDS

THE INFORMATION in this chapter was obtained largely from the 1,468 rural families with children in school. The distribution of the families by race and tenure class is shown in the accompanying table. They are representative of all rural families in

TABLE XI

RACE AND TENURE CLASS OF 1,468 RURAL FAMILIES WITH CHILDREN IN SCHOOL IN GREENE AND MACON COUNTIES, GEORGIA[1]

	WHITE			NEGRO			TOTAL
TENURE	Greene	Macon	Total	Greene	Macon	Total	Families
Owners........	154	132	286	57	53	110	396
Renters........	108	35	143	159	81	240	383
Croppers......	50	61	111	186	294	480	591
Others........	7	28	35	32	31	63	98
Total..........	319	256	575	434	459	893	1,468

the two counties, constituting a rather large percentage of the whole.

HOUSING

The vast majority of landless families move every year or so from one shabby cabin to another.

Length of Residence.—In general, the white families live longer at one place than do the Negro families. As shown by Table XII, nearly one-fourth of the whites and nearly one-third of the Negroes have been living in their present dwellings one year or less. The shorter residence for both races in Greene County seems directly due to the more unstable farm conditions there.

Of the 213 families with periods of residence exceeding fifteen years, 151 are owners—110 white, 41 Negro; 35 are renters

---

[1] The writer filled in a blank for each of these 1,468 families. Except when other source is mentioned, the data in subsequent tables in this chapter were assembled from these blanks.

[59]

TABLE XII

PERCENTAGE DISTRIBUTION OF 1,468 RURAL WHITE AND NEGRO FAMILIES
IN GREENE AND MACON COUNTIES BY LENGTH OF
PRESENT HOUSE RESIDENCE

LENGTH Of RESIDENCE	WHITE			NEGRO		
	Greene	Macon	Total	Greene	Macon	Total
1 year..................	24.1	21.9	23.1	33.7	30.3	31.9
2 to 3 years	23.5	23.8	23.7	24.6	25.7	25.3
4 to 7 years.............	15.7	13.7	14.8	20.5	20.0	20.3
8 to 14 years............	18.8	14.8	17.0	10.8	14.2	12.5
15 to 29 years............	16.0	19.2	17.4	9.5	8.3	8.8
30 and over..............	1.9	6.6	4.0	0.9	1.5	1.2
Total...................	100.0	100.0	100.0	100.0	100.0	100.0

—9 white and 26 Negro; 24 are croppers—3 white and 21
Negro; the 3 others are, 1 white overseer and 2 Negro wage
hands. The owners, constituting hardly one-fourth of the white
and Negro farm families, thus account for almost three-fourths

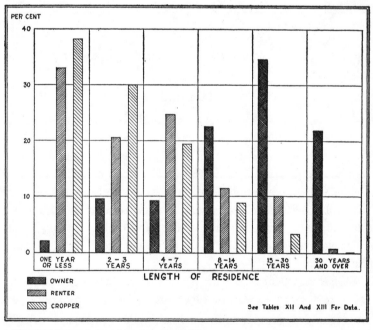

LENGTH OF PRESENT HOUSE RESIDENCE OF NEGRO FARM FAMILIES
BY TENURE CLASSES IN GREENE AND MACON COUNTIES, GEORGIA

MOVING TIME—A WAGON-BED FULL OF WORLDLY
GOODS—A COOK STOVE, A FEW CHAIRS, BEDS, POTS, PANS

IN TEN YEARS SIX FAMILIES HAVE LIVED HERE: THE SMALL WHITE OWNER WI
LOST IT TO CREDITORS, AND SINCE THEN FIVE TENANT FAMILIES,
THREE NEGRO AND TWO WHITE

SPLIT PINE BOARDS ARE USED WHEN MONEY IS SCARCE; GALVANIZED IRON WH
TIMES ARE GOOD

of all families who have been living in the same house more than fifteen years.

The distribution of median length of residence of each tenure class by color is presented for both counties in Table XIII. It will be noted that the Negro owner lives longer in one house than the white owner, the Negro renter longer in one house than the white renter, the Negro cropper longer in one house than the white cropper, and the Negro wage hand longer in one house than the white wage hand. Thus we see that the longer residence of the whites is due to the larger proportion of owners

TABLE XIII

MEDIAN LENGTH OF PRESENT HOUSE RESIDENCE OF 1,468 RURAL FAMILIES, BY TENURE CLASSES AND RACE, IN GREENE AND MACON COUNTIES

TENURE CLASS	WHITE			NEGRO		
	Greene	Macon	Total	Greene	Macon	Total
Owners................	10.0	14.0	11.6	11.2	12.4	11.9
Renters................	3.2	2.4	2.9	3.5	3.9	3.7
Croppers...............	2.5	2.4	2.4	2.6	2.9	2.8
Others................	2.3	3.0	2.7	2.9	3.4	3.2
All Families............	4.6	5.2	4.8	3.3	3.5	3.4

among them, approximately one-half, whereas scarcely one-eighth of the Negroes are owners. Length of residence, then, varies with tenure class and farm conditions rather than with race.

Rural Dwellings—Types.—With the exception of a half-dozen brick and a score or so of log houses, all dwellings in the rural areas of these counties are frame structures. Some are made of first-class oak and pine timber, others are little more than the hurried nailing together of discarded and almost valueless boards from local sawmills. Tenant houses ten years old often appear fifty. The rural dwellings of white owners erected since the Civil War have been inferior to many of those built before 1860. Most of the prosperous owners now live in the towns.

In both counties the sturdy, stolid log cabins which once stood behind the big house have been replaced by small frame houses of the "shot gun" type, which rest on stones or blocks furnishing a sheltered place for perhaps a hound or two, a couple of bony porkers, a half-dozen chickens. As a rule, the difference in appearance of long-residence and short-residence tenant dwelling is due not to differences in the houses but in upkeep. Tenants who move every year or so, whether white or black, seldom take much interest in the appearance of their dwellings. The presence of flowers, shrubs, and vines about a farm cabin suggests lengthy residence rather than the tenure or color of the family living there.

Rural Dwellings—Sizes.—Taking the two counties as a whole, the rural dwellings have an average of between three and four rooms; the white owners have the largest houses and the croppers and wage hands, irrespective of race, live in the fewest rooms. There are exceptions, particularly in the abandoned plantation areas of Greene, where a Negro or white tenant now lives in the house formerly occupied by a plantation owner. As a general rule, the tenant family uses only two or three rooms on the first floor. In several instances the upstairs windows are gone and rough pine boards have been nailed over them to keep out the rain. Sometimes the unused parts of these houses are entirely neglected.

The roofs of abandoned plantation houses are nearly always in poor repair. In more than one instance an inner roof of long boards had been constructed on the floor of the second story to keep two or three of the downstairs rooms dry enough to live in; water still ran down the walls, but the middle of the room was kept dry.

The vast majority of the houses occupied by tenants fall in one of three distinct classes: houses built by landlords for tenants, with two or three rooms; houses built by small owners for themselves, with three to five rooms; houses built by planters for themselves, with a half-dozen or more rooms.

With an average of nearly six persons to the tenant family, the overcrowding in the typical tenant house is evident. It is not unusual to find a family of ten living in two or three rooms.

In most tenant houses the kitchen is also the dining-room, while the living-room is the bedroom for the parents and the smaller children. The kitchen may serve not only as dining-room for the entire family, but as a bedroom for two or three of the older children.

What is a room in a farm house, anyway? In the better houses the rooms are well defined. In the tenant shack a partition of rough and irregular boards divides the house into two rooms; a third room for this type of house is sometimes made by "slapping" a "shed" on to the back side of the two rooms.

The Inside Finish of Farm Dwellings.—Ceiled or plastered houses as defined by this study are those in which every room—excluding pantries and storerooms—is either ceiled or plastered. No distinction is made as to type of ceiling. For example, a house with inside ceiling of rough boards direct from the saw-mill is reported as ceiled; neither is there a distinction made in type or condition of plastering. Part ceiled means that some of the rooms are ceiled or plastered and others are not. An unceiled house has no inside finish and the removal of a single plank from the outer wall lets in sunshine or the rain.

The gaudy display of newspapers and magazines upon the walls of unceiled houses serves a purpose other than decoration. The papers are often put on in fall and winter and scratched off in spring and summer. In winter, even when so papered, the houses are distressingly airy.

The Negro dwellings, it will be observed from the following table, are decidedly inferior. Approximately half of them

TABLE XIV

PERCENTAGE DISTRIBUTION BY RACE, OF 1,468 RURAL DWELLINGS BY TYPE OF INSIDE FINISH, IN GREENE AND MACON COUNTIES, GEORGIA

INSIDE FINISH	WHITE			NEGRO			GRAND TOTAL
	Greene	Macon	Total	Greene	Macon	Total	
Ceiled or plastered............	81.5	79.7	80.7	37.8	53.1	45.7	59.4
Part ceiled..................	4.7	9.4	6.8	4.1	5.3	4.7	5.5
Unceiled....................	13.8	10.9	12.5	58.1	41.6	49.6	35.1
Total.....................	100.0	100.0	100.0	100.0	100.0	100.0	100.0

are unceiled, as compared with one-eighth of the white dwellings. The white owners and renters have much better houses than the Negro owners and renters. In fact, white croppers live in ceiled houses almost as often as Negro owners. There is a greater difference between the dwellings of whites and Negroes within the same tenure class than there is between the tenure classes within the same race.

In Greene there are more unceiled houses among both white and Negro families than in Macon. That Greene has poorer dwellings than Macon is further shown by the table below, which indicates the percentage of unceiled dwellings in each county by color and tenure.

It must not be overlooked, however, that approximately three-tenths of all white croppers live in unceiled houses. A

TABLE XV

PERCENTAGES OF 1,468 FARM DWELLINGS UNCEILED, BY TENURE CLASSES AND BY RACE IN GREENE AND MACON COUNTIES, GEORGIA

TENURE CLASS	WHITE			NEGRO		
	Greene	Macon	Total	Greene	Macon	Total
Owners..................	9.9	6.1	8.0	37.3	13.2	26.4
Renters.................	9.2	5.7	8.4	57.9	37.0	50.8
Croppers................	30.0	29.5	29.7	62.4	48.6	53.9
Others..................	57.1	0.0	11.4	71.9	35.5	54.0
All Dwellings............	13.8	10.9	12.5	58.1	41.6	49.6

tenant cabin often houses a Negro family one year and a white family the next.

Leaking Roofs, Glassless and Screenless Windows.—Leaky roofs are very common. In fact, slightly more than two-thirds of the houses occupied by Negroes and one-fourth of those occupied by whites have leaky roofs. Here, again, the owners make the best showing, the renters the next best, the croppers next to the worst and the wage hands and day laborers the worst. In general the roofs on tenant houses are better in Greene, while on owner houses they are better in Macon. In the years when the farmers have most money, galvanized iron

A TYPICAL NEGRO TENANT HOUSE

WHITE TENANTS, TOO, OFTEN LIVE IN POOR HOUSES

THE "BIG HOUSE" OF A GREENE COUNTY PLANTATION—A NEGRO TENANT FAMI
NOW LIVES IN A FEW ROOMS DOWNSTAIRS

AN OLD GREENE COUNTY PLANTATION HOMESTEAD—VACANT EXCEPT FOR TWO
ROOMS OCCUPIED BY WHITE TENANTS

roofing is used; in typical years split pine shingles are most common.

The windows in practically all owner dwellings and in many tenant houses are equipped with sash and glass; in some, broken panes have been replaced with tin or pasteboard. About a third of all rural dwellings have no window sash or glass—only board shutters. They are airy and balmy on sunny days, and very dark and damp on rainy days.

Screened houses are very rare, except among the larger owners. Of tenant houses scarcely one in twenty is even partially screened; those occupied by whites make little better showing than those occupied by Negroes. In and out of such houses, the children and flies—often the chickens and pigs—move at will. They are quite open; a mad dog can trot through one of them. Or a tenant mother with a four-day-old baby may awake from an afternoon nap to find in her bed a snake attempting to nurse her full breasts.[2]

HOUSEHOLD FURNISHINGS AND SANITATION

In some homes the furnishings are quite ample and include beautiful old pieces antedating the Civil War. With very few exceptions there are cook stoves, beds, and chairs in all homes. In some of the tenant and wage hand families the stoves are little more than fire-boxes with just enough stove-pipe to reach the nearest window; some of the beds are made by nailing rough planks to the wall of an unceiled house; some of the chairs are stovewood blocks with slabs from the sawmill nailed on a flat side to make a back.

Household Furnishings by Race and Tenure Class.—The white tenants as a whole seem to have better furnishings than the Negro tenants, but some of the latter have considerably more than any of the landless whites. The Negro rural family often has the savings of a lifetime invested in household furnishings, including showy enlarged pictures of relatives and friends, sew-

---

[2] This case was reported by the Macon County physician who found the young mother suffering from severe shock.

ing machines, phonographs, organs and pianos, gilt bedsteads, ornate bureaus, and expensive cook stoves. Whereas more land is an available and attractive repository for the cash surpluses of a considerable element of the owners and some few tenants of either race, the typical landless Negro usually puts his savings, when he has any, in a "big time"—which includes some "Sunday" clothes and an automobile—or in household furnishings. Some Negro families have valuable old pieces which came into their possession when landed white acquaintances secured new furniture or moved to a distant community. This collecting and hoarding of miscellaneous furnishings is most noticeable among old women who have made their living by doing the weekly wash and other housework for prominent white families.

Of the Negro families studied intensively, 82 per cent have dressers or bureaus; 55 per cent have sewing machines; 23 per cent have pianos or organs, most often the latter; 19 per cent have phonographs; and 15 per cent have ranges to cook on. All the families use oil lamps, and not one of them has a radio. Some furnishings—bureaus, dressers, sewing machines, pianos, and organs—appear most often in Greene, while others—ranges and phonographs—are more common in Macon, the phonographs being most numerous among the cropper families. The slightly greater amount of furniture per family in Greene is apparently due to the fact that migrant families left much of their furniture behind with kinsfolk.

Printed Matter in Negro Homes.—Of the 323 Negro homes studied in 1927, 68 had no printed matter of any kind. The findings in 1934 were similar. A family's reading material, though a cultural index, provides a measure of its plane of living.

Bibles and schoolbooks make up the reading material in the majority of the homes that have any at all. Two-thirds of the families have Bibles; less than one-fourth have schoolbooks of one kind or another; a little more than one-fourth have one or more books other than the Bible and schoolbooks; about one-eighth subscribe to newspapers and magazines, slightly over one-tenth to agricultural papers, and less than three in a hundred to church papers.

Three Negro families have small libraries. One of these, numbering 600 volumes, was the gift of a white landlord to his Negro servant who became a preacher and is now living on a rented farm in Macon County making a very decent living by the double income from the three churches he serves on Sunday and the farm he cultivates during the week. The two smaller libraries are in Macon County also, one belonging to a Negro landowner with a liking for books, and the other to a cropper who is a lodge leader in the eastern half of the county.

Bibles, schoolbooks, and other books are most prevalent among owners, least prevalent among wage hands and day laborers. The owners subscribe to newspapers and magazines almost twice as frequently as any other tenure class. The families having no printed matter include one-twentieth of the owners, one-eighth of the renters, one-sixth of the croppers, and two-fifths of the wage hands, the distribution in each county being about the same, except that slightly more Macon families in nearly every tenure class were without printed matter. In each tenure class in each county, the whites had more printed matter than the Negroes. Only an occasional white family is entirely without any. For example, three-fourths of the white families studied were subscribing to newspapers or magazines, in contrast with one-eighth of the Negro families.

Water Supply and Sanitary Facilities.—Approximately one-sixth of the rural families secure their water from springs; the remainder use wells. A spring or well may be sanitary or not, depending upon its location in relation to drainage and seepage from the farm lot and, most important, the privy or its substitute. Some of the springs, practically all of which are in Greene, are little more than puddles at the foot of the hill below the house, others flow boldly from the root of a great tree, left to shelter it, or from under a projecting rock. The typical farmer's well is right at the house, and so is everything else—his livestock, chickens, and dogs. The farmyard is usually a pretty dusty place in dry weather, and sloppy when it rains. Probably less than one-fourth of the wells are properly boxed and banked to keep surface water from running into them when heavy rains fall.

The farm families in both counties have very inadequate facilities for the disposal of human excrement. Until the recent construction of a few score of modern privies by relief agencies as work relief projects, scarcely two per cent of the rural families had fly-proof privies, about two-thirds had open privies, while the remaining one-third had none.

The families with none included Negro and white tenants in about the same proportion, and some of the smaller owners. The family with an open surface privy may suggest some little advancement over the family with none, but no real progress has been made, except in so far as it is necessary to tolerate the surface privy for a time in order to get the fly-proof one later. There is an element of truth in the landlord's complaint: "Why, after I build sanitary privies, they won't use them." Public health education as well as sanitary physical equipment is needed; public health officials of the rural South should be educating the rural people, white as well as Negroes, to an appreciation of the importance of proper sanitation about their homes. At present the open privy and the unscreened window characterize the vast majority of the South's small farm owners and tenants—over three-fourths of the total farm population of the region. Rural sanitation is a field for further assistance by federal agencies looking for constructive projects upon which to utilize relief labor.

Composition of Rural Households

Only recently has the collection of complete vital statistics in Greene and Macon counties been attempted. As late as 1927, the director of the Georgia Bureau of Vital Statistics pronounced all reports from these counties and many others wholly unreliable. It seemed well, therefore, to secure specific facts on the number of births, the number of living children, and the number of dead children from each of the 1,468 rural families with children in school.

Children per Family—Living and Dead.—The rural families of both races are large; the number of births per family, as can be seen in Table XVI, ranges from 5.33 to 8.14, and the children still living average from 4.68 to 6.58.[3] The size of these families is better appreciated when it is remembered that the averages include younger as well as older couples with children in school. The Negro families are a little larger than the white. No appreciable differences in number of total births are noticeable between the tenure classes within either racial group.

The greater number of deaths of children in Macon than in Greene County families, white and colored, seems to be accounted for in part, at least, by the greater prevalence of malaria in Macon.[4] The highest percentage of dead children in any tenure class for either race occurred among the white croppers of Macon County, where more than one-fourth have died. More children have been born per family in this group and fewer are now living than in any other white tenure group in either county. The lowest percentage of deaths is for the Negro owners of Greene County. In general, however, a greater proportion of the Negro than of the white children have died.

[3] By leaving off the miscellaneous group, consisting of the ninety-eight families entered in the tenure classification as "Others" and limiting attention to the 1,370 owner, renter, and cropper families, every class except one has fifty or more families in it and consequently the averages given in the table on the following page can be relied upon as representative of the various tenure classes by color. See the first table in this chapter for number of families by color and tenure.

[4] A white baby born in Greene County, according to vital statistics from the Georgia Department of Health for 1933, did not have as good a chance to live a year as the average Georgia white infant, but in Macon County he had a better chance. The Greene County Negro infant fared considerably better than the average Negro infant of Georgia, but the Negro child born in Macon County had less chance at life than the average Negro infant in the state. The infant mortality rates for 1933 for whites were per thousand: for Georgia 59.4, for Greene County 120.0, for Macon County 26.7. For Negroes the rates were: Georgia 78.2, Greene 57.1, Macon 87.7. Taking each county as a whole, the rates are higher than the rate for the entire state, Georgia (1933) 67.2, Greene 80.0, Macon 75.7. Registration, new to this area, is probably incomplete, and unreported deaths would be more often Negro deaths.

TABLE XVI

AVERAGE NUMBER OF BIRTHS, CHILDREN LIVING, AND CHILDREN DEAD PER
FAMILY, AMONG 1,370 RURAL FARM FAMILIES BY RACE AND TENURE
CLASS IN GREENE AND MACON COUNTIES, GEORGIA

	AVERAGE NUMBER OF CHILDREN PER FAMILY			PERCENTAGE OF CHILDREN LIVING AND DEAD		
	Owners	Renters	Croppers	Owners	Renters	Croppers
WHITES						
Greene County:						
Children living......	4.88	5.14	4.84	87.9	89.2	84.0
Children dead.......	.67	.62	.92	12.1	10.8	16.0
Total births.....	5.55	5.76	5.76	100.0	100.0	100.0
Macon County:						
Children living......	4.76	4.85	4.68	87.2	91.0	74.5
Children dead.......	.70	.48	1.60	12.8	9.0	25.5
Total births.....	5.46	5.33	6.28	100.0	100.0	100.0
NEGROES						
Greene Couty:						
Children living......	5.85	4.83	4.92	95.0	81.2	79.6
Children dead.......	.31	1.12	1.26	5.0	18.8	20.4
Total births.....	6.16	5.95	6.18	100.0	100.0	100.0
Macon County:						
Children living......	6.58	5.65	5.25	80.8	77.2	77.1
Children dead.......	1.56	1.67	1.55	19.2	22.8	22.9
Total births.....	8.14	7.32	6.80	100.0	100.0	100.0

When the percentages of dead children by tenure classes are considered it is evident that in each county most deaths occurred among the croppers and fewest among the owners. That the owners as a class are older than the croppers only increases the significance of the difference. The fact that the majority of all rural Negro mothers and many white mothers, especially in the cropper group, are attended only by a midwife results in the death of many children and mothers who would live if a trained physician were present. The small cash income of most rural families not only necessitates the use of the midwife rather than the physician, but, when coupled with the small amount of food-stuffs grown, means a very inadequate diet for mother and child.

Children Living with Their Parents and Elsewhere.—The

children in 1,323 of the 1,468 families were living with their own parent or parents. In the remaining 145 cases the children were living with their grandparent or grandparents in ninety-two instances, with other relatives in forty-eight, and with people of no blood relation in the remaining five.

More Negro than white children lived with people other than their parents. This is due largely to the greater migration of Negroes and their higher death rate, particularly in the middle-age groups. Moreover, the fact that more Negroes are

TABLE XVII

PER CENT OF WHITE AND NEGRO FAMILIES IN WHICH CHILDREN LIVE WITH THEIR PARENTS, WITH RELATIVES, AND WITH OTHER PEOPLE, IN GREENE AND MACON COUNTIES, GEORGIA

CHILDREN LIVE WITH:	WHITE			NEGRO		
	Greene	Macon	Total	Greene	Macon	Total
Own Parents...........	95.6	95.6	95.6	84.5	88.5	86.6
Grandparents...........	2.8	2.0	2.5	9.9	7.6	8.7
Relatives..............	0.9	2.0	1.4	5.1	3.9	4.5
Others................	0.7	0.4	0.5	0.5	0.0	0.2
Total Families...........	100.0	100.0	100.0	100.0	100.0	100.0

croppers and renters, and live on a lower economic level renders it more difficult for the remaining parent to maintain a home, and thereby dictates that the children be cared for by relatives or friends.

Then, too, there is more illegitimacy among the Negro group and consequently more children dependent upon one parent, at whose death or desertion the child becomes an orphan, without as good a chance of institutional care as the white child. In general, the Negro family is not so stable as the white. However, in view of his slave background and his subsequent dependent rôle, with exploitation on all levels, the wonder is that the plantation Negro's family life is not less stable than it is. For a number of reasons, including modern birth control practices and a growing race pride even among rural Negroes, there is less direct crossing of the races now than formerly. Nonetheless, it is still not unknown for a white man—

who may have a legal wife and children—to "keep up" a Negro woman—who may have a legal husband and children. The clandestine father occasionally shows some interest in the "bright" child born of such a union, using him for a servant or overseer, and in rare instances sending him to high school and even to college.

The greater migration of Negroes than whites naturally disorganized family life within the Negro element, especially in Greene. Many a Negro couple, upon going to Atlanta or a more distant city, left their children behind. If everything went well, which was by no means universal, the parents usually sent back for their children. Of the children now living with relatives, absence of parents is the chief cause: in 56 cases, 46 Negro and 10 white, both parents are living outside the county; in 35 more, 31 Negro and 4 white, one parent is living outside; in 26 cases, 17 Negro and 9 white, one parent is outside the county and one lives in the county but does not provide a home for child or children. In only three cases, all Negroes, do both parents live in the county without providing a home for their child or children.

When the rural family unit is dissolved by the death of a parent or for some other reason, the responsibility for the support of the children is assumed most often by the owner class

TABLE XVIII

PER CENT OF FAMILIES BY RACE AND TENURE CLASS WHO HAD CHILDREN OTHER THAN THEIR OWN ATTENDING SCHOOL, GREENE AND MACON COUNTIES, GEORGIA

TENURE CLASS	WHITE		NEGRO	
	Greene	Macon	Greene	Macon
Owners........................	5.8	3.3	19.3	18.9
Renters........................	2.8	5.7	18.9	4.9
Croppers......................	4.0	3.3	12.9	10.2
All Families...................	4.4	4.4	15.5	11.5

of family. They have more property and are in position to be of more assistance in the emergencies which arise among the landless and propertyless families. The Negro owner families, it will be noticed in the preceding table, are rearing children other than their own more than three times as often as the white owners; Negro renters and croppers, too, care for the children of other people much more frequently than the white families of the same tenure class.

Concerning the present relation of school children to the people with whom they live, there is evident a greater family disorganization among the Negroes, especially in Greene; the disproportionately large share of responsibility assumed by grandparents, particularly among the Negroes, and the paucity of cases where children live with people not related to them by blood; and finally, the extent to which owners, especially Negro owners, assume responsibility for the rearing of other people's children.

Composition of 323 Households.—Of the 323 rural Negro families studied intensively, 198 were composed of parents and children only, while in the other 125 there lived 228 persons not of the parent-child relation. These 228 were related as follows to the head of the house: grandchildren, 121; nephews and nieces, 43; brothers and sisters (including in-laws), 18; parents (including in-laws), 16; uncles and cousins, 3; unrelated by blood, 27—10 of whom had been adopted. Verily, "blood is thicker than water," a formula often heard among rural dwellers, particularly Negroes.

The general distribution of these 228 persons by tenure class only further corroborates the materials presented above. Since the 323 families are not limited to school patrons, an additional contrast occurs: While the owner household in Greene most often contains persons not of the immediate family, it is the wage hand and laborer households in Macon which most often have them. The reason for this is not far to seek: the least well-established households, usually composed of an old woman and her grandchildren or nephews and nieces, have remained intact in Macon. In Greene, "hard times" forced the younger members of these households to leave the county to find employment, thus leaving behind many older and younger people who became dependent upon the local community; the owners were in better position than any other tenure class to shelter them.

Moreover, the Negro rural community cares for its defectives. Now and then a violently insane person is sent to the State Insane Asylum, and once in a very great while a handicapped child may be placed in some state or denominational institution. In general, however, the maimed, halt, and blind live with their relatives or friends. The feeble-minded child and the idiot are cared for by parents or kinsmen. Senile grandparents and helpless grandchildren always find some place to stay. With no public welfare officer in either county, the rural Negroes, now as formerly, take mental and physical cripples as a matter of course. They have little information, scarcely any encouragement, and practically no money with which to have twisted minds and limbs straightened.

The Negro Mother's Heavy Load.—The presence in the household of persons not of the immediate family nearly always represents an additional burden upon the family, affecting adversely the plane of living, and increasing the work of the mother in particular, for dependents require a great deal of personal attention. These "outsiders" may be there because the family has been kindly disposed toward orphans, because a son or daughter has moved to some distant place leaving the children, because the family is the victim of relatives who through ill health or slothfulness do not maintain a home of their own, because the family has adopted a boy or girl to help with the farm work, or because some aged kinsman or other dependent who must stay somewhere has been given a home.

The Negro mother or grandmother bears the brunt of the family's reverses. When her sister or daughter dies she takes the small children and rears them; when the family moves to another tenant house she puts up new clothes lines and clears the path to the spring or well and chops the weeds from the back door. When the busy season comes she prepares breakfast for the entire family, and, often leaving a small baby at the house with a young child, works until the middle of the day when she returns to the kitchen and prepares a hasty meal for her family. She goes back into the field in early afternoon and works until almost dark, returning to prepare supper and put tired children to bed. When the crop is poor she takes in additional washing or finds some neighbor who will give her a day's work now and then; when there is no work which she must do in the field or away from home, she gets out the family wash and attends to her housework, which usually includes the cultivating of whatever garden the family has and often the chopping of the wood for the stove. When "hard times" force the family to leave the home county, the father goes ahead to find work while the mother waits for word to come; then with bundles of belongings she gets her children on the train for a place where she hopes for an easier life but does not always find it.

The mother in the white tenant household, and even in that of the small owner, is usually the chief burden carrier, frequently working in the fields in addition to doing her housework. In the planter family, the mother nearly always has heavy responsibilities. Scarcely any farm mother leads an idle or a sheltered life. The Negro mother bears all the load that the white mother bears, plus the additional burdens which her race imposes—a less stable family life, a circumscribed economic base, and inferior services from private and public agencies.

CHAPTER V

LIVESTOCK, FARM IMPLEMENTS AND VEHICLES

THERE ARE hundreds of rural Negro and white families in Greene and Macon counties who own no horse or mule, cow or calf, pig or chicken, farm implement or vehicle.

LIVESTOCK

Of the families studied, over a third of the white families and nearly three-fourths of the Negroes have no horse or mule; one-seventh of the whites and two-fifths of the Negroes have no cow or calf; one-fourth of the families of each race have no hog or pig; one-fourteenth of the white and one-tenth of the Negro families have no chicken. This paucity of livestock in the southeastern states has been pointed to by many writers as indicative of the wholly inadequate farm organization of the region. The data presented in this chapter, while substantiating the generally well-known facts about the livestock ownership of rural families, will show the distribution of the various types of livestock in the tenure classes of each race.

Work Animals.—Practically all farm owners, and most of the renters, have one or more horses or mules, usually mules. Now and then an owner or renter family, made up of women, manages to cultivate a crop without a mule by swapping hoe work and other hand work with some white or Negro neighbor who has workstock. Occasionally a renter decides to farm as a cropper and is able to retain ownership of his mules by renting them to his landlord. In a few cases cropper families, furnished all equipment by the landlord, keep a mule to draw the buggy or wagon to the homes of relatives now and then, to town on Saturday afternoon, to church on Sundays, and to the occasional gatherings of the landless farmers—school closings,

[76]

lodge convocations, "big meetings," funerals, barbecues and mullet stews.

The number of work animals per family by race and tenure class shows but half the picture, for the families who own fewest frequently have very poor ones, the older and smaller animals. The support by the Negro renters of the poorer mules, sometimes even decrepit, is a phase of man-land relationships which through the years have crystallized to a marked degree along the color line.

Practically all the mules and horses are imported from Tennessee, Kentucky, Illinois, Missouri, and other distant points, and the Negro and poorer white family can afford only the cheap ones, that is, those least desired by the people with more money. The small farmer, whether with the cheap cotton of 1932 or the restricted poundage of 1934, finds it very difficult to repay his crop production debts in the fall, to say nothing of replacing in the spring his mule that died during the winter. A small farmer with corn in the crib and potatoes in the bin and meat in the smokehouse might find it difficult to get the desired mule, as indeed was the case of a Greene County Negro renter in the spring of 1932. His chances would have been little better in the spring of 1935, for a larger price per pound for fewer pounds still left him with little cash. Unable to replace the mule, the renter becomes a cropper—a common occurrence in recent years.

Since 1930 a few renters and occasionally even small owners, without the money to replace mules, have maintained their tenure status by yoking steers born in their own farmyard.[1] Low cash income, whether from cheap cotton or restricted cotton, may reduce the family's tenure status or it may reduce the family's status within its tenure class. In 1927-1928 oxen were

[1] It is rather common for death to befall the poor man's mule, particularly during the winter and early spring. In one instance a plow was being pulled by a mule and a man. The man, with the long end of the beam, explained that his other mule had just died, that he had no money to buy another, that by helping to get the cotton planted he could make out with one mule until he sold his cotton.

very rare in both these counties. Not so now, and the number is increasing. The shift from mules to oxen is a shift toward peasantry: a result of the ever dwindling status of the cotton farmer in the national economy. The Rural Rehabilitation of the Federal Emergency Relief Administration has furnished oxen to some families in these counties.

 Cows, Hogs, and Hens.—Except for mules, the cotton farmer's livestock costs little money. Though often not so well fed, the cows, hogs, and chickens of the poorer farmers are otherwise not unlike those of the best farmers from whom he secures young stock at low cost.

The ownership of cows, pigs, and chickens can be taken as a direct measure of a family's plane of living. The rural family with a cow has a regular, though often small, supply of milk to be used or sold to buy other things more desired. The hog and hen also provide food for the table. Moreover, livestock can be used to obtain credit, thus affording the family a better chance to maintain its independence.

The owner families have cows most often and the wage hands least often, with the renters and croppers occupying their usual places between. As noted above, one-seventh of the white families studied have no cow, while less than one-sixth of the owners in Greene and three-sevenths of those in Macon own more than three cows. A third of the Negro families in Greene and over half of those in Macon have no cow or calf. Most of the other farmers have one to three cows, one-sixth of them having four or more. By tenure class, nearly half the Negro owners in each county have four or more cows, whereas five-sixths of the wage hands and over one-third of the croppers in Greene have none.

The family ownership of pigs and hogs is practically the same in each county, if taken as a whole, for the larger percentage of families with no hogs in Macon is balanced by the larger percentage of those with more than eight. Among the Greene County Negro families, one-sixth have no hog, and one-fiftieth have more than eight; among those of Macon,

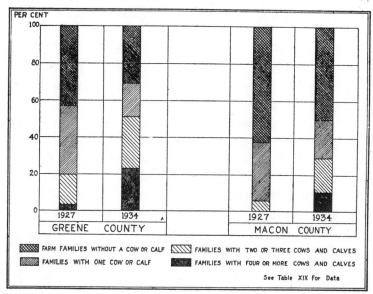

OWNERSHIP OF COWS AND CALVES BY NEGRO FARM FAMILIES IN
GREENE AND MACON COUNTIES IN 1927 AND 1934

nearly one-third have no hog, and one-ninth have over eight. Two-sevenths of the white families have no hog, while one-third of those in Macon and one-fifteenth of those in Greene have more than eight. Here again, the tenure classes fall into their accustomed places.

As in other instances, so in the ownership of chickens, the owners make the best showing and the wage hands the worst, fewer of the white families having none. Chickens, like pigs, and hogs, can be fed in part at least by the scraps of food from the table of the rural family. There is, however, not much scrap food from a considerable number of tables, and among them chickens are scarce. Roughly speaking, one-fourth of the wage hands of each race in each county have no chickens. Chickens not only require food scraps or grain, of which the poorest families have little, but during the nesting season they need systematic attention, of which some rural dwellers give little. Often in families where food is not plentiful all eggs are eaten or sold, and consequently the flock is not replenished.

One of the chickens dies, another is eaten, and after awhile all are gone.

The Farm Family's Dog.—Dogs are more common about the houses of rural Negro families than either work animals or cows and calves, but not so numerous as pigs and chickens. The mule pulls the farmer's plow, the cow furnishes the milk and flesh, the hog provides meat and lard, the chicken produces eggs and meat for his table and feathers for his pillow. But what does the dog do? What is the relation between the dog and the farmer's plane of living? In Greene County the tens of thousands of idle acres covered with broom sedge, brambles, and small pines provide excellent coverage for rabbits; the dog enables the gun-carrying hunters to get a larger booty. The dog is not without meaning in terms of race relations: white men and black men sometimes hunt together—and a dog leads them.

It is interesting to note the value placed on the Negroes' dogs in the tax digest. In 1919, for example, the Negroes' dogs in Greene were assessed at $2,480 and those of the whites at $1,570. This is the only instance in which the Negroes' property in either of these Black Belt counties exceeded that of the whites. The Negro's dog may afford his children a pet, his household some protection, or his all too-scant table a rabbit or 'possum now and then. But not all Negroes have dogs, in fact more Negroes than whites have none—four-sevenths of the Negroes and three-sevenths of the whites. Dogs are more prevalent in Greene than in Macon, and much more common among owners and renters than among croppers and wage hands in each county—roughly, four-fifths of the owners, three-fifths of the croppers, and one-fifth of the wage hands.

At country stores and other "hang-outs" there is considerable conversation about dogs; the Negro is allowed his greatest freedom of expression at this point, often vieing with white men in establishing the superior qualities of his dog. These arguments are institutions peculiarly adapted to wintry weather. Whites and Negroes crowd in; they laugh together heartily as one extravagant claim after another is set forth; they favor this disputant, then that one. Quite oblivious of race during the excitement, they sit there mutually bespattering the hot sides of the stove with tobacco spittle. Then at length the claims are less exciting, there is a shifting, and presently the Negroes are all on one side of the stove and the whites on the other. Extravagant claims for a dog, if set forth once in a long time, always attract attention, but woe to him who claims too much for his dog too often! "Why, he's a fool; he thinks he's got the only dog in the county."

Farm Animals in 1927 and in 1934.—Among the Negro farmers of Greene and Macon counties there was a decrease of work animals between 1927 and 1934, which can be taken as an index of the shift of families from renter to cropper status. The increase in ownership of cows may be due to the depressed prices of beef in recent years, or may reflect a tendency to raise

TABLE XIX

PERCENTAGE DISTRIBUTION OF LIVESTOCK OWNERSHIP AMONG 323 NEGRO
FAMILIES IN GREEN AND MACON COUNTIES, GEORGIA,
IN 1927 AND 1934

TYPE OF LIVESTOCK	GREENE		MACON	
	1927	1934	1927	1934
MULES AND HORSES:				
None	56.1	56.9	76.6	83.2
1	20.3	20.7	9.1	4.2
2 and over	23.6	22.4	14.3	12.6
COWS AND CALVES:				
None	44.6	31.0	62.8	51.1
1	35.8	17.2	32.6	20.2
2 – 3	16.2	27.6	4.6	18.6
4 and over	3.4	24.2	....	10.1
PIGS AND HOGS:				
None	11.5	17.3	28.0	28.6
1 – 3	61.5	61.2	42.3	38.6
4 – 8	22.3	19.8	25.1	21.0
9 and over	4.7	1.7	4.6	11.8
CHICKENS:				
None	9.4	10.3	18.9	8.4
1 – 4	8.7	12.1	10.9	9.3
5 – 14	35.2	51.7	33.1	50.4
15 – 44	34.5	25.9	31.4	30.2
45 and over	12.2	....	5.7	1.7

more of the family's food on the farm. A decrease in ownership of hogs will be noted in Greene, and in Macon an increase.
There has been a general decrease in the ownership of chickens,
particularly in flocks of forty-five or more.

The two facts of importance about these data are: first, the
large element which owns no livestock, the higher percentages
in Macon reflecting the larger proportion of wage hand and
cropper families there; second, the still larger group of families which own but one mule, or one cow, or less than four
pigs, or less than fifteen chickens—better than no livestock, but
quite inadequate to the needs of the typical rural family.

FARM IMPLEMENTS AND VEHICLES

Approximately one-fourth of the white families and half the
Negro families own no farm implements, not even a hoe. Three-
sevenths of the white and five-sevenths of the Negroes own no
automobile.

There are 125 tractors in these two counties, with two-thirds
of them in Macon. The big planters in eastern Macon, particularly those who use wage hands and have peach orchards or
asparagus fields, use tractors, gang plows, riding cultivators,
drills, and other modern farm machinery. Windmills for
pumping water at plantation headquarters appear in the same
areas as the tractors. On the big plantation, worked by croppers
and devoted largely to cotton and corn, there is an occasional
tractor. Cotton gins, peanut pickers, sawmills and the like,
though not always part of the plantation equipment, are usually
owned by the planter class. Aside from an occasional truck for
public hauling and a pea thrasher operated for toll, the poorer
whites and Negroes own nothing more than cotton planters,
fertilizer distributors, plows, hoes, wagons, and second-hand
automobiles.

Few and Crude Farm Implements.—Though one Negro
farmer in Macon has a windmill which pumps water into his
yard and barn, not one in either county has a cotton gin, peanut
picker, tractor, sawmill, Delco light plant, or stationary gasoline

engine. Just as the work not done by power-driven machinery must be done by work animals, that not done by work animals must be done by members of the farm family. The type and number of tools which a family owns or uses suggest the relative importance of mule-power and man-power in securing a living. In general, the wage hand and cropper families use tools belonging to their landlords and employers, and the owners and renters use their own.

About five-sixths of the owners and two-thirds of the renters of each race have cotton planters, plows, and hoes. In 1927, one-tenth of Greene's croppers, and almost none of Macon's, owned the farm implements of the typical renter—evidently the boll weevil had driven some Greene County renters into the cropper class. The fact that in the fall of 1934 a few croppers of each race in each county had renter equipment reflects the recent downward shift of tenure status.

In the planting, cultivating, and harvesting of most farm crops, the same amount of labor by the farmer with ample workstock and farm machinery will produce two, three, or four times as much crop value as that produced by the man who is solely dependent upon hoes and one-horse plows. The value of planting and cultivating machinery decreases, however, when there is no satisfactory harvesting machine. This fact reveals the situation which confronts the small cotton farmer. With a minimum of tools, he can plant and cultivate as much cotton as his entire family can take care of at picking time. Consequently, the machinery of the small cotton farmer is very crude—hoes, plows, cotton planter.

The largest farmers can afford to own labor-saving machinery for the planting and cultivating of cotton because they have for the fields at picking time the laborers who have been used in the production of peaches, asparagus, watermelons, and other crops. The small farmer cannot share in these specialized crops except through coöperative marketing, of which there is almost none in either county.

Coöperative buying and selling, crop rotation and livestock

farming combined, however, can disrupt the cotton farming system only when the farmers themselves are either educated into the value of a change, or forced into it by dire necessity. To date the rotation of crops and livestock farming advocated by the County Farm Agents, coupled with the boll weevil, cheap cotton, and latterly the restrictions of the AAA, have weakened rather than dethroned king cotton.

A One-Horse Civilization.—The cotton farms with planters and fertilizer distributors are far from mechanized; these machines are very simple, frequently drawn by a single horse, and used only a few days each year. Except on the largest and most modernly equipped plantations, practically none of the land is turned with two-horse plows. It is ridged with a one-horse plow, made ready for planting with a one-horse "buster," planted with a one-horse planter, cultivated with a one-horse "scooter"—verily a one-horse civilization. Always following this horse, which is usually a mule, is a man who walks in fresh plowed ground more than twenty miles for each acre of cotton he grows. The other processes are even more primitive: a person chopping cotton with a hoe, or picking cotton by hand and placing it in a sack which he drags through the field. Many of these cotton folk, not owning the hoes they use, can claim as their own only an ax and a wagon full of household furnishings, among which will be bedticks filled with straw or corn husks. Many cotton farmers cannot afford cotton mattresses.

Wagons and Buggies.—The owner or renter with a wagon may be a very good or a very poor farmer, but the owner or renter without a wagon is certainly an inefficient one, for he has no means of his own for hauling wood from the wood lot to his house, for hauling the manure from his barn to his fields, for hauling commercial fertilizer from the store to his farm, or for hauling his cotton to the gin and then to market. The cropper is furnished a wagon by his landlord when he needs it; the owner or renter without a wagon is dependent upon his neighbor's bounty and convenience for the use of his.

One-third of the Negro families studied in Greene and one-

A ONE-HORSE CIVILIZATION

SECTIONS OF GREENE AND MACON COUNTIES TWO-HORSE FARM IMPLEMENTS ARE RARE

UNABLE TO WALK WITHOUT A CANE, SHE HOES ABOUT A LITTLE, WITH HER CANE ON HER

SHE RETURNED FROM "UP NORTH" TO CARE FOR HER ELDERLY FATHER

fifth of those in Macon had wagons, with nearly all of these in owner and renter families. The proportion with buggies was practically the same. The few croppers with either a wagon or buggy formerly had been renters or owners, except in rare cases. A wagon or buggy, like a mule, may be good or poor. As anyone can see by looking over the wagons and buggies at the trading centers on Saturday afternoon, many of them are almost useless, with tires held on the rims by wire, and hickory sticks the size of a man's wrist wedged in the wheel to keep it from collapsing. Tracks of these rickety wheels, literally as crooked as the trail of a snake, are common sights on every Black Belt country road.

The Automobile Reaches the Cotton Farmer.—In recent years, automobile trucks have been displacing wagons to some extent, particularly on the more mechanized plantations; in the two counties, farmers own about 300 trucks. The number of passenger automobiles has increased steadily despite hard times, indicating that they are desired above almost everything else. Automobiles in Greene increased from 847 in 1932 to 1,211 in 1934; in Macon from 975 in 1932 to 1,106 in 1934. The increase in these counties corresponds to the figures for Georgia, 310,684 in 1932 and 397,685 in 1934. The expenditures by the AAA and other federal agencies since 1932, along with Georgia's three-dollar tag, have resulted in the purchase of many new cars and the buying of licenses for many an old one which had been standing behind the house. What does it mean that the recent sharp increase of automobiles has been accompanied by a decrease of mules and an increase of oxen? There is at least the suggestion that thus far the federal agencies have failed to render as much assistance to the poorest cotton farmer as to the one not so poor.

The real meaning of automobiles in the life of these rural families is not definitely known. Some large landowners, for example, report that they have been an unmitigated curse—their purchase and operation have wrecked the economic system and made irredeemably shiftless and independent the Negro as well as the white tenant families. Other large owners state unqualifiedly that, except for the auto, local business conditions would be worse than they are, and that the tenants who have automobiles want to work regularly in order to run them. The rapid transportation which the auto furnishes the cotton farmer cannot be ignored, for something important may be taking place when otherwise propertyless white and Negro croppers can climb into their cars, poor though they be, and command half of the road while they ride whither they will and their gas permits, Saturday afternoon and all day Sunday. It is significant that poor people repair their own cars. In a later chapter are discussed the social and economic implications of the ownership of automobiles by landed and landless white and Negro families.

Home for Second-Hand Cars.—It will be seen from the table below that ownership of land and automobiles go together,

TABLE XX

PER CENT OF FARM FAMILIES WHO OWN AUTOMOBILES BY RACE AND TENURE CLASS IN GREENE AND MACON COUNTIES, GEORGIA

TENURE CLASS	WHITE		NEGRO	
	Greene	Macon	Greene	Macon
Owners......................	90.4	87.9	67.3	71.7
Renters.....................	66.3	68.6	49.7	54.4
Croppers....................	51.5	63.9	37.6	43.9
Total Families...........	74.9	78.1	44.7	47.3

for a much higher percentage of owners than of any other tenure class have cars. Moreover, the owners have the best cars.

Less than one-third of all automobiles owned by rural families in both counties were bought when new: approximately three-fourths of the new cars went to whites, one-fourth to Negroes; within each race nearly 70 per cent of these new cars were bought by landowners. In both counties the tenure classes with the smallest percentages of car ownership have the highest proportion of second-hand automobiles. In short, the families by race and tenure class with the most cars have the best ones, while the tenure classes with the fewest cars have the poorest ones.

Many of these second-hand cars are literally rattletraps, and are able to get on the roads every week-end by dint of the farm boy's barnyard repairs. By the side of the roads on Saturday and Sunday one sees these cars, surrounded by their undisturbed occupants—undisturbed because they had expected to stop along the way, patch a tire or two, change a spark plug, adjust the carburetor, find a short circuit, tape an exposed wire.

In Conclusion.—In this chapter and the two previous chapters it has been shown that while a few rural families in Greene and Macon counties live well enough, the vast majority have but little money; that they buy much of their food, and many of them are dependent upon landlords for subsistence while growing a crop; that they produce only a small proportion of the meat, milk, eggs, and cereals which they need for their own tables; that they live in unattractive and uncomfortable dwellings; that they have scant household furnishings and but little reading matter; and that they own and work with the crudest kind of agricultural tools—in short, that they maintain a very low plane of living. Throughout this discussion a direct connection between man-land relations and planes of living will be noticed, the owners regularly maintaining within each race the highest plane of living, the wage hand and casual laborer the lowest, and the renters and croppers occupying midway positions. In the following chapters, devoted to man-land relations and population movements, it will be shown why the plane of living of families in these two rural counties is determined largely by tenure and racial factors.

PART THREE

Man-Land Relations

CHAPTER VI

WHITE LANDOWNERSHIP

WHITE PEOPLE own more than 95 per cent of the acreage in Greene and Macon counties, and one-seventh of the white owners hold more than one-half of all the land. Large tracts are more or less restricted to certain areas in which nearly three-fourths of all land is in tracts of 500 acres and over; in other sections of the counties are grouped the small holdings.

SIZE OF HOLDINGS IN RELATION TO FERTILITY OF SOIL

With occasional exceptions, the large holdings have always been found on the most fertile soil and the small holdings on the least fertile soil.

Greene's Red Land and White Land.—The largest slave owners in Greene County in 1860 were concentrated in the northern half of the county, particularly in the northwest, and in a more restricted area in the northeast corner; a few large plantations were scattered along the Oconee River all the way to the southern boundary of the county; there was also a small group in the extreme southeast. Farming by the poorer whites developed in the white land section near Siloam and White Plains, where the quality of the soil has never been attractive to large planters. A few now live there, but most of their acreage is elsewhere. Just as the red land in Greene has always been taken up largely by plantation-size holdings, the white land has been the home of the small white owners.

Within the slaveholding areas, the planters often lived in rather well-defined neighborhoods, usually within a radius of a mile or two, their extensive lands stretching away in fan-like shape. One such neighborhood was in the extreme northeast corner of the county, a second in "The Forks" between the Oconee and the Apalachee rivers, and another eight miles northwest of Greensboro. The landed aristocracy and the landless whites were each class conscious, giving rise to the distinction made by Negroes who even to this day refer to one white family as being "quality folks" and another as "po' white trash." The small owners constituted the Black Belt's middle class.

Self-Sufficient Farmers Become Slaveowners.—Many of the largest slaveowners in Greene County had migrated from Virginia and the Carolinas during the last half of the eighteenth century and the early part of the nineteenth. They were people of moderate means and settled in Greene and neighboring counties which later became the northmost part of the Georgia Black Belt. R. P. Brooks gives the following interesting account of their evolution to large slaveowners:

> The first wave of frontiersmen was followed at the close of the Revolution by men in better circumstances, Virginians constituting the most important element. Exhaustion of their tobacco fields was the immediate cause of the migration. As in the case of the settlers of the Upper Piedmont, the newcomers practiced for a generation a self-sufficing economy: cattle raising, diversified agriculture, and home manufactures characterized their industrial life. But the invention of the cotton gin in 1793, and the development of the cotton industry in the two decades following, revolutionized the economic life of the Lincoln and Wilkes County farmers. Being men of large ideas, possessing more property than their fellows in the Upper Piedmont, and occupying a soil admirably suited to cotton culture, the Virginian element quickly evolved into large-scale producers of cotton. Gradually the holdings of the less efficient were acquired, cattle ranges were put to the plow, and the small farmer and herdsman moved westward to squat on fresh lands. Exhausting their original holdings, the planters soon pushed on after the frontiersmen and small farmers, bought their clearings and created new plantations. This process involved social differentiation, society becoming highly stratified, with the planter element of course at the top. Their economic dominance was reflected in political life and presently the planters controlled the State and wielded a powerful influence in national politics during the ascendency of the cotton South just prior to the sixties.[1]

Many of the direct descendants of the landed families of Greene County boast their Virginia ancestry. The epitaph be-

[1] *The Agrarian Revolution in Georgia* (Madison, Wis., 1914), p. 83.

low, appearing on the gravestone in a family cemetery of one
of the early planters, could be reproduced many times in Greene
and adjoining counties.

IN MEMORY OF
WILLIAM TUGGLE, SENIOR
BORN IN VIRGINIA
APRIL 17, 1777
DIED
MARCH 20, 1861
AN HONEST MAN IS THE NOBLEST WORK OF GOD

Stately Houses on Hilltops.—The house built more than a
century ago by William Tuggle, Sr., is still standing. There
are scores of ante-bellum dwellings in Greene County. Some
of them have been abandoned entirely, mere heaps of ruins; in
others, a tenant family occupies a few rooms on the first floor;
in a few cases Negroes have bought the "old place"; in yet
fewer instances some direct descendant of the original owner
lives in the spacious and sturdy building.

In 1860 there was a more or less pretentious dwelling on
every plantation with as many as fifty slaves. Most of the
shops, tool sheds, warehouses, barns, and even the porches and
separate kitchens have disappeared; but the shorn "big house"
may yet stand erect and suggest the cultural and financial circumstances of the family who built it. Such residences, on the
crests of hills overlooking the surrounding countryside, were
little kingdoms of benevolence or tyranny. They were centers
of graciousness to friends, unlimited hospitality to sympathetic
strangers, and unmitigated hatred for outside "meddlers." Few
of the newer dwellings in the open country of Greene County
will outlast those ante-bellum structures which have been kept in
repair. The dwellings built since the Civil War have been
noticeably smaller and of less permanent construction. This
suggests that agriculture received a setback at that time from
which it never fully recuperated. But the disruption of the
slave system was perchance less important than the excessive loss

of soil fertility through erosion which had already foredoomed
the old plantation economy.

A Plantation System in a Hill Country.—The topography of
the oldest part of the Georgia Black Belt accelerated the im-
poverishment of the soil. In Greene County, most of the
largest slave plantations were located in the hilly section along
the Oconee River and its tributaries because the soil there was
the most fertile.

Prior to 1860 cotton was grown without the use of commercial fertilizers, and rich hillsides were much preferred to
the poorer white soil, however level. When excessive erosion
had followed the constant cultivation of the clean culture crops
of cotton and corn, unproductive fields were abandoned and new
fields made by clearing away the original hardwood forests.
As the years passed the most desired areas passed into the hands
of the largest owners, were cleared, cultivated, and then abandoned. By this process much of the best land had been exhausted even before 1860 and already a considerable number
of the most alert planters were beginning to migrate to South
Georgia or into the fertile but undeveloped Southwest, where
they could grow cotton more cheaply than in the hill country
between Atlanta and Augusta.

*The Development of White Landownership in Macon
County.*—In Macon, as in Greene which is roughly fifty years
its senior, the present location of plantations corresponds with
the slave plantations in 1860. Many of the largest owners in
Macon County were from the older Georgia counties west of
Augusta, some were from South Carolina, and a few from
Virginia.

The planters from South Carolina had migrated to Macon
to secure new land upon which to employ slaves which they
already owned or hoped to buy. The earliest of these South
Carolinians settled in the Marshallville district where they were
joined by newcomers from South Carolina. Eventually practically all the landed South Carolinians congregated in Marshallville, some having come from Oglethorpe in 1862-63,

GREENE COUNTY—WHERE THE WRAYS HAVE LIVED FOR GENERATIONS

IN THIS HOUSE ON THE WRAY PLANTATION TWO SLAVE FAMILIES LIVED

MACON COUNTY—THE HOME OF THE LATE SAMUEL HENRY RUMPH,
ORIGINATOR OF THE FAMOUS ELBERTA PEACH

A MACON COUNTY PEACH ORCHARD

when the severe smallpox epidemic virtually wiped it off the map. While a number of the earliest large landowners in the county were from the Black Belt of South Carolina, perhaps a larger number were from the older parts of the Georgia Black Belt, such as Greene County, where the topography was such that the best soils had been soon exhausted.

Immediately before 1860, large plantations were developing in the area around Montezuma. The older landed families of Oglethorpe and Marshallville tended to consider the newcomers upstarts. Montezuma is the trade center of this newest and now most prosperous farming section; it has the largest stores in the county, the largest bank, a public library, a hospital, and in many respects is more modern than either Oglethorpe or Marshallville. The unsuccessful attempt made about forty years ago to move the county courthouse from Oglethorpe to Montezuma has a partial explanation in the antipathy which the two older and smaller towns felt toward their newer and more aggressive neighbor.

In contrast with Greene, there are in Macon but few pretentious dwellings which antedate the Civil War, and practically all of these are in the Oglethorpe and Marshallville communities. Whereas Greene County had "arrived," economically and culturally, by the middle of the nineteenth century, Macon County became fully developed only recently.

East and West of the River.—Macon County is bisected, north to south, by the Flint River; there are noticeable differences between the halves. With the exception of its northern tip and the strip along the river, the entire western part of the county is of relatively poor soil. Small landowners located in this part of the county when the larger slaveowners were establishing themselves on the richer level lands around Marshallville and Montezuma. The plantations are still located in the rich level portions, and the small owners are concentrated on the poorer land, much of which is hilly.

These variations, which developed early, are more marked today than ever before. West of the river cotton and corn are practically the only crops; east of the river the peach, melon, and asparagus crops are also important, but they have supplemented rather than displaced the income from cotton.

The contrasts of white landownership in Greene and Macon counties up until 1920 were due, first, to the earlier settlement of Greene, and second, to the fact that the most fertile part of Greene was the most hilly, while the most fertile part of Macon was relatively level.

Townward Shift of Plantation Owners.—In Greene and Macon counties, as elsewhere in the Black Belt, the Civil War left most of the planters bankrupt. They were without funds, or credit, and their labor was disorganized. A new system of farming had to be evolved. The high price of cotton immediately after the war offered hopes of the reëstablishment of plantation farming by replacing slaves with wage hands. This hope proved to be an illusion, for the price of cotton soon dropped; and what was equally disconcerting, the Negroes, ill-adjusted to their new freedom, were often not satisfactory laborers. Unable to cultivate their plantations in the way they had hoped, many of the planters moved into the towns and worked their lands "on halves"—cropper farming it was later called.

The excessive Negro majorities in the large plantations areas, in some instances eight or ten to one, were partially responsible for this shift; with the disruption of the old master-slave relation, the whites felt less secure. The Reconstruction government provided further motivation for the influential whites to move to the county seat town: they were outnumbered two to one in Greene, and to succeed in their determined effort to restore white rule they had to work together. The planters were slow, too, to acknowledge that they had been defeated at arms, and even slower in admitting that they had been fighting to preserve an institution discarded long before by most other civilized nations. They were in need of each other's constant sympathy. For their loss of property and power at home and prestige abroad they compensated partially by much talking and theorizing among themselves about the superiority of the southern whites. They and their less refined successors—money-lenders and time merchants—have provided a white supremacy manifesto for the racial determinists of the South.

The various grievances of the southern whites were heaped upon the inarticulate ex-slave; the white South's humiliation and poverty, its hatred of the Yankees and of the central government, along with its fears of the blacks, found a convenient scapegoat in the nominally free but defenseless Negro. And there, upon the back of the black man, most of the load has remained; for many politicians in government and business and religion have found the agitation of the race question the surest road to election.

Farm Labor Further Disorganized.—When the owners of the large plantations moved into town their land became noticeably less productive, for even by using paid overseers they could not exercise the close supervision required by the unstable Negro laborers, who had been thrilled and then disappointed by their new freedom. The plantations, including the most productive portions of both counties, were turned over largely to Negro tenants who had neither the fear of the lash, which makes slaves work, nor the hope of ownership, which is the highest motive tenant farmers can have for preserving the fertility of the land they work.

With the majority of the largest plantations cultivated by quasi-self-directed tenants, the labor supply was further demoralized. It was increasingly difficult for the planters who still worked gang labor to secure wage hands. In the meantime the price of cotton was decreasing, and the demanding Negroes rather than being offered more money for their labor were being asked to work for less. The outcome was that the cultivation of yet other plantations was left in the hands of tenants, most but not all of whom were Negroes.

The Time Merchant Exalted.—When croppers and renters displaced wage hands the time merchant was exalted to first place in the Black Belt community, for in addition to the high rates of interest which he realized when full settlement was made, he received considerable acreage and more than a few work animals from time to time when full settlements could not be made. Presently, therefore, he was a merchant and a planter and, having money, a moneylender, too. About this same time the Black Belt lawyer came into prominence as legislator and as the person who knew how to make of little or no effect the Thirteenth, Fourteenth, and Fifteenth Amendments.

Landownership becoming less remunerative and the landowning class sharing its status with merchants and moneylenders and lawyers, many of the younger members of the landed families, especially in Greene, sought their fortunes in the commercial and industrial enterprises of the cities, South and North. Frequently all the heirs of a landed family would locate outside the county, in which case the land would not uncommonly be sold to some particularly successful white tenant who had been renting the entire place and subrenting portions of it. In some instances the ancestral possessions were held for sentimental reasons.

The Plantation Reaches Its Zenith.—The plantation system in Greene had reached its zenith about 1850,[2] and the number of large holdings remained constant for thirty years. During this time from fifty to seventy landlords owned one thousand or more acres of land in contrast with less than twenty such owners before 1825 and forty since 1900. Holdings of two thousand or more acres further define this period: twelve to sixteen from 1850 to 1880 against three or less before 1825 and eight or less since 1900. By the end of the period, the white population had stopped decreasing and the Negro population had stopped increasing.

In Macon the concentration of lands into larger and larger holdings continued until about 1920, when there were fifty-two owners with one thousand or more acres. Since that time these largest acreages have numbered: forty-seven in 1921, fifty in

[2] According to the Greene County tax digest of 1853, the 8,402 slaves in the county were valued at $3,537,965.00. The county's total taxable property for that year was $7,038,301. The county's total taxable property in 1925 was $3,570,549; in 1928 it was $3,116,165; in 1934 it was $2,567,310.

1925, forty-eight in 1927, forty-nine in 1932, and forty-eight in 1934. Holdings of two thousand acres or more also reached their greatest number at the same time with fourteen, while since then they have varied from ten to thirteen.

Macon County being a half-century younger than Greene, it is not surprising that Macon but recently reached what seems to be the zenith of its plantation system. At any rate it now occupies a tableland quite similar to that of Greene between 1850 and 1880. The recent increase of renters in the big plantation area of Macon further suggests that plantation farming has attained its full stature. Moreover, Macon's Negro population is now decreasing for the first time and her white farm population is increasing at a greater rate than heretofore. Whether Macon's plantation system will follow the pattern of Greene and decline after a decade or two remains to be seen.

THE INCREASING NUMBER OF LANDOWNERS

Since 1880 in Greene and 1920 in Macon, there has been much changing of ownership, particularly of large plantations

TABLE XXI

NUMBER OF WHITE LANDOWNERS BY SIZE OF HOLDINGS,
GREENE COUNTY, GEORGIA, 1827-1934[3]

YEAR	ACRES								
	0–19	20–49	50–99	100– 249	250– 499	500– 999	1000– 1999	2000 Plus	Total
1827.......	4	12	54	272	173	100	18	3	636
1828.......	8	11	41	239	145	106	20	3	573
1853.......	19	21	17	135	110	108	62	13	485
1874.......	21	22	58	185	180	89	45	12	612
1884.......	19	35	90	222	161	89	30	16	662
1894.......	21	40	116	291	151	92	35	12	758
1899.......	25	54	116	279	152	78	34	9	747
1904.......	34	45	121	318	154	65	34	11	782
1909.......	40	72	146	294	134	58	31	8	783
1914.......	29	81	155	318	145	60	32	8	828
1919.......	24	87	197	335	128	63	40	6	880
1921.......	39	97	200	352	132	65	35	5	925
1925.......	42	96	203	352	133	68	37	5	936
1927.......	44	97	206	358	129	74	39	5	952
1932.......	50	91	204	399	125	70	30	9	978
1934.......	53	103	216	421	123	68	29	4	1,017

[3] Data compiled from the Greene County Tax Digests.

which often remain intact even when forfeited to creditors. Mortgage companies now hold the titles to over 17,000 acres in Greene and 20,000 acres in Macon. Prior to 1921 in Greene and in 1928 in Macon, the loan companies held few or no titles. A few large holdings have been divided, particularly in Greene, offering opportunities for the emergence of additional small owners.

Number of Landowners by Size of Holdings.—The total number of landowners has steadily increased in Greene since about 1860 and in Macon since 1909. The owners in Greene

TABLE XXII

NUMBER OF WHITE LANDOWNERS BY SIZE OF HOLDINGS, MACON COUNTY, GEORGIA, 1838-1934[4]

YEAR	ACRES								
	0–19	20–49	50–99	100– 249	250– 499	500– 999	1000– 1999	2000 Plus	Total
1838.......	1	4	10	165	76	48	14	2	320
1852.......	18	9	27	208	94	54	34	8	452
1874.......	10	7	39	210	122	83	29	10	510
1884.......	8	13	51	223	160	64	32	8	559
1894.......	19	26	66	243	138	69	29	9	599
1899.......	23	36	87	236	144	73	29	11	639
1904.......	22	29	83	236	135	74	31	11	621
1909.......	19	47	62	223	119	63	29	13	575
1914.......	30	50	81	258	124	62	27	11	643
1919.......	60	47	87	259	131	74	38	14	710
1921.......	92	56	85	269	131	85	34	13	765
1925.......	145	45	93	238	136	80	40	10	787
1927.......	88	42	89	241	126	80	36	12	714
1932.......	160	60	99	252	126	76	36	13	822
1934.......	167	60	111	267	121	92	36	12	866

increased from 485 in 1853 to 662 in 1884; 782 in 1904, 828 in 1914, 936 in 1925, to 1,017 in 1934. In Macon from 575 in 1909 to 710 in 1919; 765 in 1925, 822 in 1932, to 866 in 1934.

This large increase in number of holdings was made possible by the disintegration of plantation farming and the breaking up of a few of the largest holdings. For example, in 1884 Greene had 16 holdings of over 2,000 acres and 312 holdings of from 50 to 250 acres, while in 1934 there were 4 of the former and

* Data compiled from the Macon County Tax Digests.

703 of the latter. Though more recent, the same trends are noticeable in Macon: in 1919, 14 holdings of 2,000 acres or more and 346 of from 50 to 250 acres; in 1934, 12 of the former and 378 of the latter. The number of holdings of between 20 and 50 acres in Greene increased from 35 to 116 between 1884 and 1934; in Macon from 47 to 60 between 1919 and 1934.

The Disintegration of Largest Holdings.—To comprehend fully just what has happened, attention is devoted to the varying conditions within each county; for, as suggested already, there are greater differences within each county than between them. The data in the following table make it clear that in

TABLE XXIII

PER CENT OF TOTAL ACREAGE IN TRACTS OF 500 OR MORE BY DISTRICTS IN GREENE COUNTY, IN 1919 AND 1927[5]

MILITIA DISTRICTS	PER CENT OF ACREAGE IN TRACTS OF 500 OR MORE ACRES		
	1919	1927	Per Cent Change 1919–1927
All Districts.....................	50.6	50.4	− 0.2
DISTRICTS:			
Number 144.................	15.4	20.4	5.0
" 142.................	17.1	34.1	17.0
" 141.................	21.2	40.4	19.2
" 163.................	27.9	52.2	24.3
" 162.................	37.1	57.9	20.8
" 160.................	41.1	20.0	−21.1
" 145.................	42.1	39.5	− 2.6
" 140.................	42.9	45.0	2.1
" 137.................	44.6	46.2	1.6
" 147.................	62.6	51.9	−10.7
" 143.................	62.6	63.1	0.5
" 146.................	63.7	30.2	−33.5
" 149.................	65.0	49.9	−15.1
" 138.................	66.8	45.0	−21.8
" 161.................	68.8	84.1	15.3
" 148.................	69.6	66.8	− 2.8

Greene between 1919 and 1927 the percentage of the total acreage in large tracts increased in the small-holding districts and decreased in the large-holding districts. This simply means that the small owners became more common in the old plantation areas and a few large owners appeared in the white land

[5] Data from Greene County Tax Digests.

section, characterized since the settlement of the county by small white owner cultivators.

The average and median acreage per holding in Greene further demonstrates the trend. The average acreage was 260.8 acres in 1919 and 248.7 acres in 1927; the median, 159.4 acres in 1919 and 154.2 in 1927. By militia districts the process is still further illustrated: in the four white land districts in the southeastern part of the county where holdings are smallest, there were 331 holdings in 1919 and 330 in 1927, the median acreage remaining almost constant at 127 acres; while by contrast, in four big holding districts in the red land section the number of holdings increased from 240 in 1919 to 274 in 1927, and the median acreage per owner dropped from 194.4 in the former year to 164.7 in the latter. The trends noted here continued in evidence between 1927 and 1934.

Macon showed an increasing proportion of all acreage in tracts of 500 acres between 1919 and 1927, and large holdings

TABLE XXIV

PER CENT OF TOTAL ACREAGE IN TRACTS OF 500 OR MORE ACRES BY
MILITIA DISTRICTS IN MACON COUNTY, IN 1927 AND IN 1934[6]

MILITIA DISTRICTS	PER CENT OF ACREAGE IN TRACTS OF 500 OR MORE ACRES		
	1927	1934	Per Cent Change 1927–1934
All Districts.....................	59.7	58.6	— 1.1
DISTRICTS:			
Number 740.................	15.2	19.0	3.8
" 757.................	24.5	28.7	4.2
" 1070.................	48.4	55.7	7.3
" 814.................	54.3	46.7	— 7.6
" 1002.................	64.2	56.7	— 7.5
" 543.................	72.0	58.9	—13.1
" 770.................	79.9	76.9	— 3.0

in Macon began to break up only after 1927. By militia districts, too, the trend in Macon after 1927 corresponded to that in Greene, with the number of holdings remaining about constant in the small owner areas and increasing from 227 to 261 in the two largest plantation districts east of the Flint River, reducing the median acreage per holding from 319.6 acres in 1927

[6] Data from Macon County Tax Digests.

to 289.1 acres in 1934. We reserve for future chapters the discussion of the effects of the boll weevil and subsequent cheap cotton upon the ownership of land.

OWNERSHIP AND USE OF LAND

Landownership does not mean that the land is cultivated by the owner. Of the 837 white owners in Greene having more than fifty acres, only 278 were listed as farmers by the 1930 Agricultural Census; of Macon's 702 white owners 320 were listed as farmers. Although there were several resident white owners who rented out all their acreage and consequently were not entered as farmers, there was a much larger number of absentee owners, particularly in Greene, who lived in Atlanta, Athens, Macon, or even farther away.

Absentee Landlordism.—Since absentee ownership emerged in Macon only after 1928, this discussion is limited largely to Greene County, where it has been prevalent for a quarter of a century or more. Absentee ownership is associated with the disintegration of plantation farming and involves but little acreage outside the big plantation areas.

The volume of Greene's absentee landownership in tracts of 500 acres and over, shown in the table below, increased roughly from 26,000 acres in 1919 to 36,000 in 1934, nearly half of which is in the hands of loan companies. During the same

TABLE XXV

RESIDENT AND ABSENTEE OWNERSHIP OF TRACTS OF 500 OR MORE ACRES
IN GREENE COUNTY IN 1919, 1927, AND 1934[7]

	RESIDENT OWNERS			ABSENTEE OWNERS		
	1919	1927	1934	1919	1927	1934
Number of owners...................	82	84	79	27	34	36
Total acreage owned.................	89,788	86,166	81,045	26,261	33,114	36,235

period the aggregate acreage owned by large resident owners decreased from roughly 90,000 to 81,000 acres.

By an intensive study of the county tax digests from 1919

[7] Data from Greene County Tax Digests and interviews with tax assessor and local citizens.

to 1927, a period of adverse farm conditions, it was found that a larger proportion of the resident owners than of the absentee owners lost their farms. The latter could retain their acreage better because the majority of them had incomes independent of their land.

Some of the tracts held by absentee owners are used for growing timber, some are held as investments, some are rented for the fourth share or for a cash or cotton rent. Many tracts can be bought by anyone who has satisfactory credit, while others —old home places—are held for sentimental reasons and are not for sale. Though Carver, in his *Elements of Rural Economics*, speaks of absentee landlordism as an unmitigated evil, it is proving of some benefit in the long run to Greene County, for new owner cultivators of both races emerge most often in the absentee owner areas where the land is for sale.

Absentee landlordism is most harmful to a community when it persists irrespective of the revenue received from the land; that is, when large tracts are held for sentimental rather than economic reasons. They cannot be bought by prospective new owners, and often rent at a very low rate, simply because a little something is just so much more than nothing; in that way, it works a hardship upon near-by resident planters who are dependent upon their rents for a livelihood.

Occupying a position midway between the absentee owners and the owner cultivators are a number of resident white people who own land, but like the absentee owners, pay very little personal attention to its cultivation. This relation of landowner to his land, fairly prevalent in the red land area of Greene and not uncommon west of the river in Macon, might be classed as quasi-absentee landlordism. These owners control more acreage in Greene than the absentee owners. It is a reasonable estimate that not less than one-third of the entire acreage in Greene and about one-fifth of the acreage in Macon is held by either absentee or quasi-absentee owners.

Owner Operators.—The number of white owner operators

in Greene County decreased from 474 in 1910 to 278 in 1930;[8] even then, however, the proportionate loss of owners was not as great as that of the tenants. In 1935, there were 349 owner cultivators in Greene. Macon County, on the contrary, had 272 white owner operators in 1910 and 338 in 1925, the number dropping to 320 in 1930 and to 300 in 1935. Macon's white tenant element, too, increased to 1925 but decreased slightly between 1925 and 1930, only to increase nearly 30 per cent by 1935.

The whites in these counties who cultivate their own land are, for the most part, those who have always lived in communities of small owners or have come up out of the tenant class. In Greene the majority of owner cultivators live in the white land section and in those portions of the red land area where the large holdings have been subdivided; the western half of Macon is the home of the white owner-cultivators.

Approximately one-sixth of all white owner cultivators in these counties moved in from the Piedmont and mountain counties of Georgia and Alabama. Some of these newcomers purchased farms with money which they secured by selling land they owned in the hill country, and a few more saved and bought after settling in the Black Belt, but the vast majority came without property or credit and merely swelled the ranks of the white tenants already present. Most of these north Georgians and north Alabamians, whether owners or tenants, have settled in localities where the large estates are being rented, rather than cultivated by croppers as formerly. In Greene a group of these families are located midway between Greensboro and Penfield, a second group seven miles west of Greensboro in the lower part of "The Forks," a third in the extreme southern part of the county. In Macon the newcomers who have bought land are on the outskirts of the peach section east of the river. In the past five years considerable plantation acreage around Marshallville has been taken over by loan companies. A number of white families from north Alabama now

[8] United States Census.

live there as renters, the relation of man to land most conducive to ownership.

West of the river in Macon and in the white land section in Greene the children of the small white owners tend to take up all available land. As a general rule the younger members of these families who remain in the community begin farming as tenants on the land of relative or neighbor, and sooner or later purchase some tract.

In addition to these outsiders and children of resident small owners who become owner cultivators, a white tenant now and then rises into ownership. This happens most often in cases where the land belongs to an absentee owner who needs the income from the rent or sale of his land. Occasionally a successful tenant on the holdings of an absentee owner purchases the entire tract, which, if large, makes of him a landlord who secures revenue from his investment by supervising tenants and wage hands. As a general rule, however, the tenant who rises into the owner class purchases a relatively small tract and cultivates it himself, with the assistance of little or no labor from outside his immediate family. In a later chapter is discussed the disillusionment of the tenant families who lost all they had in unsuccessful attempts at ownership during the inflation period of the World War.

Planters and Farm Managers.—Since 1890 the number of tracts of 500 acres or more cultivated under the supervision of the owner or his agents has decreased in Greene and remained about constant in Macon, as is shown in the accompanying table.

TABLE XXVI

FARMS OF 500 OR MORE ACRES IN GREENE AND MACON COUNTIES, GEORGIA, 1880-1930[9]

YEAR	GEORGIA	GREENE	MACON
1880	10,508	82	76
1890	8,819	83	66
1900	6,576	44	60
1910	5,471	28	65
1920	4,244	29	66
1930	3,639	32	71

[9] United States Census.

Practically all farm managers and overseers are found on these large farms; in 1930, Greene had six in contrast with thirteen in 1910; Macon had sixty-one against sixty-three in 1910. Though small in number, the importance of these farms under the supervision of managers and overseers is appreciated when one notes that they averaged over 550 acres, more than ten times the size of the typical tenant farm. Moreover, the best land in each county is in these largest units of cultivation.

More than four-fifths of the Georgia farms with managers and overseers are located in the Black Belt, and two-thirds of these are in the southern part of it; that is, in the newer counties, including Macon and surrounding area. In fact, six of Georgia's seven counties which had more than thirty-five managers and overseers were in the immediate vicinity of Macon County; this concentration is accounted for largely by the peach, melon, asparagus, and pecan industries.

It is not without significance that when Peach County, one of the smallest, was formed in 1925, only two other counties in Georgia had a larger number of farm managers and overseers, and one of these was Bleckley which, like Peach, was called into being in 1913 by a group of large planters who wanted a county of their own. The rôle of the plantation owner in the Black Belt may be not so all-inclusive as formerly, for merchants and money lenders have been powerful factors for decades; but the planter is still king to his overseer and tenants and wage hands. A later chapter carries a discussion of landlord-tenant relations.

The Overseer.—The landlord decides what shall be planted, when it shall be planted, and how it shall be planted. The overseer, seldom with training beyond the seventh grade and usually with less, merely sees to it that the landlord's instructions are followed. The overseer functions as an extension of the landlord's eyes; he has no authority other than that which is his as the representative of his employer. Some overseers secure permission from the county sheriff to carry a pistol, and are termed "pistol-totin' deputies."

In so far as farm management is concerned, the hired white

overseer, usually the twenty-five to thirty-five year old son of a distant tenant, is the direct descendant of the slave driver, and like him is not much better off economically or culturally than those whose labor he directs. He is paid a meager salary, ranging from $30 to $90 per month.

The Number and Significance of Negro Overseers.—Can as much work be got out of Negro laborers by Negro supervisors as by white supervisors? Many planters think not, but within the acquaintance of these men there are prosperous landlords who use Negro overseers. In 1910 there were two Negro overseers in Macon County, in 1930 there were eight, while Peach had four and Sumter had three. Roughly speaking, one-tenth of the overseers in Macon and surrounding counties are Negroes. In Greene and environs the Negro overseers have not decreased so rapidly as the white. All of them are in the employ of white landlords and usually they are long-time acquaintances.

The practice of entrusting the supervision of Negro workmen to a Negro rather than a white man is not new by any means, for in slave times the planters used certain of their most trustworthy Negroes as agents. It has not been unusual for a landlord to call aside one of his oldest Negro tenants to find out just what the "racket is about" between the new white overseer and some Negro workman. But publicly to place a Negro in a position of responsibility by giving him a salary for his services is a rather late development, and is practiced even now only by a few planters and in places where practically all the farm laborers are Negroes.

As a general rule, the Negro overseer has had an active part in stabilizing labor conditions on the plantation through the development of the local Negro institutions—church and school and lodge. There is quite a contrast between the white man and the Negro who become overseers: The Negro overseer is a leader in the life of his community and is able to function as agent for the landlord because of the respect which the farm workers have for him personally; the white overseer may be the type of propertyless white man who needs employment and is willing to contract his time to some landlord who wants a man to "stay on the place" and see that his instructions are followed. In short, the white owner can secure the services of the most capable Negroes for his agents; but the wages he pays will hardly attract a white man with qualities of leadership.

Another difference between the white and Negro overseer is that the white feels it is not his business to work; he directs the wage hands or tenants by telling them what to do and how to do it. The landlord expects the Negro overseer to work while directing the activities of others, and there is nothing in his background and but little in his present situation which prevents his doing so. In those instances where a son or nephew of the landlord acts as overseer, the supervision is on a basis of proprietary interest and what has been said about the characteristics of a hired white overseer does not apply.

For every whole-time or part-time Negro overseer there are a score of unpaid Negro tenants who function as landlords' agents. The landlord frequently capitalizes the paternal interest which some well-established tenant feels toward the other families on the place, and makes of him a sort of guardian of his local interests by encouraging him to see to it that each family produces a good crop. This type of quasi-overseership obtains particularly in Greene, where the owners leave their farming operations largely in the hands of tenants. Throughout the Black Belt the Negroes themselves have dubbed these patronizing members of their own race "white folks Niggers." Individuals from this group more often than from any other rise into the landowning class.

CHAPTER VII
THE NEGRO BECOMES A LANDOWNER

WHAT can be said about Negro landownership in counties where approximately three-fourths of all farmers are tenants and three-fourths of all tenants are Negroes?[1] By what means can Negroes become landowners in these Black Belt counties, and with what results to themselves and to the community?

THE OWNERSHIP OF LAND BY NEGROES

The freedman's hope for forty acres and a mule has remained unfilled—the Negro has been given no land. Such acreage as he owns he or his father has bought, and usually the purchase has been the result more largely of a personal equation than of a purely business transaction. Here and in other rural Black Belt counties, where primary contacts prevail and master-slave patterns are not altogether absent, the white owners choose their landowning neighbors. Though a Negro is tolerated now and then, and in some few instances even welcomed, the number of Negro owners is not large and their combined acreage is small.

One-Eightieth, One-Sixteenth, One-Twentieth.—Sixty-five years ago, in 1870, seven Negroes owned less than 800 acres in Greene and Macon counties; four years later fifty-two owned 6,118 acres, one-eightieth of the land area of these counties. There followed a gradual increase until 1921, when 409 owned 30,862 acres, one-sixteenth of the total. Since 1921 Negro owners have decreased, and 1934 showed 365 with 22,599 acres, which is less than one-twentieth of the land area. This loss since 1921, it will be observed in the following table, is restricted almost wholly to Greene; the Negro there was heir,

---

[1] In Greene County 76.1 per cent of all farmers were tenants, and 71.6 per cent of all tenants were Negroes; in Macon County 78.4 per cent were tenants, 76.5 per cent of whom were Negroes. These data were compiled from the 1930 United States Census.

along with the white man, to all the financial strain and readjustment which came with the boll weevil depression of the
early twenties.

TABLE XXVII

NUMBER OF NEGRO-OWNED TRACTS OF LESS THAN TWENTY ACRES, OF
TWENTY OR MORE ACRES, AND THE TOTAL NEGRO-OWNED ACREAGE
IN GREENE AND MACON COUNTIES, GEORGIA, FROM 1870 TO 1934[2]

YEAR	GREENE			MACON		
	Less than 20 Acres	More than 20 Acres	Total Acreage	Less than 20 Acres	More than 20 Acres	Total Acreage
1870........	1	3	421	..	3	375
1874........	2	27	3,537	4	27	2,581
1884........	9	34	4,722	5	31	3,478
1894........	27	48	7,560	23	52	7,147
1904........	34	119	11,705	28	53	7,241
1914........	41	127	13,672	34	72	9,634
1919........	50	155	15,898	40	93	10,338
1921........	73	173	18,977	60	105	11,885
1925........	53	135	12,741	45	98	11,353
1927........	69	123	11,315	47	119	11,637
1934........	85	126	11,543	44	110	11,056

The Development of Negro Landownership.—Almost without exception, the earliest Negro landowners had the same name
as the white people from whom they secured their land. Most
of them became owners through the advice and assistance of
their ex-masters. In Greene the Stocks and Saunders—in the
vicinity of the Stocks and Saunders plantations—the Ellingtons,
Watts, Murdens, Rowlands, and Fambroughs were of this class.
All were located in the heart of the old slave plantation areas.
Only a handful of the descendants of these earliest owners came
out of the boll weevil depression with their land. In Macon,
where the boll weevil was not so severe, there are a half-dozen
of the old tracts still held by a score of the descendants of the
original owners. Near Marshallville are the Ned Frederick
and Rumph homesteads—while in the western half of the county
are the Harrises, Lewises, Tookes, Turners, McDonalds, and
Jordans—all out from Oglethorpe in the plantation area of that
time.

[2] From the Tax Digests of Greene and Macon counties.

Most of the larger Negro-owned farms in Greene are still in the old plantation area, but the greatest increase since 1890 has occurred just outside the white-land section in the south-eastern part of the county, where the small white owners live. In Macon County the owners have increased scarcely any in the Marshallville and Montezuma districts, and have become most common in the Garden Valley and Englishville areas, where the plantation system is breaking down, and also among the smaller white owners in the hill region around Ideal.

While the largest Negro-owned tracts in both counties are located at a distance from the towns, the majority of the smallest

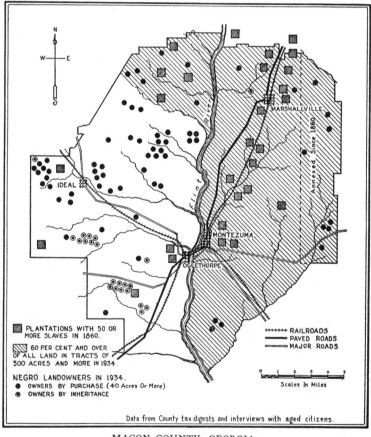

PLANTATIONS WITH 50 OR
MORE SLAVES IN 1860.

60 PER CENT AND OVER
OF ALL LAND IN TRACTS OF
500 ACRES AND MORE IN 1934.

NEGRO LANDOWNERS IN 1934.
● OWNERS BY PURCHASE (40 Acres Or More)
◉ OWNERS BY INHERITANCE

RAILROADS
PAVED ROADS
MAJOR ROADS

Scales In Miles

Data from County tax digests and interviews with aged citizens.

MACON COUNTY, GEORGIA

ones—two to twenty acres—have been, since their emergence about 1890, located near the towns. Nearly half of the eighty-five smallest tracts in Greene are near Greensboro, Union Point, and White Plains; in Macon, over half of its forty-four are within a mile and a half of Montezuma, Oglethorpe, and Marshallville. The smallest homeowners are of little economic importance in so far as their farm ownership is concerned, for they make practically all their living by working in town or on adjoining farms, but they are not without social meaning: They have permanence of residence, and the opportunity to choose between available employment, to control their own time, to receive cash for their work, and to trade where they like. Of all owners, this group has best withstood the depression.

Decrease in Greene from 1921 Through 1927.—The total acreage owned by Negroes in Greene County, it will be noted, dropped from 18,977 in 1921 to 11,315 in 1927, and there it has remained. The total loss of acreage in Macon during this period was less than 300 acres. For these reasons, the discussion of farms lost is limited to Greene County, and to the 1921-1927 period.

The 7,662-acre loss which occurred during these six years involved only four of the smaller owners, with a total of fifty-six acres, as contrasted with twenty-eight of the larger owners, with an aggregate of 5,843 acres, who saw their farms sold or taken over to satisfy indebtedness, and an additional eighteen with an acreage of 1,763, who, after having made one or more payments, allowed their farms to revert to their former owners. More land was lost between 1921 and 1927 than was cultivated by resident owners in the latter year.

It was unavoidable that many of these farms should be lost because of indebtedness, or allowed to revert to their former owners. Many had been bought at boom prices during the three years that the boll weevil delayed its coming. Then the weevil arrived and wrecked crops and land values in an outworn farm system that was already tottering.

Just as the owners with less than twenty acres did not suffer

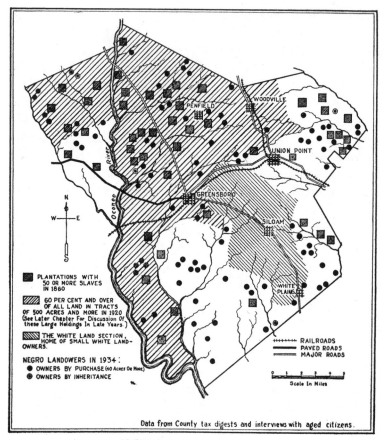

GREENE COUNTY, GEORGIA

so much as those with over twenty, the smaller owners of the
latter group retained their lands more often than the larger
ones.   This middle-sized farmer, in addition to producing a
larger proportion of foodstuffs for his family and stock, could
often earn enough from sawmills and odd jobs at spare times to
take care of his small indebtedness.   In several cases these
smaller owners, upon the advice of their creditors, went to
Florida or elsewhere to secure through employment the cash
needed to hold their property.   The larger owner could not so
readily follow this procedure because of his larger indebtedness
and the greater need for his presence on his farm.   In short,

the small owner kept his land in spite of the boll weevil, deflation, and bank failures because he was not entirely dependent
upon the products of his farm to satisfy his creditors. When
the larger owner did not receive enough money from his cotton
to satisfy his creditors, the land he gave as security for his borrowings was lost.

Losses Most Common Among Largest Owners.—The table
below reveals that the holdings lost because of debts averaged
more than twice the size of those forfeited to former owners.
It will be noticed, too, that seven of the county's eight largest
owners lost their lands during this period; these large tracts
were sold under mortgage to satisfy indebtedness (usually to
supply merchants). The bankrupt condition of the largest
Negro farmers parallels the experience of the largest white

TABLE XXVIII

NUMBER AND SIZE OF NEGRO LAND HOLDINGS OF TWENTY OR MORE ACRES
IN GREENE COUNTY IN RELATION TO DECREASE OF OWNERS
FROM 1921 THROUGH 1927[3]

	CULTIVATED BY OWNERS IN 1927	LOST BECAUSE OF INDEBTEDNESS, 1921–1927	FORFEITED TO FORMER OWNER, 1921–1927
Number of holdings.............	73	28	18
HOLDINGS BY SIZE:			
20– 49 acres................	23	4	3
50– 99 acres................	18	8	5
100–174 acres................	23	8	10
175–259 acres................	8	1	..
260–499 acres................	..	5	..
500–999 acres................	1	2	..
Total acreage....................	7,562	5,843	1,763
Average acreage................	103.6	208.7	97.9

planters, for like the whites they had financed the planting and
cultivation of the profit-consuming crops of 1921 and after, by
mortgaging their property. The only way they could have
kept their land would have been to change their money crops,
shift to self-sufficient farming, or quit the farm in 1920 and
seek remunerative work elsewhere to pay taxes and outstanding

[3] Data from Greene County Tax Digests and personal interviews.

debts. Except among the smaller owners, rarely was any one of these things done, for they hoped in 1923, in 1924, and again in 1925 to retrieve what they had lost. Cash was consumed; credit evaporated with the deflation of land values and the closing of banks; forced sales were frequent.

In both counties, but particularly in Greene, there were scores of prospective owners arising out of the tenant class, white and colored, who put into land their amassed savings of a lifetime, most of which were accumulated between 1915 and 1920. Then came the depression, and in their plight they reluctantly deserted their farms, rather than lose still more money on them. Some families think that exacting and unsympathetic creditors stole their land; many more feel that fate tricked them out of their savings. They have experienced a profound disillusionment and now work and hope for nothing more than "just a livin'."

The foreclosures do not necessarily mean that the former owners have permanently lost possession of their farms, for many still live on them as tenants. With a few good crop years, or with a loan service adapted to their needs and offering slow amortization and low interest, many could repurchase their former acreage. Under present conditions, however, little of it will be regained.

Resident and Absentee Owners.—There are still in Greene County sixty-six Negro owners with forty or more acres who now live at the same places and own the same farms as in 1919. The losses were not uniform over the county. The four militia districts which include the "white land" area had a decrease of 30 per cent, as contrasted with a decrease of 45 per cent in the remaining twelve districts, four of which lost more than 50 per cent. Furthermore, the losses in the white land districts were in direct relation to the percentage of red land in them: the district between Union Point and Siloam, with the least red land, had a loss of 3.6 per cent, whereas the White Plains district, with the most red land, had a loss of 32.7 per cent. This relation of type of soil to landownership, migration, and other factors is discussed fully in another chapter.

TABLE XXIX

Tracts of Twenty or More Acres Owned by Negroes in Greene and Macon Counties, Georgia, 1934[4]

	Greene	Macon
Cultivated by Owners:		
Owners by inheritance..............................	5	20
Owners by purchase...............................	68	58
(Under 20 acres)................................	19	8
Residence of Absentee Owners:		
In Northern States................................	5	2
In Georgia cities..................................	19	2
In rural Georgia..................................	3	1
In home county (quasi-absentee).....................	14	8
Undivided Estates..................................	5	6
Additional tracts owned by persons listed above.............	7	13
Total..	126	110

At present, it will be observed in the table, 73 of the 126 tracts in Greene of over 20 acres and 78 of the 110 in Macon are cultivated by resident owners. Negro absentee ownership is most prevalent in Greene.

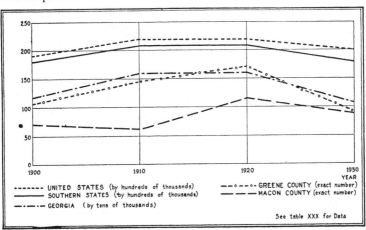

NUMBER OF NEGRO FARM OWNER-OPERATORS, 1900-1930

[4] Data from Tax Digests of Greene and Macon counties and personal interviews.

Greene and Macon Counties Are Representative.—The accompanying table shows that from 1900 through 1935 the rise and fall of Negro owner-operators in Macon and Greene counties followed in general the rise and fall of Negro owner-operators in the United States, in the southern states, and in Georgia. In view of these parallel fluctuations from decade to decade, the two counties seem to be representative of Negro landownership in so far as numbers are concerned. In the loss

TABLE XXX

NUMBER OF NEGRO FARM OWNER-OPERATORS, 1900-1935[5]

	NUMBER OF NEGRO FARM OWNERS				
	1900	1910	1920	1930	1935
United States............	187,797	218,972	218,612	202,270	
Southern States..........	179,418	211,087	212,365	182,019	150,967
Georgia.................	11,375	15,698	16,040	11,081	10,571
Greene County...........	108	147	171	92	115
Macon County...........	72	68	123	86	73
Average for Greene and Macon Counties	90	107	147	89	94

of acreage between 1920 and 1930 the similarity continues: Negro owner-operators in the South lost 19.7 per cent; in Georgia, 33.7 per cent; in Greene and Macon combined 8,263 acres, or 26.8 per cent. The loss in Greene was nearly 40 per cent, in Macon scarcely 7 per cent. During the past five years owners have increased in Greene and decreased in Macon.

The ninety-two owner-operators in Greene were divided as follows: nineteen with less than twenty acres, seventy-eight with more than twenty. Of Macon's eighty-six, eight had less than twenty acres, seventy-eight had over twenty.

A Contrast of Owners by Inheritance and by Purchase.—The five owners by inheritance in Greene who have retained their land have done so in nearly every instance by leaving the county to secure the money with which to pay off accumulated debts, and now live in Atlanta, Chicago, or elsewhere, holding their lands at a loss. The story of the Ellingtons is representative: The Adam Ellington estate of 160 acres, in the northwest part of the

[5] United States Census.

county, was divided among the seven heirs in 1920. By 1925, all except two of the heirs had left the county, and only three had retained ownership of their land. Since that time two more have lost out, leaving but one of the seven an owner. On his acreage, one-seventh of the paternal estate, two of the heirs now live: One is a widow with four children under six years of age; the other is a bachelor farmer-preacher who finished the fifth grade in the local one-teacher school. He now hitch-hikes to Porterdale, fifty miles away, where he conducts a service once a month at a salary of $65.00 a year. These people do some patch farming, and live in small leaky houses which are unpainted and unceiled.

The presence of twenty inheritor owners in Macon County, in contrast with five in Greene, seems to be the result almost solely of the greater economic strain upon Greene County farmers since 1920. As will be seen by referring to the map of Macon County showing the location of owners, practically all the twenty inheritors live in two communities.

The data in Table 31 present quantitative measurements for definite contrasts of the Macon County owners by inheritance and by purchase. Each measurement indicates that the inheritors are living on a lower economic and cultural plane than the purchasers. In addition to supporting themselves on fewer acres and living in relatively inferior houses, they purchase additional acreage less often, hold fewer offices in the local church, school, and lodge, and have fewer life insurance policies. Despite the fact that the inheritors have on an average scarcely one-third the acreage of the other owners, and have equally poor soil and follow equally poor farm practices, they secure their whole income from their own land more often than the purchasers.

Some Notable Exceptions.—Not all owners by inheritance, however, are characterized by the deterioration in evidence here. It is noted in a later chapter that the son of one of Macon's early Negro landowners now owns and operates one of the best country stores in the county.

TABLE XXXI

A CONTRAST OF RESIDENT OWNERS BY INHERITANCE AND PURCHASE
IN MACON COUNTY, 1934[6]

	INHERITORS		PURCHASERS	
	Number	Per Cent	Number	Per Cent
TOTAL HOLDINGS...............	20	100.0	58	100.0
Average acreage.............	51.1	....	155.9	....
Over 100 acres..............	2	10.0	37	63.8
Additional purchases.........	3	15.0	11	18.9
HOUSES:				
Four rooms and more........	6	30.0	36	62.1
Painted outside.............	..	....	10	17.2
Ceiled inside...............	2	10.0	19	32.7
INCOME:				
All from own farm...........	13	65.0	33	56.9
All meat home raised........	3	15.0	12	20.7
HEAD OF FAMILY:				
Local church officer..........	6	30.0	26	44.8
Local school trustee..........	..	....	26	44.8
Local lodge officer...........	3	15.0	14	24.1
Life Insurance...............	2	10.0	7	12.1

There are notable exceptions, too, in counties adjoining
Greene and Macon. Perhaps the best known is the Hubert
family at Springfield, Hancock County, six miles southeast of
White Plains. A large family of sons and daughters attended
high school and college, and assumed places of responsibility in
widely separated communities; in later years they have become
greatly interested in the opportunities which farm life now holds
for Negroes. They have contributed of their time and money,
with evident wisdom, in encouraging ownership and the improvement of farming in the home community. Negroes now
own several thousand acres in the Springfield community and
are gradually acquiring more. The range of crops, the quality
and quantity of livestock, the near absence of crime, the high
type of teachers in the four-room local school and the regular
attendance of the pupils, the construction and use of a community house and the upkeep of farm dwellings—all make this
an attractive Negro landowning community, which has devel-

[6] Data from Macon County Tax Digest and personal interviews with
owners.

GREENE COUNTY—A NEGRO LANDOWNER'S HOME

HE BOUGHT HIS FARM FROM WHITE RELATIVES

THE ROSENWALD SCHOOL AT SPRINGFIELD

THE "LOG CABIN" COMMUNITY CENTER AT SPRINGFIELD; A SHORT SUMMER SCHOOL
IS CONDUCTED HERE, AND MANY OF GREENE COUNTY'S NEGRO TEACHERS ATTEND

SPRINGFIELD NEGRO COMMUNITY IN HANCOCK COUNTY—STORE, CHURCH,
AND HUBERT HOMESTEAD (OFF TO THE LEFT)

oped largely because of the constructive assistance rendered by the heirs of an early Negro owner.

Explanations Are Needed.—The low status of most owners by inheritance in Greene and Macon counties may be due in part to the filtering off to urban communities of the more alert inheritors. This possibility is suggested by the materials in a later chapter, which show that the population movement from Greene County between 1920 and 1930 was highly selective, the best educated and most ambitious persons leaving the county in the greatest numbers.

The inferior dwellings of these inheritors seem to be due in no small degree to the fact that they usually live in houses they built for themselves, while a considerable proportion of the purchasers live in houses built by landowning whites for themselves. Moreover, there is evidence that the owners by inheritance tend to reflect the standards of their landowning fathers' youth more than those of their own day. It is easily explained why the original acreage of the inheritor is small—even 200 acres divided equally among a large family can result only in a small acreage for each.

But what is the explanation of the larger number of additional purchases by owners who have bought their land than by inheritors? It is barely possible that these earliest Negro owners, to keep themselves and their families acceptable to the white community, exercised a supervision so exacting that their children were without opportunity to develop the resourcefulness and self-direction needed to carry on successfully where their patriarchal fathers left off. The children of the landowner would also have less opportunity for that type of contact with landed whites so necessary to the Negro purchaser.

Factors Regulating Negro Landownership

There is considerable evidence that the discipline which the Black Belt Negro tenant gets as a landless farmer affords him the sort of training he needs to maintain himself in landownership in this area. As we shall see in the following pages, Negro landownership—even now—can be achieved only by means of a most exacting and highly selective procedure: the would-be-owner must be acceptable to the white community, have a white sponsor, be content with the purchase of acreage least desired by the whites, and pay for it in a very few years.

The Prospective Owner Must Be Acceptable.—The Negro buys land only when some white man will sell it to *him*. Just because a white man has land for sale does not mean that a Negro, even the one most liked and respected by him, can buy it even if he has the money. Whether a particular Negro can buy a particular tract of land depends upon its location, its economic and emotional value to the white owner and other white people, the Negro's cash and credit resources, and, doubtless most important of all, his personal qualities in the light of the local attitudes: He must be acceptable.

Being acceptable here is no empty phrase. It means that he and his family are industrious and that his credit is good. It means that he is considered safe by local white people—he knows "his place" and stays in it. Though it varies somewhat from one community to another and from one individual to another, the definition of "his place" hedges the Negro landowner about by restrictions similar to those which define and enforce the chronic dependency of the landless Negroes: The Negro landowner is an independent Negro farmer rather than an independent farmer. The economic and cultural advantages which the Negro can secure through the ownership of land are limited by local racial dogmas, which insist alike upon the Negro's submerged status and upon his acceptance of it.

The Negro Landowner's White Man.—Of the resident Negro landowners by purchase who had more than twenty-five acres, nearly nine-tenths reported that they bought their land from white men, and that in three-fourths of these cases the white man had taken the initiative—had approached the prospective buyer, advised him to buy, and offered to assist him. About three-fifths of the Negro buyers were sold their land by former landlords, the white men upon whom they have been most confessedly dependent. In over half the remaining cases the white men who sold them land had sold them groceries and fertilizer when tenants, or had loaned them money to produce a crop.

We cite here typical instances of the Negro's emergence into ownership. Said one of the largest planters in Greene County to a grandson of an ex-slave of his father's: "Seab, I got a corner down there you ought to buy." After persistent encouragement from his landlord, Seab Kimbrought bought it. In another case a Greene County planter wrote into his will that Abe Johnson, a favored Negro tenant, should be allowed to remain on a certain tract of land with the privilege of buying it. Some years later he bought it. In Macon County an elderly white owner without heirs said to his only tenant, a Negro: "Now, Herbert, I have just a good one-horse farm here; I want you to work and be smart and save up some money, for when I die I want you to own it." Not many years later the white man died and was buried in the near-by family cemetery. His grave, and those of his parents, are kept in order by Herbert Griffin who now owns the farm. Another case is Willis Rumph, son of one of the earliest small Negro landowners in Macon County, who grew up with two white boys who later became large peach growers and shippers. When a small boy he learned to graft trees, and in later life was very valuable to the peach growers, who made him an overseer on one of their farms. Over a period of years he had put some money in the bank. Upon the advice of one of his white employers he took it out and gave it, with other savings, to his employer to secure for him a farm, which after a few years was bought and delivered. In five instances, mulatto owners had been sold their farms by white relatives.

The White Man Takes the Initiative.—In interviewing the Negro landowners it was not unusual, particularly in Greene where absentee ownership is prevalent, to find that ownership had been first considered by the Negro when the absent landlord, by letter or otherwise, suggested the idea to him by remarking, "Why not just buy that place?" When asked if he knew the man from whom he bought his land, a Macon County Negro landowner exclaimed, "Why, Lord God Almighty, yes; I raised part of 'im." Young men of landed families, especially when in successful businesses in distant cities, now and then assist into ownership a certain favored Negro family. Such a transaction guarantees to the young man—familiarly called "young master"—a most enthusiastic and cordial reception upon his occasional trip to the old home place. The Negro who comes into ownership in this way, however, not only flatters the vanity of his young master, but also has been the best possible market for the land, which the owner may have needed to sell. Debt-ridden local whites, too, will sometimes sell land to neighborhood Negroes. The local banker, merchant, or money lender also may find the capable Negro renter the best available market for some particular tract which he wishes to sell.

It will be observed in each of these representative cases how the active interest and oversight of some white man protects the Negro purchaser. This, of course, does not mean that no Negro is ever sold land without clear titles, that no Negro is ever forced by local white people to abandon his farm, or that no Negro is ever deprived of his property by untimely foreclosures and scheming traders. Such things do occur, but they are reduced to a minimum by the fact that the prospective Negro owner must be acceptable to the community and that he is so dependent upon some particular white man. There is little weeding out of Negro owners, as they are usually hand-picked before the purchase. In brief, landownership by a Negro in the Black Belt community is not an experiment; it is the culmination of a business transaction based on a personal equation, and thereby destined to be achieved by only a small select group so long as the whites desire to own the land.

Important as a white sponsor is, the Negro does not automatically move into ownership just because he has one. For the white man who would like to help him may own no land, or he may own land but wish to keep all of it, or the land which he would sell may be located in a community where Negro ownership would not be tolerated, or where the particular Negro under consideration would not be acceptable.

Without a White Man's Interest.—A few Negroes, however, by reason of their own suggestions and propositions have come into the ownership of land. The largest owner in Greene County went to a white man and asked the sale price of a large tract of land, and a relatively high figure was mentioned. The Negro surprised the owner, first, by saying: "I'll take it," and again, by paying for it two years ahead of his contract. A smaller Negro owner in the same county, who had just returned from a northern city, approached a white man, asked the price of a small farm, and paid cash for it. From a sheriff's sale in Macon County, a Negro bid and bought without assistance from anyone the farm on which he now lives.

Fourteen of the counties' 126 resident Negro owners by purchase, who had more than twenty acres, secured their land from Negroes: three from a Negro administrator of a Negro estate; five from Negro owners, who, because of indebtedness or inability to continue purchase payments, sold part of or all their acreage to Negro friends; six from established Negro owners who bought land for and sold it to their sons or sons-in-law. But such purchases as these involve only tracts of land where Negroes are convinced that ownership by them will be acceptable.

The Location of Available Acreage.—The land least desired by whites, for whatever reasons, is the land most available for Negro ownership. Except in areas where the white community organization has almost completely broken down, there are scarcely any Negro owners in the vicinity of the white churches and schools, near the railroads, on the leading highways, or on the most fertile soil.

In Greene County, it will be observed from the map, Negro owners are scattered throughout the old large plantation areas. The explanation is that absentee ownership is prevalent here, and white community organization is at a low level. As a result of the boll weevil depression and subsequent hard times, many of these absentee owners have become convinced that landownership is an expensive luxury. With its economic value gone, the old home place sooner or later loses most of its emotional value, and is for sale. The local independent renters are the best available market. Moreover, in their capacity as renters they have exercised considerable self-direction, and some of them have accumulated farm animals and equipment. There are available to Negroes now some tracts of productive land, but they are located in depopulated areas where the church, schools, and roads have been allowed to deteriorate.

In the white land section of Greene County there are no Negro owners. The small white owners in this area, as already noted, have been more successful than any other farmers in the county in holding on to their land during the boll weevil depression and since; consequently there has been no land for sale to Negroes.

The map of Macon County on page 112 makes it clear that the Negro owners are concentrated west of the river in the hilly region around Ideal, where the soil is relatively poor, and in the Garden Valley and Englishville sections, both characterized by the distintegration of white landownership and community organization. Moreover, it will be observed that there are scarcely any Negro owners in the big plantation area around Marshallville and Montezuma.

There is high probability that Negroes will be able to purchase land in this area only as the plantation system crumbles. In short, the Negro has the opportunity to buy what was the most desirable land only when it has become less desirable. It is by no means an accident that the big plantation section of Macon and the small white landowning area of Greene have no Negro owners—Negroes buy land where it is available to them, the tracts least desired by the whites.

Some Concrete Cases.—The involved and tedious procedure by which the Negro becomes a landowner is further illustrated in the following cases.

Case 1. The statement below clipped in 1928 from *Georgia,* a publication of the Georgia Power Company, introduces a

Negro renter who in that year was asked by a Greene County planter if he would like to buy a farm.

GREENE COUNTY COLORED TENANT
FARMER SUCCEEDS WITH
DAIRY COWS

Sam Baugh is a tenant on a farm belonging to Judge James B. Park in Greene County. . . . In 1922 the boll weevil had destroyed his cotton crop and there didn't seem to be any market for any other crop that he could grow. The outlook was dark. . . . Sam, thinking County Agent W. H. West could help him in this went to him for advice. . . .

On May 2, 1923, a sour cream station was opened and Sam was the first man to show up with cream. He had six young cows and after he had saved enough for his family his first check was for $2.00. But he was not discouraged and continued in this and improved in milking and in the care of his milk as time went on. . . . From a beginning of six milkers he now has ten besides five heifers that will come in the spring. After using all that he needs at home he now receives each week $15.00. Sam says that he has never borrowed a dollar from the day that he began to sell cream and besides has paid all of his old debts that were caused by making all cotton.

This Negro renter's opportunity to purchase a farm came when a white planter, who was a friend of his landlord, received, in lieu of a promissory note, a small tract of land in a community where there was no objection to ownership of land by Negroes. The proposition made to the Negro was as follows: "Pay what you can cash and as much as you like each year— you will be charged 10 per cent on the unpaid principal, and I will not sell you out." The Negro decided to continue as a renter, but the case illustrates the type of Negro who is acceptable for ownership, the kind of land available to him, the initiative of the white man who wanted him to buy, and the reasons why he was given this opportunity to own.

Case 2. Because of an accumulated indebtedness, an old plantation in Greene County on the Greensboro-Athens State Highway was advertised for sale. It was divided into twenty-six plots of sixty to ninety acres each. The advertisements, appearing along the highways in no less than a dozen counties, read:

AUCTION SALE!
EACH LOT TO BE SOLD ON THE BLOCK
TO THE HIGHEST BIDDER
NOW IS THE TIME TO BUY A HOME
EASY TERMS
PUBLIC INVITED——FREE BARBECUE
FOR EVERYBODY

Two Negroes wanted to purchase the two lots which lay adjacent to a Negro church and lodge. Six weeks before the sale date they went to the owner and offered him a price nearly double the market value of the land. He sent them to the auction company's officials, who told them that it "can't be done" because of the company's contract with the owner. The Negroes then went to a local white friend and asked him if he would bid in the two lots for them at the auction, whereupon he advised: "Now, I am going to help you get some land, for you fellows ought to have some; but, I don't believe I would try to buy any of those lots—you know there aren't any Negro owners right in there, and besides that land is right on the main road. Now understand, I want to help you—you just keep in touch with me and I will help you locate some land in a neighborhood where you will like it better."

On the day of the auction, the two Negroes were on the ground. Neither of them made a bid and no one bid for them. They heard each of the twenty-six tracts knocked off to the highest bidder—and not one of them brought the price they had offered.

Significantly enough, either the owner or the auction company was qualified under the contract to sell before the sale date such lots as could be disposed of at a fixed price, which price had been doubled by the Negroes in their offer. Clearly, the economic considerations here rest on social factors: It doubtless would have been poor "business" for the owner or the auction company to sell these lots to the Negroes either prior to or at the sale. The lower price which the other tracts would possibly have brought forcibly suggests the attitude of the typical white prospective buyer toward Negro landowners as neighbors. As this case demonstrates, the "safest" policy to follow when racial factors are undefined is that procedure which would be satisfactory to those whites who are most bitter toward the Negro.

Incidentally, the "Free Barbecue for Everybody" was for white people only. To all practical purposes, as this story well demonstrates, the effective definition of "everybody" and "public" does not include the Negro.

Case 3. West of the Flint River in Macon County, two boys, one white and one colored, decided that they wanted to own land. Twenty years later when they were thirty-five, the white man arranged for the purchase of 200 acres from a loan company for $2,500. The white man kept one hundred acres and sold the other to his boyhood friend for $1,400. The Negro considered the trade quite fair, for the white man arranged the trade, secured the deeds, and gave him the better half.

Negroes Buy Where Renters Are Prevalent.—Negro ownership emerges in areas where land is rented, rather than where it is worked by croppers or wage hands. Renters do not cultivate the "proud acres" of the plantations. They are common only where the tracts of land are too small, too unproductive, or too distant to warrant supervision; or where the owners, because of other remunerative business, make little effort to secure maximum revenue from their lands. On the out-of-the-way, or neglected tracts, in the nooks and corners between creeks and between white communities, and in areas where white community organization is disintegrating—these are the places where renters are most prevalent, where they move least often, where they are most independent and self-directed, where they accumulate most cash and credit. These are the tracts which are most often for sale to the Negro.

By militia districts in both counties, the prevalence of Negro owners and the percentage of land owned by them is greatest where renters are most common, and least where croppers and wage hands are most common. To illustrate, in the five Negro school districts in Macon County with the largest number of owners more than one-fourth of all Negro farmers are renters; whereas, in five school districts with no owner, only 1.4 per cent are renters. In Greene practically all the Negro tenants in the white land section are croppers; in the remainder of the county, with Negro owners scattered throughout, practically 50 per cent of the tenants are renters.

There is every reason to believe that in Greene County the ownership of land by Negroes would be increasing rapidly, except for the excessive ravages of the boll weevil. But Negro ownership is circumscribed by the limited ability of the landless farmer to secure enough money to buy the land *when* it is available to him.

He Buys When He Can.—The Negro has the greatest opportunity to buy land when it is most difficult for him, or anyone else in the community, to buy it. The absentee owner, for example, is most anxious to sell his land only after the income from it has ceased—which, of course, is when his renter has been least able to pay rent and consequently is least able to buy.

Bargaining for land is one thing and paying for it is another. The permanent increase of Negro landownership turns upon the farms bargained for in periods when payments can most easily be made; that is, when farm incomes are on the rise. It will be seen from the accompanying table that a larger number of the present Negro owner-operators bargained for their farms between 1910 and 1914 than in any five-year period since, for most of them completed the payments during the period of rising prices. Out of the larger number who bargained for land during the prosperous years, 1915-1920, fewer were able to make payment with the shrunken farm incomes of the subsequent years.

A study of the distribution of Negro owners in Georgia throws additional light upon the factors of place and time as related to Negro landownership. While owners are distributed throughout Georgia as they are throughout Greene and Macon

TABLE XXXII

NUMBER IN 1933 OF NEGRO OWNER-OPERATOR FARMERS BY PURCHASE, IN
GREENE AND MACON COUNTIES, GEORGIA, SHOWING
YEAR OF PURCHASE[7]

YEAR OF PURCHASE	GREENE	MACON	TOTAL
–1879	..	1	1
1880–1889	2	2	4
1890–1899	9	6	15
1900–1909	8	5	14
1910–1914	14	12	26
1915–1919	10	8	18
1920–1924	9	4	13
1925–1930	6	13	19
1930–1934	9	7	16
Total	67	58	126

counties—only five counties having none[8]—they are most numerous in the six coastal counties,[9] in the six counties in the
extreme southwest corner of the state,[10] and in the lower Piedmont area, particularly the fourteen counties lying between
Augusta, Atlanta, Athens, and Dublin.[11]   In these twenty-six
counties, comprising approximately one-sixth of the area of the
state and containing about one-fourth of all Negro farmers, were
located nearly 40 per cent of Georgia's 11,153 Negro owners in
1930.

These three areas were the sites of the largest slave plantations and are the sections now characterized by plantation disintegration.   By 1875, the plantations along the coast were
literally abandoned; by 1900, many of the largest plantations
in the southwest counties were being used as winter homes and
hunting preserves; by 1925, hundreds of plantations in the fourteen counties east and south of Atlanta and Athens were being
forfeited to loan companies and other creditors, and excessive
farm migrations were under way, indicating the low vitality of
the plantation system in this area when the boll weevil arrived.

[7] Greene and Macon County Tax Digests.
[8] Dawson, Forsyth, Pickens, Towns, Union—in the mountains.
[9] Camden, Chatham, Glynn, Liberty, Long, McIntosh.
[10] Brooks, Decatur, Grady, Mitchell, Seminole, Thomas.
[11] Baldwin, Burke, Greene, Hancock, Jasper, Jenkins, Jones, Morgan,
Oglethorpe, Putnam, Screven, Taliaferro, Washington, Wilkes.

There is a Negro-owned farm to every seven persons (which includes women and children) in the Negro farm population of the coastal counties; there is an owner to every twenty-two in the southwest counties, and one to every sixty-six in the counties east of Atlanta. The smallest farms and the poorest owner-dwellings are in the coastal counties; the largest farms and best dwellings are in the counties east of Atlanta. In general, the earlier the breakdown of the plantation system the greater the number of Negro owners, the smaller the farms, the poorer the owner-dwellings. Thus does peasantry emerge when the Black Belt plantation collapses.

The specific data gathered in Greene and Macon counties, and the general information for the state, suggest that Negro ownership is severely limited because its emergence is so largely restricted to areas characterized by economic deterioration, which usually sets in when the original fertility of the soil has been exploited—as in the counties east of Atlanta—or when the chief money crops are lost to other regions—as in the case of the coastal counties.

Older Negroes Preferred.—The very procedure by which the Negro in Greene and Macon counties escapes his landlessness requires a number of years, for in addition to being industrious and acceptable to the white community and having a white sponsor, he must have abundant labor within his family. It takes time to meet such qualifications, and it is not surprising that three-fourths of the owners were over thirty-five years of

TABLE XXXIII

AGES OF RESIDENT NEGRO OWNERS IN GREENE AND MACON
COUNTIES, GEORGIA, AT TIME OF PURCHASE

AGE	GREENE	MACON	TOTAL
Less than 25 years	1	1	2
25–34 years	15	13	28
35–44 years	36	25	61
45–54 years	12	14	26
55–64 years	3	4	7
65 and over	1	1	2
Total	68	58	126

age when they bargained for their land. Except for the few instances mentioned above where the older landowning Negroes arranged the purchase of farms for sons or sons-in-law, scarcely any were under thirty.

How Negroes Pay for Their Farms.—From case studies of the owners in these counties, it is clear that as a whole they paid about the market price for their land. In about one-tenth of the cases, however, the Negro purchaser paid well above the market value. Because of the dependency of the typical purchaser upon some local landed white man, it is not unusual for "understandings" to exist which give the white sponsor gratuitous labor at times when he particularly needs it. Not infrequently, the Negro owner's contributed labor is altogether unsolicited—is a sort of thank offering to the white man who made and keeps ownership possible for him. Many of the white landowning neighbors of Negro owners readily comment upon their willingness to help out in "pinches." These neighborly "lifts" are not always donations; often the white owners reciprocate in kind.

As to the method of payment, out of the 126 purchasers in both counties, approximately 60 per cent paid some cash and gave notes for the rest; about 25 per cent made full cash payments when the sale was made; in the remaining cases notes were given for the entire purchase price.

Over half of those who paid cash had accumulated it while renting farms. Two had worked in the North and saved money; in one instance a father used the money he had received as damages from a railroad for his son's accidental death; another farm was purchased by a widow who received war insurance upon the death of her husband in France. A few others obtained part or all of the money from sources other than farming, such as domestic service and home laundry work by women and sawmilling or other public work by men.

The number of annual notes given varied from two to twelve. Out of the seventy cases with information on this point, the notes in twenty-four ran from one to three years, in twenty-nine from four to six, in fourteen from seven to ten, and in only three cases for more than ten years. These annual payments were usually of the same amount, and fell due in October or November. For the last decade or two, most of these annual notes have been payable in money. Before 1900 many payments were in cotton. To illustrate: A Macon County white landlord in 1888 decided to sell his 800-acre farm and go to Texas. He sold it to one of his Negro tenants, Tom Williams, for fifty-five bales of cotton, payable over a period of twenty years. The purchaser, with several grown boys, "pitched in" and paid for the place in three years.

When the Negro Purchaser Cannot Meet His Payments.— What happens if the Negro cannot make his annual payments? That depends upon several things, especially the creditor's attitude toward him. Some cases were investigated where foreclosures had been made as soon as the law would allow. In one locality in Macon County, the tenants laughed heartily at a Negro purchaser for beginning a new house before the last payment was made and the deeds duly recorded: "Why Will, you fool, what do you mean? Going to give him back his land with a house on it?" In another instance, for the third successive time Negroes had bargained for a farm belonging to an absentee owner. The first two, after paying more than half the price agreed upon, had been forced to let it revert to the absentee owner because they could not make a particular yearly payment on account of boll weevil conditions, droughts, or excessively cheap cotton. The third Negro fooled the absentee owner, so the report goes, by paying for the farm two years ahead of time. In doing so he lost interest on two payments, but this was gladly borne. In general, the Negro purchasers have thrown all other considerations and obligations to the winds, while paying for their farms. Many of them seem to be afraid of all inquiring comers, save only the United States Census Enumerators. These things they have learned through experience.

As a general rule, however, foreclosure was the last resort. There is no evidence that the creditors in Greene and Macon counties have been inclined to "sell out" the Negroes more than the whites. Even the reverse may be true, since the Negro's credit is more than just commercial credit. As a general proposition, an owner loses all his acreage or none. Of the counties' 151 resident owners with over twenty acres, 135 have never sold or lost any land; five lost part of their acreage because of debt; two allowed a portion of their holdings to revert to previous owners; and eleven sold part of their acreage to Negro relatives or friends.

Out of ninety cases of present owners reporting on punctuality of payments, about four-fifths had completed them; more than one-half had finished on schedule time, a little less than one-fourth had finished ahead of time, and the others had had the time extended. In this latter group, about equally divided between the two counties, many of the larger owners appeared. Eight or ten per cent interest was usually charged on these deferred payments.

It is strikingly evident that in all but a few of the cases in both counties, whether the purchases were made in recent years or earlier, the periods of payment have been limited to a relatively few years. Some plan, perhaps arranged through a governmental agency, should be formulated which would distribute the payments over a longer period and arrange for lower interest rates.

Taxes on Negro-Owned Land.—The Negro landowner pays tax at about the same rate as the white owner, as will be seen in the table below. In Macon the Negro average was regularly

TABLE XXXIV

TAX VALUATION PER ACRE BY RACE OF OWNER IN GREENE AND MACON COUNTIES[12]

YEAR	GREENE		MACON	
	White	Negro	White	Negro
1919	$9.88	$9.29	$6.77	$5.26
1921	8.33	8.99	8.26	6.72
1925	5.66	6.84	7.34	6.43
1927	5.70	6.83	7.30	6.54
1934	4.21	5.34	5.43	5.52

[12] Computed from Greene and Macon County Tax Digest.

below that of the white until 1934, when both were considerably less than in 1927. In Greene the Negro rate has been
higher in every instance since 1921; the explanation of this
seems to be the slower adjustment downward of Negro-owned
lands. This retarded adjustment is accounted for in large part
by the Negro's restricted opportunity to be felt politically: he
cannot go into a Black Belt courthouse office and demand a tax-
valuation adjustment from a county official he did not help to
elect—he is equally impotent should he wish to help unseat
some office-holder for lack of proper consideration to him. A
further indication that the Negro's higher tax is due primarily
to the slower adjustment for him than for the white owner is
the fact that the Negro rate in Greene was almost uniformly
lower than the white prior to the beginning of land deflation
in the early twenties: in 1914, the white rate was $6.30, the
Negro $6.11; in 1899, white $3.88, Negro $3.02; in 1894,
white $3.61, Negro $3.40.

The average Negro-owned farm is decidedly smaller than
the average white farm, but each has a dwelling and farm buildings. The lower value of Negro-owned land, due to its inferior
location or quality, is generally offset by the greater per-acre
value of the buildings on it.

The Negro Owner Reflects His White Neighbors.—In both
counties the Negroes' largest tracts and best dwellings are in the
areas where the white farms are largest and the dwellings best;
the smallest Negro farms with the poorest dwellings are located
where the white farms are smallest and the dwellings poorest.

In the plantation area of Greene the resident Negro operators have an average of nearly 120 acres. In 1920, before the
loss of the largest farms in this area, the average was over 160
acres. By contrast, in the four white land militia districts,
characterized by the small white holdings, the Negro owners'
average acreage has remained constant at a little over eighty
acres. In the eastern half of Macon County, where three-
fourths of the acreage owned by the whites is in tracts of over
500 acres, every one of the Negro owner-operators had more

than 100 acres, and the average for the ten was nearly 250 acres. In the western half of the county there are sixty-eight owners, with an average of scarcely ninety-five acres; only three of them have more than the average for the eastern half, and two of these are in the northern plantation district, where over 60 per cent of the land is in tracts of 500 acres or more, as contrasted with scarcely 30 per cent in the remainder of the western half.

TABLE XXXV

SIZE AND CONDITION OF 151 RESIDENT OWNER DWELLINGS
IN GREENE AND MACON COUNTIES

	GREENE		MACON	
	Number	Per Cent	Number	Per Cent
SIZE OF HOUSE:				
1 room....................	..	....	1	1.3
2 rooms...................	2	2.7	6	7.7
3-5 rooms.................	53	72.6	63	80.8
6 and over................	15	20.6	5	6.4
Unknown..................	3	4.1	3	3.8
Total..................	73	100.0	78	100.0
OUTSIDE FINISH:				
Painted...................	21	28.8	10	12.8
Unpainted.................	49	67.1	68	87.2
Unknown..................	3	4.1	..	....
Total..................	73	100.0	78	100.0
INSIDE FINISH:				
Ceiled and plastered.........	35	47.9	21	26.9
Part ceiled.................	32	43.8	27	34.6
Not ceiled.................	4	5.6	30	38.5
Unknown..................	2	2.7	..	....
Total..................	73	100.0	78	100.0

Even after Greene has lost all but one of its eight largest Negro owners, a bigger proportion of the owners live in the plantation areas than in Macon, and the dwellings are generally superior to those of Macon in size, and in outside and inside finish. The dwellings of the ten owners, however, in the eastern half of Macon, where white plantations are larger and more productive than any in Greene, are superior in every way except in size to any ten in Greene.

SOCIAL AND ECONOMIC BENEFITS OF NEGRO
LANDOWNERSHIP

Despite the restricted life of the Negro owner, he stands
head and shoulders above his landless Negro neighbors. He is
known by all the people of the community, whether white or
black. He knows how to get along; he has credit and influential
friends; in three-fourths of the cases he is over fifty years of
age; he lives at the same place year after year, and is a permanent fixture in an otherwise constantly shifting population.

Longer Residence—A Better Citizen—A Mediator.—In
many localities owners are the only Negroes who remain at one
place long enough to become identified with the life of the com-

TABLE XXXVI

LENGTH OF PRESENT HOUSE RESIDENCE OF 140 OWNERS, 240 RENTERS, AND
480 CROPPERS IN GREENE AND MACON COUNTIES

LENGTH OF RESIDENCE	OWNERS (Per Cent)	RENTERS (Per Cent)	CROPPERS (Per Cent)
1 year or less.........................	2.9	32.9	37.7
2 – 3 years...........................	9.3	20.4	29.8
4 – 7 years...........................	9.3	24.2	19.2
8 – 14 years..........................	22.8	11.7	8.9
15 – 30 years.........................	34.3	10.0	4.4
30 years and over.....................	21.4	0.8	.0
Total.............................	100.0	100.0	100.0

munity. A comparison of the length of present house residence
of owners, renters, and croppers in the two counties indicates
the owner's natural position for institutional and community
leadership. Over 55 per cent of the owners show a residence
of more than fifteen years, while nearly 55 per cent of the
renters and over 65 per cent of the croppers have lived in their
present houses less than three years.

The owner's interests are grounded in his community. In
commenting upon the general standing of Negro landowners in
southern communities, T. J. Woofter, Jr., said:

There is no doubt that the backbone of the rural Negro population is the group of successful Negro owners and renters who have
demonstrated their productivity and usefulness to the community.

The Negro race looks to this class for its leaders and supporters of rural institutions.   The low incomes of wage hands and tenants preclude their participation to any marked degree in the financing of institutions and their initiative, undeveloped because of the dependency of their position, is not sufficient to make them successful leaders.

In race relations, also, the existence of this class of farmers, permanently attached to the land, is very beneficial.   The fact that they are taxpayers heightens the respect which members of the white race have for them.   The fact that their occupancy is more permanent allows acquaintanceship to grow and stimulates confidence in their activities.[13]

A Negro with land usually considers himself a kind of father to the community.   He functions as a mediator between the mass of whites and Negroes.   He becomes the spokesman for the local school trustees when they go to the county superintendent for assistance; he intercedes with the court officials for Negro defendants from his community; he explains to the whites any unusual behavior of the local Negroes, and vice versa, always pleading for understanding and good will, for his continued ownership depends upon his remaining acceptable to the whites, and his institutional leadership depends upon his popularity among his own race.

The Owner Provides Institutional Leadership.—Although only one Negro farmer in ten is a landowner in the two counties, more than one-third of the church officers, about one-fourth of the school trustees, and more than two-fifths of the lodge leaders are owners.   Moreover, from the owner group comes a disproportionate number of the key officials—presidents and treasurers of lodges, and chairmen of the various church and school boards and committees.

The owners are in virtual control of all Negro institutions in both counties, except in the big plantation area of Macon and in the "white land section" of Greene where there are no owners. In many communities the few owner families form a kind of oligarchy.   The fact that local church or lodge leadership is satisfactory to headquarters in proportion to its effectiveness in

<hr>

[13] *Negro Migration* (New York, 1920), p. 90.

maintaining a large paid membership puts a premium upon the owner's ability to solicit the participation of the entire community. The motivation for a thriving institution is not solely from without, however, for Negro owners, like men everywhere, wish to be in positions of leadership and to receive popular acclaim. It is no mean honor for a Negro, in a Black Belt county where political participation is prohibited, to become the ranking deacon in the Baptist Church or the president of the Brothers and Sisters of Love.

More Money and More Food.—The Negro owner is as near a live-at-home farmer as one finds in the Black Belt: he has hogs, cows, chickens, and a permanent garden. That he is fundamentally correct in having his farm animals and miscellaneous crops is borne out by statements of bankers and merchants, who agree that he is a good financial risk. It is not unusual for a local banker, fertilizer dealer, or merchant, to say he would as soon take this or that Negro owner's personal note as any man's in the county.

When considering the economic significance of Negro ownership in these two counties, it must be remembered that less than one acre out of twenty is involved, and that this small acreage is made up for the most part of the poorer and more inaccessible tracts. That the Negro home owner is of social significance is largely due to his relative economic independence and his greater opportunity for self-expression and self-direction.

The Prospects for the Future.—Whether Negro ownership will increase in these counties will depend upon the economic and social conditions of the future. The attitude of the white owner toward his own land will determine the availability of land for Negro purchase; the ability of the Negro to buy land will rest upon economic conditions and upon the restrictions placed upon him because of race and tenure. Though the fluctuations in ownership in any single period may be traced to shifting economic conditions, the volume and benefits of ownership over the decades are fixed by social tenets. The Negro cannot become an independent buyer on the land market of the

Black Belt or an independent farmer in the community so long as he must ingratiate himself upon some influential white man and keep himself acceptable to a white community which holds racial dogmas that limit his benefits in ownership.

"But, if the Negro wanted land he could buy it," some say, "it costs no more than to run an old automobile." But the Negro, even as the white man, likes to ride in an automobile, use tobacco, send his children to school, wear shoes and the like —and these things take money, all he has during hard times.

The typical Negro tenant hardly considers the ownership of land possible. Though the owner has a larger income, lives in a bigger house, eats better food, sends his children to school longer and more regularly, and controls his own time, he leaves the landless masses with little hope of achieving a similar status. They seem to realize that Negro landownership in these counties is still limited to those few whose exceptional contacts with some landed white man which lead him to violate the plantation system to the extent of doing for the particular Negro what he would least consider doing for them all.

A Workable Plan is Needed.—The Negro needs additional motivation for ownership: he needs to be convinced that he will be allowed to enjoy in tenancy and ownership the benefits which might accrue to him from the application of initiative and hard work; he needs the opportunity to be a responsible member of his community.

The Federal Land Bank and Land Bank Commission have rendered some assistance. They have been utilized by Negro owners in the two counties, when taken together, in about the proportion of their numbers and acreage. In Greene nineteen Negro owners received $20,000 from the two agencies, nearly one-eighth of the county's total loans; in Macon fifteen owners borrowed $17,100, less than one-thirtieth of the total loans.[14] Temporarily, at least, these loans have helped to stabilize Negro landownership; without them some of the largest owners in

[14] These data were compiled from records in the office of the Clerks of Court in Greene and Macon counties.

both counties would have lost their farms recently. If a comparable service could be offered for the reclamation, at a fair price, of the farms lost between 1923 and 1927, Negro ownership would be greatly increased—particularly in Greene—and some of the disillusionment and fatalism of the landless masses would be relieved.

A workable plan to increase ownership will supply credit for purchase at a low rate of interest and a long period for repayment. Advice and supervision, too, will be needed. Any plan worthy of adoption will make it feasible for the Negro when still a young man to purchase good land. These combined services can doubtless best be provided by some state or federal agency, especially designed to meet the need. Such a plan would render a much needed service to the few local people who now want to become owners, to the larger number who would become interested under a convincing demonstration, and to those who have lands for sale—local people, absentee owners, banks, life insurance companies. An increase of owners would mean greater support of local institutions, larger business enterprises. Neither the Negro nor the white man can be expected to devote himself wholeheartedly to the maintenance and improvement of social and economic conditions until he is made to feel that he is a responsible part of the community.

CHAPTER VIII

FARM TENANTS AND WAGE HANDS

THE LANDLESS agricultural workers, farm tenants and wage hands, constitute the most numerous economic class in the typical Black Belt county. The contrast between tenancy and home ownership, meaningful in any community, is most significant in areas where the products from the soil are the chief source of income.

FARM TENANCY BY RACE

Prevalence of Tenants.—More than half the white farmers and more than nine-tenths of the Negro farmers in Greene and Macon counties in 1930 were tenants. A high proportion of tenancy is a corollary of the plantation.

TABLE XXXVII

PER CENT OF ALL FARMS OPERATED BY TENANTS IN GEORGIA AND IN GREENE AND MACON COUNTIES, 1900-1935[1]

YEAR	GEORGIA		GREENE		MACON	
	White	Negro	White	Negro	White	Negro
1900........	41.8	86.0	53.7	91.5	44.5	89.2
1910........	50.2	87.1	51.2	92.0	41.7	94.1
1920........	51.5	87.6	56.7	91.2	43.3	89.5
1930........	58.5	87.1	54.8	90.1	52.4	91.7
1935.......	56.9	85.5	55.0	88.3	54.3	91.9

In the Black Belt plantation area of the lower South there are not only more landless farmers than elsewhere in these states, but a greater percentage of the landless farmers, white as well as Negro, are croppers and wage hands, at the bottom of the farm tenure ladder.

Increases and Decreases Since 1900.—White tenants in Georgia increased from 63,317 in 1900 to 98,754 in 1930, to 101,649 in 1935. The picture in Macon County was similar, and in Greene until 1920 when a sharp decrease set in, offset in part by

[1] United States Census.

the increase since 1930. The number of Negro tenants in Georgia increased from 71,243 in 1900 to 113,938 in 1920, but had decreased to 75,636 by 1930, and to 62,682 by 1935. Negro

TABLE XXXVIII

NUMBER OF FARM TENANTS AND PER CENT GAIN FROM DECADE TO DECADE IN GEORGIA, AND IN GREENE AND MACON COUNTIES, 1900-1930[2]

YEAR	GEORGIA		GREENE		MACON	
	White	Negro	White	Negro	White	Negro
Number of Tenants						
1900...................	63,317	71,243	433	1,194	280	624
1910...................	84,242	106,738	512	1,684	238	1,123
1920...................	93,016	113,938	589	1,788	304	1,082
1930...................	98,754	75,636	337	849	352	1,022
1935...................	101,649	62,682	428	868	393	832
Per Cent Increase						
1900–1910..............	33.0	49.8	18.2	41.0	—15.0	79.9
1910–1920..............	10.4	6.7	15.0	6.2	27.7	— 3.7
1920–1930..............	6.2	—33.6	—42.8	—52.5	16.0	— 6.4
1930–1935..............	2.9	—17.0	27.0	2.2	11.6	— 18.6

tenancy in Macon and Greene counties also reached its highest point in 1910 and 1920, and since then has declined; the greatest losses occurred in Greene between 1920 and 1930 as a result of the boll weevil and deflation, in Macon since 1930 as a result of the loss of tenure status which accompanied the cotton restriction programs.

Greene and Macon counties present very similar and very different pictures of Negro farm tenancy. In 1920, which was just before the beginning of the migration from Greene, more than three-fourths of the county's 3,000 farmers and Macon's 1,912 farmers were tenants, and approximately three-fourths of these tenants were Negroes. Ten years later the situation was much the same in Macon; but in Greene the total number of farmers had dropped to 1,557, a loss of 250 owners and 1,193 tenants, 941 of whom were Negroes. Even after this tremendous loss, Negro tenant farmers outnumbered white owners and tenants and Negro owners combined. Any discussion of farm conditions in the Black Belt or of the recent migration of

[2] United States Census.

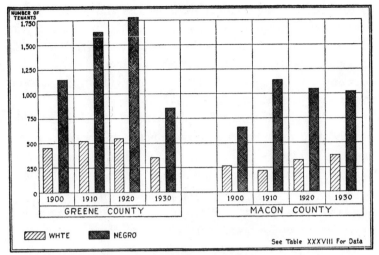

FARM TENANTS BY RACE IN GREENE AND MACON COUNTIES
FROM 1900 TO 1930

Negroes from the rural South to the industrial urban centers involves an interpretation and description of Negro farm tenancy.

The Growth of Negro Tenancy.—Greene and Macon, like other counties of the Georgia Black Belt, "turned black" in the nineteenth century in response to the development of the slave plantation system; the Negro population first exceeded the white about 1825 in Greene and about 1855 in Macon.

Then came the Civil War; slave labor was outlawed. The high price of cotton in 1865 (43.5 cents) and in 1866 (31.6 cents) caused many planters, as suggested in an earlier chapter, to attempt the operation of their plantations by hiring the ex-slaves as wage hands. Some few were partially successful, but by 1870 many of the large plantations already had been sub-divided into small holdings.[3]

There were several reasons for this.[4] The Negroes, wanting

[3] Brooks, *op. cit.*, pp. 19-29.
[4] For a full analysis of "The Evolution of the Cotton System," see R. B. Vance's *Human Factors in Cotton Culture* (Chapel Hill, N. C., 1929), pp. 34-80.

to be free from supervision, were restless and shiftless; they were not acquainted with the meaning of contracts; the price of cotton continued to drop; the local planters were competing among themselves for wage hands,[5] and labor agents from the Mississippi Valley and the Southwest were bidding for laborers in the Georgia Black Belt counties.

Brooks suggests that, "The luxury of having their erstwhile owners compete for their services did not make for the economic efficiency of the Negroes. . . . In the unsettled condition of labor, it became a common thing for Negroes who had contracted to one planter to be enticed away by promises of higher pay elsewhere. It was a matter more of chagrin than of surprise if one's entire plantation force disappeared over-night."[6] A new relation of man to land was the outcome.

Three systems of tenancy developed, share cropping, share renting, fixed or standing renting. As a general proposition, wage hand and cropper farming came to dominate in areas where the land was most productive, while the less productive areas were rented for the third or fourth, or leased for a fixed cash or cotton rent.

Forms of Tenancy

The three fundamental forms of tenure—the cash (or standing produce) renter, the cropper, and the share renter—were well defined by Boerger and Goldenweiser[7] as follows:

Method of Renting

Share Cropping (Cropping)	Share Renting	Cash Renting (Fixed Renting)

[5] John Townsend Trowbridge, *The South* (Hartford, Conn., 1866), p. 465, cites the case of a Macon County planter who, in 1865, was fined $150 for enticing farm hands.

[6] Brooks, *op. cit.*, pp. 30, 31.

[7] *A Study of the Tenant System of Farming in the Yazoo-Mississippi Delta* (U. S. D. A. Bulletin No. 337, 1916).

LANDLORD FURNISHES

Land	Land	Land
House	House	House
Fuel	Fuel	Fuel
Tools	One-fourth or one-third of fertilizers	
Work stock		
Feed for stock		
Seed		
One-half of fertilizers		

TENANT FURNISHES

Labor	Labor	Labor
One-half of fertilizers	Work stock	Work stock
	Feed for stock	Feed for stock
	Tools	Tools
	Seeds	Seeds
	Three-fourths or two-thirds of fertilizers	Fertilizers

LANDLORD RECEIVES

One-half of crop	One-fourth or one-third of crop	Fixed amount in cash or cotton

TENANT RECEIVES

One-half of crop	Three-fourths or two-thirds of crop	Entire crop less fixed amount

TABLE XXXIX

PERCENTAGE DISTRIBUTION OF FORMS OF TENANCY BY RACE IN GREENE AND MACON COUNTIES, GEORGIA, 1930[8]

FORM OF TENANCY	GREENE		MACON	
	White	Negro	White	Negro
Total Tenants.................	100.0	100.0	100.0	100.0
Cash Tenants.................	35.1	12.8	13.4	2.9
Croppers....................	32.1	54.0	60.5	79.0
Other Tenants*..............	32.8	33.2	26.1	18.1

*Largely share renters.

Upon first glance, it will be observed that Macon has more croppers than Greene, that more Negroes than whites are in the

[8] United States Census.

cropper class in each county. Cash renters are most common in Greene and more prevalent among whites than Negroes.

Significant Rôle of the Fixed-Rent Tenant.—As stated in the chapter on Negro landownership, it was through cash renting and its equivalent, produce renting, that a considerable number of the new owners, white and Negro, came into possession of their farms. Fixed renting naturally emerges on the acreage of absentee owners and of resident owners who care little about their land.

The rôle of the cash or standing renter distantly approximates that of the owner, and for the same reasons: he lives at one place longer than any other type of tenant; he owns more property; and he is more nearly the master of his own time.

In 1930, there were 216 cash renters in Greene and only eighty-one in Macon. Cash renters reflect the distintegration of plantation farming. This is illustrated by their greater number in the old plantation section of Greene and by their recent emergence in the Marshallville community on the lands which have fallen into the control of loan companies.

Croppers Most Prevalent in Macon.—In 1930, as for decades before, croppers were much more prevalent in Macon than in Greene. In fact, a larger proportion of the white tenants in Macon were croppers than of the Negro tenants in Greene. The figures appear in the table above. Croppers are most common in Macon because farming, generally more remunerative there, is more closely supervised.

The presence of landless Negroes in the Black Belt does not improve the condition of the average white man in relation to the soil. The percentage of white tenancy is almost as high in the Black Belt as in other parts of the state, and the proportion of white tenants who are in the lowest tenure class—croppers—is higher in the Black Belt than elsewhere. Since the plantation system forces white tenants and Negro tenants into competition, there is but little possibility of either group rising unless both rise.

Croppers, the most dependent of all tenants, are little more than wage hands. The Georgia statutes, into which have been crystallized the economic facts of cropper farming, recognize croppers as share hands or wage earners rather than as tenants.[9] As has been seen already, the croppers, with the exception only of wage hands and day laborers, have a lower plane of living than any other element of the rural population. Cropper farming, requiring close supervision, demands obedience and servility and gives small reward to individual initiative and self-expression.

Negro croppers are often preferred to white croppers for two reasons: first, they are more easily supervised; second, since they do not advance into ownership as readily as the white tenants, they provide a higher type of labor. Several large planters mentioned the necessity for having all white croppers or no white croppers. Supervision is often difficult when Negro and white croppers are located on the same plantation, for while the white cropper objects to being treated on a parity with the Negro cropper the landlord cannot satisfactorily supervise him in any other way. The outcome is that most large planters in each county either use only Negro tenants, or work the Negroes as croppers and the white tenants as share or fixed renters, which further demonstrates that the form of tenancy is an index of social as well as economic conditions.

Share Renters in Greene.—The share-renting system of farming, where the tenant owns his work animals and pays one-fourth or one-third of his crop for rent, is historically a white institution, while cropper farming is a Negro institution. Share renting developed in the mountain and Piedmont counties prior to the Civil War, and is still most prevalent in the Piedmont counties with the fewest Negroes. Cropper farming sprang up in the Black Belt with the breakdown of the hired labor plantation régime which occurred within a decade or two after the Civil War. Macon County, in the lower part of the Black Belt, has but few Negro renters, while Greene, in the upper Black Belt, has many.

[9] 46 Georgia Reports, pp. 584-85, and 61 Georgia Reports, pp. 488-89.

The share renters are not so self-sufficient as the fixed-rent tenants nor so dependent as the croppers. They become owners less often than the fixed-renters and more often than the croppers. In general, the share renter occupies a middle position between the wage hand and the owner; the wage hand takes no risk and gets none of the surplus; the cropper takes some risk and gets half; the share renter takes more risk and gets two-thirds or three-fourths; the cash tenant takes yet more risk and gets all above the rent price; and the owner assumes the entire risk and gets the whole benefit accruing from price and weather, and from any application of personal insight, resourcefulness, or industry.

Approximation of Forms of Tenancy by Race.—Though the whites regularly have larger proportionate placements in the higher tenure groups, there is a tendency for tenure types of the two races to parallel each other in the same area. White croppers appear most often where Negro croppers are most common, and Negro share renters are most in evidence in the same localities where white renters are prevalent. Further emphasizing the similarity of tenancy by race is the fact that the greatest decrease of white and Negro tenants between 1920 and 1925 occurred in the same areas—in the same districts of Greene County, in the same counties of Georgia.

The greatest decrease of each race was in the upper part of the Black Belt. Of the eleven counties losing more than 30 per cent of their white farm tenants between 1920 and 1925, nine were in this area. The excessive decrease of Negro tenants in the upper Black Belt is strikingly set forth in Table XL.

Later chapters, devoted to population movements, show why the people migrated in such great numbers from Greene and other counties characterized by cash and share renting. Most population movements, and particularly the forced movements of rural people, usually reflect pathological man-land relations.

Wanted—a New Type of Tenancy.—A Macon County planter who is interested in his plantation as a source of regular income reports that he wants to try out a new type of tenancy:

WHITE AND NEGRO FARM TENANTS—WHERE THERE
IS LITTLE HOPE THERE IS LITTLE ENDEAVOR

GREENE COUNTY—PLANTATION HOUSES IN DECAY

TABLE XL

NEGRO TENANT FARMERS IN THE SOUTHERN STATES, SOUTH ATLANTIC
STATES, GEORGIA, AND GREENE AND MACON COUNTIES, 1920-1925[10]

	NUMBER OF NEGRO TENANTS		PER CENT INCREASE*
	1920	1925	1920 to 1925
Southern States..................................	703,555	636,248	— 9.6
South Atlantic..................................	280,212	228,472	—18.5
Georgia..	113,938	72,206	—36.7
45 Georgia counties with more than 1,000 Negro tenants in 1920......................................	70,691	43,386	—38.6
23 in Upper Black Belt............................	35,408	18,726	—47.1
22 in Lower Black Belt............................	35,283	24,660	—30.1
114 Georgia counties with less than 1,000 Negro tenants in 1920......................................	43,247	28,820	—33.3
Macon County**................................	1,082	1,022	— 3.5
Greene County..................................	1,788	930	—48.0

*Minus sign (—) indicates decrease.
**A small part of Macon's territory was incorporated into Peach County, when it was formed January 1, 1925.

that he will take graduates of Negro agricultural colleges, set them up as croppers and let them move into the status of renters just as soon as they can; that he will be glad for them to keep their own accounts, mix the fertilizer for their crops, plant certified seed, have pure-bred stock, and as many tractors, riding cultivators, and other modern equipment as they can use profitably. The planter proposes, further, to let a family live at one place as long as it likes, and not to raise the rent as the farm improves. The planter's imperatives are three: the rent must be paid, the planting of kudzu vines is prohibited, no land will be sold. The tenant, on the other hand, is to do just as he likes, plant what he pleases, sell where he chooses—he is to be his own boss. "Now," said the planter, "if you know any graduates of Negro agricultural schools who want to farm on this basis, we'll begin next year."

It took only casual inquiring at Negro agricultural schools to be convinced that any Negro with the qualifications to make a success of this type of tenancy is the type of man who would

[10] United States Census.

be satisfied only with ownership. Said the head of a Negro school, "If the planter will let his best renters buy the places they live on, I can get him any number of our graduates."

And so the case rests—a planter wants to be rid of the tedium of the petty and meticulous oversight of dependent tenants, and the most capable Negroes want an opportunity to direct their own farms. But the planter will not sell his acreage because the ownership of land has been the evidence of aristocracy in his community for generations—to part with his plantation would be to desecrate the memory of his father and his grandfathers. The Negro agricultural graduate remains uninterested in types of farm tenancy which do not lead toward ownership because the dependence of landless agricultural workers is a constant reminder of slave times—to accept the tenant's lot would be to flout the efforts of his parents and his grandparents to escape servitude.

Wage Hands and Casual Laborers

Until the last two years, the distintegration of southern plantation farming has been accompanied by the transformation of wage hands into tenants.

Fluctuations in Number of Wage Hands.—Farm wage hands, hired by the day or month, are more common in Macon than in Greene. In both counties, the number varies from decade to decade, even from year to year, in response to the demands of the plantation. Prior to the advent of the boll weevil many of the resident planters in Greene used a limited number of wage hands to cultivate their most productive fields. By 1928, with the exception of a few small dairies and one large farm, there was practically no demand for them in Greene County. The number of wage hands in Macon has been determined largely by the peach industry. With two or three years of successful peach growing and marketing the demand for these laborers increases; when the peach crop is noticeably short or the market is poor, the demand decreases. As a general proposition in each county, the number of wage hands has increased when the large landowners have been most prosperous and has decreased when they have been less prosperous.

The most dependent rural dwellers, almost always on the largest and most closely supervised plantations, have little choice but to occupy the tenure status the planters want them to. One year they will be wage hands—"Mr. George is doin' wages." Another year they will be croppers—"Mr. George is halvin' 'em."

Since 1933, in response to the AAA and other federal emergency activities, wage hands have been on the increase.

It is estimated that there are now between forty-five and seventy wage hands in Greene and between 400 and 500 in Macon, most of whom are Negroes. In addition, there is the greater number of Negro and white tenants and small owners who do work for wages now and then throughout the year, the income from which was shown in an earlier chapter.

A few large planters employ a squad of wage hands; most of the peach, melon, and asparagus shippers have at least a few regular hands, while the bulk of their labor is secured from their own tenants, most of whom are Negro croppers. Outside the peach belt in Macon and in Greene, the landlords have some work for which they pay wages—fixing fences, chopping wood, draining the swamps, terracing the fields.

Croppers as a Labor Reserve for Landlords.—There is a tacit agreement that the tenant will work for the landlord at a certain price at any time he needs him. When the tenant is not working at his own crops and the landlord does not desire to hire him, he is at liberty to hire himself by the day to some near-by planter or sawmill operator, the landlord always reserving the right to request the tenant to take care of his own crop.

The tenants in Macon County are hired by their own land-lords more often than in Greene, for absentee owners seldom hire any wage hands, and landlords who share-rent their acreage need but few. The peach and asparagus crops in Macon usually afford employment for croppers when they are least busy with

their own crops. But even if there is some conflict in the mind
of the cropper who wants to work his own cotton rather than
spray the peach trees of his landlord, there is no conflict in the
mind of the landlord. It is the general consensus of opinion
among Negro croppers, however, that landlords seldom keep
them from their crops when they should be working in them.

The activities of the croppers on the big plantations in eastern Macon County are directed throughout the year—as day
laborers—in winter they work in the orchards, in spring they
work in the asparagus fields, in summer they pick peaches, in
late fall they gather pecans. In the meantime, as croppers, they
have planted and cultivated a crop of cotton and corn. During
the entire time, whether employed as day laborers or croppers,
they work under the direct supervision of the landlord or his
hired overseer. To all practical purposes they are wage hands.

Casual Day Laborers on Increase.—By the term casual day
laborers reference is made to those who depend for a livelihood
upon finding work from day to day, or week to week, or month
to month throughout the year. With croppers now tending
toward wage hand status, former wage hands tend to be pushed
into the casual labor group. Employment in the city is a weekly
or daily proposition; in the rural Black Belt, except for the
casual laborers, it is a yearly proposition, for even the wage
hand, though paid only for the days the landlord wants him,
must be available at all times and it is on this condition that he is
furnished a farm cabin in which to live.

Casual laborers are recruited from rural families not wanted
as tenants or wage hands and from the families of the smallest
landowners, most of whom live, as shown already, in the vicinity
of the small towns. With the exception of the relatively few
who own only a house and lot in the open country, there are
scarcely any families whose labor supply is not directly or im-
plicitly contracted for during the entire year. The farm owner
must pay taxes and feed his family and stock; he must apply
his labor to his own farm or else be penalized by his ownership.
The fixed-renter is dependent upon the application of his labor

to the tract of land he rents. The only time a cropper's family has labor for the open market is when there is but little demand for it.

The Negroes and whites living in the country who own but a house and lot can apply their labor where they choose only because they own their living quarters and do not own any land. The share renters provide a second source of casual day laborers; for while the head of the house and the women work at the crop, the sons of the family not infrequently work by the day or week wherever they can find employment. With the decline of sawmilling in Greene and the increase of wage hands in Macon, the demand for casual laborers is small; most families dependent on casual labor find it difficult to house themselves in the open country. Landowners provide houses only for those whose labor they wish to use. With only abandoned houses available, the casual laborer ends up by drifting into town and in recent years by getting on relief.

The Plantation's Busy Season.—It is a tradition in Black Belt counties that all Negro workers, including the casual laborers about the towns, be subject to the call of the cotton fields at chopping time and at picking time. Sometimes they voluntarily go out to help relatives who live on owned or rented farms, while at other times there is an element of coercion in it, as when federal relief is discontinued in order to assure plenty of cotton pickers, or when police on Saturday night release the participants of a "crap game" on promise that everyone of them will find work in the cotton fields on Monday morning. Field hands, women and men, are hauled in trucks to the fields of some local planter who offers them thirty, forty, fifty, or sixty cents a day.

These busy seasons sometimes take on the semblance of a festal occasion. Everybody is at work, usually in a group, doing the same thing. There is at times much loud talking, some unison singing of the spirituals, and incidentally some very exceptional individual accomplishments, for while the majority of laborers tend to work along together, there are always certain individuals who insist upon demonstrating their claim of being the "fastest chopper" or the "biggest picker" in the whole crowd. In some instances planters attempt to speed up the whole gang of laborers by encouraging a few key workers to set a faster pace. But woe to the pacesetters if their fellows learn why they are so industrious, for despite the occasional loud talk and unison singing of the gang laborers, they do not find their task easy or their day short. Moreover, they seem to feel that there is something of slavery in gang labor.

In addition to the cotton-chopping and cotton-picking seasons in both counties, many urban dwellers in Macon County go to the peach orchards in late June and July to help pick and pack the peaches. While in some instances only Negroes are employed, on most peach plantations both whites and Negroes are used; the division of labor by color is in conformity with a general pattern—the Negroes work in the orchards under the summer sun, the white people work at the packing house in the shade.

These evidences of racial differentials, to be seen at almost every turn in the Black Belt counties, seem to find fullest expression in landlord-tenant relations, their antecedents reaching back into slave times and their consequences circumscribing the movement of present day landless agricultural workers, white as well as Negro.

CHAPTER IX

LANDLORD-TENANT RELATIONS

THE RELATION of landlord and tenant is the human phase of man-land relations. It retains in Greene and Macon counties something of the quality of the master-slave régime.

The increase of white tenants in recent decades has done little to modify the traditional patterns which grew up along the color line in the years following the Civil War. The white and Negro tenants, competing within the system for farms, are now the common heirs to its impositions. Their resulting dependence helps to maintain the régime that continues to rob them of self-direction.

THE BASIC ASSUMPTIONS

In general, both races and all tenure classes accept things as they are. The basic assumptions of the planter—the tenant needs to be looked after like a child, he is improvident, and he works only when in need of food—find a complement in the tenant's somber sequel: "What's the use? I don't get nothin' but a livin' nohow."

The "Childlike" Tenant.—"Why, my tenants would starve to death if I didn't keep an eye on them," said a Macon County planter recently. He had to tell them what to plant, when to plant it, and how to cultivate and harvest it; he had to take care, he said further, that the backbands did not make sores on the mules' backs and that the trace chains did not rub the hide off their legs; he could risk the tenants to care for nothing, they were so dependent and childlike. They looked to him and would call upon him day or night—a bottle of medicine for the baby's colic, or bail for the rambling son in the Americus jail, or a coffin for "old grandma."

Such an estimate of tenants is quite common, particularly on the big plantations of Macon County. With few exceptions, the planters in all parts of both counties assume that the tenants, whether white or Negro, are naturally lazy and shiftless and would be unable to make a living if farms were given to them.

The Tenant's Improvidence.—The typical tenant, asserts the typical landlord, will take no interest in a garden, nor assume any responsibility for his own house; unless he is told specifically to do it, he will not fix a leak over his head, mend the hearth at his feet, nail on a board, repair the garden fence, or build a pig pen; the tenant simply does not see that he would benefit by a good garden instead of a poor one, or that it is to his advantage to have a cow even if he does have to keep it on a chain.

One planter complained that the tenants will not stay put—always moving around—and that it is next to impossible to get them to coöperate even in the production of foodstuffs which they later secure from the plantation commissary, at one-third to one-half below the local market price. "Why," said he, "they wouldn't drive a cow out of my turnip patch from which they are cutting greens that I'm giving to them."

Many landlords justify a rather close oversight of any money surplus the tenant family may have at settlement time on the grounds that if not supervised the tenant will spend his money foolishly. "Yes," said one planter, "you've almost got to force them to save—I'm bodily holding $100 for one of my tenants now. He has a wife and seven children, and rents a two-mule farm; he wants to operate a three-mule farm next year, and I'm holding his money and told him I'd give it to him to buy another mule. Oh, if he came and asked me for it I'd give it to him; but, he'll not do that for he knows I want him to buy a third mule—if I didn't hold the money, he'd not do it; why, I'm continually protecting them from their own foolish use of their meager resources."

Hunger—Best Guarantee of Regular Labor.—The typical wage hand or tenant, asserts the typical landlord, will work when he has to—when he is hungry or about to get hungry; his improvidence is so thorough that a little money in hand causes him to work irregularly or not at all. His wife, too, it is said, will help him get off to work if there is little or no food in the house, not so if there are provisions on hand for more than a few days; the pinch of hunger, as nothing else, will get the shiftless, child-like tenant into the fields and keep him there.

"The man working for food not only works regularly," explains the planter, "he works gladly; he takes orders cheerfully, is seldom sullen—all in all, he's the most satisfactory farm laborer."

The Tenant's Somber Sequel.—These assumptions have a sequel in the typical tenant's assumption that the world has "nothin' but a livin'" in it for him. To prove it, he recites his experiences: one year his half of the crop barely settled his debts for fertilizer and for furnishings, a whole year's work for a bare existence; another year he had a cash surplus, with which he bought two mules; for three years he paid a cash rent; then came a dry year, or cheap cotton, or the weevil and it took all of his cotton to pay the rent, his mules to pay the fertilizer bill, and his cow to satisfy the merchant's account. "Well, Lizzie," he confided to his wife, "we'd just as well 'a' bought that Ford, for we ain't got nothin' as it is."

Some tenants have even bargained for land, and now and then one has held on to it. Most tenants, already convinced that they get "nothin' but a livin'" anyway, put whatever money they have into automobiles, or phonographs, or a short period of "high living," or more sensibly into family necessities—food, clothing, schoolbooks.

CONCRETE CASES

The landlord can demonstrate why he says tenants are child-like and improvident: they make foolish purchases, they get credit on a credit, they contract all the debts they can, they take everything they can get and give as little as possible in return.

The tenant, too, points to concrete situations: the landlords and merchants have the books and most of the crops go to settle accounts for fertilizer and food and clothing.

Credit on a Credit.—The average tenant not only lives on the advances which are provided for him and his family by the landlord, but he lives on the promise of those advances. It works this way: A tenant who is to get a credit allowance the first day of March goes to the storekeeper on the tenth or twelfth of February and asks for some provisions. If the storekeeper refuses him he goes to another store and gets what he wants. Competition between stores bidding for tenant trade forces them to comply with the wishes of the tenant. The result is that they usually owe most or all of their allowance when they get it.

Another common transaction: A tenant went into a store in Siloam and tried to get a knife on credit. He failed. He then tried at each of the other stores in this small town. Being unsuccessful, he returned to the first store and asked if he could get "that thar ole razor" on a credit. The storekeeper, glad to see it go for the promise of seventy-five cents, handed it to him. He went to the next store and pawned it for twenty-five cents—promising to pay fifty cents for it at the end of the week —and bought the knife. How much did the tenant pay for the twenty-five cent knife?

One Saturday a storekeeper sold two dozen dollar watches on credit. By closing time that night, six of these watches were in the hands of the merchant next door. The tenants had come into his store and secured loans of fifty cents on the watches, promising to redeem them at the end of the week for seventy-five cents, which is an interest rate of over 2,500 per cent per annum. Five of the watches were redeemed, and the sixth was sold for fifty cents to break even. The merchant stated that he disliked to traffic in this kind of business, but that he had to do it or the tenants would get mad and trade somewhere else: "They refuse to spend their money with any one who will not help them when they get in a 'tight,' and they are in a 'tight' most of the time."

Some landowners, particularly the smaller ones, and also some of the better established tenants, condemn severely the short-sighted ways in which the majority of the landless workers run through all they get. A Greene County Negro landowner, after telling how his nephew bought five-dollar silk shirts in 1920, and now, though working regularly and hard, is scarcely able to make a living, added with astute certainty: "I'll des tell you—if a man's haid ain't quite right it puts a terrible strain on his body."

Foolish Expenditures.—The landlord points out that the tenant not only misuses the advance which he secures, but he literally throws away most of whatever money he gets at settlement after his rent and debts have been paid. The following case is not unique: A white tenant, with wife and three young children, had $75 cash in hand upon settlement, $65 of which he used to make an initial payment on a second-hand automobile priced to him at $116. At the end of the first week the car was in need of repairs. Three years later the car—with no tires, top broken, and most of the upholstering gone—still stood back of the cabin, and was the prized toy of the children of the Negro tenant family which had moved in when the white family moved to another plantation three miles away. The dealer left the car there because he had already gotten more out of it than it was worth, and besides the needed repairs would cost more than the car could be resold for.

This white tenant's foolish expenditure was made in spite of his landlord's effort to get him to use his money on his family. The tenant listened to the landlord politely enough, but he wanted an automobile, and it was his own money and he would spend it as he liked. Numerous cases more or less like these can be recited by any large planter. A suit of furniture, a piano, a cooking range, a victrola, an automobile will absorb the greater part of any cash surplus the typical landless family receives. Most noticeable of all, once in a very long while a Negro with cold cash in the bottom of his pockets will journey to Augusta, or Atlanta, or Albany and return with a gold tooth or two in the front of his mouth.

The More Creditors the Better.—Strange as it may seem at first, many tenants like to be in debt to some man other than their landlord. Accustomed to being furnished and to getting only that part of the crop which is left after rent and advances are taken out by the landlord, the tenant's ability to get additional credit is proof positive that the merchant or banker has faith in his personal integrity, for the lender knows he can collect only after the rent and advance claims are settled. Further than the stamp of personal worth which a loan implies, there is the fact that the tenant who is in debt to two or more influential people has secured for himself some protection against exorbitant claims. The tenant family which is furnished by the landlord likes to have an independent account at the local store, for the merchant's interest in the tenant's crop may regulate the demands of the landlord.

The accepted definition of color precludes the Negro's right to question the landlord's account, but the merchant can and does look into the matter if the tenant does not have enough left to settle the store account. In cases where the landlord agrees to give the merchant first claim on the crops to furnish tenants, the landlord investigates if there is not enough left for the rent. A Negro woman who wants to keep the laundry work of a certain white family often manages to stay in debt to the "white folks" so that "the wash" will not be sent to some other Negro woman. The landlord's answer to all this is that the tenants merely want to get all they can, and for their purposes, the more creditors the better.

Getting All They Can.—The planter states positively that the tenants never have the welfare of the planter in mind, never decide that their wage is too high or that they have received more than their share of the crop; many of them even have to be watched during cotton picking and corn gathering to prevent serious "seepage." The credit merchant insists that to protect himself he must ride out several times during the summer and make certain that there are crops with which to settle the store accounts. The absentee landlord, too, says he needs to know something about the crops on his land, otherwise he stands a high risk of learning in the fall that there was nothing left when the food, feed, and fertilizer bills had been paid.

Wage hands, too, according to the man who employs them, get what they can. All along during the year they get things from the garden—collards, turnips, roasting ears, beans—and from the kitchen—buttermilk and leftover food. Yet, whenever they sweep the yard, clean the barn, or pick up a bucket of pecans they expect pay for it. Even on hog-killing days, when the women get the chitterlings for larding them and the men carry home enough feet and heads and other "odds and ends" to last the whole family a week, the men never suggest that their pay be left off.

"Moreover," says the planter, "they call upon you without any claim on you: Lizzie, a wage hand, picked cotton for us a week or two a few years ago, yet the other day she came to me for $10 to get her boy, Sam, out of jail for cutting a Negro woman. I told her I'd see what I could do. She came by the next day and said it would take $15. It didn't sound right, so I inquired around and found she had already secured $5 from another white man—obviously she had decided not to use it when she found me sympathetic. She got nothing out of me! Why bother with her troubles when she's not doing what she can?"

Another case was this: A tenant with a good crop, deciding that he would rather pay a rent of one bale than divide his cotton in half, maintained that he was a standing renter rather than a cropper. The landlord was greatly surprised at the suggestion, for the tenant owned no workstock and his half of the crop for two years had been scarcely a half-bale each year. Upon reflection the planter saw how to resolve the tangle: "All right, if you are a standing renter pay me the rest of the rent for last year and the year before; if you're a cropper pay me half of this year's crop." The tenant decided he was a cropper—"Ah, but you've got to watch 'em; they get all they can at every turn."

THE SANCTIONS

The assumptions of the landlord that tenants and wage hands are childlike and improvident became established when

these tenure groups were still made up almost solely of Negroes; and consequently the fundamental bases of present as of
past landlord-tenant relations in Greene and Macon counties
root back into the race relations of slavery. The whole plantation structure rests upon social, political, and theological sanctions, each of which upon analysis proves to be little more than
a rationalization.

". . . *A Servant of Servants Shall He Be*. . . ."—The
economics of the Black Belt rests upon customs and practices
which maintain the plantation system with its few landlords
and numerous landless workers. These customs and practices
are in need of justification; to the typical white man of the Black
Belt the Bible provides it. The vast majority of the white
people, whether landed aristocrats or tenants, believe that the
Negro was made to serve the white man. A Biblical sanction
for this they find in the latter part of the ninth chapter of
Genesis:

20. And Noah began to be an husbandman, and he planted a
vineyard;

21. And he drank of the wine, and was drunken; and he was
uncovered within his tent.

22. And Ham, the father of Canaan, saw the nakedness of his
father, and told his two brethren without.

23. And Shem and Japheth took a garment, and laid it upon
both their shoulders, and went backward, and covered the nakedness
of their father; and their faces were backward, and they saw not
their father's nakedness.

24. And Noah awoke from his wine, and knew what his
younger son had done unto him.

25. And he said, Cursed be Canaan; a servant of servants shall
he be unto his brethren.

26. And he said, Blessed be the Lord God of Shem; and
Canaan shall be his servant.

27. God shall enlarge Japheth, and he shall dwell in the tents
of Shem; and Canaan shall be his servant.

This story, which makes no mention of anybody's being
turned black, is well-nigh universally used in the Black Belt
as Biblical proof that the Negro was created to serve the white

man. It is pathetic to hear a person unaccustomed to reading the Bible or anything else elaborate upon the meaning of this passage and then not be able to find it. And then when he realizes that it says, "And he (Noah) said, Cursed be Canaan"; instead of, "And God in his wrath cursed Ham and turned his skin black," he falls back upon his well-established impression of the meaning of the passage and disposes of the matter by saying that Noah was God's prophet and that the curse was black skin and that he doesn't want to talk with anybody who does not believe in the Bible. The real rôle of the Bible in this connection was clearly revealed by the young white man who, when asked what the Bible said about the Negro, replied emphatically: "Well, I don't know exactly what it says but I know what it means."[1]

The majority of the white people, assuming that the Negro is actually and potentially less than a normal human being, quite naturally feel that he commands and deserves a different treatment from the white man. Said a Greene County school man, "The Negro should have justice as a human being, but in the light of the kind of a human being he is." With this kind of special creation theory to support the hang-overs of the slave régime there is but little wonder that the Negro's political status is what it is, that the Negro schools of Greene and Macon counties receive such a small proportion of the public school funds, and that the Negro tenant is supposed to accept without question the statement of his landlord at settlement time.

Election Must "Go Right."—The second sanction is the political one—white supremacy must be maintained, and consequently elections must "go right" every time. It is the expressed belief of nearly all the white people in these counties that the Negroes should not be allowed to vote, especially in local elections, and that if necessary force should be used to

---

[1] The Bible is a positive control in some cases: A Greene County white farmer was convinced that a certain Negro had set fire to his barn. The white man got his gun and waited behind a bush by the side of the road. Before the Negro's wagon reached the bush, however, the white man—according to his own report—had decided that spending eternity in hell was too big a price to pay for the privilege of killing a "nigger."

keep them from the polls. The outcome is obvious, practically no Negroes vote in county and state elections and but very few in the national elections.

From 1865 until the present day some extraordinary things have happened. It is not unusual to hear the leading older white men tell how they stood guard at the courthouse to see that the count was not "disturbed," or how the white men from one county would go and vote in another, or how all the white boys over eighteen were advised to vote, or how the poll holders would change the Negroes' ballots and so on. The most unusual incident was when one of the largest ex-slave owners of Macon County, soon after the end of the War, ate scores of Negro votes—the little town of Marshallville was faced with the necessity of making the election "go right" when there were 375 Negroes and only 118 whites qualified to vote. A local planter told how he "stole" a tax receipt to keep a Negro from voting: The planter demanded that the Negro present his tax receipts, and he did. The planter then took out the receipt for 1882 and handed back the others. When the Negro could not produce the receipt for 1882 he could not qualify to vote— and within a few years no Republican votes were cast in local elections at Marshallville.

Negro Votes for Sale.—Montezuma is reported to have failed to secure enough votes to move the courthouse from Oglethorpe because of three things: first, the older communities of Marshallville and Oglethorpe and Englishville united to keep the courthouse at Oglethorpe; second, the Montezumian who was corralling the imported Negro voters from Americus (Sumter County) got satisfied too soon and did not vote them enough times;[2] third, contrary to instructions, the train halted at Oglethorpe on its return trip long enough for the Negroes to vote there. And Oglethorpe is still the county seat.

Even the white men who have been instrumental in providing better schools for the Negroes at both Montezuma and

[2] The county historian terms this election ". . . a blot in the 'scutcheon of Macon County." Hays, *op. cit.*, pp. 366-68.

Greensboro express the opinion that it is best not to let the Negroes vote. They point out that the mass of Negroes, having no training in the use of the ballot, would, were they allowed to vote, place political control in the hands of the vote-buying element of the white people, the element in the community least qualified to administer the affairs of the county and to train the Negroes in citizenship. They further state that it would be practically impossible to let only a small proportion of the Negroes vote, for, once they begin to register, every white man in the county will bring in his following to offset some other, and then when some sorry white man begins to round up the votes the decent people will get disgusted and leave the election to the buyers and sellers.

White Votes, Too, for Sale.—The purchasable vote in these counties has not been confined to Negroes. It is enough to relate one incident: A white man went to a storekeeper at Siloam and told him that several people down about Veazey would vote "right" if he would speak to them. Explaining why he did not follow the suggestion he said, "Yes, they'll vote 'right' next Wednesday, but next Saturday they'll be up here wanting me to credit them. After voting the way I want them to they'll feel they have a right to ask just anything of me. I've decided not to bother with them." The bald fact is, a certain type of white man feels that he should be given something to vote "right."

National politics in these counties is usually taken very seriously, for the local whites have inherited a fear of "nigger-lovin'" administrations in Washington. This fear is capitalized in many ways by politicians and others. State politics is of relatively minor import, except when some local man is in the race for a state office, or when the Negro question is dragged in, as in the Talmadge-Pittman gubernatorial campaign in the fall of 1934. Judge Pittman was accused of being a party to a penitentiary sentence for an alleged Negro rapist; but the Judge, not to be outdone, assured an audience before the courthouse at Greensboro on the afternoon of August 31, 1934, that he had

helped secure a prison sentence instead of the death penalty only
because he was convinced of the Negro's innocence: "I shall
have the blood of no innocent man on my hand; he was not
guilty of rape, if he had been the case need not have come into
my court." The Superior Court Judge's open suggestion of
lynch law elicited from his audience the most enthusiastic ap-
plause of the afternoon.[3]

County politics affords an opportunity for personal and community rivalries, and although county offices do not pay fabulous
salaries, since 1920, especially in Greene, they have been looked
upon with favor by many of the best citizens as sources of ready
cash with which to support land.

In one respect Negroes have been of other than negative
political import in these counties: Local Republican patronage,
though always going to the whites, has been somewhat subject
to the local Republican Committeeman, a Negro. One Macon
County man put it this way: "It is a long jump from 'my slave'
to 'my fellow-citizen'."

The Negro Who Votes.—It is estimated that over a hundred
Negroes in Macon County had qualified to participate in the
presidential election in the fall of 1932, but less than half that
many voted. Although the Democratic primary virtually ex-
cludes the Negro from participation in local politics, some few
have been voting the Democratic ticket in the national election
and occasionally in the local election. A recent sheriff of Macon
County stated that on the eve of his election a group of Negro
voters came to him and said they wanted to vote for him. He
thanked them for their interest, and advised them that the best
way they could help him was to stay away from the polls—
their participation might be used against him.

For the most part the Negroes who vote are home owners.
They might be expected to vote, for as was shown in an earlier
chapter, most of them have already proved themselves accept-

[3] For further information about Judge Pittman's attitude toward lynching,
see Raper, *The Tragedy of Lynching* (Chapel Hill, N. C., 1933), Chapter
XV, especially pp. 304-12.

able to the white people. At a Republican mass meeting held in the Macon County courthouse to which whites and Negroes were invited, a very astute property-owning Negro rose to answer the accusation that the federal government was doing nothing to help the rural Negro. He deftly pointed out the Smith-Lever and Smith-Hughes appropriations along with other things, ending with the argument that the great need of the rural Negroes of Macon and surrounding counties was more potatoes and peanuts and corn and chickens and cows, rather than algebra, rhetoric, philosophy, and Latin. "We need," said he in closing, "more food and better houses, not more books and bigger books. You know, I like substance better than sound: I like a whole lots better a fellow who says 'dem taters' and has some, than a fellow who says 'those potatoes' and has none." His remarks were enjoyed almost beyond measure by the local white people, most of whom went there to see what "niggers" and white Republicans could talk about. The speaker is the kind of Negro who votes most often in the rural Black Belt.

Little Patches of the "Solid South."—Greene and Macon counties are two units of the "Solid South." They always vote Democratic by an overwhelming majority. In 1928, when 56.6 per cent of Georgia's ballots were for candidate Al Smith, he drew 71.9 per cent of Greene's votes and 76.1 per cent of Macon's. The real backbone of the "Solid South" is Protestant rather than Catholic and votes dry rather than wet, but above all it is Democratic. White fathers tell their children that the best Republican is not so good as the worst Democrat, and angry schoolboys sometimes call each other Republicans.[4]

Greene and Macon counties exhibit the disfranchisement which characterizes the "Solid South," for not only do scarcely any Negroes vote, but less than half of the whites. In 1932, the largest poll on record, the total presidential vote in Greene was a number equal to but 35.0 per cent of the whites of voting

[4] *Ibid.*, p. 150: "Hicks District is proud of the distinction of having been the only voting precinct in Georgia where not a single Republican vote was cast in the heated [presidential] election of 1928."

age; in Macon 49.8 per cent. Less exciting elections draw hardly half this many. Thus it is evident that the political sanctions of the plantation system rest upon the race situation as do also the theological sanctions, and that politics and theology, creations of the landed oligarchy, penalize the white tenant along with the Negro.

Providentially Inferior.—The social sanction of landlord-tenant relations, that the Negro is providentially and irredeemably inferior, springs logically from the theological and political sanctions discussed above.

Hand in hand with the white man's determination to keep the Negro from voting is the assertion that he cannot get or use an education. The planter, of course, is not altogether mistaken when he affirms that education has ruined many a "good nigger." It has, for it makes him less servile and better able to keep up with his accounts. Furthermore, if one assumes with a Greene County school official that the Negro can have no place in American life except that of a non-landowning farmer, or casual laborer in the city, or preacher or teacher for his own providentially incapable race, one might logically agree with him that the Negro's education should be limited to the elementary forms of the three R's.

The majority of the white people in these counties believe that the Negro is irredeemably inferior, naturally unappreciative of his own needs, and improvident of everything he gets, and they believe that the white people of the Black Belt are of a particularly high type. At almost any country store one can hear the white people speaking of the disproportionately large number of America's leading statesmen who came out of the old South and expressing their belief that the section would still maintain virtual control of American politics but for the degrading influences of outsiders, particularly following the Civil War, upon the South.

Such are the rationalizations and defense mechanisms which the controllers of the plantation system have fabricated into a philosophy which justifies and maintains the politically sterile

"Solid South" and its outmoded agricultural structure based upon the human relations of a distintegrating feudalism.

THE PRICE IS PAID

The assumptions and sanctions of the plantation system have their price, and Greene and Macon counties have paid with one-crop farming, excessive erosion and depleted soil, low incomes for shifting landless workers, frequent bankruptcies for landowners, emigration, and, most devastating of all, human relations built upon the idea that the vast majority of the population—the landless, whether white or Negro—are incapable of self-direction.

The Black Harvest.—The improvidence and dependence of plantation workers rest primarily upon the demands of the plantation: They must be amenable to instructions, must live in the houses provided, must accept the merchant's and landlord's accounting, must remain landless. The very life of the plantation system is threatened when tenants accumulate property, exhibit independence. A large tract of land—whether centrally owned or not—which is cultivated by propertied, self-directed farmers is not a plantation; it is a community of farms.

The plantation system, while raising the level of workers to a certain point, insists that they shall not go beyond it. To illustrate, the slaveowner taught his labor to plow, to hoe, to pick cotton, to fix wagon wheels, to build houses, to slaughter animals, to make corn bread, and cook turnip greens; and the sooner these tasks were mastered the better. But the development was cut short when it reached the point of greatest usefulness to the plantation. The system lifted its workers to the level of good plantation labor and then attempted to hold them there; the plantation was a civilizing force as long as it was teaching its workers; since then it has been a millstone about the neck of the civilization which it cradled.

The typical wage hand or tenant is the victim of an enforced arrested development, is the product of the plantation, is the fruit of the tree. Said Johnson, Embree, and Alexander recently: "The mobility of the tenant, his dependence, his lack of ambition, shiftlessness, his ignorance and poverty, the lethargy of his pellagra ridden body, provide a ready excuse for keeping him under a stern paternalistic control. There is not a single trait alleged which, where true, does not owe its source and continuance to the imposed status itself."[5]

No Easy Escape.—The tenant has little opportunity of escaping his status. For the plantation owner, though selling a small tract now and then, as long as possible holds his acreage—the very foundation of his relatively privileged position. Nor can the tenant always leave the plantation at will, despite his theoretical right, for state legislation designed to protect the landlord's interest has virtually made it impossible for tenant families to move except in the fall after the crops are harvested.

Added to this yearly detention, justified by those who control the plantation on the basis of the tenants' dependence and improvidence, is the practice some planters have of making their tenants responsible in subsequent crops for any deficit in rent or in settlement for furnishings. This practice is rendered effective by a kind of gentleman's agreement among the planters that they will accept a wage hand or tenant from another plantation only when the change meets with the approval of his landlord, in which case the new landlord assumes his indebtedness to the old, applying it against the tenant's future crops. Naturally enough a tenant far in arrears is not wanted by another landlord, and a planter can readily keep his tenants in arrears. Thus robbed of his normal right to move, the propertyless farm worker can escape his lot only by fleeing the community, which involves considerable risk. Threats of flogging, murder, and lynching follow and sometimes overtake the "debtor" who "slips off like a thief." If he gets safely out of reach, the violence originally meant for him may descend upon his relatives and friends, for little mercy is shown those who dare challenge the plantation controls.

No Surplus for Tenant or Landlord.—Plantation labor being

[5] *The Collapse of Cotton Tenancy* (Chapel Hill, N. C., 1935), pp. 21-22.

confined within its landless and changeless bounds, there ensues a sort of grim game in which the landlord and tenant get all they can out of each other, the tenant carrying home all the provisions he can and the landlord furnishing him as little as possible. The tenant, frequently receiving little or no cash settlement in the fall, often proceeds upon the assumption that he had better get all he can as he goes along, for irrespective of how much he gets he loses no money, as he puts no money in. The planter, on the other hand, puts up all the money and is saddled with the responsibility of seeing that the tenant's bills do not get too great and that he has a crop with which to settle accounts and pay rent.

The landlord may become very autocratic and dictatorial, but never wholly beyond the reach of his dependent tenants, many of whom, particularly the Negroes, have become past masters at getting things. They know when to approach him, where to approach him, how to approach him. The tenant, in keeping with his station, makes each year take care of itself— seldom applying the savings of one year to the crop of the next. The cash outlay of the landlord, therefore, is great each year, and his interest centers in the money crop. The outcome is inevitable; no substantial surpluses in foods or feeds or money accumulate for either landlord or tenant. The fat years consume themselves and the lean years go hungry.

That plantation farming is a precarious business no planter in Greene or Macon counties would deny. Few of them, however, seem to see any connection between man-land relations and human relations. The high costs of the plantation system are paid in response to its imperatives—that its workers remain dependent, servile, and landless.

Some Innovations

The established relation between landlord and tenant has made a puny dictator of the one and a fatalistic plodder of the other. Before there can be any significant change, the tenant must have reason for feeling that he can improve his lot by the application of industry and intelligence; the planter must realize that he has more to gain by ending the present parasitic tenant system than by maintaining it, for the plantation first impoverishes its workers and then disinherits its owners. Any institution or practice which modifies present landlord-tenant relations might mean a readjustment of man to land, might mean an improvement in social and economic conditions.

Brief comment is made upon four innovations: the automobile, the cash advance to tenants, the holdings of loan companies, and the New Deal.

Automobiles Give Tenants a Sense of Power and Importance.—The tenant's automobile may have been bought with money which might better have gone into food, or clothing, or education, or doctors' bills. Be that as it may, an understanding of the landless farmer's plight leaves one little surprised at his purchase. He needs food, clothing, education, medical service; he wants release, immediate release from his meager, drear, changeless life, and for him the automobile provides it. The feel of power, even in an old automobile, is most satisfying to a man who owns nothing, directs nothing, and while producing a crop literally begs food from his landlord.

The tenant's automobile, however, has other effects. First of all, it teaches him about machines. Many of the cars have poor light connections, engines requiring constant attention, brakes which need adjustment, and tires that are punctured readily. The tenant and his boys do most of the repairs. They are becoming "machinery wise," and can the better operate tractor-driven farm equipment.

In his car the tenant has a right to half of the road whether he is meeting another tenant, a traveling salesman, or his own landlord. Only in automobiles on public roads do landlords and tenants and white people and Negroes of the Black Belt meet on a basis of equality.

Scarcely ever before have rich and poor, educated and ignorant, self-styled superiors and acknowledged inferiors, landlords and landless, white folks and black, ridden in the same type of vehicle; and never before have they ridden so fast that they could not see who was approaching. When master and slave met along the road, whether in ancient Rome, or in Greene and Macon counties, each acted in keeping with his station. Prior to the coming of the automobile, when landlord met tenant or when white man met black man, each knew his relation to the other and acted accordingly. But today when the landlord, speeding down the road at forty miles an hour, sees an old automobile coming he does not know whether he is meeting his tenant or the richest planter in the county who takes pride in his ability to go as fast in an old car as his neighbor in a new one. And even if he could see just whom he was meeting, the nature of his vehicle would force him to steer on his side of the road or run the risk of killing himself.

Within limits determined by ability to buy gas, the tenant can go where he pleases on the public road, and after he gets twenty or thirty minutes from home he travels incognito and is subject to his own wishes. Whether to the city to find work, to the church, to the moonshine still, to the brothel, or to any one of a hundred other places, he goes and comes and nobody knows where he has been. It is a thesis too pretentious for development here, but the opportunities afforded by the automobile provide a basis for a new morality for whites as well as Negroes, based upon personal standards rather than upon community mores—upon what the individual wants to do rather than what the community does not want him to do. This type of morality is more fundamentally democratic than anything the world has known. The automobile in these counties, as elsewhere, is significant because it is providing the mechanical means for a greater degree of self-direction and self-expression.

An additional reason why the automobile is so popular with Negroes, even among those who have achieved relative economic independence, is that it affords them an escape from the irritations of the unequal transportational facilities provided by train and bus and plane. The Negro driving his own automobile is not so constantly reminded of the meaning of his color.

The tenant who drives an automobile in the Black Belt is being introduced to one estate where he has equal rights with all who come and go. Will this make the tenant jealous for rights in other fields? The possibility that it may has not been wholly overlooked—a white man in Macon County advocated that the cars be taken from the Negroes or that the county maintain two systems of roads, one for the whites and one for the Negroes!

Cash Advances and Landlord-Tenant Relations.—The method by which a dependent family secures its provisions while producing a crop, referred to as a "run," reflects landlord-tenant relations. Families in the more dependent tenure classes, croppers and share renters, receive rations or a weekly credit allowance, called a "limit," at a near-by store. The more independent renters, though frequently furnished by "rations" or "limit," may receive a monthly check or cash advance, the spending of which is determined by the tenant. This latter practice is less prevalent now than a few years ago.

In 1928, in both Greene and Macon counties nearly half the tenant families were furnished by cash or check. About 1910, with the impact of modern business methods upon the rural Black Belt, a few planters without commissaries began the practice of furnishing their tenants by monthly cash advances, rather than by a credit slip to some store. With the cessation of immigration from Europe and the industrial expansion of the World War period, a shortage of workers prevailed in the North and East; agents went through the South recruiting labor; many planters found they could better retain their tenants by furnishing the monthly allowance in cash.

The automobile further contributed to the popularity of the cash advance; first, the tenant needed money to buy gas, second, the more stores he saw, particularly "bargain sales," the less satisfied he was with the commissary. Then, too, the development of the chain store method of distributing groceries and other merchandise crippled the wholesale merchant system which had supplied the commissary with its small stock of goods.

By 1928 there were but few commissaries in Greene and Macon counties. They were passing because they were becoming less satisfactory to the tenants at the same time that they were becoming more expensive to the landlords.

What changes were taking place in the landlord's and in the tenant's thinking when cash instead of rations was provided? In the landlord's, at the outset, perhaps nothing more than that he was practicing a new method of furnishing his tenants because it was cheaper; in the tenant's, at the outset, perhaps nothing more than that he was going to have a little ready cash for gas and bargain sales. But as the practice continued to be followed, the dependent family began to acquire training in personal and family responsibility and in discriminating buying. The family seemed to take on a sense of self-direction: When furnished through a commissary, the head of the house and other members went several times a week to get this or that, each time acknowledging their dependence and usually stressing it in order to get what was wanted. When a cash allowance was given the tenant, he reported to the landlord at the first of the month to get what was his by agreement. With this money he went forth to buy where he thought he was getting the best values for his money, and where he was treated with most consideration. Merchants were quick to realize this, for they knew that when a tenant walked into the store with cash he would not buy unless he wanted to. The one who came for rations might be ignored or put off for an hour or two—he had to stay until he got his order. A tenant with cash in his pockets had a different attitude toward the merchant from one who got rations each week or month—the latter essentially a beggar, the former a buyer.

The monthly cash allowance also made it possible for the tenant to question the landlord's statement at settlement time, for the tenant or his child could probably multiply fifteen dollars —the amount of the monthly check—by five, the number of months the advance was made. It was not so easy to dispute a commissary account, with its hundreds of charges for fatback and fertilizer, plow points, and chewing tobacco. When the landlord knew that the tenant could estimate his status as a debtor, when the merchant knew that the tenant would trade somewhere else unless he received courteous treatment, and when the tenant knew that he was personally responsible to his landlord and to his own family and could buy where he pleased —with all this understood, an innovation which seemed revolutionary was emerging in 1928 when cash allowances were given to tenants in Greene and Macon counties.

But conditions changed. Commissaries and store credit came in vogue again. To escape immediate and complete disintegration, since 1930 the controllers of the prevailing plantation system have had to reduce cash expenses to the minimum. Three things have happened: the landlord is growing more foodstuffs, distributing them to his tenants through his commissary; the cost of the advance per family has been reduced; the number of families furnished has declined. So the rise and fall of the monthly cash advances, with whatever meaning it may have had, has been little more than an incident in the changing requirements of the plantation system, which above everything else seeks continued life against its impending dissolution.

Loan Company Holdings and Landlord-Tenant Relations.— A third factor modifying landlord-tenant relations in Greene and Macon counties is the increase of land owned by loan companies, approximately 17,000 acres in Greene, acquired since 1920, and 20,000 acres in Macon, acquired since 1928. The distribution of this acreage by location and ownership is shown in a later chapter; here we are concerned solely with its effect upon landlord-tenant relations.

The acreage which falls into the control of loan companies is good land and in large tracts, and much of it is being cultivated. The loan companies seldom provide rations or production credit for their tenants, and the rent on the loan company land is usually lower than that on adjoining acreage—with the result that it attracts the most independent renters. When there are not enough local self-sufficient renters to utilize this land, as has been the case in recent years around Marshallville in eastern Macon County, the agents of the loan companies import renters from other areas. Thus scores of white tenant families from North Georgia and Alabama have been brought into that area of the county where the tenants have been most closely supervised, most dependent, and most wholly of the Negro group. Were whites imported because there were no local Negroes who wanted these farms, or because the local Negroes who wanted them could not get the credit to cultivate them, or because the agents—local whites—did not want to compete with the local planters for the best Negro labor?

It should be borne in mind, however, that the present situation may be quite transitory. The loan companies may sell their acreage at a loss, or, with an increase of land price, they may sell at a profit, or they may go into the farming business, which most likely would mean a new kind of plantation, thoroughly centralized and mechanized, with places in it for a few mechanics, scientists, and managers and a great horde of semi-skilled but dependent and propertyless workers. Everything else being equal, more and more of the best land of the cotton plantation belt will fall into the hands of loan companies. These tracts are virtually inviting some public agency to purchase them and develop owner-cultivator farming. With large acreages of good land being forfeited to loan companies and sold for taxes, and thousands of capable farmers slipping down the tenure ladder, can the South, and the nation, do other than conserve its natural resources and strengthen its people through devising constructive procedures for assisting landless families into farm ownership? This question brings us to the New Deal and its significance in terms of man-land relations and their human aspect, landlord-tenant relations.

The New Deal and the Plantation.—Is the New Deal going to make farm tenants more dependent or more independent? Will it result in a wider ownership of land, or a further concentration of it? Will it aid in the transformation of the old plantation or will it merely extend its life past the time of its natural and otherwise inevitable death?

Before the effects of the New Deal in Greene and Macon counties are discussed, the population movements will be reviewed in order that one may better understand why the New Deal's meaning in these counties turns so largely upon whether it helps point a new way or temporarily energizes the old.

PART FOUR

Population Movements

CHAPTER X

POPULATION AND PLANTATION

THE POPULATION movements in Greene and Macon counties typify respectively the older and the newer sections of the Georgia Black Belt.

POPULATION RESPONSIVE TO PLANTATION

In 1920 more people were living in Greene and Macon counties than ever before. According to census reports, the total population of Greene had increased from 10,761 in 1800 to 18,970 in 1920, a gain of 76.3 per cent in one hundred and twenty years. The population in Macon increased from 5,045 in 1840 to 15,427 in 1920, a gain of 205.5 per cent in eighty years. This greater gain in Macon suggests its later settlement and more rapid development.

Population Movements Incident to Plantation Development.—The growth of the two races decade by decade throws into relief the population movements incident to the development of the cotton plantation system of the South. The Negro population in Greene rose from 3,664 in 1800 to 11,974 in 1880, a gain of 277.0 per cent; during this same period the white population decreased from 7,097 to 5,573, a loss of 21.5 per cent. From 1880 to 1920 the Negro population decreased 6.4 per cent, while the white population gained 39.4 per cent. The proportion of white people in the total population decreased from 66.0 per cent in 1800 to 31.7 per cent in 1880; between 1890 and 1920 the white element rose from 31.3 per cent to 41.0 per cent. With the development of the plantation system the number of Negroes increased, and the number of white decreased; but, with the subsequent partial disintegration of the plantation régime in Greene County since 1880, the number of Negroes has decreased slightly while the number of whites has increased. R. P. Brooks, G. G. Smith, and others have commented upon the emigration of small farm owners and landless whites from Greene and adjoining counties between 1800 and 1860 as farm land became concentrated into the control of fewer and fewer owners who depended more and more upon slave labor.

As is shown in the following table, the numerical relation of the two races in Macon from 1840 to 1920 is strikingly similar to that which obtained in Greene from 1800 to 1880. Macon County was formed about fifty years later than Greene, and

TABLE XLI

WHITE AND NEGRO POPULATION IN GREENE AND MACON* COUNTIES, GEORGIA, THROUGH 1930[1]

YEAR	GREENE			MACON*		
	White		Negro	Total	White		Negro	Total
1800	7,097	66.0%	3,664	10,761	.....	....	.....	.....
1810	6,398	54.8	5,281	11,679	.....	....	.....	.....
1820	6,599	48.6	6,990	13,589	.....	....	.....	.....
1830	5,026	40.1	7,523	12,549	.....	....	.....	.....
1840	4,641	39.7	7,049	11,690	3,553	70.4%	1,492	5,045
1850	4,744	36.3	8,324	13,068	4,088	58.0	2,964	7,052
1860	4,229	33.4	8,423	12,652	3,575	42.3	4,874	8,449
1870	4,298	34.5	8,156	12,454	3,975	34.7	7,483	11,458
1880	5,573	31.7	11,974	17,547	4,288	36.7	7,387	11,675
1890	5,332	31.3	11,719	17,051	4,001	30.3	9,181	13,182
1900	5,325	32.2	11,217	16,542	4,302	30.5	9,791	14,093
1910	6,875	37.2	11,636	18,511	4,434	29.3	10,581	15,015
1920	7,771	41.0	11,200	18,971	**5,639	31.9	**12,028	**17,667
1930	5,988	47.1	6,628	12,616	5,451	32.8	11,192	16,643

*Macon County was formed in 1837.
**This includes the area annexed from Houston County between 1910 and 1920.

there are many indications that the development of the plantation system in Macon had reached a point by 1920 not unlike that reached by Greene forty years earlier. The fact that the white population remained more constant in Macon than in Greene doubtless resulted from the larger area in Macon of unproductive land, the lower edge of the sand hills in the northwestern section, which could not be profitably cultivated by plantation owners.

[1] United States Census.

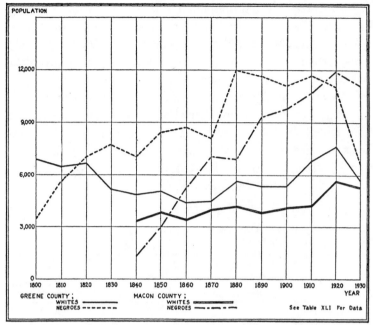

POPULATION BY RACE IN GREENE AND MACON COUNTIES, GEORGIA

The Georgia Black Belt Whitens.—It will be observed that the percentage of white people was greater in 1920 than in 1910 in both counties. This was true in thirty-four of the seventy Black Belt counties in Georgia. A still greater change, however, occurred between 1920 and 1930, when the proportion of white people increased in all but nine of the Black Belt counties. The greatest change took place in the upper and older half of the Black Belt. Most of the counties became whiter because the Negroes migrated in greater numbers than the whites, some because the number of whites remained constant or increased slightly while the Negroes decreased, and some few because the whites gained more rapidly than the Negroes. The whitening process in the Black Belt was at its height between 1920 and 1925.

Plantation Disintegration Brings Increase of Whites.— Some causes of the bleaching of the Black Belt may be learned by examining the fluctuations of the civil divisions within

Greene County during the period 1900-1920, before the migration of the twenties. In the five militia districts in the plantation area the total population increased from 4,478 to 4,685. This net gain was the result of a decrease of 386 Negroes and an increase of 595 white people. In the three districts where small owners predominate the total population decreased 144, for while 332 fewer Negroes lived in the area the white population gained by 188. The white population increased in both areas, but faster in the plantation area, because the disintegration of the plantations afforded additional opportunities for self-sufficient renters and small home owners.

TABLE XLII

WHITE AND NEGRO POPULATION BY PLANTATION AND SMALL OWNER
AREAS IN GREENE AND MACON COUNTIES, GEORGIA[2]

	YEAR	GREENE		MACON	
		Plantation Area: Five Red Land Militia Districts*	Small Owner Area: Three Gray Land Militia Districts**	Plantation Area: East of River	Small Owner Area: West of River
White......	1900	1,100	1,357	1,459	2,843
	1910	1,454	1,629	1,648	2,786
	1920	1,695	1,545	2,764††	2,843
Negro	1900	3,378	2,762	5,472	4,319
	1910	3,218	2,292	5,820	4,762
	1920	2,990	2,430	7,514‡	4,514
Total....	1900	4,478	4,119	6,931	7,162
	1910	4,672	3,921	7,468	7,548
	1920	4,685	3,975	10,278†	7,357

*Militia districts 145, 146, 147, 148, 149.
**Militia districts 141, 142, 144.
†2,239 of this number from territory annexed between 1910 and 1920, leaving 8,039.
†† 292 of this number from territory annexed between 1910 and 1920, leaving 2,470.
‡1,945 of this number from territory annexed between 1910 and 1920, leaving 5,569.

In Macon, from 1900 to 1920, the total population increased in both the plantation and the small owner areas. It will be noticed, however, that while the Negro population increased but slightly in both areas and the white population in the small owner area remained constant, the white population in the plantation area increased from 1,459 in 1900 to 2,470 in 1920.

[2] Compiled from a special tabulation of white and colored population in Greene and Macon counties, Georgia, by militia districts for 1920, 1910, and 1900, which the writer obtained from the United States Census Department.

Within both counties, then, the partially disintegrating plantations were attracting white farmers before 1920.

White Families from the Hill Country—In Table XLIII is
shown the birthplace and length of residence in Greene and
Macon counties of the oldest child in the white and Negro
schools from 319 rural white families in Greene and 256 in
Macon, and from 434 rural Negro families in Greene and 459
in Macon. Of the 319 oldest children from white families in
Greene, fifty-six were from the Piedmont and mountain counties
of Georgia and four from other states. More than half the
ninety children born outside of Greene had come from the hill
country of Georgia, and sixty-nine of them had been in Greene

TABLE XLIII

BIRTHPLACE OF OLDEST CHILD IN SCHOOL FROM 319 RURAL WHITE AND
434 RURAL NEGRO FAMILIES IN GREENE COUNTY, AND FROM 256 RURAL
WHITE AND 459 RURAL NEGRO FAMILIES IN MACON COUNTY, GEORGIA

CHILDREN BORN IN:	WHITE		NEGRO	
	Greene	Macon	Greene	Macon
Present county......................	215	165	369	382
Adjoining Counties..................	29	13	47	55
Elsewhere in Black Belt..............	11	25	8	12
Wiregrass—Coastal Counties..........	4	8	..	7
Piedmont—Mountain Counties (Ga.)..	56	18	7	2
Piedmont—Mountain Counties (Ala.)..	..	21	..	..
Other States........................	4	6	3	1
Total.........................	319	256	434	459
RESIDENCE IN PRESENT COUNTY:				
1 – 2 years.........................	19	21	16	28
3 – 5 years.........................	20	19	22	28
6 – 9 years.........................	32	30	19	9
9 years and over....................	33	21	8	12
All life............................	215	165	369	382
Total.........................	319	256	434	459

less than nine years, indicating that the movement of white
families to Greene did not stop with the depression caused by
the boll weevil and land deflation in the early twenties. The
cheaper land resulting from the depression has made Greene
County relatively more attractive to the hill people of Georgia,
many of whose progenitors had been pushed out of this same
area by the development of the plantation.

In Macon County, of 256 oldest children from rural white families 45 were born in the Piedmont and mountain counties of Georgia and in other states, 21 of them in Alabama, mostly in the hill country east of Birmingham, especially Clay County. The Atlanta, Birmingham and Coast Railroad which crosses Clay County, Alabama, first reaches the Upper Coastal Plain at the Macon County line.

Just as the principal increase of rural white families in Greene was from the hill counties of Georgia, in Macon it was from the hill counties of Alabama and Georgia. This would be

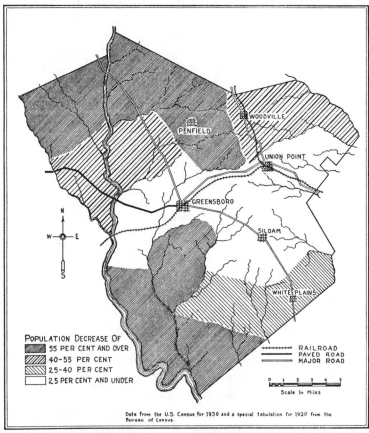

MIGRATION OF WHITE POPULATION FROM GREENE COUNTY
BETWEEN 1920 AND 1930 BY MILITIA DISTRICTS

expected, for the Piedmont Region of Alabama is nearer Macon County than is the upper Piedmont Region of Georgia. The disintegration of the plantation system in the Black Belt and the rapid erosion of land in the hill country seem to be the fundamental factors back of the recent movement of white families from north Georgia and Alabama into Greene and Macon and other Black Belt counties.

The rural Negro children in school were practically all from the local county or adjoining counties, only twenty out of the 893 having been born outside the Georgia Black Belt. Thus

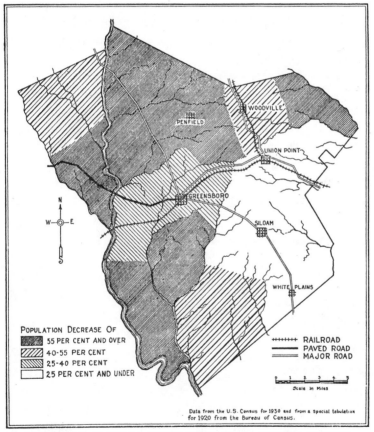

MIGRATION OF NEGRO POPULATION FROM GREENE COUNTY
BETWEEN 1920 AND 1930 BY MILITIA DISTRICTS

far the Negro population movements in these counties have been determined almost solely by the labor needs of the plantations.

The Greene County "Exodus"

The volume of the migration from Greene County is indicated in the first table in the chapter, which shows 18,971 in 1920 and 12,616 in 1930, a decrease of 33.5 per cent, the whites decreasing 23.0 per cent and the Negroes 43.0 per cent. Hundreds of farm families moved out of Greene County in 1922, a large number left in 1923, and still more in 1924 and 1925 when the "exodus" reached its zenith; even in the late twenties families were still boarding trains, hoping to find in Atlanta, Birmingham, Chicago, or Detroit some ready money with which to buy food and clothing.

Areas Most Affected.—The migration, though considerable from all parts of Greene, was greatest from the old plantation area and least from the white land section in the southeastern part of the county characterized by small holdings; the white losses, though uniformly less, paralleled those of the Negro. It will be observed that the white population decreased 44.0 per cent and the Negro population 67.3 per cent in the five militia districts with the largest landholdings; whereas, the

TABLE XLIV

POPULATION IN GREENE COUNTY, GEORGIA, IN 1920 AND 1930 BY RACE AND BY MILITIA DISTRICTS[3]

	Whites		Negroes		Whites	Negroes
	1920	1930	1920	1930	Percentage Increase from 1920 to 1930*	
Greene County................	7,771	5,988	11,200	6,628	—23.0	—43.0
Five Plantation G. M's**.......	1,695	950	2,990	978	—44.0	—67.3
Three Small Owner G. M's***..	1,545	1,499	2,430	1,572	— 3.8	—11.6
Remainder of county..........	4,531	3,529	5,780	4,078	—22.1	—29.4

*Minus (—) indicates decrease.
**Militia districts 145, 146, 147, 148, 149.
***Militia districts 141, 142, 144.

whites lost but 3.8 per cent and the Negroes but 11.6 per cent in the three militia districts with the smallest landholdings. In

[3] United States Census.

the remaining eight militia districts the losses were about midway between. The basic causes are pursued further in the chapter immediately following.

Though the population loss of Macon County in the decade was comparatively small, it is significant to note that it occurred in the big plantation area, and involved Negroes much more than whites. In Macon, then, as in Greene, the population decrease of the last ten years has intensified the whitening

TABLE XLV

POPULATION IN MACON COUNTY, GEORGIA, IN 1920 AND 1930 BY
RACE AND MILITIA DISTRICTS[4]

	WHITES		NEGROES		WHITES	NEGROES
	1920	1930	1920	1930	Percentage Increase from 1920 to 1930*	
Macon County	5,639	5,451	12,028	11,192	— 3.4	— 7.0
East of River**	2,796	2,658	7,514	6,642	— 4.9	—11.6
West of River ***	2,843	2,793	4,514	4,550	— 1.8	— 0.8

*Minus (—) indicates decrease.
**Militia districts 543 and 770—big plantation area.
***Militia districts west of Flint River.

process already under way in 1920, prior to the havoc wrought by the boll weevil.

Virtual Refugees.—The people who left Greene County in 1921 and thereafter were virtual refugees. They were *fleeing from* something rather than being *attracted to* something. They were fleeing from hunger and exposure, they were going to . . . they didn't know what. The same white landlords who sheltered their landless Negro tenants from the extravagant inducements of labor agents from 1916 to 1920 confessed to them in 1921 and thereafter that they would have to furnish themselves and farm with a minimum of fertilizer and stock and implements, or go somewhere else and get along the best they could. Some stayed; others went.

Approximately half the Negro migrants left the county in 1923, 1924, and 1925, the peak of the white migration coming nearly two years later, presumably because the whites were a little less dependent than the Negroes. The fact that the

[4] United States Census.

Negro migration was greatest in 1924 and 1925 does not mean that conditions were worse in those years than earlier for they were not, but rather that the accumulated effects of the depression could no longer be withstood.

Population Movements are Selective.—By their very nature, population movements are selective. A relatively large number of the migrants had been wage hands and laborers, while but few were from the owner class. The Negro renters in the county with children in school numbered 159 in 1928, while 188 had migrated; croppers numbered 186, while 275 had migrated; and wage hands and laborers numbered 32, while 193 had

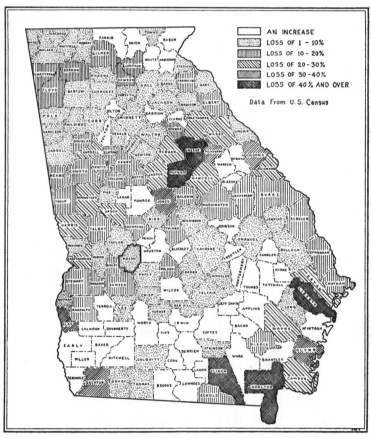

INCREASE OF WHITE FARMERS FROM 1920 TO 1930

migrated. Only one tenure class, the owners, had more living in the county in 1928 than had migrated. The reason why persons from the lowest tenure groups migrated in greatest numbers is not far to seek—they were most dependent, and consequently most helpless when the planters, for lack of cash or credit, discontinued farm operations.

The illiterate and most poorly educated adult Negroes tended to remain in the home county more often than those with a better education. Of 19 adult illiterate Negroes reported by a younger brother or sister in school, 9 left Greene County and 10 remained at home; by way of contrast, 75 of the 126

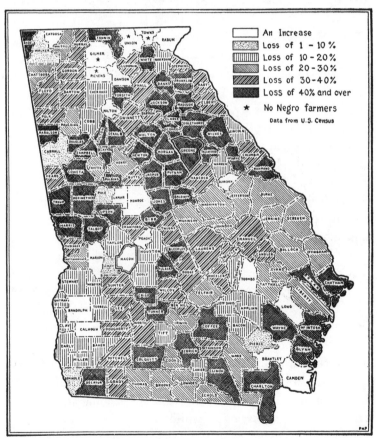

INCREASE OF NEGRO FARMERS FROM 1920 TO 1930

with a high school education migrated, and 7 of the 9 with more than a high school education. A quick comparison is this: 27.3 per cent of the Negroes remaining in Greene County and

TABLE XLVI

SCHOOLING OF 420 NEGROES OVER 18 YEARS OLD WHO MIGRATED COMPARED WITH THAT OF 617 REMAINING IN GREENE AND MACON COUNTIES, GEORGIA

GRADE COMPLETED	GREENE				MACON			
	In County		Migrated		In County		Migrated	
	Number	Per Cent	Number	Per Cent	Number	Per Cent	Number	Per Cent
Illiterate............	10	5.2	9	4.5	26	6.1	13	6.0
1 – 3 grade.......	24	12.4	16	7.9	96	22.7	18	8.2
4 – 6 grade.......	107	55.1	95	47.0	225	53.2	109	50.0
7 –11 grade........	51	26.3	75	37.1	73	17.3	66	30.3
12 and over........	2	1.0	7	3.5	3	0.7	12	5.5
Total.........	194	100.0	202	100.0	423	100.0	218	100.0

40.6 per cent of those who migrated had schooling beyond the sixth grade; on the other hand, 17.6 per cent of those remaining in the county and 12.4 per cent of the migrants had not finished the third grade.

From Macon County, where the migration was more gradual and involved individuals rather than families, the selection as measured by education was even more marked: 18.0 per cent of those remaining in the county and 35.8 per cent of those migrating had finished the sixth grade, while 28.8 per cent of those remaining in the county and but 14.2 per cent of the migrants stopped school before they had finished the third grade.

From both counties nearly 60 per cent of the migrants were males. Unattached males between twenty and thirty moved off first; then the younger couples with few or no children; next the unattached females; and then the families, the wife and children frequently remaining behind until the husband could find work and living quarters; many wives soon joined their husbands. In both counties there were deserted wives who had little or no hope of their husbands either sending for them or returning to aid in rearing the children. Left behind, too, were most of the aged and handicapped people. Old men and cripples and children leave home when taken. Frequently the migrants were scarcely able to pay passage for themselves and their immediate families, to say nothing of invalids and defectives who could be sent for later—or never.

The Direction of the Negro Migration.—Between 1920 and 1930, Negroes from Greene County, a political unit of less than 500 square miles, were scattered all over eastern America, South and North, the vast majority of them still in the South. Of the 1,826[5] Greene County migrants reported—kinsmen of children attending school in 1928—33.5 per cent were living in Atlanta in 1928, 53.0 per cent within Georgia, and 74.7 per cent in the southern states. Only one out of four was living north of the Mason and Dixon Line. Almost none went into the Northwest, and but two were living outside of the United States.

Six times as many Greene County migrants were living in Atlanta as in any other city, and eight times as many lived in Georgia as in any other state. Florida was second most popular, with but 6.3 per cent; then follow Illinois with 6.1 per cent, Ohio with 5.9 per cent, Tennessee with 4.6 per cent, New York with 3.9 per cent, Michigan and North Carolina with 3.8 per cent each, and Alabama with 3.7 per cent. It will be observed that most of the migrants in these various states are concentrated in the largest cities.

The migrants from Greene County were virtual refugees and so stopped at the first place they could, which accounts for one-third of them being in Atlanta, and the next largest numbers in Athens and Augusta—the three nearest cities with which Greene County had direct railroad connections.

The residence in 1928 of the 1,483[6] migrants from Macon County indicates that even though there was no one southern

[5] This number represents about one-third of all Negro migrants from Greene between 1915 and 1928, most of whom left the county between 1922 and 1927.

[6] This number approximates the total migration of adult Negroes from Macon County between 1915 and 1928. That a smaller proportion of Greene's migrants were reported by school children is due to facts already mentioned; namely, the migration from Greene involved unattached persons

city which attracted such a large number as did Atlanta from Greene, nearly 70 per cent of the Macon migrants still lived in southern states, and almost 40 per cent in Georgia alone. Just as the largest number of Greene's migrants went to near-by Atlanta, Athens, and Augusta, a large percentage of Macon County's migrants went to the near-by cities of Macon, Columbus, and Albany. Of Macon County's migrants outside the state in 1928, 18.8 per cent lived in Florida, 7.0 per cent in Michigan, 6.5 per cent in Pennsylvania, 5.0 per cent each in Alabama and Ohio. Though only 5.2 per cent of the migrants from this county lived in Atlanta in 1928, but one city, Detroit, had more.

Adjustment of Rural Negro Families in Cities.—Upon reaching the city the rural Negro family is unable to function efficiently. From a study of the Negro clients of Family Welfare Societies in Atlanta, Augusta, and Savannah from 1922 through 1928, and miscellaneous information from other family societies in the South and North, it was obvious that the rural Black Belt Negro was not prepared for what he found in the city. The city's labor shortage of the late teens and early twenties had been satisfied before the arrival in 1922-1927 of the rural refugees from Greene and adjoining counties; in general, the men secured only irregular work as day laborers, and women found employment in the more poorly paid types of domestic service.

From the Family Welfare Society of Atlanta the case records of 485 Negro families were secured, from Augusta 171, and from Savannah 245. Of the 485 Atlanta families, 456, or 92.2 per cent, were born outside Atlanta; of Augusta's 171 families, 121 or 70.8 per cent were born outside Augusta; of Savannah's 245 families, 143, or 58.4 per cent, were born outside Savannah.

Of the 456 non-Atlanta families served by the Atlanta family society, 367 were from the small towns and open country of

---

at first and later families, while the Macon migration was limited almost solely to the movement of individuals. The movement of families from Greene frequently resulted in the migration of whole kinship groups, excepting many aged and handicapped persons (nonschool groups) temporarily or permanently left behind.

TABLE XLVII

DIRECTION OF THE MIGRATION, AS INDICATED BY THE RESIDENCE IN 1928 OF
3,309 ADULT NEGRO MIGRANTS FROM GREENE AND MACON
COUNTIES, GEORGIA

DESTINATION OF GREENE AND MACON COUNTY MIGRANTS	GREENE		MACON	
	Number	Per Cent	Number	Per Cent
GEORGIA:				
Adjoining Counties........................	84	4.6	149	10.0
Other Black Belt Counties..................	70	3.8	73	4.9
Piedmont and Mountain Counties............	33	1.8	7	0.5
Wiregrass and Coastal Counties.............	40	2.2	116	7.8
Atlanta..................................	611	33.5	77	5.2
Augusta, Athens, and Savannah.............	114	6.2	23	1.5
Macon, Columbus, and Albany..............	15	0.8	147	9.9
Total...............................	967	53.0	591	39.8
OTHER SOUTHERN STATES:				
South Carolina...........................	9	0.5	2	0.1
North Carolina...........................	70	3.8	8	0.5
Washington, D. C.........................	16	0.9	2	0.1
Virginia, West Virginia, Maryland, and Delaware	19	1.0	10	0.6
Jacksonville..............................	10	0.6	54	3.7
Miami and Tampa.........................	6	0.3	46	3.2
Remainder of Florida......................	98	5.4	191	12.9
Chattanooga, Nashville, and Knoxville........	45	2.5	29	2.0
Remainder of Tennessee....................	39	2.1	11	0.7
Kentucky................................	12	0.7	...	...
Birmingham..............................	4	0.2	43	2.9
Remainder of Alabama.....................	51	2.8	31	2.1
Mississippi, Louisiana, Oklahoma, Arkansas, and Texas.............................	17	0.9	8	0.5
Total...............................	396	21.7	435	29.3
MIDDLE ATLANTIC AND NEW ENGLAND STATES:				
Philadelphia and Pittsburgh.................	53	2.9	66	4.5
Remainder of Pennsylvania.................	6	0.3	30	2.0
New Jersey..............................	9	0.5	33	2.2
New York...............................	71	3.9	40	2.7
New England States.......................	5	0.3	9	0.6
Total...............................	144	7.9	178	12.0
EAST NORTH CENTRAL STATES:				
Cincinnati...............................	55	3.0	30	2.0
Cleveland................................	32	1.8	18	1.2
Remainder of Ohio........................	21	1.1	26	1.8
Indiana..................................	13	0.7	25	1.7
Chicago..................................	91	5.0	15	1.0
Remainder of Illinois......................	21	1.1	1	0.1
Michigan................................	69	3.8	104	7.0
Total...............................	302	16.5	219	14.8
ELSEWHERE IN THE UNITED STATES..............	12	0.7	22	1.5
OUTSIDE THE UNITED STATES....................	2	0.1	...	...
UNKNOWN...................................	3	0.1	38	2.6
GRAND TOTAL............................	1,826	100.0	1,483	100.0

the upper and older part of the Georgia Black Belt, lying across the state immediately south of Elberton, Covington, and New- nan. The greatest number of clients were from Greene, Mor- gan, Putnam, and near-by counties, the area with the greatest population losses between 1920 and 1930. Many of the Augusta clients, too, were from the part of this area which lies closest to that city; some of Savannah's clients had formerly lived in this area, others in South Carolina, and places throughout south Georgia. Reports from other cities, South and North, further indicate that the rural Black Belt Negro often fails to support himself in the city, and that the cities of the nation can no longer

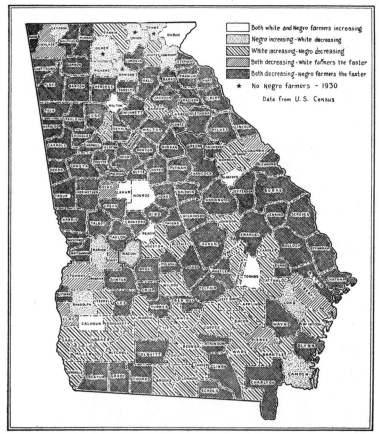

INCREASE AND DECREASE OF FARMERS BY RACE FROM 1920 TO 1930

ignore conditions in the rural Black Belt except at their own expense.

The great bulk of Atlanta's Negro relief clients in 1923-1928 not only came from the exodus area, but they arrived in Atlanta between 1922 and 1927. Nearly two-thirds of all the families of the Atlanta organization had been living in Atlanta less than ten years when they first asked for assistance. Ten families sought aid before they had been in Atlanta three months, 31 had a residence of from three to six months, 60 a residence of six months to one year, 108 a residence of two to five years, and 110 a residence of five to ten years. The short residence of the average Negro family reporting for help to the Atlanta Family Welfare Society tells but half the story, for doubtless the need develops prior to the time this agency is approached, and the family would report earlier if it knew how. Rural Negro families, accustomed as they are to the loneliness of their solitary farm dwellings and their crude hand tools, find everything in the city strangely new, impersonal, indifferent, and complicated, and it takes them some time to become acquainted with the fact that there is a Family Welfare Society, and a longer time to learn where it is and how to get to it.

Practically one-fourth of the cases were closed within four months after they were opened, another fourth were open less than eight months, roughly a third less than sixteen months, and a sixth over sixteen months. Some families needed nothing more than the constant friendly advice of the case worker, who was accustomed to helping the poor adjust themselves to the city. A large number, however, needed regular employment and better wages. Family disorganization further complicated the support of these families. The following statement is taken from an unpublished report (1926) of Ada S. Woolfolk, executive secretary of the Atlanta Family Welfare Society:

One of the most serious aspects of Negro family life is the desertion of the father. 25 per cent of all the families presented this problem. . . . Almost the entire group of families present the problems of the broken home. In only 9 per cent of the families under consideration were we dealing with a family group including two parents and children, where the father was carrying the burden of the support of the family without the aid of the wages of the mother. In 25 per cent of the families father and mother were present and contributing to the support of the family. In 66 per cent of the families the woman was left to support the children without the aid of the father. 44 per cent of these women were deserted wives, 40 per cent were widows. . . . 96 per cent of these women are in some type of domestic service. . . . The wage scale among these women workers in the various lines of domestic service is as follows:

Maids . . . .$2.50 to $10—Median wage $5.50
Launderer . . . . 1.50 to 10—Median wage 4.50
Cooks . . . . 3.00 to 10—Median wage 6.00
General house maids . . . . . .   —Median wage 7.00

It is obvious that a function of the Family Welfare Society of Atlanta, even prior to 1929, was the supplementing of the wages of Negro widows and deserted wives. The Negro husband's poorly paid and irregular work appears to be an underlying cause of desertion.

In 1929 came the stock market crash, and since then the breadline. Being the last hired, many of the migrants with work lost their jobs when the first employees were laid off. Conclusive data are not available, but there is every reason to believe that a thorough study of the backgrounds of Atlanta's present unemployment would reveal an excessive number of families who came in from the upper part of the old Black Belt before 1930.

The next chapter is devoted to a study of the causes of the wholesale cityward movement of rural families from Greene and adjoining counties during the twenties.

CHAPTER XI
CAUSES AND CONSEQUENCES OF
THE EXODUS

WHEN NEARLY one-fourth of the white population and over two-fifths of the Negro population leave a county within ten years, as was the case in Greene County between 1920 and 1930, there must be some very evident reasons. There were fundamental causes, making migration inevitable, and immediate causes, determining the time and intensity of the migration.

THE IMMEDIATE CAUSES OF THE EXODUS

A combination of boll weevil ravages and excessive deflation of land values was the immediate cause of the Greene County exodus in the twenties.

Cotton and Corn—King and Vassal.—During the first quarter of this century, roughly half of the improved acreage in Greene County was devoted to the single cash crop of cotton. About half of the remaining improved acreage was planted in corn, all of which was consumed within the county by the people who chop and pick cotton, by the work animals that pull the cotton plows, by the pigs that the cotton producing families eat. Corn serves rather than rivals cotton: where cotton is king, corn is vassal.

Depredations of the Weevil.—To a rural people who devoted three-fourths of their acreage to cotton and its support, corn, came the boll weevil. A glance at the accompanying table will indicate what havoc was wrought in Greene. From an average of 16,844 bales a year from 1910 through 1915, the production of cotton in Greene dropped to 11,964 bales in 1916, when the weevil first reached the county.

Between 1917 and 1919 the weevil was less in evidence and the number of bales reached a new high mark in 1919, about which comment will presently be made.

TABLE XLVIII

NUMBER OF BALES GINNED IN GREENE AND MACON
COUNTIES, GEORGIA, 1910-1934[1]

YEAR	GREENE	MACON
1910.............	13,862	11,499
1911.............	23,015	19,097
1912.............	13,782	13,502
1913.............	17,350	17,358
1914.............	18,092	20,733
1915.............	14,581	11,285
1916.............	11,964	15,098
1917.............	14,396	14,233
1918.............	18,773	12,859
1919.............	20,030	6,853
1920.............	13,414	10,042
1921.............	1,487	9,139
1922.............	333	9,588
1923.............	1,490	8,360
1924............ ..	4,279	12,901
1925.............	4,877	13,702
1926.............	5,969	20,134
1927.............	4,538	13,246
1928.............	4,380	10,831
1929.............	7,394	13,188
1930.............	8,674	17,684
1931.............	6,825	13,676
1932.............	4,577	7,246
1933.............	5,123	11,279
1934.............	5,167	12,444

Though the 1920 crop was somewhat below par, 13,414
bales, prices were fairly good and most of the planters determined to make back by the next crop their relatively small loss.
For the 1921 crop great sums were spent in fertilizer, and later
in the year for weevil poison; provisions for tenant families
were still high—nearly at war-time prices. To satisfy the outlay, there was a crop of but 1,487 bales, less than one-tenth of a
normal crop; the cultivation of some plantations was abandoned,
the expensive crop having consumed the cash and credit of a
score of the largest planters in the county. There was a rem-
nant, however, who hoped to retrieve from the crop of 1922 a
part of their loss in 1921. But in 1922 the weevil was even

[1] Data copied from the annual cotton reports issued by the United States
Department of Agriculture.

more relentless than the year before, and only 333 bales, or about 2.0 per cent of an average crop, were harvested. Debts and taxes went unpaid; credit vanished; chaos reigned.

The Fates Tricked Greene.—Greene County doubtless would have suffered less if the boll weevil had remained when it first appeared in 1916; but with fewer weevils in 1917 than the year before, and practically none in 1918 and 1919, many of the local farmers felt that the weevil had found Greene County and environs unsuited to its way of life. Cotton farmers forced off their lands to the south and southwest looked with greedy eyes

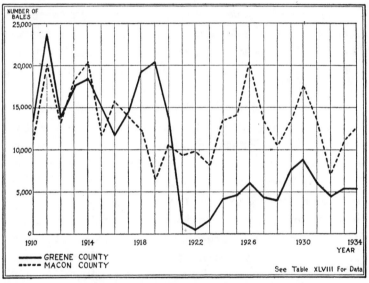

ANNUAL COTTON PRODUCTION IN GREENE AND MACON COUNTIES, GEORGIA, FROM 1910 THROUGH 1934

upon this proclaimed weevil-proof area. In Macon, farther south and infested since 1916, the cotton crop was smaller in 1919 than any year between 1910 and 1934. Land prices in Greene County were already inflated by the relatively good yields and high prices of cotton during and immediately after the World War. Everybody, even tenants, had money and wanted land. Prices were boosted by occasional extravagant offers made by prospective buyers from distant counties. Presently everybody wanted more land.

During the summers of 1919 and 1920 land buyers rushed from one part of the county to another. They offered from $75 to $200 per acre for the best tracts. When the owner did not sell, as was often the case, he usually was holding his place for yet better prices, or was determined to remain on his land and reap the returns of his good investment. When an owner did sell he joined those who rushed about looking for a farm which could be cultivated or sold for a nice profit. Landowners, bankers, lawyers, doctors, and merchants—to say nothing of tenants who bargained for land or made first payments on automobiles or wore silk shirts for the first time in their lives—all were intoxicated with their prosperity. Greene County was on a spree, and everyone was speculating on why the area was "weevil-proof."

And Then the Weevils.—But while the people speculated, the weevils, elusive and small, floated across the Oconee River from Morgan and Putnam counties; they came up the national highway from Hancock County, and through the woods from Oglethorpe County, and up the little creeks from Taliaferro County; they seemed to come up out of the very ground. The winged demon, as it were, had descended upon the planters over night. Their valuable farms became unproductive; their cash was consumed by costly fertilizers and furnishings for extravagant tenants; their crop did not pay the bills; their credit dwindled as their lands continued to decrease in value; their optimism of 1919 had turned into despair by the fall of 1922.

Every effort to retrieve in 1922 the losses of 1921 had been mocked by the pestiferous little weevils on the one hand and the evaporation of credit on the other; by 1925, land prices had dropped to one-fifth of what they had been in 1919. As the crops grew poorer, the tenants became more and more dependent upon the landlords, who were less and less able to carry them. The fertilizer cost alone of each bale of cotton produced rose

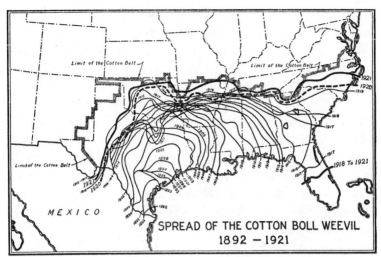

SPREAD OF THE COTTON BOLL WEEVIL
1892 — 1921

NOTE THAT THE WEEVIL REACHED GREENE COUNTY IN 1916, AND
THEN RECEDED. DESPITE THE MAP, GREENE COUNTY'S COTTON
CROP WAS NOT AFFECTED BY THE WEEVIL IN 1919 TO ANY APPRE-
CIABLE DEGREE, THE CROP FOR THAT YEAR HAVING BEEN LARGER
THAN FOR ANY YEAR SINCE 1911. (MAP REDRAWN FROM *U. S.
Department of Agriculture Yearbook, 1921*).

from approximately $16 in 1919, $23 in 1920, $190 in 1921,
to $665 in 1922.[2]

Land and Labor Unproductive.—Land bargained for at high
prices gave no relief, for the payments which had been made
prior to the slump were either dissipated in the inflation or
consumed by the expensive crops of 1921 and 1922, while with
the slump these purchasers preferred to relinquish their equity
rather than continue payments. More and more land was for
sale at distress prices; the banks throughout the county were
paralyzed; the two largest ones, both at Greensboro, closed,
as did most of the smaller ones.

The crops of the croppers were not sufficient to repay the
advances made to them; white and Negro renters were unable

[2] These sums were arrived at by applying three-fourths of the total expenditure for commercial fertilizers to cotton for each of the years from 1919
to 1922; it was assumed that the expenditure for fertilizers was the same for
1920 as that reported by the census for 1919, namely, $431,503, and that the
cost decreased to $400,000 in 1921, and to $200,000 in 1922.

to pay the promised cash or cotton; owners could neither meet their financial obligations nor secure more credit. Emergency relief crops, such as peanuts and peas, gave little relief. Labor not being needed, many wage hands and croppers had no choice but to leave the county to secure the bare necessities of physical existence; many renters had to sell their stock to make even partial payment of promised rents, and then either revert to wage hand status or leave the county.

Many of the migrants left Greene only upon the pinch of hunger. Think of people leaving a Georgia county for the bare necessities of life—a county where peaches, pears, pecans, peanuts, potatoes of two varieties, peas, beans, corn, oats, wheat, molasses, melons, tomatoes, asparagus, and a hundred other vegetables and cereals and fruits can be produced in great profusion, and where the countryside is well-watered and admirably adapted to livestock farming. The whole economic organization of the county was dependent upon cotton, and when cotton could not be produced everybody suffered.

Two Representative Cases.—On one plantation eight miles northwest of Greensboro, the owner-operator had accumulated a cash surplus of nearly ten thousand dollars by 1919. A 180-bale crop in 1920 just about paid for itself, leaving the cash surplus intact. Only twenty-four bales were produced in 1921; the landlord could not get back even the advance which he had made to his croppers to say nothing of the enormous expenditures made for feed, fertilizers, and weevil poison.

This one lean year consumed the fat of the previous years: the owner could not finance another crop; the tenants could not live through the winter without an advance; an exodus occurred, all the tenant families leaving the plantation except a mere handful employed at the sawmill which the owner had set up to get what cash he could from the timber on the plantation. After sawing and selling his timber, and after buying and sawing and selling the timber on other plantations, he moved his sawmill to Alabama. Since 1922 the old column-fronted mansion has been empty. The deeds for the land have fallen into the hands of a life insurance company, in settlement of a loan. Only two of the tenant houses are now occupied: in one of these live an aged Negro man—the ex-mule feeder about the barn—and his wife, the ex-cook in the kitchen of the "big house." Another aged Negro couple live in the second house. Each of these families cultivates a few patches of the best land, paying the insurance company, which furnishes them nothing, a small cash figure for the privilege.

A second representative case is the old William Tuggle place, a few miles northeast of Union Point. For a number of years a Negro by the name of Tuggle, formerly a slave of the family, had leased the place for ten bales of cotton a year. The lessee cultivated part of the land; on the remainder he used six Negro families who worked on halves with him. For several years, with cash or bank credit, he had financed the furnishings of his cropper families, bought fertilizer for the whole crop, and fed his stock. In the early summer of 1921, in addition to other property, he owned six fine mules, for each of which he had paid $250 the year before, and had a balance of $3,000 in a Union Point bank. The weevils began to drop his cotton squares in midsummer, but he would not pick up squares or use poison, for he was not going to be a party to any interference with "the doin's of the Almighty."

As the summer wore on, his six fine mules stood in the stalls eating costly bought feeds; the expenses for furnishing his croppers and fertilizing his cotton had all been met with cash. He was a cotton farmer, and a successful one, but the squares continued to fall.

At length the cotton was picked and sold, and the croppers did not have enough to repay the advances; the bank which held his remaining cash was closed; he could not pay the ten bales of rent. Late in the fall he refused $199 for a team of his mules; in the spring, unable to feed them longer, he sold five of them for $200. Now he is a cropper on the same place. Five of the six families who worked with him moved off to find some means of securing a livelihood.

Why They Went to North Carolina.—Only one instance was found in either county where any considerable number of Negroes migrated because of race conflict. This was in Greene County, and involved only three of the county's sixteen militia districts, the two lying between the Appalachee and Oconee rivers, commonly called "The Forks," and the one immediately east of them. A Negro and a white planter, at the planter's barn on a rainy afternoon, got into an altercation. Threats were followed by demands for retractions, and finally shots, the planter sustaining a slight wound. The Negro fled. Within a few hours, and for nearly a week after, a determined group of whites scoured the countryside. Unable to find him,[2a] the enraged whites killed one Negro man who was suspected of harboring "their nigger" and threatened all the Negro homes in the locality, shooting in the yards at night and intimidating whole families, giving as an excuse for their threats that they knew the offender was being sheltered some place and they meant to find him.

The Negroes were frantic; they congregated nightly at a few places for safety. More than twenty-five stayed in the home of the leading Negro landowner in the community, while about twice that many went to the home of a local white farm overseer who was sympathetic.

Not many days after the trouble had subsided a white man from Cleveland County, North Carolina, was in the community looking for cotton pickers, and after the white overseer and his wife accepted an offer from him many of the Negroes decided to go. It will be realized that this was in 1920, a year before the migration started. The Negroes began to leave, many of them packing out at night on foot, lest the creaking of wagon wheels attract the attention of whites who might do them violence if caught "running away like thieves." The white overseer was still in Cleveland County a short time ago, as were also most of the Negroes who followed him there.

[2a] It is common report that a local white man, for the sum of $30.00, took him secretly to Marietta the night of the shooting.

Some of the Negro families remained in the community, particularly the half dozen who owned farms; a few have drifted back. The area is still well-nigh depopulated, yet not more so than many other districts in Greene and adjoining counties where there had been no recent intense racial conflict.

Why Macon Had No Exodus.—From the standpoint of schools, courts, landlord-tenant practices, and race relations, there are, as will be seen in later chapters, little or no grounds for believing that the Negro would want to migrate from Greene and would want to stay in Macon.

It seems clear that Macon's cotton output is the most important reason why her population remained relatively stable between 1920 and 1930, while Greene's decreased so much. The three poorest cotton crops in Greene came consecutively and ranged from 2 to 10 per cent of a normal preweevil output; in Macon no two of the three poorest crops came in succession, and they ranged from 40 to 55 per cent of a normal preweevil crop. Every year the Macon County cropper repaid all or at least the greater part of his advances. The cash and standing cotton renters were usually able to settle their rent in full by the end of the second year at least. With most rents paid and most croppers settling their accounts, the Macon landlords were able to pay some or all of their bills, and their credit was left more or less intact to finance another crop.

The question arises, why didn't the weevil reduce cotton production as much in Macon County as in Greene? There seems to be no conclusive answer. The intensity of the weevil infestation varied all over the South. Macon County farmers, particularly those west of the river, did not use more modern farm methods, or better fertilizer, or more poison, or pick up and destroy more squares than the Greene County farmers. Nor does diversification of crops account for the difference, for while there was considerable shipment of peaches, asparagus, and melons from many plantations east of the river and a few west of it, the great bulk of farmers grew only cotton and corn.

The most probable explanation is that the soil of Macon

County, which is generally more open and has a larger gravel content than that of Greene, reflects more of the sun's heat and kills a bigger proportion of the larvae in the infected fallen squares. Moreover, Macon County has a relatively smaller area than Greene in sedge, brambles, pines, and other undergrowth affording hibernation for weevils.

SEQUELS OF THE EXODUS

Just as the exodus was a sequel of the depredations of the weevil, the exodus itself had sequels—cheap land, sawmills, sheriff's sales, mortgage company holdings, low rents, "old-field" rabbit industry, fatalism of rural dwellers.

Cheap Land.—The boll weevil made the land cheap; the exodus has helped to keep it cheap. The Ellington Place, a tract of 1,650 acres on the Greensboro-Athens Highway, was purchased in 1919 for $52,000. The weevil got there pretty soon after the new owners. After they had paid about half the purchase price and invested in work stock, implements, fertilizer, and furnishings for tenants, the crops of 1921 and 1922 were almost total losses. In 1923 the new owners relinquished their equity, for at that time the land could not be sold for half the amount still owed. The tenants moved away; cultivation ceased; the fields were left to the gullies and pines.

In 1928, a Union Point bank with a claim on the place for $5,000 interested a land sale company in selling the land for half the sum remaining after the claim was paid. The sale was advertised widely. The acreage was divided into sixty and ninety acre plots, each facing the highway. At the sale one local white said to another, "Jim, you ought to buy that sixty acre tract and put up a filling station." All but two of the twenty-nine tracts, selling at an average of $5.04 per acre, were bid in by Greene County people who already owned land. They bought it because they thought they could not afford not to buy it—surely the price of land would rise.

Though this particular acreage is generally hilly, the same relative drop in prices occurred during the ten-year period in all parts of the county and for all types of farms. Some of the land near Carey which sold for $150 to $220 per acre could be bought in 1928, and at present, for $35 and less. Farms off the roads, and otherwise generally unattractive, decreased from around $25 per acre in 1919 to as little as $2 in 1928.

Sawmills Everywhere.—Another sequel of the land deflation and exodus was the phenomenal growth of the sawmill industry in the early twenties. Hard-pressed landlords turned to their woodlots for salable timber.

The great expanses of land thrown out of cultivation between 1870 and 1900 in the old plantation area, along with rough and hilly acreage not cultivated, had by 1920 grown pines large enough for saw logs. By 1923 sawmills were puffing away all over the county. They had become Greene County's major source of income. From the car windows of the Atlanta-Augusta train, as it ran across the county, one could see a score of sawdust piles in 1925.

These represented the dissipation of Greene County's last resource which could readily be turned into money. Had it not been for the sale of timber and the employment which sawmilling offered, the exodus would have been even worse than it was. But the relief was temporary; the income from this source was absorbed by the continued deflation just as the county's cash and credit resources of 1920 had been swallowed up by the boll weevil. At present there is but little marketable timber left in the county.

The "Old-Field" Rabbit Industry.—Another sequel of the weevil and exodus was the emergence, in the middle twenties, of a new industry in Greene County—the trapping of "old-field" rabbits. In the winter of 1927-1928 over fifty thousand wild rabbits were shipped from Greene, locally proclaimed the nation's number one rabbit-shipping county. More than two-thirds of them were sent from Penfield, the site of Mercer University prior to 1860, in the area where cultivation had been abandoned because of the boll weevil. Here the sedge, brambles, young pines, and blackberry thickets which soon sprang up provided excellent coverage for rodents and other game.

By 1929 enterprising storekeepers in Greene and adjoining counties were showing boys and men how to trap the rabbits, but the supply was exceeding the demand and the price was falling. Soon thereafter the rabbit industry was wiped out by the outbreak of tularemia, the "rabbit sickness." Since then the rabbits have been largely decimated by some distemper: "Things have changed, not even but a few rabbits now, and them mostly sick," was the heavy complaint in 1934 of an elderly Negro man living in a depopulated area and in 1927 preferring rabbit to pork—"more fun to get it, and cheaper besides."

Fifteen Thousand Acres Sold for Taxes.—Though the sale price of land by 1928 had dwindled to less than one-fifth of what it was in 1919, the assessed valuation decreased but one-third to one-half—$9.88 per acre in 1919 and $5.70 in 1927. And while the taxable value remained thus relatively high, the total tax rate increased from roughly twenty-one mills on the dollar in 1921 to more than twenty-eight in 1928. This means that the tax rate per actual dollar's worth of land more than trebled during the period. Greene County schools, roads, and police service had to be maintained even if "hard times" had come, and land was the chief source of taxation.

Many owners defaulted in their taxes. By 1927 a total of 15,785 acres had been sold by the sheriff at the county courthouse for taxes. The acreage sold in 1922 was for 1921 taxes alone; the acreage sold in 1923, for example, may have been for just 1922 taxes or for 1921 and 1922 taxes and so on, until by 1927 some of the land in the county was hardly worth the amount of the accumulated taxes. The unpaid taxes on the 15,785 acres amounted to $5,870, an unpaid per acre tax of $0.37. The greatest number of the sales were made to a few of the largest resident landowners in Greene County, the next largest number to local mercantile establishments, and the remainder to smaller local landowners and local industrial enterprises.

The tax delinquent has the privilege[3] of redeeming the title to his land by paying to the tax-sale purchaser all back taxes, with interest at 8 per cent, and to the county its cost of the sale, usually about 10 per cent of the tax-sale price. If the land is redeemed, the tax-sale purchaser gets a good interest on his investment; if it is not redeemed he has secured land at a very low figure.

More than 95 per cent of all lands sold for taxes in Greene County is located in the red land where the big plantations are, about 70 per cent of it being in the militia districts which border on the Oconee River. Practically no lands were sold for taxes in the white land area in the southeastern part of the county.

Seventeen Thousand Acres Forfeited to Mortgage Companies.—While 15,785 acres of the cheapest land in Greene County were sold for taxes between 1922 and 1927, the titles to nineteen tracts, aggregating 12,786 acres, and including some of the best land in the county, had been forfeited to loan companies, by 1934 thirty-six tracts, aggregating 17,207 acres. More than 85 per cent of the acreage now owned by mortgage companies is located in six militia districts in the plantation area of the county.[4]

Besides their holdings, the loan organizations have an equity exceeding the present sale price of the land in an acreage several times as great. With the price of land generally lower than the amount of the indebtedness, the loan companies have usually come into complete ownership only where the owners insisted upon being relieved of keeping up even the interest and adjusted principal payments. Generally speaking, the life insurance companies and other loan organizations are willing to consider any offer by which they can sell their lands for the amount of the loans. As has been suggested in another chapter, these lands

[3] Although the statutory right of the delinquent taxpayer to redeem his land ends with twelve months, certain court decisions have been handed down which permitted the delinquent taxpayer to redeem his land any time within seven years.

[4] See next chapter for names of companies to which land has been lost.

are the natural beginning place for the government to assist tenants into ownership.

Low Farm Rents.—Between 1922 and 1932, there were scarcely a score of large landowners in Greene County who had the cash and credit and inclination to put any considerable sum of money in anything so uncertain as a Greene County cotton crop. Nearly all owners wanted to rent to tenants who could take care of their own expenses, and, as we have seen already, the boll weevil virtually consumed the stock and credit of many of the most independent renters. The inevitable result was that rents dropped very low. Soon lands were rent free, for a small number of the larger owners, thinking it wise to offer some inducement to keep their tenants on the plantation, offered them everything they produced. This rent-free land kept some tenants from migrating, and would have retained more except for the announcement at the same time that no furnishings would be available. Even the promise of rent-free land for next year's crop is of little relief to the tenant family who is without food or credit for the winter.

The tracts belonging to the loan companies provided further cheap-rent land. Assuming no responsibility for work stock or fertilizer or furnishings for tenant families, the loan companies would rent their land for a very low figure. The acreage sold for taxes, too, could usually be rented for almost nothing.

Numerous renters in Greene County living on lands belonging to absentee owners have been paying little or no rent since 1921. When asked what rent they pay, they answer: "Well, that depends." It develops that their rent "depends" upon their labors, their crops, and their integrity. Prior to 1921 these families paid their absentee landlords one-third of the corn and one-fourth of the cotton they produced; since 1921 the landlords have had to take what they could get.

Complicating the collection of the rents promised has been the method by which the renters have been furnished: the merchants would advance provisions only when the landowners

GREENE COUNTY—THIS PLACE, OF MORE THAN 150 ACRES, IS ON THE GEORGIA RAILROAD AND STATE HIGHWAY MIDWAY BETWEEN GREENSBORO AND UNION POINT. A LOAN COMPANY OWNS IT AND RENTS IT FOR $60 PER YEAR

GREENE COUNTY—RE-ROOFING THIS HOUSE WITH SHEET IRON COST A RECENT PURCHASER MORE THAN HALF AS MUCH AS THE HOUSE AND THE 100 ACRES OF LAND UPON WHICH IT IS LOCATED

THE CYCLE—AFTER THE BOLL WEEVIL THE SEDGE, AND AFTER THE SEDGE
THE SILENT REDEEMING PINES

FROM PINES BACK TO COTTON

would waive their lien upon the renters' crop up to the amount advanced.

Note a representative contrast of rents in 1919 and 1928: The Nelson Armour plantation of 1,300 acres, located about six miles southwest of Greeensboro, was rented for twenty-five bales prior to 1921. The rent received from this plantation each year between 1924 and 1928 was as follows: $250 in 1924, $500 in 1925, and $175 in each 1926, 1927, and 1928. In the last three years, the rent from this plantation did not pay the taxes on the place. The owner wanted to sell it but could find no buyer.

Fatalists of the First Order.—As a result of all this, Greene's people are pessimistic. To the general feeling of helplessness and disillusionment among the landowners is added the fatalistic philosophy, largely inarticulate, of those white and Negro tenants who lost their meager savings of years by trying to finish payments during the deflation period on land bargained for at high prices. They are not particularly bitter about their losses, but they have experienced a profound disillusionment and now many of them propose to spend everything they get as soon as they get it. To the vast majority the urge for home ownership is gone. They are fatalists of the first order.

Here is a typical story. A white tenant from north Georgia moved into Greene County in 1915. He was about fifty years old. For the first three years he farmed as a cropper. With a little over six hundred dollars in the bank in 1918 he looked about for a farm. Unable to find one of a hundred acres, such as he wanted, he decided to buy a tract containing nearly two hundred acres. He made a payment of $600, leaving a balance of $3,000 to be paid by yearly installments. By the end of 1920 he had an equity of $1,800 in the property. The next year he was unable to make the payment. His creditor threatened to sell him out, whereupon he sold the land to a banker for $1,800, the amount he still owed on it. The $1,800 lost by trying to buy land represented the family's savings of a lifetime. At present he is a cropper; he does not want to own land.

Aggravating the disillusionment of the owners and the fatalism of the tenants is the disproportionate number of dependents in the rural population, left behind by the exodus. Still further depressing the Greene County folk, particularly the Negroes, has been the returning migrant, often in broken health and not infrequently with reports about the hardships in the city—"no job and no friends." Though there are numerous cases of Greene County migrants who have regular work at fair wages in cities, South and North, the total impression seems to have convinced the rural Negro that there is no certain haven for him "up North." This is a severe blow, for in the early days he was a free man if he could get across the Ohio, and even until lately he had a job anytime he would board the train for Atlanta, Birmingham, Chicago, New York, or Boston. But by 1928, to say nothing of 1934, the distant haven had been blurred, and not for Negroes only. Whites could not go to the city as formerly and pick up a job and earn enough cash to tide over a hard winter.

Greene and Macon Counties Contrasted in 1928.—A terse contrast of conditions in these two counties in 1928 further emphasizes the sequels of Greene's weevils and exodus. Land values in Macon had dropped 30 to 50 per cent in contrast with a drop of 80 to 90 per cent in Greene. Of sawmilling there was but little in Macon; commercial rabbit trapping, none. Practically no Macon County farms had been sold for taxes, and the land forfeited to loan companies between 1922 and 1927 in Macon was 603 acres. Rents were good in Macon County; for the best lands around Marshallville and Montezuma, it was not uncommon to obtain ten bales for 180 acres, nine bales for 209 acres, $450 for 150 acres. The poorer land rented for lower figures, but never so low as in Greene.

FUNDAMENTAL CAUSES OF THE EXODUS

The boll weevil was the straw—a heavy one, 'tis true—which broke Greene County's cotton back. For years the load had been accumulating. As early as 1854 George White wrote,

"There is much worn-out land in this county; but it is the confident belief that by judicious management, it may be redeemed; . . ."[5] The "judicious management" failed to emerge, and when the large planters moved into the towns after the Civil War they gave less attention rather than more to conservation of soil. With the land becoming poorer and poorer and the surpluses from farming smaller and smaller and the dependence upon cash crops greater and greater, the population movement of rural dwellers was already decreed long before the coming of the weevil.

The Increasing Dependence Upon Cotton.—That Greene County farmers have relied upon cotton is a historical fact. In the years when cotton was plentiful and the price was good there was no immediate need for a different crop; when cotton was scarce or when it was cheap, there was no ready cash or credit to buy new equipment and teach labor to grow a new crop. The situation is like that of the lazy old man who was convinced only when the rain began that he should have fixed his leaky roof while the sun was shining. The explanation of why the planters did not resolve the quandary lies in the fact that they were operating on borrowed money, and in excessive amounts. The amounts were excessive because they proceeded on the basis that the tenants would not work if they had money or provisions. The tenants, in turn, convinced that they could be certain of getting out of their crops only what they had got out of the landlord as "furnishings," thought it foolish to apply the savings of one year's crop to the production of the next. So the landlord must risk a great deal of money in producing a crop. To get his money back he organizes his whole plantation around the cash crop—cotton.

Landlord-Tenant Relations.—Whether the landlord's estimate of the tenant was a product of the racial situation is a matter too complicated for complete analysis here. But the prevalent belief that the Negro would work only when his money and rations were all gone was doubtless based upon the

[5] *Op. cit.*, pp. 476-77.

planters' experience with ex-slaves immediately after the Civil War, and upon their belief that the Negro was innately inferior and therefore had to be taken care of. With this kind of situation, it was only natural that the business relations of the landlord and tenant should be characterized by no contract other than a general verbal agreement concerning the rent to be paid, the crops to be planted, and the amount of advances.

Landlord-tenant practices became so stereotyped and so completely in the control of landlords that a tenant often moved from one plantation to another without knowing which house he was to live in, which land he was to cultivate, and what his wife and children were expected to do on the farm or at the landlord's or overseer's house, or even what rate of interest he was to pay. Any controversy which arose was disposed of in accordance with the traditional practices of the community, varying with the personalities involved. The tenant, almost without legal status and with no effective redress, had no choice but to accept the landlord's decision. It was because of his vague and unequal contract that the tenant was certain only of getting his furnishings. And so he made no effort to furnish himself. Could there have been devised a relation of landlord to tenant which would have put a greater premium on improvidence and dependence?

The white tenant, though not so defenseless as the Negro, of necessity competed with him for a farm within the general landlord-tenant pattern, with its white-black basis.

The tenants were constantly on the move, some because they did not like their landlord, some because they had been advised by their landlord to find another place, and some because they always move. Anyone who travels extensively in the Black Belt during the winter months cannot but be impressed by the number of wagons and trucks filled with the scanty household furniture of landless and unattached families, white and Negro, seemingly motivated by a vague hope rather than an active expectation of finding something better. Their characteristic improvidence was to no small degree simply their adjustment to the demands of a system of farming which insisted that they be landless, that they be servile, and that they be dependent.

There was a prevalent feeling among tenants that it did not pay to improve the house they lived in or the land they worked. An old saying among English tenants,

> He that havocs may sit
> He that improves must flit[6]

expressed the feeling of many tenants. In the near future the American people may find it advantageous to follow England's lead and allow tenants some recognition and remuneration for permanent improvements made on rented land, or use Denmark's example and make it possible for tenants to become owners through governmental assistance. The tenants' lack of interest in the land which they cultivated was a fundamental reason why tenant farming produced such small surpluses and why Greene County's economic fabric was disintegrating even before the weevil came.

Renters—Miners of the Soil.—With the partial disintegration of the plantation system in Greene, types of renting developed which consumed the fertility of the soil much quicker than cropper farming, where better tools, better mules, and more fertilizer were used. When a fixed cash or cotton rent is paid, a premium is put upon reducing production costs to a minimum, which usually means that as little fertilizer as possible is used, that cheap work animals do shallow plowing, and that only the best patches are cultivated.

The landlords who supervise croppers or wage hands and the small owners who cultivate their own acreage also produce at the lowest cost possible, but they are not altogether oblivious of the future when planting a crop. Not so with the renters, who might move next year and not get the benefits. They produce each year's crop as cheaply as possible, regardless of the consequences to the land. The next year they do the same

[6] Quoted from H. C. Taylor's *Agricultural Economics* (New York, 1919).

thing. The result is inevitable: the land gets poorer and poorer. Where the nonresident owner assumed no risk and got as much rent as he could from the tenant who in turn got as much as he could each year at as little expense as possible, there existed a type of farming which mined the soil. Could there have been devised a relation of man to land which would have put a greater premium upon the consumption of soil fertility?

The Cycle from Cotton to Cotton.—The acreage left in the hands of the average standing renter in Greene eventually became so impoverished that the rent price had to be lowered, and owner and renter approached the time when it would be more profitable to leave the land uncultivated. Thus the rented acreage tended to be exploited and then abandoned. But as soon as it was left idle, sedge grew profusely and within two or three years young loblolly and short leaf pines were over the whole area, except where there were gullies. After thirty or forty years the pines were large enough for logs. In the meantime the soil had improved, and after the sawmill was gone parts of the land would be cleared and planted in cotton and corn. It was not, however, as fertile as when cleared originally and could not be cultivated as profitably.

There seems to be a well-defined cycle leading from cotton culture, through impoverished soil, sedge, pines, sawmill, and back again to cotton. Throughout Greene County, especially along the Oconee River, there are evidences of each of these stages. Much of the land has been logged within the last ten years, some of which is now planted in cotton or corn; some of the land is in pines but half big enough for logs; there are smaller tracts of land which have been logged, cultivated, and again left to the silent redeeming pines. Only a few pieces of ground have been in cultivation ever since the original hardwood forest was cleared away. It seems that this cycle, leaving the land poorer with every turn, will not be disrupted so long as the land is in the control of owners who virtually encourage a system of farming which mines the soil.

Systems of Farming vs. Fertility of Soil.—As further evidence that the boll weevil and the accompanying deflation of
land values were only the immediate causes of the Greene
County exodus and that the fundamental causes were the methods and practices of farming which produced no surpluses for
landlords or tenants, it will be well to emphasize a fact mentioned in the last chapter, namely: that while the majority of
the large plantation owners on the best lands in the county have
gone into bankruptcy and abandoned the operation of their
farms, the smaller farm owners in the less productive white
land area in the southeastern part of the county have continued
to operate their farms. The most important difference in farm
practices in the two areas was that the large owners urged their
tenants to confine themselves almost entirely to cotton and corn
while the small owners have always produced, in addition to
these crops, a considerable portion of the food for their families
and the feed for their livestock. The result was that the greater
part of the exodus was from the big plantation areas, from the
most fertile land.

Another evidence of the significance of man-land relations
in terms of population movements was that the ten large plantations in Greene which remained in cultivation throughout the
twenties and consequently from which there was no migration
were, without exception, operated by tenants under the close
supervision of resident owners. Nearly everyone of these either
had their tenants produce a considerable part of their food or
had some source of cash income other than the farm. These
plantations were located in various parts of the county, several
of them being surrounded by abandoned plantations.

What has been said in these last two chapters may be reduced to this: the larger the plantation the greater the emphasis
upon cash crops and the more likelihood of its disintegration.
The truth of this formula in Greene has been demonstrated
already. Macon, as we have seen, is now not unlike Greene
four decades ago. Could a New Deal in 1890 and thereafter

have kept Greene from losing one-third of her population between 1920 and 1930?   Will the New Deal forestall the imminent disintegration of the Macon plantations?   What has the New Deal done thus far for the various tenure groups of each race?   In short, what is the effect of the New Deal upon the various elements within these two rural Black Belt counties?

PART FIVE

The New Deal

CHAPTER XII

STATE AND FEDERAL ASSISTANCE FOR FARM AND HOME

THE PROGRAM of the Georgia state executive has not always paralleled the efforts of the National Administration. Governor Talmadge has sponsored cheap automobile tags, defended low wages for farm and industrial labor, advocated the discontinuation of relief standards which compete with even poorly paid labor, reduced state taxes, and lowered the rates on public utilities. The federal government, on the contrary, through its production credit for farmers, National Recovery Administration, Agricultural Adjustment Act, and loan services such as the Reconstruction Finance Corporation, Federal Land Bank, Land Bank Commission, and Home Owners Loan Corporation has attempted to help the local people become self-supporting by providing them with credit with which to pay higher wages and thus increase the buying power of the consuming public. In the interim, the Public Works Administration, the Federal Emergency Relief Administration, and the Works Progress Administration have provided work or relief for the unemployed.

There is an essential difference between the present state and federal programs. The state program proposes to lower taxes and then let each community shuffle for itself, while the federal program proposes to establish national creature-comfort standards by federal subsidy and by federal resources to stimulate the local governments to share increasingly in meeting their own needs. The effects of these two approaches in Greene and Macon counties are noted in the following pages.

GOVERNOR TALMADGE'S PROGRAM

Advertised throughout the nation for his use of troops in the textile strike of 1934, for his attacks on the New Deal, for his red "galluses," and for his advocacy of low taxes, the present

[225]

governor of Georgia is far from unpopular among widely separated groups in Green and Macon counties.

The Three-Dollar Tag.—"Yes, the rural people will vote for Talmadge," said a well-informed Greene County man in the early fall of 1934. "They'll vote for him because he gave them cheap automobile tags." The observer went on to say that the typical voter would reason that Talmadge had saved him money and consequently had earned his vote.

The three-dollar tag for all cars really penalized the poor man by making him pay the highest relative tax and by reducing the state's income, thus adversely affecting the public schools and other state services. "You know," remarked a Macon County citizen, "the typical owner of a cheap car sees and understands little more than that he now pays three dollars for a tag which formerly cost him ten or twelve." Clearly the owners of expensive cars and trucks and busses support the governor for even better reasons than do the owners of small cars. The owners of the cheapest cars never have considered seriously the possibility of graduating the price of tags from three dollars up, a plan which would allow them cheap tags without robbing the state treasury of a sizable income from tag taxes on expensive cars, trucks, and busses.

Prevailing Wages.—That relief should be so low as never to compete with prevailing wages has been Governor Talmadge's contention. Here, again, the poor man is penalized and the wealthy man is given the advantage, for when relief offers no competition to prevailing wages, labor has no choice; it must accept a rate of pay based upon unemployed labor, while the employer temporarily benefits by the low wage.

The prevailing wage of from thirty to seventy-five cents a day for farm laborers, who are paid only when employed and employed only when needed, leaves many rural families with gross incomes of between $75 and $150 per year. So small an income inevitably means inadequate food, dietary diseases, little service from physicians and nurses, poor clothing, few school books, almost no contributions to church or club, nothing laid aside to help the family through illness and death.

Cheaper Electricity and Telephones.—The cheaper rates for electricity and telephone service, sponsored by the Governor, make little difference in either of these counties, except in the largest towns and among the people least in need of relief. In 1935, there were 437 families in Greene County using electricity, less than one-sixth of the total; in Macon 412, less than one-seventh. There were telephones for only 304 families in Greene and 355 in Macon, scarcely one in ten, even including the towns.

The reduction of electricity and telephone rates was not a blow to these utilities, for their loss of income was offset by the accompanying reduction in the state tax rate.

Relief through Lower Taxes.—Governor Talmadge's reduction of state taxes by one mill penalized Greene and Macon counties along with scores of other rural counties which receive more from the state treasury than they put into it. Actually the reduction has resulted not infrequently in higher taxes.

In 1928 the state tax rate was 5 mills, in 1934 it was 4 mills. In the meantime the county-wide school tax in Greene has remained at 5 mills, but the special school tax districts within the county increased their special tax as follows: from 7 mills to 8 mills, from 7 to 10, from 5 to 10, from 2 to 5, from 4 to 5, and from 3.5 to 13. Even after this increase of taxes the public schools had less money than they would have had if the state tax had been collected and allocated on the pre-Talmadge basis. Whatever relief there has been from this type of tax policy has been enjoyed by the wealthy counties which put more into the state treasury than they get out of it.

The only relief Greene County ever got was by cutting its budget and lowering the county tax rate more than the increase necessitated by the shrinkage of state funds. In short, the county gave itself a present of a tax decrease from 15.4 mills to 8 mills, only to see half of it swallowed by the special school tax districts' adjustment to the Governor's one-mill reduction of state taxes. The real meaning of the Governor's reduced taxes is to be seen in the expenditure of $1,600,000 federal funds in the spring of 1934 to keep the rural schools of Georgia from closing, while full term schools in the richer urban counties were financed by local taxes.

In the use of troops to break strikes, in the three-dollar tag, in the prevailing wage, in the reduction of utility rates and taxes, the Governor has consistently befriended the city rather than the farm, the rich rather than the poor. It is clear why the society woman told the society editor, "Gene's all right."

FEDERAL PRODUCTION CREDIT FOR FARMERS

In recent years the farmers of Greene and Macon counties have secured a considerable part of their production credit from the federal government's Emergency Crop Loan Department and its Production Credit Association. Except for these loans many farmers could not have planted crops.

Production Credit Association Loans.—To secure loans from the Production Credit Association the borrower purchases $5.00 worth of stock in a local Production Credit Association, and becomes a member of a stock company with the privilege of voting and attending all meetings. His application for a loan, which he secures by mortgage on his livestock or other property, is passed upon by the association which he is joining. He repays the loan, with interest at five per cent, when his crops are harvested.

This service has been used by farmers in both counties, particularly Macon. A few Negroes have joined these credit associations and have received the financial benefits which they offer. Other federal loan services providing credit for the larger farmers were the Regional Agricultural Credit Corporation of Raleigh and similar loan services made possible through the Reconstruction Finance Corporation.

Emergency Crop Loan Department.—The Emergency Crop Loan Department was designed to finance small farmers who otherwise could not plant a crop. The number of these loans has increased rapidly; in 1932, for example, about 44,000 were made in Georgia; in 1933, nearly 100,000; the increase was made possible by a reduction in the size of the individual loans and an increase in the total amount available.

In numerous localities in Greene, Macon, and other counties, well-informed people reported that scarcely any farm operation could have been carried on without these loans. In some instances solvent planters put their tenants on this loan service simply because they did not wish to take the risk involved in farm operation.

The loans have been variously administered. In some communities the tenants themselves received and spent their loans: they bought their feed, seed, and fertilizer at cash prices, and accordingly had smaller debts in the fall. Usually, however, the planters got control of their tenants' checks. In some instances the landlord virtually forced the tenant to deliver the check to him by explaining that since he waived his rent to the government—one of the requirements for the loan—the tenant would have to bring the check to him. Not infrequently, when the tenant's check arrived he took it to the landlord and then and there endorsed it, or being unable to write his own name, "touched the pen" when the landlord endorsed it for him.

In other instances the planter took the money and deposited it to his own account, and issued cash back to the tenant as he thought he needed it. The planter usually charged him eight or ten per cent interest. Thus the tenant paid double interest: about six per cent to the government for the money and a larger amount to the planter for keeping it for him! It was a still more expensive method for the borrower when the planter secured the money upon its arrival and then repaid it to the tenant in feed, seed, and fertilizer at credit prices. Actually these planters secured their operating capital through the loans of their tenants, who not only paid the interest on it to the government but also a "ten per cent" credit charge to the planter on the goods bought with their borrowings.

Dividing the Landless Farmer's Loyalty.—In these and

other Black Belt counties some few planters got the loan money from their tenants and applied part of it to old debts.   Since any farmer who could not otherwise finance a crop was eligible for the loans, the planter had only to refuse advances to his tenants to qualify them.   Occasional cases have been reported where planters secured loans on the names of tenants who never saw the money, some of these cases coming to light when the tenants received receipts from the government for repaid loans of which they knew nothing.   The reported abuses of these emergency loans were not nearly so common in 1933 and 1932 as in 1931, when first administered.

When some few landlords who misused the emergency farm loan service were prosecuted and when the tenants came to understand that their production credit was coming from the federal government by reason of their own qualifications, the authority of the planters began to be undermined and even remotely challenged.   The landless farmers were beginning to realize that the planters were not so indispensable as they had appeared to be when they personally arranged the debt structure by which the Black Belt's cotton crop was produced.   In the meantime, many of the tenants knew that their landlords held their acreage only by the suffrance of creditors, usually insurance companies, who already held more land than they wanted and accordingly were agreeing to concessions and adjustments to keep the debtor-landlord from abandoning his farm.   The insecurity of the planters and the divided loyalty of the tenants— who for the first time owed an obligation to an outside agency— foreshadowed a vast deal of adjustment.

Excessive Losses of Land

That the pressure which the farmers were feeling may be better understood, there follows an analysis of the losses of farm lands to loan companies by 1932 in Greene and Macon counties —over 17,000 acres in Greene, over 20,000 in Macon.[1]

[1] The data on this and the following pages were secured from the Tax Digests of Greene and Macon counties and from interviews with county tax collectors.

Distribution of Land Losses.—Practically all the 20,278 acres owned by loan companies in Macon County in 1934 had come into their possession between 1928 and 1932. Nearly nine-tenths of them were in the Marshallville and Montezuma militia districts—the big plantation area—and included eight tracts of over one thousand acres each and four more of between 500 and 1,000 acres. In the western half of the county, the small owner area, the loan companies owned 2,197 acres in the county seat district of Oglethorpe, no tract in three militia districts, and but 381 acres in a fourth.

In Greene, too, beginning with the boll weevil depression and continuing through 1933, the greatest losses to loan companies had occurred in the plantation area and involved the largest holdings.

Some Concrete Cases.—The following instances from eastern Macon County are typical: Case one borrowed all he could get on his land, invested it in Florida real estate, and lost it; he is now trying to get a government job. Case two kept trying to retrieve his losses in peaches by the further production of peaches; he lost his plantation and is now selling mules. Case three, an elderly man, lost most of his land through accumulated yearly deficits, and is now living on his remaining acreage, selling dairy products. Case four bought his land at inflated prices and lost it when land prices dropped; he retained some city property, and is now attempting to buy back a small part, 200 acres, of his former holdings. Case five lost out by having too many peach trucks and by spending too much for peach spray; he retained part of his acreage, and may be able to buy back another portion. Case six, formerly an overseer, bought a plantation at inflation prices and for a few years made considerable profit on peaches, losing first his profit and then his land with the decline of the peach industry and the deflation of land values. Case seven, an absentee owner, has forfeited to loan companies a considerable portion of his very extensive holdings.

In general, the larger the holding the greater the probability of its falling into the hands of the loan companies. Plantation farming, though utilizing the best lands, provided the least economic security for its owners as well as workers.

Loan Companies Represented.—The largest acreages were held by life insurance companies and mortgage companies, the Federal Land Bank holding relatively little.   In Greene the John Hancock Life Insurance Company owned eight tracts aggregating 5,842 acres; the Metropolitan Life Insurance Company three tracts, 3,063 acres; the Scottish American Mortgage Company seven tracts, 2,305 acres; the Atlanta Joint Stock Land Bank three tracts, 2,343 acres; the Federal Land Bank four tracts, 1,117 acres; most of the other 2,537 acres was owned by the Penn Mutual Life Insurance Company, Canadian-American Mortgage Company, the Federal Intermediate Credit Bank, the Citizens and Southern National Bank, and the Federal Reserve Bank.

In Macon the Metropolitan Life Insurance Company held 7,335 acres, the Atlantic Joint Land Bank 4,152 acres, the First Joint Stock Land Bank 2,662 acres, the John Hancock Life Insurance Company 1,884 acres, the Federal Land Bank 1,041 acres; an additional 3,204 acres was owned by the Equitable Life Insurance Company, the Penn Mutual Life Insurance Company, the Prudential Life Insurance Company, and other agencies.

Loan Company and Local Taxes.—The planter who still owned his land might regret the presence of the loan company acreage near-by which could be rented for a relatively small sum, and the local church and school might be penalized by the bankruptcy of a leading farmer, but the courthouse officials found the taxes on the property of the loan companies promptly paid.   Between 1924 and 1932, the tax collector of Greene County was regularly uncertain about the amount of tax which would be collected, and consequently would welcome the check from the John Hancock Life Insurance Company, the county's largest landowner.   In Oglethorpe County, northeast of Greene, where a very large acreage was owned by loan companies, the county tax collector in 1931 reported that except for the regular payment of taxes by loan and finance companies the public services of the county would have been hopelessly curtailed.

By 1932, cotton was down to five and six cents; the work relief created by the Reconstruction Finance Corporation was restricted largely to the urban communities; the Red Cross was attempting to distribute enough food and clothing to insure against starvation and nakedness.

ENTER THE NEW DEAL—LOANS FOR FARMS AND HOMES

At this juncture the New Deal came into being with its expanded Federal Land Bank, Land Bank Commission, Home Owners Loan Corporation, National Recovery Administration, Agricultural Adjustment Act, and Emergency Relief Administration. A picture of the working of these agencies in Greene and Macon counties gives a fairly representative idea of their meaning to the various elements in the population.

Many well-informed people in each county, and particularly in Macon, stated unhesitatingly that there would have been a great deal of suffering and that the majority of the large owners, even the county itself, would have gone into bankruptcy before the fall of 1934, except for the money from the plow-up, the land rented to the government, the ten-cent and twelve-cent cotton of 1933 and 1934 respectively, the money from the relief program, and the loans through the Federal Land Bank, the Land Bank Commission, and the Home Owners Loan Corporation.

The Federal Land Bank.—The Federal Land Bank had been making some loans in these counties before the beginning of the present depression, but most of them have been made since 1932. They bear 5½ per cent interest and permit slow amortization, and consequently are more attractive than loans by local banks. Moreover, many owners could secure no further local credit.

Through October 1934, sixty-three loans had been made in Greene County aggregating $87,715,[2] of which amount $77,515

[2] Data presented here were secured from the records of the clerk of court and other county officials in Greene and Macon counties.

went to fifty-four white owners and $10,200 to nine Negro owners. In Macon, by mid-November 1934, the Federal Land Bank had made loans of $371,389 to ninety-three owners; of this amount all was to white owners except $4,200 to two Negro owners.

Land Bank Commission.—Supplementing the services of the Federal Land Bank were loans by the Land Bank Commission, bearing 5 per cent interest, permitting slow amortization, and deferring reduction of principal for two years.

Through mid-September 1934, sixty-four loans had been made in Green County totaling $76,290, fifty-four white borrowers with $66,490 and ten Negro borrowers with $9,800. By November 21, 1934, nearly $200,000 had been loaned to 106 Macon owners, ninety-two whites receiving $183,255 and thirteen Negroes $12,900.

Race and Areas Served.—In the two counties and for both loan services, the Negroes contracted for approximately one-twentieth of the loans, a proportion which corresponds to their ownership of acreage. When taken separately the counties present quite different pictures, one-eighth of Greene's $164,007 and one-thirtieth of Macon's $567,544 having been borrowed by Negroes.

The loans of these two federal agencies, while distributed throughout both counties, were more or less concentrated in the big plantation areas, particularly of Macon, where the mortgage companies already had large holdings and except for these federal loans would now hold the titles to a much larger acreage. In Macon, for example, nearly two-thirds of the loans have been made in the big plantation area east of the river. The Negro owners in this section, though few in number, borrowed more than those in the remainder of the county.

Home Owners Loan Corporation.—By mid-November 1934, the HOLC had made nearly eighty loans in the two counties, aggregating approximately $130,000. Of Macon's forty-six borrowers, forty-three whites received $80,624.41 and three Negroes $1,204.22. In this service, as in that of the Federal

Land Bank and Land Bank Commission, the Negroes in Greene fared relatively better than those in Macon, seven out of thirty-one borrowers in Greene being Negroes.

In both counties the HOLC loans were concentrated in the larger towns. In Macon, for instance, Montezuma homeowners borrowed nearly 70 per cent of the county's total while in Greene practically all of it went to Greensboro and Union Point. Many large landowners, living in the towns, secured Federal Land Bank loans on their farms and HOLC loans on their town houses.

Something of a Boom.—The refinancing of farm and home indebtedness through the Federal Land Bank, the Land Bank Commission, and the HOLC has resulted in the payment of all back taxes, in the settlement of most loans held locally, in lower interest rates, in longer periods in which to repay debts. All these things taken together, plus the fact that in some cases more money could be borrowed than was owed, have increased the indebtedness in each county and have created, temporarily at least and for the borrowing class, a period of relatively good times.

Proceeding on the yearly basis of financing, as the Black Belt has done and probably will do, the present good times may be aforedoomed to short life, for it would seem impossible to continue to get relief through paying off one debt by contracting a larger one, with the difference between the two constituting a chief hope for better times. It should not be overlooked, how-ever, that the source of the present loans may result in the central government's striking a better balance between agricul-ture and urban industry to safeguard its farm loans.

Loan Services for Small Owners Needed.—The need for low-interest and slow-amortization loans is not confined to the large landowners and large towns. The truth is, the large owner, whether applying for a loan on his farm or his home, has a natural advantage. The credit of ten small owners may be as good as that of one large owner, or even better, but to serve the ten is a more tedious task and requires more administrative personnel.

When through lack of administrative machinery the smaller owners do not secure federal assistance comparable to that available to the large owners, it means an added handicap to them, and eventually an increase of propertyless families and the further centralization of ownership. There is urgent need that the present federal loan agencies adapt themselves to the requirements of the small owners, and of those who could come into ownership through federal assistance; or that additional agencies be created to meet the need.

But what has been the effect of the National Industrial Recovery Act and the Agricultural Adjustment Act?

CHAPTER XIII

THE NEW DEAL IN INDUSTRY AND AGRICULTURE

THE EFFECTS of the Agricultural Adjustment Act have been felt throughout Greene and Macon counties; the National Industrial Recovery Act, though affecting fewer people, has been of some significance.

THE NATIONAL INDUSTRIAL RECOVERY ACT IN THE BLACK BELT

Windows big and little throughout both counties displayed the Blue Eagle and its "We Do Our Part." With patriotic enthusiasm for the measures of the Democratic Party, the Black Belt embraced the NRA which proposed to increase wages and shorten hours for certain industrial and commercial employees. In these counties as elsewhere in the South, the Negroes usually referred to the letters as meaning "Negro Removal Act," "Negro Rarely Allowed," and the like, while white men have been heard to call it the "Negro Relief Act," and even "No Roosevelt Again."

Restricted Scope of the NRA.—Of the 11,976 persons of both races gainfully employed in Greene and Macon counties in 1930, nearly three-fourths, as reported by the Census, were engaged in agriculture or domestic service,[1] neither of which came under any code or wage agreement of the NRA. Over half the remainder were in small businesses for themselves, such as retail stores, gas stations, and pressing clubs, or were workers not under the code, such as curb service and delivery boys at drug stores

---

[1] Approximately nine-tenths of the employed Negroes and about one-half of whites in these counties were engaged in the two non-NRA occupations of agriculture and domestic service. Of all Negro workers in the thirteen southern states, 66.5 per cent were employed in these two occupations in 1930; in Georgia and Alabama about 70 per cent, while in Arkansas, South Carolina, and Mississippi nearly 80 per cent.

and retail establishments working on commission or solely for tips, yard tenders and family laundresses, outside workers and janitors at cotton mills. A considerable number of the remaining eighth of the workers were exempt because they were members of the owner's or operator's family.

By the time the various exemptions had been taken most of the Blue Eagles in the store windows of these counties meant just about nothing, except that the proprietors were loyal Democrats and that they liked President Roosevelt. Except for a few of the larger stores and automobile agencies and filling stations, the employees coming under the NRA were limited to cotton mills, sawmills and planing mills, oil mills, railroads, and a fertilizer factory.

In 1930 the racial distribution of the chief types of non-agricultural workers in Greene was: textile, 690 whites and 30 Negroes; wholesale and retail trade, 145 whites and 25 Negroes; sawmill and wood, 35 whites and 69 Negroes; railroad, 58 whites and 41 Negroes; building industry, 25 whites and 13 Negroes; telephone and telegraph, 20 whites and 1 Negro; restaurants and rooming houses, 14 whites and 7 Negroes; laundry and pressing, 5 whites and 2 Negroes. In Macon the figures were about the same, except that cotton mill employees were fewer, 101 whites and 2 Negroes, and sawmill hands were more, 76 whites and 158 Negroes, as were also chemical fertilizer and oil mill workers, 18 whites and 42 Negroes.

The Discontinuation of Marginal Jobs.—When the NRA first reached these counties it was taken seriously, and many small businesses instituted the eight-hour day and—unwilling or unable to pay more—discontinued many marginal workers. The white clerk in the grocery store became the "sweeper," too; the more efficient of two employees was asked to take over the work of the other; the soda jerker began to deliver packages—the NRA was doing for the smaller enterprises of the Black Belt what the efficiency experts long ago had done for big business.

Slavery, and later cheap Negro labor, has caused many a Southern white man to use a Negro or two at a very low wage to do almost nothing. In many cases these employees were of value to the white man's status rather than to his business. The NRA, however, did not discontinue all marginal jobs, for before the adjustment had gone far it became evident that most of the codes could be ignored with impunity. The marginal worker, sensing that he would most likely lose his job if he protested his non-NRA wages and hours, became a party to making the NRA of no effect in most smaller enterprises where employer and employee knew each other personally and where the employee, for whatever reason, became convinced that the employer could not or would not reduce hours and pay the minimum code wage.

Circumventing the Codes.—Another reason why the Negro, along with the white workman, did not receive the full benefits of the NRA was found in the various techniques which the employers early utilized to circumvent the minimum wage provisions of the codes. In the fall of 1933, for example, the cotton ginners in a south Georgia community requested of the officials in Washington the privilege of paying labor fifteen cents per hour, and proceeded to pay at this rate. It was with open levity that the county NRA representative, a local chamber of commerce official, told of having filed this request, observing that it would be turned down but that in the meantime the cotton ginners would have completed the year's work. Shoe shops and barber shops effected a circumvention almost immediately and one was frequently told by the bootblack that he was not hired by the shoe shop or barber shop owner, but that he had rented the shoe shine equipment and was "in business" for himself.

In some instances where wages were raised to the minimum, the recipients of these larger wages had agreed to pay a visit to a "hand-me-back-man" and leave with him an agreed-upon amount; to conceal the procedure a check for the full amount usually had been given to the employee. Another device was for the employee to sign a receipt for more wages than he received.

The employees in some lumber camps and other places complained that under the NRA they worked three or four hours a day, instead of twelve as formerly, and that they had to do practically the same amount of work. It should be noted, however, that in such instances the employees received approximately the same wage for the few hours under the NRA that they had received formerly for the entire day. All kinds of practices were being employed to operate with the Blue Eagle and without increased costs.

The Plight of the Small Business.—Many small business enterprises which attempted to live by the NRA were soon in a desperate plight. If they paid the minimum wages they could not successfully compete with bigger businesses. The small industry using small machines, for example, has a distinct advantage over the industry using hand processes; by the same token the large industry using big machines has a distinct advantage over the industry using small or obsolete equipment, not infrequently that discarded by the larger units. The NRA, by fixing wages solely on the man-hour basis, threw considerable strain upon the smaller and less mechanized industries. For example, the operator of a small feed mill using obsolete machinery had a smaller output per man-hour than the larger and more mechanized concerns in the industry and so could not compete with them if he had to pay the same man-hour wage.

The NRA wages often increased the production cost of the small operators from fifty to one hundred per cent, or more; whereas, the added cost in large factories with modern machinery was much smaller. The workers in the plants with the most productive machines were receiving somewhere near the minimum wage prior to the application of the code. The smaller and obsolete machines could compete successfully with the larger machines only when cheaper labor was used. It can scarcely be denied that the NRA, by dealing solely with man-hours rather than with units of production, has accelerated the discarding of hand processes and obsolete machinery in American industry, thus further mechanizing industry—which means fewer employees and, everything else being equal, longer bread lines.

The Dictates of Economic and Racial Factors.—The industry employing the largest number of workers in either Greene or Macon counties is a cotton mill at Greensboro. Before the NRA the daily wage of workers in this mill was about seventy-five cents for ten or more hours; afterwards, wages ranged from $2.00 to $2.40 for eight hours, a daily wage increase of about three hundred per cent and an hourly wage increase of nearly five hundred per cent. The machinery in this mill was obsolete. To all practical purposes there existed a mill in Greensboro simply because labor was so cheap there that even on obsolete machines a product could be manufactured at a cost comparable to that of products from the factories with more modern machines, where labor costs are higher per hour but not per production unit. With the coming of the NRA the mill at Greensboro had three choices: to operate at a loss and eventually close; to ignore the NRA stipulations; to install more productive machinery and pay the code wage to fewer workers. Time recorded the choice—six months after the coming of the Blue Eagle larger machines were installed; the number of employees was decreased by twenty, thus increasing the number of Greene County families in urgent need of relief.

Inside this cotton mill at Greensboro there were twenty Negro employees whose hours under the NRA were decreased and whose wages were increased in accordance with code stipulations. Six months later when the modern machines were installed and the number of employees was reduced, it was the Negroes who lost their jobs. Here is a formula of South-wide importance: Economic factors dictated the installation of the more productive machines at Greensboro; racial factors dictated the discontinuation of the Negro employees first.

The Black Belt and Industry.—Throughout the Black Belt, the cheapest labor area in the South, the small manufacturing establishments making products on obsolete machines with cheap labor are faced with the same choices as the Greensboro mill.

Further complicating the problem for the rural county, however, is the fact that as long as there is rank unemployment in
the large industrial centers, industry can not afford to place modern equipment in the Black Belt where labor has had so little
experience with machines of any sort and consequently is without the skill required to operate complex machines productively.

Our discussion poses two questions: First, did the NRA, by
arbitrarily fixing wages solely on the man-hour basis, preclude
the expansion of industry in this low-wage area, and in doing so
virtually make permanent the chronically low wages of the
rural Black Belt? Second, if the national government does not
set hour and wage standards, will not the standards of even the
urban South seek the low levels of the Black Belt?

NRA Wages and Hours for Negro Labor.—NRA wages for
industrial labor cause complications when the industry is located
in an agricultural region with a low wage scale. Difficult situations therefore arise: When farmers all around are paying from
thirty to sixty cents for a long day's work—ten to thirteen hours
—it is a rather delicate proposition to hire workers at NRA wages
for a short day—eight hours—according to the foreman of a
bauxite mine in Sumter County, just across the boundary of
Macon. The foreman explained that he would hire a colored
man after the crops were sold, but during the year he hired no
one until certain he was not wanted on a farm. "You see," he
said, "these planters around here are my friends."

At this mine are employed 6 white men and 125 Negroes,
23 of whom are residents of Macon County. The miners live
in barracks at the mine, and are required to eat at least two
meals a day from the barrack's mess. The meals cost the miners
from eleven to fifteen cents each, never exceeding $3.75 for a
two-weeks' period. Without them, according to the foreman,
the Negroes would not have the strength to perform their tasks.
"They've got to be watched," he said, "or they'll buy old automobiles for three or four times what they are worth and not
have enough to eat, even working regularly at $12.00 a week."

The Mixed Emotions of the Black Belt Whites.—By and

MACON COUNTY—THIRTY CENTS AN HOUR AT THE BAUXITE MINE

ON COUNTY—FORTY TO SIXTY CENTS A DAY ON THE PLANTATION, BUT THERE
ARE SLACK-WORK SEASONS AND THERE ARE RAINY DAYS WITH NO PAY

MACON COUNTY—NEGRO OVERSEERS ARE USED BY SOME OF THE LARGEST PLAN

THE GREENE COUNTY CONVICT CAMP—"CHAIN GANG" IS NOT A MISNOMER H

large the response of the Black Belt employer to the NRA was better than might have been expected. A Democratic administration in Washington has not been without practical significance. In fact, it is quite uncertain whether under other political auspices the orthodox southern employer would have coöperated at all in a federal program which proposed to pay the same wage to white and Negro labor. The southern employer found himself with mixed sentiments: he was a Democrat, and also a believer in racial differentials; he was personally enthusiastic about the president, who in neighborly fashion calls Georgia his southern home; and at the same time he was traditionally and well-nigh unalterably opposed to any person or scheme which proposed to tell him what he should or should not pay his labor, particularly his Negro workers. Moreover, the single minimum wage scale implied that the needs of the white and Negro laborer were similar, a theory not in harmony with the Black Belt white man's assumption—rather his rationalization—that the Negro does not need so large a wage as the white man because he does not need so good a diet, so good a house, so good a school, or so good a suit of clothes.

It is interesting to reflect that whatever success the NRA had in Greene and Macon counties was due, in no small degree, to the traditional loyalty to the Democratic Party, a loyalty grounded in the peculiar hopes and fears which have given substance to the "Solid South" with its white supremacy, segregation, and racial differentials.

THE AGRICULTURAL ADJUSTMENT ACT

The AAA has been generally satisfactory to the Black Belt's leaders—to the planters, to the business men, to the cotton factors, to the professional people. This agency has paid the farmers to plow up cotton, to refrain from planting cotton; moreover, it had doubled the price. Most current bills and some back debts of recent years have been paid.

The Plow-Up.—In the late summer of 1933, with cotton in bloom or already heavy with bolls, hundreds of farmers in

Greene and Macon counties coöperated in the plow-up. Their first reaction was one of amazement, but when the proposition was fully explained to them they began to show sympathy with it.

The reasons are not far to seek: six cents per estimated pound, with the possibility of additional money from it in the fall should the price of cotton be boosted by the plow-up, was attractive to the farmers who the year before had sold their cotton for five and six cents. Moreover, hail storms and heavy rains can cause great damage. When they saw that they would lose no money and perhaps gain some, their patriotic loyalty to the Democratic administration was all the more effective. The fact that advances to tenants could be collected from the tenants' share made the proposition very attractive to the planter.

"Let's Swap Work That Day."—The aversion which the landowners felt at first to plowing up cotton remained with many of the tenants, who year in and year out had been taught above everything else to treat the cotton plant with respect. The following case, from Greene County, is typical: A planter got in his automobile one mid-afternoon and rode to the plantation where his six tenants were waiting for him under a chinaberry tree at the corner of a cotton field. He placed a cord 210 feet long in the hands of two tenants and told them to stretch it across the ends of the rows. That measured one side of one acre. The man at the far end marked the place by knocking his heel in the soft ground and moved on another length of the cord. This time, when he marked the spot by pulling up a handful of cotton stalks, a glum look came over the tenant at the other end of the cord—it was his cotton. Five lengths carried them to the corner of the field, where the man at the back swung across the rows to take the lead, and now having got beyond his own cotton, marked the end of the cord five times with a green pyramid of pregnant stalks. Turning back up the other end of the rows for five cords and then down the rows for five cords, to the starting point, the party measured off the twenty-five acres to be plowed up.

As he left the field, the planter told them that he was expecting to receive final instructions any day and he would let them know when to plow it up. The tenants looked out over their twenty-five acres of good cotton without any show of pleasure and without any suggestion that they would do other than follow their landlord's instructions.

In low tones, one tenant said to another: "You know, I ain't never pulled up no cotton stalks befo', and somehow I don't like the idea." "I been feelin' sorter funeral-like all afternoon," said another. A third relieved their gloom somewhat by suggesting: "Let's swap work that day; you plow up mine, and I'll plow up yours."

The Plow-Up Pays Bills.—When the money came, approximately $10 per acre for the twenty-five acres, practically all of it found its way into the hands of the landlord. One-half of it belonged to him as rent, while the other half was used to reduce the tenants' indebtedness to him for furnishings.

As was anticipated, the destruction of ten million acres of cotton boosted the price from six to ten cents, creating an option of four cents per pound for the cotton destroyed. When the option check arrived it was sometimes divided between landlord and tenant, while in other instances the landlord took it, with the explanation that he had arranged for the plow-up and had taken out the option himself. This latter practice amounted to the tenant's getting but three cents per pound for the cotton plowed up while the landlord got seven cents. The cotton which was not destroyed brought around ten cents per pound, one-half of which went to the cropper or toward the settlement of his debts.

The total rental and benefit payments made by the AAA to Greene County farmers through December 31, 1933, amounted to $41,632.50; to Macon County farmers $84,587.25.[2]

Renting Cotton Land to the Government.—In the spring of 1934 the AAA proposed to hold the cotton crop to ten million bales by renting land from the farmers to keep it from being

[2] *Agricultural Adjustment* (U. S. D. A.—a report of the administration of the Agricultural Adjustment Act, May, 1933 to February, 1934), p. 300.

planted in cotton. By August 31, 1934, Greene and Macon County farmers had participated in this program to the extent of nearly $50,000 rentals[3]—for Greene farmers $21,628.33 and for Macon farmers $27,854.85. All of this was for cotton, except a little over $1,000 in the latter county. Thus for 1933 and through August 31, 1934, nearly $200,000 had come to the farmers of these two counties from the AAA. The sums for the entire state were: $11,546,120 for cotton, $1,432,820 for tobacco, $5,332 for wheat, and $1,285 for the corn-hog program.

Some of the larger planters in Macon County expressed the belief that this land which could not be planted in cotton would result in a larger production of food and feed stuffs. Thus far, however, there has been little indication that anything short of dire necessity will establish and maintain a system of self-sufficient farming in this area, so completely dominated by the cotton economy that efforts at crop rotation have amounted to but little and livestock farming is no more in evidence now than a decade ago.

The Tax-Free Bales.—The Bankhead Allotment Bill put teeth into the AAA's cotton restriction. Under its provisions tax-free certificates for about 10,000,000 bales were issued and distributed to the various cotton states on the basis of their production in recent years. Each of the state allotments was next distributed to the cotton producing counties, and the county's allotment in turn to the cotton producing farms.

If a farm produced less cotton than was allotted to it, the farmer holding the surplus tax-free certificates could sell them, at not over four cents a pound, to any farmer who produced cotton in excess of the tax-free certificates allotted to his farm. This arrangement made it easy for tax-free certificates to flow from areas with a poor crop to areas with a good crop. Any cotton for which a tax-free certificate could not be secured was to be subject to a tax levy of nearly 50 per cent.

Greene County was allotted tax-free certificates for 3,832 bales, Macon for 8,879 bales. There were rumors, especially in

[3] Associated Press release in the *Atlanta Constitution*, October 10, 1934.

Greene, that kinsmen and friends of some persons associated with the administration of this bill received more than their part; in one instance, ran a rumor, an elderly woman whose plantation had been largely uncultivated in recent years received a sizable allotment of bales. Be this as it may, farmers in another part of the county bought certificates in considerable numbers from the persons under suspicion.

The confusion which would have resulted without the Bankhead Allotment Bill will be readily appreciated by the fact that in the spring of 1934 the farmers of Greene County signed to rent to the government an acreage almost equal to the total acreage planted in cotton in 1933, despite the instructions that only 40 per cent of the acreage of each farmer would be eligible. The County Agent explained that the great majority of the farmers had made correct entries; that discrepancies occurred among only 112 of the county's 1,034 participating farmers. He added that the Bankhead Allotment Bill, while irritating some by its police qualities, served a good purpose in restraining those few farmers who would try to take undue advantage.

Renter, Landlady, Merchant.—The tax-free bales necessitated considerable adjustment between landlords and tenants. In some instances the landowners claimed all or most of the tax-free cotton, while in others the tenants claimed it.

For some years a Greene County landlady had been renting 250 acres to a tenant for two bales. In the spring of 1934 the tenant rented some of the land to the government, from which he received all the money. The farm was allotted two tax-free bales by the county committee. For the convenience of the renter, the landlady waived her claim upon his first bale to a merchant who was "running" him.

The crop was harvested. The merchant got the renter's first tax-free bale and reduced his indebtedness accordingly. The landlady, expecting the second tax-free bale, then went down to get her first bale of rent. Upon arriving, she was informed that the renter had sold the tax-free certificate for that bale to his son whom he wanted to help get out of debt. The landlady told the renter he had no right to sell it, for it was to cover her rent bale; she would give him a few days to pay the tax and free her bale. After a few days it was free; the landlady put it in a bonded warehouse and got a twelve cents per pound loan on it. She then went to the merchant who was "running" her renter, only to find that the renter had borrowed from him the twenty dollars with which he freed her rent bale, saying that it would be paid by the landlady when she sold the cotton. She was infuriated; she would assume no responsibility for the twenty dollar debt, and after this the storekeeper was to be on his guard and never make an unauthorized loan which involved her. Next day she went to the ginner to see that the renter's next bale went to the merchant. Abandoning hope of receiving her second rent bale, she informed the tenant that every grain of his corn and other crops were tied up and that he could be put on the chain gang if he touched any of it until he applied his third and last bale to his store bill. When she had explained it all to the renter, he thanked her profusely and said that he appreciated the advice very much and all the trouble she had gone to, to show him just how it was. "Now what would you do," she asked, "with a polite cuss like that?"

Nineteen Cents Mistaken for Nineteen Dollars.—Another case will illustrate further how landlord-tenant relations are being affected by the entrance of the government into the cotton picture. In the fall of 1932 a small landlord took the last of his tenant's cotton to settle a loan which the tenant had secured from the government for feed, seed, and fertilizer. A few weeks later the tenant received a notice from the governmnt of an unpaid debt of $0.19 which he misread for $19.00. He wrote a letter to the government accusing his landlord and the county agent of stealing his money. Within due time the tenant's letter came back to the county agent and then to his landlord, who was literally shocked, for he felt that in case of any question the tenant should have come to him and learned the meaning of it. He took the letter to his tenant, who hung his head. Assuring him that he had paid the bill as promised, the landlord told him to leave his place immediately. "But the debt which you are quarreling about," said the landlord, "is nineteen cents instead of nineteen dollars—a small amount to be raising a row about." The tenant then begged to remain; the landlord agreed, but told him that he was keeping the letter in case he should ever need to use it against him.

The landlord's brother, who lived near by, expressed surprise that the tenant should be allowed to remain on the place long enough to gather his crop, to say nothing of the next year. Another landlord in the community said that if one of his Negro tenants did him that way he would hardly live to accuse any other white man of misappropriating funds.

Large Owners, Small Owners, Renters, Croppers.—In both counties most of the large owners were enthusiastic supporters of the AAA's cotton program. The small owners were either indifferent to or against the plan, often feeling that the county committee had been partial to the large owners. A considerable number of the small owners pointed out that their tax-free certificates were for less than one bale.

The renters who were paying cash rent seemed to be well enough satisfied, for they could apply to their rent the rental benefits which they had got from the government and their twelve-cent cotton. Many of those paying a fixed cotton rent were dissatisfied because the amount of cotton which they were paying under the restricted production program was usually the same as they had paid when cotton was cheaper and they could raise more. In many instances it took all or most of their tax-free certificates to clear the rent bales.

The croppers had very little to say, since they were dependent upon the landlord, accustomed to following instructions, and usually expecting their share of the crop to do little more than settle the advances which they had already received.

They All Voted on the Bankhead Allotment Bill.—When it was first suggested that an election be held on the Bankhead Allotment Bill, it was generally believed in Greene and Macon counties that there was so much opposition to the plan that the

Administration would never permit it to come to a vote. A few weeks before the election, however, an additional ten per cent allotment of tax-free certificates were received in each county. In the distribution of these certificates the county committee corrected some of its worst mistakes, winning to the support of the bill a large proportion of the smaller farmers who had been undecided or hostile, but who had felt that the plan could work if properly administered. About the same time President Roosevelt, then at Warm Springs, suggested that the small farmers be given larger allotments in 1935. These developments dispelled most of the opposition to the Bankhead Allotment Bill.

In the meantime, the price of cotton seed had increased to the point where it would just about pay for the tax-free certificate. Moreover, the rental benefits from the government for the land not planted in cotton, if applied to the purchase of tax-free certificates, would usually deliver the whole crop at twelve cents. Greene County farmers sold their 3,832 tax-free bales at twelve cents and above, their 1,335 surplus bales at eight cents and above. Macon farmers had 3,565 surplus bales above their quota of 8,879 bales. With relatively good yields and relatively good prices for their cotton, practically all the tenants in both counties paid their rent and settled their furnishing accounts. The planters, merchants, and bankers were more prosperous than they had been in several years—more new automobiles, larger bank deposits.

Immediately before election day it was not unusual to hear large planters openly state in the presence of their tenants that if the Bankhead Allotment Bill failed to pass they would plant no cotton; in fact, that they would let their plantations grow up in weeds if the people failed to endorse the bill, the only means yet found to give the cotton farmer a chance to live. "Nothing," one planter said, "can be worse than five- and six-cent cotton. The Bankhead Bill has given us twelve-cent cotton, and the folks working with me had better vote for it."

On the day of the election the farmers swarmed to the polls

and expressed themselves overwhelmingly in favor of the bill. Scarcely any objection was registered by the white farmers in these counties to the Negroes' voting. The reason is clear: Many of the Negro owners and cash renters favored the bill, and the Negro croppers voted for it in accordance with the expressed wishes of those who control the plantations.

Noncoöperators—Texas Drought.—With tax-free certificates available for all the cotton produced, the farmers of Greene and Macon counties who disregarded the instruction to limit their acreage were the ones who profited most by the higher price resulting from the cotton restriction program. In Greene four large farmers demonstrated that they could profit by the program by ignoring it, for they produced large crops and sold them at twelve cents, less the cost of ginning certificates.

These circumstances raise this question: To what extent did the success of the Bankhead Allotment Bill in 1934 rest upon the drought in Texas? Because of it the nation's cotton crop fell slightly below 10,000,000 bales. Without it the nation's cotton crop would have exceeded 10,000,000 bales, the amount for which tax-free certificates were issued. More cotton than certificates would have meant that some of the cotton would have been subject to a tax levy of nearly 50 per cent. This would have been very distasteful to the typical cotton farmer.

As it turned out the drought in the Southwest and the good crop in the Southeast left everybody happy about the Bankhead Allotment Bill: plenty of tax-free certificates for sale in the good crop areas to market the surplus produced there, meaning that none of their cotton sold for less than eight cents; plenty of purchasers for tax-free certificates not needed in the drought area, meaning that the farmers there got twelve cents for the cotton they produced and four cents for what they failed to produce within their allotment. Despite the general satisfaction of farmers in the Southeast and in the Southwest, there is somewhere something sinister in legislation implemented by droughts!

Down the Tenure Ladder.—The cotton reduction program and other federal emergency agencies operating in Greene and

Macon counties have caused a kind of boom. There are more new automobiles and other evidences of cash than at any time since the early twenties. The controllers of the plantations, in particular, are better off than in recent years.

At the same time there has been a distinct tendency for people who were poor in 1928 to be even poorer now, despite the federal money which has either gone through their hands or missed them. The money which came into the county for rental benefits in most instances went directly to the landlords. Of all the landless farmers only the independent renters, rare in Macon County and constituting only a small proportion of the farmers in Greene, received any appreciable benefit from these federal expenditures. Naturally enough, croppers, always dependent upon the landlords, had little claim upon these benefits and wage hands had none. Moreover, since the government was renting land and also issuing ginning certificates, the situation made it advantageous for the landlord to use wage hands instead of croppers and in many instances, even during the summer, the cropper's status was transformed into that of wage hand. The planter need only send word to his croppers that he will pay them a daily wage or allow them so much credit per day for their labor, rather than advance them so much per week against their crop. Thus the cropper is changed into a wage hand, leaving the landlord in control of the tax-free certificates and the benefit rentals. Furthermore, the planter can tell a wage hand at any time that he does not need his service, and the wage hand has no choice but to get out of the house which belongs to the planter.

Except for the special consideration shown to farmers with two bales or less, more of the croppers in the big plantation areas shortly would have been reduced to wage hands. Even with this added incentive for landlords to retain the number of farmers, the trend in these counties is toward fewer agricultural workers and a lowering of tenure status.

Bankhead Allotment Bill Enforces Greene's Depression.—It was noted in an earlier chapter how the cotton production in

Greene County fell from an average of 16,000 bales between 1910 and 1920 to 333 bales in 1922, and less than one-tenth of a normal crop in 1921 and 1923. This resulted in the excessive deflation of land values and great migration from the county, described already. Since that time the county has been recovering from this shock; by 1930 it had a cotton crop of 8,674 bales.

The Bankhead Allotment Bill, by fixing the allotment of tax-free bales on the basis of crops in recent years, tends to make permanent the depression from which Greene County was emerging. Macon County, with no more cotton between 1910 and 1920 than Greene, had an allotment over twice as great. In short, the Bankhead Allotment Bill by using the cotton record of the last few years crystallizes the present differential between Greene and Macon instead of giving Greene the opportunity to recover.

The large acreages in Greene County which have been idle since the early twenties can scarcely be got back into cultivation under the Bankhead Allotment Bill unless some plan is made for this particular purpose; for the "new farmer" plan of 1934, by which surplus certificates were made available to new farmers, can scarcely be effective without further curtailing production on land already in cotton unless there should be another drought in the Southwest.

The New Deal's efforts to increase farm and industrial incomes in Greene and Macon counties left many people without means of a livelihood. For them the relief program was designed to maintain creature-comfort standards.

CHAPTER XIV

THE RELIEF PROGRAM

PRIOR TO 1931, when the Red Cross first gave out food and clothing to needy families, there was no relief service in Greene or Macon counties except the county poor fund. Since the fall of 1933 the Federal Emergency Relief Administration has operated in both counties.

THE COUNTY POOR FUND

The antecedents of the county poor fund are to be found in the English Poor Laws, which in 1388 established the principle that the poor should remain at the place of their birth and be aided by local alms. In 1547 the local authorities were authorized to provide convenient houses for the "impotent poor," and in 1563 legal machinery was effected for the collection of the poor "taxe" even from the "obstinate person." Counties unable to provide indoor relief, a "poorhouse," provided outdoor relief, the poor fund.[1] Most of the populous Georgia counties have poorhouses, while the remainder, including Greene and Macon, have only outdoor relief.

"On the County."—In 1928 there were twenty-four persons on Greene County's Poor Fund, or pauper list—four elderly white women, all widows, and twenty Negroes, sixteen women and four men. Over half the Negroes on the list lived at Greensboro, the county seat; in nearly every instance they were old and decrepit. In Macon there were about thirty, four-fifths of them Negroes.

The combined sum received by the twenty-four persons on the pauper list in Greene was less than $700 during the year of 1927. The four white women were allowed from three to five dollars per month; the Negroes got from one and one-half to

[1] Stuart A. Queen, *Social Work in the Light of History* (Philadelphia and London, 1922).

two dollars, in many instances scarcely enough to pay the tobacco bill. One crippled Negro man, receiving $1.75 monthly, lived alone; each day he hobbled to one of three houses for his dinner, usually getting there about noon; it took him the whole afternoon to get back to his shack a quarter of a mile away.

The investigation made of an applicant for the fund usually consisted of little more than having him swear he was without property, without property-owning relatives, and unable to work. The receipt which the clerk of court gave the county commissioners for the small amount of money given to the pauper during the year constituted the only case history of the client.

There were scores of other old people who would have been entirely dependent upon the county except for their children and friends and former employers. It was not unusual to find an aged couple living in a house provided by some sympathetic landowner, or an aged Negro put on the pauper list at the request of a white landlord. Persons who got on the pauper list were spoken of as being "on the county" and usually remained on it until death.

"One Year and One Month to Live."—In November, 1934, there were fifty-five on Macon's pauper list, nine whites and forty-six Negroes; the whites received an average of $2.38 per month, the Negroes an average of $1.79. In August, 1934, Greene's pauper list stood at forty-nine, six whites and forty-three Negroes; the whites received an average of $2.71 per month, the Negroes an average of $1.82.

Obviously these small amounts, though often of some assistance, are insufficient to support life, and it is not surprising that of the 115 persons who were put on the pauper list in Macon County after January 1929, sixty had died before November of 1934, one-fourth of whom died within four months. The average life of the sixty clients was thirteen months—one year and one month to live after getting "on the county." In 1934 a little over $1,200 was provided for Macon's fifty-five, a little over $1,000 for Greene's forty-nine paupers. "The Poor Fund" is a very poor fund, indeed: eighteen clients in Greene and twenty-four in Macon were receiving $1.50 and two in Greene and five in Macon $1.00 per month.

THE RED CROSS' FOOD AND CLOTHING

The reactions of the planters to the distribution of food and clothing by the Red Cross are symbolic of their fear and subsequent adaptation of most innovations which reach the Black Belt.

Free Food Will Ruin Labor.—By the fall of 1931 considerable amounts of food and clothing were being distributed to the needy families of these counties. Many of the larger landlords expressed misgivings, even disgust, upon seeing able-bodied men stand in line for free flour and cloth. "They'll never work again," was the general prediction. When asked if the recipients needed assistance they reluctantly replied, "Well, yes. But anybody who knows these people knows they won't work unless they have to."

Confirming the planters' predictions were reports from the cities of Macon, Montgomery, Memphis, and smaller towns in the heart of the cotton belt, that planters had gone to these bread lines and frequently found the people there unwilling to pick cotton or do other farm work for the prevailing wage. With the price of cotton low and farm prospects generally gloomy, the planters felt that the casual labor supply, living largely around the towns, should not be disorganized by the hope of living without work. Washerwomen, weekly cleaners, yardmen, and pick-up laborers were commonly said to be getting careless about their occasional opportunities to work. The following dialogue is credited to many communities: "Oh, Manda, why didn't you come for the wash?" "Who, me, Miss Jane? Why, didn't you know I done quit washin' when I got on de Cross?"

A Nuisance and then a Convenience.—The weeks wore on; bales accumulated; settlement time was at hand, and the price of cotton was so low that many tenants could not pay the rent and settle their furnishing accounts. Under these conditions the planters found the Red Cross to be a convenience rather than a nuisance, for they could more easily secure full settlement from their tenants when Red Cross food and clothing were available for the winter. On many plantations all crops had gone into the settlement. The Red Cross had given the landlords, in sore need of money, a chance to squeeze their tenants drier than they could have done otherwise.

In many instances the same planters who, before and during cotton-picking time, had lamented and sometimes even protested the distribution of food and clothing to town-dwelling casual laborers, after settlement time advised their own tenants to apply for assistance, went to the office to certify their need, had the Red Cross flour and cloth taken to their plantations by their own trucks and distributed by their own overseers. The free food and clothing which threatened their cheap labor supply one month were serving their own ends in the next. Scarcely any Red Cross flour or cloth went on the plantations until after settlement time, and then not on all of them.

The economics of the situation is clear: The planters had found a means of shifting to the Red Cross part of the expense of maintaining their dependent workers. The formula was well expressed in these words: "The more the tenants get from the Red Cross, the less they'll have to have from the landlord."

At Montezuma there was a chapter of the Red Cross which constituted a sort of miniature family welfare society. A small budget was raised and thirty families, nine white and twenty-one colored, were provided with food. The coming of the federal relief service dried up local contributions for this private charity.

THE FEDERAL EMERGENCY RELIEF ADMINISTRATION

The Federal Emergency Relief Program reached Greene and Macon counties in the late summer of 1933, with Greene coöperating but half-heartedly at first, and consequently not getting as large a number of the CWA workers in the winter of 1933-1934 as she would have got otherwise. The various phases of the emergency relief program—direct relief, work relief,

distribution of surplus products, rural rehabilitation, employment of unemployed teachers, the maintenance of rural school
terms, and nursery schools, and the improvement of school
grounds and plants—present a spotted picture.

The Relief Load by Race.—Unlike the situation in Georgia's urban counties, where there is a larger proportion of
Negroes than of whites on relief, in Greene and Macon, as in a
majority of the state's other rural Black Belt counties, more
whites than Negroes have been on relief, as is shown in Table
XLIX, which includes the rural rehabilitation and other types of
service rendered by the FERA. Negroes in Macon had the
higher proportion only during the first months, and in Greene
only for a month now and then.

TABLE XLIX

PER CENT OF POPULATION ON RELIEF BY RACE IN GREENE AND MACON
COUNTIES, GEORGIA, AUGUST, 1933-MARCH, 1935[2]

MONTH	GREENE		MACON	
	White	Negro	White	Negro
August 1933	*	*	5.2	10.0
March 1934	11.2	9.9	6.6	7.0
April 1934	7.8	7.2	9.5	5.6
November 1934	10.7	14.2	8.4	7.4
March 1935	13.5	8.7	11.2	7.8

*FERA not yet functioning in this county.

No one in authority at the relief offices thought that the
Negroes had more opportunities to work or more surplus resources than the whites. The most common explanation of the
higher proportion of whites on relief was that the Negroes could
live on less, and that even though more of them had been cut
off during cotton-chopping and cotton-picking time, it was in
response to the prevalent belief of the planters that "most any
nigger who wants to work can get something to do." In view
of the farm incomes by race and tenure class, and in view of the
employment of scarcely any Negroes in the cotton mills at
Greensboro and Union Point and in the knitting mill at Monte-

[2] The data in this table and on subsequent pages were compiled from
records in the FERA offices in Atlanta, and from data obtained from the
offices of the FERA Administrators of Greene and Macon counties.

"ON THE COUNTY"—THIS EX-SLAVE REMEMBERS A GREAT DEAL ABOUT
SLAVERY IN GREENE COUNTY

"ON THE COUNTY"—$1.50 A MONTH

ROOSEVELT HURT—HE IS THE YOUNGEST OF SEVEN LIVING CHILDREN (TWO DEAD
THE OLDEST OF WHICH IS THIRTEEN. HE WAS BORN THE DAY THE FAMILY GOT
RELIEF AND WAS NAMED FOR THE PRESIDENT

zuma—the three largest nonfarm employers in these counties—
it is evident that the proportion of Negroes will exceed the
proportion of whites when the relief is administered on a basis
of need.

During the period of the textile strike, September and October, 1934, the white proportion was much higher, particularly
in Greene, than during any of the months shown. In one month,
October, over two-thirds of all expenditures were for textile
workers. By November 5 only four of the mill families were
still on the relief roll, and two of these had temporary sickness. The other two, with records of ineffective work in the
mills, seemed to be more or less chronic relief cases.

Geographic Distribution of Relief Cases.—The small town
dwellers have received the lion's share of the various monies
spent in these counties for relief. Of Macon's 491 CWA workers during the winter of 1933-1934, over three-fifths were residents of Montezuma, Marshallville, Oglethorpe, and Ideal,
which have roughly one-fourth of the county's population; of
Greene's 124 CWA workers over two-thirds were residents of
the towns, which contain scarcely one-fourth of the county's
population. The total relief load in November, 1934, showed
about the same distribution, with a tendency toward an increase
in the open country. As the rural rehabilitation program becomes more extensive, it is to be hoped that the needy families
living on the farms will receive a service commensurate with
that which is already available for town dwellers.

Relief in the rural communities is still controlled largely by
the landlord: first, the tenants and wage hands hardly dare ask
the relief office for help unless the landlord concurs; second, the
applicant often has little chance of securing aid unless recommended, "vouched for," by the leading white farmer of his community; third, a complaint from a landlord that a relief client
refused to work for him may result in his being dropped from
the roll.

Types and Amount of Relief by Race.—In general the white
person on relief has fared much better than the Negro. In

March, 1934, the average monthly expenditure for direct relief in Greene was $2.89 per white person and $2.30 per Negro, in Macon $2.52 per white and $1.19 per Negro. The CWA expenditures from November to April (1933-1934) in Greene averaged $130.80 per white and $74.00 per Negro worker; in Macon $173.05 for the white and $134.14 for the Negro.[3] Of Greene's forty-seven skilled CWA workers only two were Negroes; of Macon's ninety skilled workers, sixteen were Negroes —twelve from Montezuma alone. In November, 1934, the average white work-relief family in Greene received a total of $7.73, while the Negro received $7.25; in Macon the figures were $11.62 and $6.24 per white and Negro family respectively.

The distribution of surplus food commodities further reflects the racial differential in relief. In Greene, November 1934, 186 of the 196 white families on relief received money either for work relief or for direct relief. But of the 225 Negro families on relief 143 received money, while 82 received only beef and rice. The amounts of these surplus products per white and Negro family, however, were practically the same, between five and six pounds of each per family per month. In Macon, too, money went more often to the whites and surplus foods more often to the Negroes.

Emergency Relief Teachers.—Since the Fall of 1933 some unemployed teachers have been on the payroll of the FERA in these counties, first at a salary of $60 per month and later between $40 and $60, depending upon their qualifications, with the same salary scale for white and Negro teachers. In March 1934, Greene had three such teachers, all white, and Macon seven, five white and two colored; the three white teachers in Greene were employed to relieve the congestion in white schools. When asked why no Negro teachers were used to relieve the greater congestion there, the county school superintendent an-

---

[3] The CWA wages were the same for whites and Negroes; the difference in total wages resulted from: (1) the greater proportion of skilled workers among the whites, (2) the greater number of work hours given the whites (due largely to the laying off of Negroes before whites in the spring of 1934).

swered that there were no extra rooms for them to teach in. In mid-September 1934, Greene had four whites and no Negroes; Macon had three whites and one Negro. By March 1935, due in part at least to instructions from the central office, five of Greene's twelve[4] were Negroes, as were also five of Macon's twelve.

Even after this improvement there was an average of 1,323 Negroes per teacher in Greene and 2,232 in Macon, in contrast with 854 and 779 whites per white teacher in the respective counties. On the basis of illiterates there was one white teacher in Greene to every 12.1 white illiterates and one Negro teacher to every 223 Negro illiterates; in Macon there was one white teacher to every 16.3 white illiterates and one Negro teacher to every 491 Negro illiterates. These figures, representative of scores of counties in Georgia alone, define a project in which the Federal Emergency Relief Administration might well have utilized a larger number of the unemployed Negro teachers who have accumulated around Atlanta, Nashville, Raleigh, New Orleans, and other cities. The state FERA officials would have found it much easier to get the county school superintendents to accept Negro teachers from other counties if the Washington office had ruled that in counties without qualified teachers on relief surplus unemployed teachers from other counties should be employed.

Rural School Term Maintenance.—With many of the rural schools of Georgia about to close at the end of January 1934, the State Department of Education secured $1,601,995.79 from the FERA to maintain regular school terms at prevailing salaries for teachers, meaning that the white teachers received larger salaries and for a longer period. The outcome was that 86.8 per cent of the total went to white teachers and 13.2 per cent to Negro teachers—the federal funds being used to finance the racial differentials imposed by Georgia's 159 autonomous county boards of education. It is to be hoped that educational

---

[4] This figure includes two white nursery school teachers.

needs rather than county-made racial differentials will be the basis for the further allocation of federal funds.

The exact data for Greene and Macon counties are presented in the following table. The Negro teachers received a much smaller salary per month, and for a shorter term.

TABLE L

FERA EXPENDITURES BY MONTH, BY RACE, FOR MAINTENANCE OF RURAL SCHOOL TERMS IN GREENE AND MACON COUNTIES, GEORGIA, SPRING OF 1934[5]

Month	GREENE				MACON			
	WHITE		NEGRO		WHITE		NEGRO	
	No. of Teachers	Expenditure	No. of Teachers	Expenditure	No. of Teachers	Expenditure	No. of Teachers	Expenditure
February	46	$ 2,571.80	45	$ 962.75	21	$1,485.67	10	$ 337.50
March	55	3,464.30	48	1,057.75	21	1,485.67	10	337.50
April	54	3,532.30	48	1,057.75	40	2,776.67	50	1,105.00
May	48	3,124.30	3	95.00	44	2,786.67	13	422.50
Total	203	$12,692.70	144	$3,173.25	126	$8,534.68	83	$ 2,202.50
Average monthly salary	..	$ 62.52	..	$ 22.03	..	$ 64.56	..	$ 26.53

Rural Rehabilitation.—In November 1934 fifteen farm families in Greene were on the rural rehabilitation list, twelve white and three colored; of Macon's fourteen families on this list, six were Negroes. In each county the Negro families were said to be doing as well as the white families, and sometimes better. The best "rehab" family in Greene was colored, the second best white, with the other two Negro families falling into third and fourth places, according to the County Administrator's statement. The extent to which the emphasis was placed on the matter of reducing their indebtedness may be surmised from the fact that the prize "rehab" had come into the relief office in the fall with nearly $100, the largest amount repaid by any one of the fifteen families.

In March 1935 Greene had seventy-five families on rural

[5] Data compiled from records in the office of the Georgia FERA Administrator.

rehabilitation, fifty-three whites and twenty-two Negroes; Macon had fifty-three, of which fifteen were Negroes. The proportions of the population on rural rehabilitation by race were: 5.2 per cent of Greene's whites and 2.1 per cent of her Negroes, 3.8 per cent of Macon's whites and less than 1.0 per cent of her Negroes. Even though the Negro and white families in this program are supposed to share alike, which they not always do, the relatively greater number of whites benefiting from it when the need among the Negro group is relatively greater further demonstrates the fact that race is a determinant of relief in these counties. As the rural rehabilitation program progresses, it will be necessary for the county, state, and federal administrators to check at regular intervals to make certain that the service is reaching Negroes as well as whites.

Civilian Conservation Corps.—The benefits of the Civilian Conservation Corps in these counties have been limited almost wholly to the whites. When the first recruits were secured the local agents in these counties assumed that only whites should make application; no word was sent from state or federal offices to correct their orthodox "Solid South" assumption, until after the first quota had been filled. Thirty white boys went from Macon, a slightly smaller number from Greene. Months later, two Negro boys went from Macon and a couple from Greene— but in these two Black Belt counties the CCC has remained a white institution, with no more coloring than landownership, which tolerates the possession of one acre in twenty by Negroes.

The CCC has been satisfactory to the whites because many of the families with eligible applicants have been accepted, and many families not needing this form of relief have been relieved of the responsibility of assisting those who did. Then, too, the boys come back from the camps hale and hearty and ready to work, which is not without meaning in some white families where the young men have felt that work was undignified and unbecoming to them.

Work Relief Projects

The CWA and FERA expenditures for work relief projects through March 1935 in Greene amounted to $43,633.45 and in Macon to $103,501.26, more than nine-tenths of which was allocated from federal funds. These projects are correctly called work relief projects, for since April 1934 less than fifty cents out of each hundred dollars spent has gone into materials, the other $99.50 being spent for labor. It has been noted already how the different communities and races shared in the wages paid. But what community and which race were the completed projects designed to serve?

Here again the bulk of the benefits went to the towns and to the white people. In the following table are shown the total expenditures by CWA and FERA in each county for projects serving the whites, the Negroes, and the general public. Included in the projects serving the general public are all expend-

TABLE LI

EXPENDITURES BY CWA AND FERA FOR WORK RELIEF PROJECTS, BY RACE, IN GREENE AND MACON COUNTIES, GEORGIA, THROUGH MARCH, 1935[6]

PROJECTS FOR:	GREENE		MACON	
	CWA	FERA	CWA	FERA
Whites only....................	$13,899.65	$11,695.83	$17,025.97	$ 4,645.66
Negroes only..................	785.42	1,421.44	3,270.52	682.28
General community............	2,837.80	12,993.31	56,495.34	21,381.49
Total........................	$17,522.87	$26,110.58	$76,791.83	$26,709.43

itures for clerical help in administrative offices and for all supervision of projects.

Projects for Whites Only.—Nearly four-fifths of the $17,-522.87 spent by the CWA in Greene was for projects which served whites only, such as the repairing and enlarging of white schools, the employment of white school teachers, and the erection of a basketball shell and dressing room at a white high school. Of the $26,110.58 spent in Greene by the FERA for

[6] Data from state FERA offices in Atlanta and from Greene and Macon County FERA offices.

work relief projects, $11,169.83 served only whites, and included sewing classes, teachers to relieve congestion in schools, renovation of school auditorium, cleaning fifteen rural schools, building a community house, conducting a nursery school and providing a playground supervisor.

In Macon the CWA spent $76,791.83 for work relief projects, with $17,025.97 going into the white community for the enlargement of a white school, the improvement of a white park, the installation of a water toilet in a white school. Of the $26,709.43 expenditure for work relief projects by the FERA in Macon County, $4,645.66 went for whites only and included the completion of a school enlargement and the employment of a vocational teacher.

Projects for Negroes Only.—The expenditure for projects which served only the Negroes were small in both counties; in Greene $2,206.86 by CWA and FERA and in Macon $3,952.80. Scarcely one-tenth as much was put into the projects in Greene County serving Negroes as was put in projects for the whites, in Macon one-seventh as much for Negroes as for whites.

The Negro projects in Greene included the employment of teachers, and the painting and calcimining of the Junior High School at Greensboro—only Negro schoolhouse in either county to benefit thus far by federal relief expenditure, in contrast with $26,859.84 devoted to the improvement of white schools in these counties. In Macon the projects serving Negroes only included a sewing class, repairs to streets and sidewalks in a Negro section of Montezuma, and employment of school teachers.

Throughout both counties, there were things which needed to be done and which the Negroes were trying to get help on. A work relief project of $1,284.00 for the East Over Negro School, in Greene, was submitted to the state administrator's office, as were also projects for a Negro community house near Greensboro and two other Negro school projects. Not one of these was approved, despite the fact that similar projects were being carried forward for the whites. The nonracial explanations of why scarcely any of the Negro projects have material-

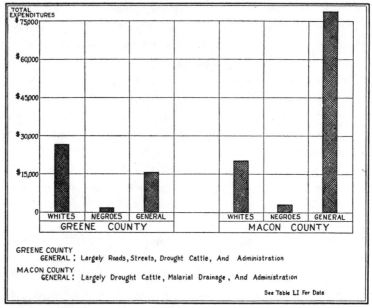

TOTAL EXPENDITURES BY THE FEDERAL GOVERNMENT (CWA AND
FERA) FOR WORK RELIEF PROJECTS IN GREENE AND MACON
COUNTIES THROUGH MARCH, 1934
SHOWING AMOUNT SPENT ON PROJECTS SERVING WHITES ONLY,
NEGROES ONLY, AND THE COMMUNITY AS A WHOLE

ized are singularly unconvincing.[7]   There is urgent need that
the federal government take care that its resources serve the
needs of all elements of these Black Belt communities.

Projects Serving the General Community.—In Greene
$15,831.11 was spent on projects serving the general commun-
ity.   This included: repairs on the relief office, road and street
repairs and construction, sewer extension, care of cattle from

---

[7] The fact that many Negro projects failed to qualify because they lacked
the "required local sponsors and material subscriptions" only emphasizes the
rôle of race as a determinant in the selection of projects, only emphasizes the
fact that the local public officials sponsor and provide resources for white
projects more readily than for Negro projects.   It is well-nigh inevitable
that such will be the case so long as the Negro is without representation on
the board of county commissioners, school board and the like.   It would seem
that the federal agency which puts up practically all the money should share
with the local officials in determining the projects upon which the money is
spent.

the drought area, fight on the screwworm, supervision of projects, assistants for the county agent, and a small amount for malarial drainage. For general projects $77,876.83 was spent in Macon, two-thirds of it for malarial drainage alone; the next largest for pit privies, and smaller sums for the eradication of the phony peach, for the emergency landing field at Montezuma, community sanitation, care of government cattle from the drought area, sewer extension, repairing the relief office, personnel and repairs of building, comforter making, clerical assistance for the administrative offices, and the supervision of projects.

A truly county-wide project was the immunization of Greene County's children against diphtheria. The immunization was sponsored by the Georgia Child Welfare Council, and was made possible in Greene by an allocation of $75 by the County Commissioners, a like amount by the County Board of Education, $25 by the Red Cross, and the donation of a trained nurse by the FERA to supervise the project. The nurse and a doctor went to each school, white and colored, in the county. A white doctor was used in the white schools and the county's only Negro doctor was used in the colored schools. Preschool children, even babes in arms, were brought. It was really a county-wide service, for even though a fee of twenty-five cents was asked, any person who could not pay it was served without cost. This project seems to demonstrate that a rural county can co-operate with the federal government in serving all the people.

Representative Reactions

At almost any place in these counties where people come together, various reactions to the New Deal and particularly to the relief program will be heard. Some will say that it is ruining labor, others that it is all wrong, or that it is doing some good, or that it is indispensable. As a general rule, the elements of the population supporting the cotton reduction program are the least kindly disposed to the emergency relief program, and vice versa.

"Just a 'Moralizing Labor."—These are the words of a

small business man in Montezuma, Macon County. "The New Deal, particularly the relief, is ruining labor—just a 'moralizing it," he said. Representative of many others, he cited case after case where some person on relief had refused work that was offered: women had stopped doing laundry work, yardmen no longer reported for their day's work a week, and it had become well-nigh impossible to go down the street and pick up a fellow to do a half-day's work when you needed him.

One case is reported of a Greene County man on relief who advised the people in his community to stop working for the prevailing wage—forty to eighty cents a day—and get on work relief at $2.40 a day, with free food when there was no work. He was warned and was promptly dropped from the relief roll. A second case, also in Greene, was that of two white boys who were accused of refusing to pick beans, but the relief office's investigation revealed that the beans were so small and so light that scarcely a dollar a week could be earned at the rate of pay offered. The boys remained on relief.

"*This Relief is All Wrong.*"—According to a large planter at Montezuma, the rural rehabilitation is no better than the other forms of relief. "In fact," said he, "it is often worse, because it puts on farms families that no planter in the community would be willing to risk money on; by helping the worst, it puts a premium upon improvidence and idleness—I tell you, this relief is all wrong."[8]

So opposed was a group of planters in eastern Macon to the emergency relief administration that they appointed a committee to investigate the matter. Thus far the investigation has amounted to little.

In Marshallville, also within the big plantation area, it was currently reported among the planters that practically all the money which the relief office spent on Negroes there found its way into the hands of professional gamblers, who came into the community each week. This was first suspected when strange

[8] But in the late fall of 1935, this planter stated that Macon County's "Rehab" families were in better condition than most other tenant families. He referred particularly to the variety of foodstuffs they had raised for the winter.

Negroes were observed in local gambling games shortly after the relief money had been received. Tending to corroborate this impression was their hurried checkup at local stores which revealed that the sales had not increased nearly so much as would be expected from the amount of relief money which came into the community.

All kinds of objections were made—it was maintained by some that the home towns of the key people in the county relief offices had secured more than their share of the approved work projects and of successful applications for relief. In Greene County, Union Point, Penfield, and White Plains were supposed to be getting more than their share, while in Macon the most unusual accusation was that the Baptist applicants in one community were accepted more readily than Methodists, who were equally numerous and equally poor. An examination of the list revealed that over four-fifths were Baptists.

Not all the propertied people, however, are opposed to federal relief. The owner of several scores of Negro houses in Montezuma found the services quite beneficial, since he had little difficulty in collecting his weekly rent of fifty cents after the relief was given. A number of merchants, too, found their business increasing appreciably; some of the planters liked the relief, for it facilitated the shift from croppers to wage hands.

"The Emergency Relief is Indispensable."—Except for the emergency relief, many of the local people claim, intense and prolonged suffering would have occurred among the poorer classes. The local methods of relief were entirely inadequate, even the Red Cross was proving to be ill equipped in personnel and resources for so large a task.

The fact that the relief office has taken care of the least capable families in the community is significant, for these are the people who, for whatever reason, find it most difficult to maintain themselves. The farm families that the plantation owners thought beyond use were the very ones in the greatest need, and it is a bit paradoxical for the planters to find fault with the relief office for taking care of the families which they could not or would not use.

Note this case: A request came to the Macon County relief office that a certain relief client in Montezuma be taken off the roll because he had refused to work when offered a job. An investigation revealed that two weeks earlier the man on relief had worked for the man making the complaint, but that his day's wage of seventy-five cents had not yet been paid. Word was sent back to the employer that he should make no request for people to be left off relief when he had used their services and had not paid them.

Commenting upon this and similar cases a leading citizen remarked that it is not wrong for the government to feed our "sorriest people"; that they are the first left off when there is a shrinkage of jobs. He went on to say that the planters who are now grumbling about the relief program do not need and will not use these people on relief; that they may give them a day's work now and then, but they do not want them in their houses and they will not assume any responsibility for them.

In both counties there were continuous complaints that improvident and lazy people were given work relief or direct relief and were otherwise encouraged to remain idle, while the most deserving people—cripples, invalids, and other handicapped persons—often were offered little or no assistance. The answer to this, of course, is that these unemployables were considered the charges of the local communities, and the federal government proceeded upon the assumption that the local communities had regular services for this group. This assumption, however, is far from true where the only assistance rendered to handicapped persons is the county poor fund, described above. Despite its many announcements to the contrary, the federal relief program has continued to render assistance to a large number of unemployables in each county.

"... *When Relief and Employment Compete.*"—One hears on every hand that the relief program pampers its clients, that often they live better than the families who work, that the Black Belt employer cannot pay wages anywhere near the work relief wage scales, that the workers will all be getting on relief

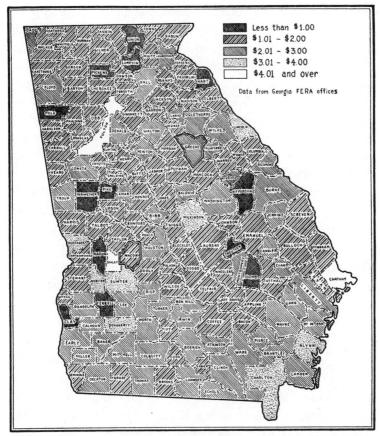

EXPENDITURES PER PERSON PER MONTH ON DIRECT RELIEF,
MARCH, 1934

if they can—in short, "Things have come to a poor pass when
relief and employment compete." Part of the answer to these
fears is that the relief, as shown above, is quite low in these
counties and seems to be geared to maintain life rather than to
raise living standards.

But even maintaining physical efficiency represents an advancement for many families, accustomed to rickets and pellagra.
When complaints came to a relief worker that the food which
her clients received was better than the workers could buy from
their wages, her reply was that if she gave them less there would

be a recurrence of the dietary deficiency diseases. The situation is simply this: the relief's minimum standards of physical efficiency can compete with regular employment only when regular employment does not provide the resources with which to maintain physical efficiency.

These and other Black Belt counties, along with the rural South as a whole, have reaped real benefits from the New Deal, for even though the South was the scene of the lowest wages under the NRA and has often had a lower rate for work relief and direct relief than other sections, the employment of CWA workers and unemployed teachers and the administration of the federal loan services and the AAA in the South have approximated the national standard. This application of national or regional standards has created relative prosperity in the Black Belt and the rural South, the area of the nation's lowest wages and lowest planes of living, by reducing the normal differential between it and the high wage areas. Herein lies the explanation of the frequent news stories that the South, particularly the rural South, is leading the nation in its recovery.

Inadequate relief will continue the rickets and pellagra, the high morbidity, the high mortality among the landless farmers of the South. Adequate relief will disturb labor conditions in many communities, because it will offer more than many of the landless farmers have been receiving from their employment. The solution of the dilemma lies in the readjustment of man to land in the local community and of the entire region to the economy of the nation.

The need for raising the general plane of living in the Black Belt is rendered the more difficult by the complacency of the dominant political, educational, and religious leadership of the region. As we shall see in the following chapters, the institutions of Greene and Macon counties are in need of revitalization. Nothing short of a shift of emphasis from land to man will release these Black Belt counties from the economic and cultural deterioration which now characterizes them.

PART SIX

Institutions

CHAPTER XV

GENERAL OR BIRACIAL INSTITUTIONS

THERE ARE MANY places in a Black Belt county where white people and Negroes mix and mingle every day of the year. Most common among the general or biracial institutions are small town and country stores, filling stations and cotton gins, cotton warehouses and banks, doctors' and lawyers' offices, post offices and county courthouses—including the courtroom and jail near by—the offices of the county relief administrator, county farm agent, and county superintendent of schools.

STORES, GINS, BANKS, OFFICES

It is the fact that the two races have the same government and the same kind of money that occasions the presence of biracial institutions. Cultural institutions—educational, religious, social—are separate and distinct for each race.

Small Town and Country Stores.—During the year more white people and Negroes come together at the small town and country stores than at any other place in Greene and Macon counties. To a great portion of the whites and Negroes the store is the place to "hang out" on cold or rainy days; it is also the place to buy food and clothing, as well as the place to meet with the people of the community to transact business.

A large proportion of the "trading" between landlords and tenants is carried on around the store, for it is generally considered bad taste for one landlord to go on the land of another to secure tenants. The sale of land to Negroes by whites is often first mentioned and eventually arranged at the country store. Many a Negro landowner copies the methods of some local white planter, and it is at the store that he asks him questions and hears how he fixes the land for the early corn, which variety of cotton he has been planting since the weevil came, what kind of land to sow in spring oats. These contacts, in many instances,

[275]

have done much to improve the farming of Negro owners and renters.

The country store is to the isolated rural Black Belt community what the county seat is to the Black Belt county, what Atlanta is to Georgia, what New York is to the United States.

Consciousness of Color.—Both races frequent the same store, at the same time, for the same purpose; whites and blacks stand together at the counter and buy. Negroes can buy anything, in any part of the store, at any time they have the money or credit to secure it. The members of the two races, however, mingle in the store only when they occupy the status of prospective purchasers, only when they are moving.

As soon as the Negroes have finished their buying, they tend to move off to themselves. When a Negro goes to sit down at the stove, he just naturally, it seems, sits by a member of his own race. Other Negroes drift in and the "Negro side" of the stove, which may be any side, reaches two-thirds around; half an hour later the "white side" may take up two-thirds of the circle. All day long this circle around the stove gradually changes its racial complexion, with almost no intermixing of the races. The seating is not prearranged, and doubtless the sitters themselves are unaware of the typical arrangement, which anyone may observe for himself by "hanging around" a store in the rural portions of either county. The fact that the Black Belt store is a social center as well as a business establishment is further discussed in a later chapter.

A Negro-Owned Country Store.—With one exception, all the open-country stores of any consequence in Greene and Macon counties are owned and operated by whites. West of the Flint River in Macon County, about three miles northwest of Oglethorpe, at a crossroads called New York, is a store owned and operated by a Negro, son of one of the county's early landowning families. The range of goods and the general upkeep of the store make it one of the best in the rural sections of the county, though not one of the largest.

In 1907, at the age of twenty-five, the present owner and

operator, after having worked a few years for a wholesale grocer in Americus, decided to open a store. He had a dozen or so accumulated dollars and he believed that if he could make money for somebody else he could make money for himself. His first store, a box-like affair, was replaced after a few years with a larger one to accommodate his growing business; about a decade ago, when the second building had been outgrown, he rolled it aside and built another. The stock of goods now offered for sale includes Gulf gasoline, lubricating oils, kerosene; salt brick for stock, mule collars, plow lines, plow points; onions, potatoes, oranges, eggs, butter; assortment of NBC products, loaf bread; salt and sugar (100 lb. bags); extracts, carbonated drinks, candy, tobacco; face powder, hair straightener, Vick's products, patent medicines; stockings, gloves, spool thread, shoe soles; knives, shot gun shells, red cedar buckets, nails, axes, and handles for all sorts of tools.

The Negro storekeeper estimated that two-thirds of his business is with white people. Just across the road is the only other building in this New York, a smaller store operated by a white man. There has never been any friction between them, so the Negro storekeeper reported. With the exception of the losses of small amounts of money, tobacco, and candy in two burglaries a decade ago, no one has ever molested him or his property in any way. When asked why there was no other Negro country store in the county, he said: "Don't want them I guess; if they would conduct their business right and tend to their own business, colored people could own stores all around here."

Turn-Taking and Its Meaning.—Turn-taking is the general practice at most places of business. Automobiles are served according to their turn at the filling stations. Except in rare cases, the color of the driver has little to do with the promptness of the service rendered.

At the cotton gins, too, the whites and Negroes are served in turn according to arrival. This practice is strictly adhered to by all the larger gins which advertise to serve the public. The cotton warehouses also practice turn-taking but serve mostly white people, for much of the Negro's ginned cotton is left in the hands of white landlords or sold to cotton agents who buy direct from the gin.

Sooner or later turn-taking may spread to all the retail business in the Black Belt communities; even now the practice is followed in some of the rural stores. The wide-awake store-keeper does not want his place to be a community lounging house, except in so far as it is necessary to tolerate the customs of the past in order to get the trade of the present and the future. One storekeeper stated that he approached every person, regardless of color, as he walked in the door. The man who wants to make a purchase appreciates quick service, and the one who never wants to buy anything, whether white or black, gets tired of being bothered and finds some other place to "hang out."

What is the explanation and probable significance of the practice of turn-taking which has developed at the filling stations and cotton gins and at some of the rural stores? The explanation, to put it bluntly, is that good business dictates turn-taking —both races have the same kind of money and cotton. If not satisfied at one station, the customer who has cash for gasoline goes elsewhere to buy. The man with cotton in his wagon is in position to pay for its ginning and expects to be treated as a buyer rather than a beggar. The practice is significant because the Negro knows his place is determined by the order of his arrival rather than the color of his skin. This gives him a taste of self-respect.

Banks.—Members of both races patronize the banks; turn-taking is usually but not always practiced. There are four state banks in Greene County, two at Union Point and one each at Greensboro and Siloam. In Macon County there is one national bank at Montezuma, two state banks at Marshallville and one state bank at Oglethorpe. The decrease of total resources and deposits in banks in these counties between 1918 and 1934 is shown in the accompanying table. Greene's deposits in 1933, it will be observed, were scarcely one-third what they were in

TABLE LII
TOTAL RESOURCES AND DEPOSITS, ON DECEMBER 30, IN ALL NATIONAL AND
STATE BANKS IN GREENE AND MACON COUNTIES,
GEORGIA, 1918-1934[1]

YEAR	GREENE		MACON	
	Total Resources	Deposits	Total Resources	Deposits
1918.........	$1,139,088	$565,558	$2,783,888	$1,707,115
1920.........	1,328,261	714,887	1,763,548	838,428
1928.........	507,064	348,747	1,039,034	725,175
1933.........	387,023	252,552	622,093*	411,511*
1934.........	525,168	342,682	1,068,435	682,015

*Estimated.

1920, Macon's scarcely one-fourth. At the end of 1934, it will be observed, the resources and deposits in each county were about 50 per cent higher than at the end of 1933, approximating in every instance the 1928 figures. That most of this increase during 1934 is directly traceable to federal loans and crop control measures is discussed elsewhere.

The deposits of Negroes, which have always been comparatively small, are reported by local bankers to have decreased even more rapidly than total deposits. While some of the Negro accounts belonged to farmers, preachers, teachers, and owners of small shops in the towns, a considerable portion of it belonged to various Negro lodges and societies. The bank officials, all of whom are white, have not been opposed to Negro depositors; some have even invited them to use their banks and in a few cases have assisted them into landownership by giving them moral backing and arranging the necessary credit.

The failures of banks in Greensboro, Union Point and White Plains between 1922 and 1925 and in White Plains and Ideal since then, coupled with the reorganization of the banks in Montezuma and Oglethorpe, resulted in considerable losses and have made a great proportion of the whites and Negroes of both counties very shy of banks. Significantly enough, the small bank at Siloam, in the heart of the white land section, is the only one in Greene which survived the depression. The

[1] Data obtained from Banker's Blue Book and from Federal Reserve Bank in Atlanta.

national bank at Montezuma, organized about six years ago, has resources (June, 1934) of $289,000 and deposits of $202,000, making it by far the largest bank in either county.

Lawyers' and Doctors' Offices.—The offices and homes of Black Belt lawyers and doctors are frequented by members of both races at almost any hour of the day or night. There being no Negro lawyer in either county, no Negro physician in Macon and but one in Greene, the Negroes are wholly dependent upon the white lawyers for legal counsel, and largely dependent upon white doctors for medical service. The single Negro physician in Greene has a large practice among his own race and occasional white patients.

There seems to be no limitation upon the Negro's calling upon the white lawyer and doctor, except that he remember his racial identity and act accordingly, which means that he will call only when he wants service and that, except in the greatest emergencies, he will not go into a doctor's or lawyer's office until the white clients are leaving. On the other hand, a group of waiting Negroes do not keep white people from taking chairs. Those waiting may then be taken according to their turn, or the late white comers may be served immediately, no one being disturbed in the least, or even realizing, apparently, that it might have been otherwise. Whether a Negro appears at a lawyer's or doctor's office does not depend so much upon his ability to pay as upon his acquaintance with and acceptance by the white professional man; much service is outright gratis, or put on books with little expectation of more than a partial settlement.

POST OFFICES AND COURTHOUSES

Negroes and whites use the same stores and banks because they have the same kind of money. They use the same post office and courthouse because they have the same government.

United States Post Offices.—Even though the post office is sometimes referred to by Negroes as "the white folks' post office," they demonstrate that they trust it more than any other institution serving both races in the Black Belt community. They often buy money orders for mail order houses; they send and receive letters containing discussions which would not be tolerated if known by the local white community. Their confidence is seldom violated. The United States Post Office is practically immune to the dominant local white assumption that the Negro's rights are nowhere outside the reach and control of white public opinion.

Why do Negroes trust the post office? There are federal standards of performance, federal employees, inspectors, and federal courts to punish offenders. Does federal patronage further help to explain the situation? It may be so, for the local Black Belt postmasters under the Republican administration have been more or less dependent for their appointment and continuance in office upon local Negro Republican leaders.[2] Still further recommending itself to Black Belt Negroes, the post offices of all larger southern cities employ considerable numbers of Negro mail carriers with civil service rating.

There are rural mail routes reaching into all parts of both counties; there are mail boxes at all owners' dwellings and they are as common among landless Negroes as among landless whites. Letters are about the only remaining ties between the people who migrated and those who remained.

The Courthouse and the County Seat Town.—In the Black Belt the county seat is a capital city and the courthouse is the capitol. Many new counties have been formed in Georgia since 1900, while two small counties have been absorbed by Fulton, already by far the strongest in the state. In practically every case the new county grew out of rivalry between the county seat and a newer town. And in other counties where the larger town is not at present the county seat, as in Macon County, an effort has been made to move the courthouse.

Greensboro is acceptable as the county seat, for it has been the largest town in Greene from the outset. In Macon, Ogle-

[2] These Negro Republican leaders, though usually unmolested by the whites, are sometimes driven out of the community and even killed. For a specific case of violence see Arthur Raper, *The Tragedy of Lynching* (Chapel Hill, N. C., 1933), pp. 172 ff.

thorpe was formerly the largest town and is still the county
. seat.   But the largest town is now Montezuma, just across the
Flint River and two miles from Oglethorpe.   Repeated attempts
have been made to make it the county seat.   If Montezuma
were on the border of Macon County instead of near the center,
a new county might be the result.   Fort Valley, just twenty-five
miles northeast of Montezuma, was the largest town in Houston
County until 1925, when it became the county seat of the newly
created Peach County.

In some of the southern states the state welfare officials have
emphasized the importance of consolidating county institutions,
such as poorhouses and jails; an effort is also being made to
interest groups of counties in the erection and maintenance of
district hospitals and other institutions which would serve several counties.[3]   Except for the emergency federal activities,
Greene and Macon counties remain sufficient unto themselves,
and whatever they are too small or too poor or too unimag-
inative to do must go undone.   There is no county welfare
officer, no full-time county health officer, no public health clinic,
no county nurse, no juvenile court judge or probation officer,
no Negro supervisor of schools, no Negro Farm or Home
Demonstration Agent in either county.

None the less, all the people of Greene and Macon counties
have business at the courthouse and the county seat town.   People buying or selling land get records of titles and deeds from
the courthouse; the property owners report there to pay taxes;
the males with and without property between twenty-one and
fifty years of age go there to pay poll taxes; persons who have
been mistreated personally or swindled out of property go to
present their case to get a court hearing; public-minded citizens
go there to request the county commissioners, or the grand jury,
or the board of education to improve roads and schools; persons
qualifying for pensions secure their checks from the federal

[3] See especially: F. W. Hoffman, *Counties in Transition* (University, Va.,
1929); and the *Biennial Report of North Carolina Board of Charities and
Public Welfare, 1926-1928*, and for following years.

government through courthouse officials; the prospective groom goes to the courthouse for a marriage license; the paupers or their friends report there to get their poor fund allowance; law violators, when apprehended, are taken by the courthouse, and, if the charge is a serious one, they are held at the county jail prior to their appearance in the courthouse, and not infrequently for a time thereafter as servants of the county at the convict camp. With the coming of the New Deal there are additional reasons for visits to the courthouse and county seat town: to receive instructions for plowing up cotton, checks for acreage reduction, ginning certificates; to make application for direct relief, rural rehabilitation, civil works employment, surplus food; to secure loans from the Farm Credit Administration, Federal Land Bank, Land Bank Commission, and Home Owners Loan Corporation; to request federal aid for schoolhouse repairs, road and bridge building, draining of swamps. Under the New Deal, even more than before, the county seat towns are the governmental, financial, and cultural centers of the masses.

Court Week a Festal Season.—Court week is still a kind of festal season in these Black Belt counties. Horse traders from miles around turn up at the county seat, along with persons securing subscriptions for the *Southern Ruralist* and the *Tri-Weekly Atlanta Journal*. At the noon recess on one side of the courthouse a patent medicine man, who takes a monkey around with him, proclaims the wonderful power of his herb concoction to relieve headaches immediately, to remove warts in two weeks, or to restore hair within two months. Another salesman, on the opposite side of the courthouse, has a black-faced white man hold a great snake high above his head and sing weird ballads until people, white and Negro alike, crowd in to see what is happening. A wonderful offer is made: The first ten purchasers can get two bottles of the world-renowned "Bitter Root Pain Remover" for the price of one. On another side of the courthouse square is a man with a five-piece band; he has books on practical medicine to sell, which explains in simple terms the most modern treatment for all the diseases known to man; each purchaser receives absolutely free, a wonderful knife sharpener. The horse traders have their stock out for exhibition and sale. The stores do a thriving business.

Not all the attractions of court week are outside the courthouse. Many cases are called. The paneling of juries makes it necessary for scores of white men to hang around while court is in session. Many of the cases coming up for trial are of general interest throughout the county; rural people with few contacts demonstrate intense interest in sensational cases, and their only way to get the latest news is to sit through the trial. Then, too, the majority of the people may be personally acquainted with some man who gets into court. When a murder is committed in a rural Black Belt community, practically everybody stops work and goes to the trial. To some extent, at least, the people of a rural county get from the courthouse and the country store what the city people are fed from day to day by sensational news writers who bring out special editions every few hours.

Levity in the "White Folks' Court."—To many white people in these counties there are few things more amusing than to hear a Negro woman tell how and why she "carved up" or "plugged" her "ole man." Levity in the courtroom is in evidence, too, when a keen lawyer begins to cross-examine a good-natured but ignorant Negro witness. Frequently the very sound of the frightened witness's voice seems to amuse a considerable portion of the white audience; and now and then when a Negro witness becomes overanxious to harmonize two different tales which a patronizing lawyer has coaxed him into telling, everybody present, regardless of color or position in the court, laughs uproariously.

Three things, it seems, account for the levity: first, the Negro is often much frightened and, being unaccustomed to cross-examination, falls into the ridiculous situation in which every lawyer tries to get his opponent; second, quite a few of the offenses for which Negroes are brought before the courts are things which many white people assume that Negroes do by

reason of their race—fornication, larceny; third, a great proportion of the whites in the rural Black Belt community seem to
assume that they are altogether unlike the Negro, and so they
do not share his anxiety.

COURTS, CRIMINALS, CRIMES

To all practical purposes, the Negro is tried in the "white
folks' court." The judge, the prosecutor, the jury, the clerk,
the sheriff, the jailer, the deputies, and the lawyers are white—
there is not a Negro lawyer in Greene or Macon County. In
the courtroom itself the Negroes sit in the balcony, or in the
corner traditionally set aside for them.

Juvenile Delinquency is Winked At.—With the exception
of minor cases disposed of by the justice of peace courts, all
men, women, and children offenders come before the superior
court in Greene, and before the county court or superior court
in Macon. There is no juvenile court; the misdeeds of children
are handled by these courts, or are ignored entirely. The superior court of Macon County sentenced a white boy convicted
of burglary to the Georgia Training School, an institution for
incorrigible youths. The general policy, however, toward the
youthful offender is to let him alone until he is "old enough" or
until he has committed such a serious offense that his case is automatically thrown into the superior court, rather than to help him
correct his habits before he gets into serious trouble.

Undesirable as this situation is, the fault does not lie with
the superior courts—they were not designed to take care of
juvenile delinquency. Since there is no public welfare officer,
no regularly organized juvenile court, no probation officer, the
counties virtually wink at juvenile offenders of both races.

Offenders by Race.—Since 1920 a marked change has taken
place in each county; the Negroes get into the courts less often
and the white people more often than formerly. In 1920 forty-
two cases came before the superior court of Greene, seven white
and thirty-five Negro; in 1927-1928 (July) there were forty-
eight cases, twenty whites and twenty-eight Negroes. This

same type of change took place in Macon in both the county court and the superior court: in 1920, there were forty-five cases, five whites, forty Negroes; in 1925, there were 166 cases, fifty-three whites, 113 Negroes; in 1927-1928 (July), there were eighty-two cases, thirty-three whites, forty-nine Negroes. The ratio of offenders by race, types of crimes committed, and punishment are said by officials to be about the same at present as in 1928.

Considering the total court cases for 1920 and 1925 and 1927-1928, the racial distribution of offenders in each county was as follows: In Greene, where approximately 60 per cent of the population was Negro during the period studied (1920-1928), 70 per cent of the cases brought before the superior court were Negroes; in Macon, where approximately 70 per cent of the population was Negro, 68.7 per cent of all offenders were Negroes.

Prosecutors and Witnesses.—In nearly half the Negro cases, as will be seen from the tables below, the prosecution was brought by Negroes. In Greene County superior court, five prosecutions against Negro defendants were brought by officers, twenty-five by white people, twenty-three by Negroes, ten not recorded. The Negro prosecutions in the Macon superior court were brought by officers in thirteen cases, by special presentment in twelve, by whites in twenty-six, and by Negroes in thirty-eight; in Macon's county court forty-five were brought by officers, eight by special presentment, nineteen by whites, and forty-one by Negroes.

It will be observed, too, that while white witnesses predominated in cases of white defendants, only Negro witnesses appeared in approximately half the cases of Negro defendants in the Macon courts: In Macon's superior court all witnesses were Negroes in twenty-nine cases, and in thirty-six additional cases part of the witnesses were Negroes; in the county court all the witnesses in fifty-five cases were Negroes. Not only do Negroes testify as witnesses when the defendant is a Negro, but in nine out of twenty-four white cases in the superior court of

Macon County all witnesses were Negroes. In one of these cases the prosecution also was brought by a Negro, and the white defendant was found guilty of intent to murder and sentenced to the roads for a period of two years; in four more of the cases where Negro witnesses testified against white defendants road sentences of from four to six months were given.

Crimes Charged by Race.—Crimes of violence, larceny, carrying concealed weapons, and burglary were the most common charges against Negroes. The violation of license laws, crimes of violence, and burglary were most common among the whites. There were six charges of rape in the two counties, two whites and four Negroes. In both white cases the prosecution was brought by whites; in all four Negro cases the prosecutions were brought by Negroes.

The solicitor of Macon County court, in commenting upon crimes of violence committed by Negroes, stated that in practically every case there is an absence of motive for murder. The usual situation is this: A crowd at a "mullet stew" or some other social affair will be possessed with a spirit of recklessness, not infrequently augmented by drinking. In the hilarity some Negro will say something of little consequence, but there will be a show of guns and razors and knives. As the crowd mills about, more drinking takes place and after a few hours they usually go home all tired out. Now and then, though, something does happen when some drunken fellow sticks his pet "Mary Anna" at another drunk, laughingly warns him: "Look out! I'll shoot!" and the snarling challenge comes back: "You shoot somebody—blah—folks what got calf livers don' shoot nobody." Later they are in court.

Threats of mob violence have occurred several times in each county since 1927. The three most recent instances in Greene are representative. A white rural mail carrier while on his route was killed from ambush. The evidence seemed to implicate a Negro man, who for safe-keeping was immediately carried to a prison in another county. In the second instance someone, said to have been a Negro, threw a rock into a parked car at night and injured the head of a white woman. In the third case a white woman, a cotton mill employee, returned to her home from the midafternoon shift with clothes mussed up, hair disheveled,

TABLE LIII

NUMBER OF DEFENDANTS BY RACE, SHOWING THE OFFENSE CHARGED, BY WHOM THE PROSECUTION WAS BROUGHT, AND THE DISPOSITION OF ALL CASES COMING BEFORE THE GREENE COUNTY SUPERIOR COURT IN 1920 AND 1927-1928[4]

Offense	Number Cases	Case Brought By				Disposition						Fines			Time				Optional Time or Fine*
		Officer	White	Negro	Unknown	Nol Pros	Not Guilty	Mistrial	Trial Pending	At Large	Bond	$10 to $49	$50 to $99	Costs	1-2 Years	5-6 Years	10 Years and Over	Unknown	
NEGRO:																			
Crimes of Violence	12	1	9	..	2	..	2	..	..	1	..	..	1	..	3	..	1	4	1
Burglary	5	..	3	2	..	..	1	2	..	1	..	..	..	..	1	..	..	..	..
Larceny	14	..	7	3	4	..	..	..	..	..	1	..	1	3	5	..	..	4	..
Forgery	1	..	1	..	..	..	..	..	..	..	..	..	..	..	..	..	..	1	..
Cheating and Swindling	3	..	1	1	1	..	..	..	3	..	..	..	..	..	..	..	..	..	..
Carrying Concealed Weapons	10	2	1	4	3	1	..	..	..	..	1	..	..	2	1	..	..	5	..
Domestic Negligence and Violence	..	..	..	..	..	..	..	..	..	..	..	..	..	..	..	..	..	..	..
Crimes vs. Morality	..	..	..	..	..	..	..	..	..	..	..	..	..	..	..	..	..	..	..
Rape	1	..	1	..	..	..	..	..	..	1	..	..	..	..	..	..	..	..	..
Disturbing Worship	..	..	..	..	..	..	..	..	..	..	..	..	..	..	..	..	..	..	..
Violating License Laws	1	1	..	..	..	..	..	..	..	..	..	1	..	..	..	..	..	..	1
Violating Prohibition Laws	..	..	..	..	..	..	..	..	..	..	..	..	..	..	..	..	..	..	..
All Others	16	1	3	12	..	..	1	..	..	..	1	7	..	..	1	..	..	6	..
Total	63	5	25	23	10	1	4	2	3	3	3	8	2	5	11	..	1	20	2
WHITE:																			
Crimes of Violence	7	..	7	..	..	4	..	1	..	..	..	..	..	2	..	..	..	..	..
Burglary	3	..	3	..	..	2	..	..	..	..	..	..	..	..	..	1	..	..	..
Larceny	6	..	6	..	..	..	..	..	..	3	..	..	..	..	3	..	..	..	..
Forgery	..	..	..	..	..	..	..	..	..	..	..	..	..	..	..	..	..	..	..
Cheating and Swindling	..	..	..	..	..	..	..	..	..	..	..	..	..	..	..	..	..	..	..
Carrying Concealed Weapons	2	..	1	..	1	..	..	..	..	..	..	..	..	..	..	..	..	2	..
Domestic Negligence and Violence	..	..	..	..	..	..	..	..	..	..	..	..	..	..	..	..	..	..	..
Crimes vs. Morality	..	..	..	..	..	..	..	..	..	..	..	..	..	..	..	..	..	..	..
Rape	2	..	2	..	..	..	..	..	..	2	..	..	..	..	..	..	..	..	..
Disturbing Worship	..	..	..	..	..	..	..	..	..	..	..	..	..	..	..	..	..	..	..
Violating Prohibition Laws	..	..	..	..	..	..	..	..	..	..	..	..	..	..	..	..	..	..	..
All Others	7	..	5	2	..	1	1	..	..	1	..	..	1	1	2	..	..	..	..
Total	27	..	24	2	1	7	1	1	..	6	..	..	3	1	2	4	..	2	..

*When a sentence was optional its disposition is listed under fines.

[4] Data compiled from records of the Clerk of Court, Greene County.

and incoherent allusions to "something terrible" having happened on the short path which lay between her home and the mill. Reports went out that she had been raped, that a Negro

TABLE LIV

NUMBER OF DEFENDANTS BY RACE, SHOWING THE OFFENSE CHARGED, BY WHOM THE PROSECUTION WAS BROUGHT, THE RACE OF THE WITNESSES, AND THE DISPOSITION OF ALL CASES COMING BEFORE THE MACON COUNTY SUPERIOR COURT IN 1920, 1925, AND 1927-1928[5]

OFFENSE	Number Cases	Officer	Special Presentment	White	Negro	White	Negro	Mixed	Nol Pros	Not Guilty	$10 to $49	$50 to $99	$100 to $499	$500 and Over	Costs	4-6 Months	7-11 Months	1-2 Years	3-4 Years	5-6 Years	7-9 Years	10 Years and Over	Institution	Optional Time or Fine*
NEGRO																								
Crimes of Violence	25	3	5	3	14	4	14	7	1	5	1	1	5	..	1	..	1	3	1	2	..	4	..	8
Burglary	21	3	..	12	6	9	3	9	2	2	..	3	2	..	1	..	2	3	2	1	3	..	..	5
Larceny	12	..	1	6	5	5	2	5	3	1	..	1	..	..	2	..	..	3	2	..	..	..	..	1
Forgery	7	3	1	1	2	1	..	6	1	1	1	1	1	1	2	..	..	2	1	..	..	..	..	2
Cheating and Swindling	..	..	..	..	..	..	..	..	..	..	..	..	..	..	..	..	..	..	..	..	..	..	..	..
Carrying Conc. Weapons	3	..	..	..	3	..	3	..	..	..	..	..	..	..	..	2	1	..	..	..	..	..	..	..
Domestic Vio. & Neglect	1	..	..	..	1	..	..	1	..	..	..	..	..	..	..	..	1	..	..	..	..	..	..	..
Crimes vs. Morality	6	..	3	1	2	1	3	2	1	..	..	1	4	..	..	..	..	..	..	..	..	..	..	4
Rape	3	..	..	..	3	..	2	1	..	..	..	..	1	..	..	..	..	1	..	1	..	..	..	1
Disturbing Worship	1	..	..	..	1	..	1	..	1	..	..	..	..	..	..	..	..	..	..	..	..	..	..	..
Viol. License Laws	2	1	1	..	..	2	..	..	..	..	..	1	..	..	1	..	..	..	..	..	..	..	..	1
Viol. Prohibition Laws	..	..	..	..	..	..	..	..	..	..	..	..	..	..	..	..	..	..	..	..	..	..	..	..
All Others	8	3	1	3	1	2	1	5	3	1	1	..	..	..	..	..	..	..	..	3	..	..	..	1
Total	89	13	12	26	38	24	29	36	11	9	4	6	13	1	7	..	5	14	6	4	6	4	..	23
WHITE																								
Crimes of Violence	2	..	..	1	1	1	1	..	1	..	..	..	..	..	..	..	..	1	..	..	..	..	..	..
Burglary	6	3	..	3	..	6	..	..	..	..	..	2	..	2	..	..	..	1	..	..	..	..	1	4
Larceny	..	..	..	..	..	..	..	..	..	..	..	..	..	..	..	..	..	..	..	..	..	..	..	..
Forgery	1	..	1	..	..	1	..	..	..	..	..	..	..	..	..	..	..	1	..	..	..	..	..	..
Cheating and Swindling	..	..	..	..	..	..	..	..	..	..	..	..	..	..	..	..	..	..	..	..	..	..	..	..
Carrying Conc. Weapons	2	..	2	..	..	..	2	..	..	..	..	..	..	2	..	..	..	..	..	..	..	..	..	..
Domestic Vio. & Neglect	..	..	..	..	..	..	..	..	..	..	..	..	..	..	..	..	..	..	..	..	..	..	..	..
Crimes vs. Morality	2	..	1	1	..	2	..	..	..	..	..	1	..	..	..	..	1	..	..	..	..	..	..	..
Rape	..	..	..	..	..	..	..	..	..	..	..	..	..	..	..	..	..	..	..	..	..	..	..	..
Disturbing Worship	2	..	2	..	..	2	..	..	..	..	..	..	..	2	..	..	..	..	..	..	..	..	..	..
Viol. License Laws	2	2	..	..	..	1	..	1	..	..	1	1	..	..	..	..	..	..	..	..	..	..	..	2
Viol. Prohibition Laws	1	1	..	..	..	1	..	..	1	..	..	..	..	..	..	..	..	..	..	..	..	..	..	..
All Others	6	..	4	2	..	..	4	2	2	3	..	..	1	..	..	..	..	..	..	..	..	..	..	..
Total	24	6	10	7	1	12	9	3	4	3	1	3	2	2	..	4	..	3	1	..	..	..	1	6

*When the sentence was optional its disposition is listed under fines.

[5] Data compiled from records of the Clerk of Court, Macon County.

was the offender. Suspect after suspect was taken before her
without identification. Three days later, despite the fact that
the report had been given credence by many of even the most

TABLE LV

NUMBER OF DEFENDANTS BY RACE, SHOWING THE OFFENSE CHARGED, BY
WHOM THE PROSECUTION WAS BROUGHT, THE RACE, OF THE WITNESSES,
AND THE DISPOSITION OF ALL CASES COMING BEFORE THE OGLE-
THORPE CITY COURT (MACON COUNTY COURT)
IN 1925 AND 1928[6]

OFFENSE	Number Cases	Case Brought By				Witnesses				Disposition										
												Fines				Time				Optional Time or Fine*
		Officer	Special Presentment	White	Negro	Officer	White	Negro	Mixed	Nol Pros	Not Guilty	$10 to $49	$50 to $99	$100 to $499	Costs	3 Months or Less	4-6 Months	7-11 Months	1-2 Years	
NEGRO																				
Crimes of Violence	6	1	..	..	5	..	1	5	..	2	..	..	2	..	2	..	..	..	..	4
Burglary																				
Larceny	15	4	..	6	5	1	3	10	1	3	2	..	3	..	5	..	2	..	..	4
Forgery																				
Cheating and Swindling	2	..	..	2	..	..	2	..	..	..	..	..	2	..	..	..	..	..	..	2
Carrying Concealed Weapons	25	10	5	1	9	6	3	16	..	7	2	..	9	2	2	..	1	1	1	13
Domestic Violence and Neglect	2	..	..	..	2	..	..	2	..	..	..	..	..	..	2	..	..	..	..	..
Crimes vs. Morality	2	..	..	..	2	..	..	2	..	2	..	..	..	..	..	..	..	..	..	..
Disturbing Worship	10	..	..	..	10	..	..	10	..	2	1	1	1	..	4	..	1	..	..	3
Violating License Laws	16	15	..	..	1	..	13	3	..	..	5	..	1	..	7	3	..	..	..	3
Violating Prohibition Laws	7	4	..	1	2	3	1	2	1	1	..	2	1	..	3	..	..	..	..	5
All Others	28	11	3	8	6	12	8	8	..	3	2	4	5	..	12	1	1	..	..	9
Total	113	45	8	19	41	35	21	55	2	25	7	8	23	2	37	4	5	1	1	43
WHITE																				
Crimes of Violence	7	5	..	2	..	5	2	..	..	2	..	..	..	..	5	..	..	..	..	1
Burglary	1	1	..	..	..	1	..	..	..	..	..	..	1	..	..	..	..	..	..	1
Larceny																				
Forgery																				
Cheating and Swindling																				
Carrying Concealed Weapons	1	..	..	..	1	..	..	1	..	..	..	..	1	..	..	..	..	..	..	..
Domestic Violence and Neglect	3	..	..	3	..	..	3	..	..	..	..	..	..	..	3	..	..	..	..	..
Crimes vs. Morality																				
Disturbing Worship																				
Violating License Laws	19	16	..	3	..	16	3	..	..	8	..	1	..	..	10	..	..	..	..	1
Violating Prohibition Laws	5	3	..	1	1	1	3	..	1	..	1	1	1	..	2	..	..	..	..	2
All Others	31	21	2	6	2	18	11	1	1	7	1	1	..	..	15	5	2	..	..	2
Total	67	46	2	15	4	41	22	2	2	17	2	3	3	..	35	5	2	..	..	7

*When the sentence was optional its disposition is listed under fines.

[6] Data compiled from records of the Oglethorpe City Court.

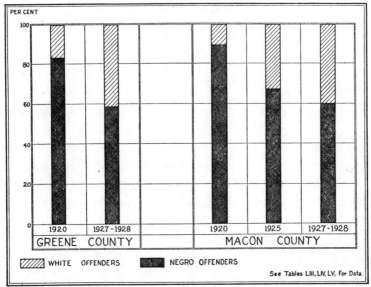

DISTRIBUTION BY RACE OF OFFENDERS BROUGHT BEFORE THE
COURTS OF GREENE AND MACON COUNTIES IN 1920, 1925, 1927-28

sober whites of the county, the sheriff reported that a full investigation had convinced him that the woman, addicted to dope,
had collapsed on her way home, and that some busybody jumped
to a conclusion of what had happened and spread the false
report.

COURT FINES AND CHAIN-GANG SENTENCES

Taking the two counties as a whole the Negroes received
longer road sentences than the whites. In Greene, however, as
will be seen by referring to the tables above, the Negro terms
did not average so long as those of the whites. The long sentences for Negroes in Macon seem to be due, in part at least, to
the more serious offenses of which they were convicted—murder,
and other crimes of violence, and burglary being common.

As is shown in the table below, the percentage of accused
Negroes convicted was but a little more than for the whites.
It will be observed, too, that except for the county court in
Macon approximately the same proportion of each received fines

TABLE LVI

THE PERCENTAGE DISTRIBUTION, BY RACE, OF DEFENDANTS WHO WERE
CONVICTED, SHOWING THE TYPE OF SENTENCE[7]

COURT	CONVICTED		FINED		OPTIONAL		CONVICT CAMP	
	White	Negro	White	Negro	White	Negro	White	Negro
Greene County Superior Court.......	37.0	42.8	14.8	20.7	0.0	3.1	22.2	19.0
Macon County Superior Court.......	70.8	77.5	8.3	7.9	25.0	25.8	37.5	43.8
Macon County Court..............	71.5	71.6	50.7	23.9	10.4	38.0	10.4	9.7

and optional fines or chain-gang sentences, and that a slightly
greater percentage of the white defendants than of Negro defendants were sent to the convict camp from the Green County
superior court and from the Macon County court.

The Optional Sentence and the Negro.—The actual number
of Negroes getting on the chain gang is much larger than is
suggested by these figures. The option of paying a fine or
serving time on the chain gang accounts in part for the excessive
number of Negroes serving road sentences, for, because of their
poorer economic condition, the Negroes cannot arrange to pay
the fine so easily as the whites. In the two counties there
were eighty-one optional sentences, thirteen to white defendants
and sixty-eight to Negro defendants. In Macon's superior court
some of the optional sentences were: 90 days or $25, 6 months
or $100, 6 months or $50, 12 months or $100, 12 months or
$150, 12 months or $60, 9 months or $150, and 12 months or
$1,000. This last case is the only instance in either county
where the defendant could make more than fifty-five cents per
day by going to the convict camp. In the typical sentence,
twelve months or $100, the defendant works off his unpaid fine
at the rate of twenty-seven cents per day. The relation between
size of fine and optional road sentence was practically the same
for Macon's county court. There were but two optional sentences in Greene.

Given the option of paying a fine or serving a road sentence,
all defendants with property, credit, or propertied friends pay

[7] Computed from Tables LIII, LIV, LV.

the fines. Also the defendants who are desirable workmen can get their fines paid, if workmen are needed. A white landlord will not let his cropper or renter who has received an optional sentence go to the roads when he is needed on the farm. Moreover, in some instances, optional sentences seem to have been given by the courts to protect the landlords against the loss of their tenants' labor, rather than to be lenient with the defendants.

Accommodating Courts.—At times when laborers have been in greatest demand in Greene and Macon counties, certain landlords have made it a practice to pay fines and get out on bail, when possible, any defendants who seemed to be desirable workmen. This practice has been virtually abandoned in Greene since 1923, in Macon since 1925. Prior to the weevil depression, in a county adjoining Greene an understanding existed between certain court officials and two or three big planters whereby Negroes lodged in the county jail were bonded out to them; other laborers were obtained by them through the payment of court fines. In at least one of these cases there is evidence to support a rumor that bonded-out and fine-paid Negroes were kept in the employ of the planter by coercive means. The bonding-out practice is essentially pernicious, for without close supervision offenders often skip trial and desert their families; with close supervision they are little better off than slaves.

It is not unusual for a Negro or white tenant's case, in all but the most serious offenses, to be delayed from the spring or summer term of court to the winter term. When a tenant's case is delayed to a later term the court places the defendant in the custody of the county sheriff or his landlord. The crops of such tenants are unusually well cultivated and harvested, for practically every tenant realizes that his landlord is the best possible friend before the courts. To what extent the interest of a white landlord influences a case cannot be measured, but a Negro defendant who has an influential local white man at court to testify to his good character has an invaluable ally. Just any white man, however, cannot be of service; unless the Negro defendant can secure the testimony of some very highly respected white man, he doubtless stands a better chance of "getting off light" by having only testimonials from members of his own race.

Judges in these two counties follow the general practice of appointing counsel for any defendant who comes before the court without a lawyer. Since there are only a few lawyers in these rural counties, the counsel thus provided is often as good as the defendant could have secured had he had the money to employ counsel. Here, as elsewhere, however, even a good lawyer makes a better presentation when he gets some money for his services and has had time to work on the case prior to the court hearing.

Despite the Negro's lower economic status and his lack of representation among the court officials, he comes into the courts only a little in excess of his proportionate numbers in the total population; he is found guilty by the courts in about the same proportion of cases as the white defendant; he serves road sentences more frequently than the white largely because he cannot so often pay the fine imposed. That he receives a longer road sentence than the white seems to be accounted for in large part by the more serious offenses of which he is convicted. There is always the probability, of course, that the charges brought against the defendants may reflect the dominant white community attitudes rather than measure the types of crimes committed. This possibility, however, does not help explain the Negro's more serious charges evident from the preceding records, for most of them involved only Negroes, and white public opinion is by no means so determined to keep the Negroes from committing crimes within their own group as outside of it.

Chain Gang Not a Misnomer.—There is a convict camp in both Greene and Macon counties, units of the state prison system, and chains are used in both. Some of the convicts will be seen without chains; others have shackles and double shackles, which have been welded upon their legs and which they wear for months at a time. From sun-to-sun, with one hour off for rest at noon (two hours in a few of the hottest months), these

men work with iron ankle bands connected by a chain to keep
them from taking a full step.

The real meaning of the chain gang, however, can best be
felt by seeing the Greene convicts put on the chain when they
come in at sundown. They form a line under the guards'
guns; each shackled convict steps upon a block, calls his number,
while the iron bands about his ankles are twisted and his shackle
chain is jerked to make certain the bands are tight; the convict
then takes the long chain from the convict in front of him and
passes it through the big central link of his shackle chain and
hands it back to the convict behind him, and so to the last one,
in whose shackles one end of chain is padlocked, as was the
other end in the shackles of the first man in line. Interestingly
enough, the ankle bands and shackles are usually tested by a
Negro convict, a trusty (commonly called a "trustee"). With
much clanking, the chain of men walk wide-legged through a
door, across the guards' observation quarters, and into a barred
room where they take their fill of convict's fare: fat-back meat,
corn bread, peas, and molasses, with now and then some vegetables and biscuits. After supper those who have bunks in this
room are taken off the big chain while eighteen are left on it
and are marched back through the guards' quarters to an adjoining shed room where there is a four-wheeled iron cage, about
six feet wide, eight feet high, and twenty feet long. Here they
are taken off the big chain, but never relieved of their iron ankle
bands and shackles. In this cage there is no heat, tarpaulins are
rolled down in cold weather; no running water; an open tub
under a hole in the floor serves all sanitary purposes. This
"Four Wheeler," formerly part of a movable camp, has been in
a shed under the camp's central roof for more than a decade.

In the back of the main room, where all the prisoners eat
and some of them sleep, there are wooden stocks, used to "break
the spirit" of prisoners not amenable to camp discipline. In
the yard, apart from the camp proper, there is a small building
like a box car. It can be used to segregate a sick prisoner, or
for solitary confinement; the door and four small port-hole

windows are equipped with solid, four-inch, tight-fitting shutters which make the enclosure light proof and well-nigh sound-proof, the walls and floor being of concrete.

In each county the public health officer, a part-time employee, provides medical service for the convicts. It is commonly reported that Greene County has been making money on its convict camp by getting more money from the state prison system than it has been spending on the state's prisoners within its care.

Chain-Gang Negroes and Kangaroo Courts.—With a few exceptions, all of Greene's thirty convicts and all of Macon's sixty are Negroes. Formerly it was unusual for a white man in either county to receive a road sentence. Although this is no longer the case, the convict population remains largely Negro through the policy of sending the whites to camps where all the convicts are whites. Likewise, Negroes from other counties are sent in.

There are intraprison governments in both camps. The following case of a chronic "lifter," referred to below as Alex, serves to illustrate the effectiveness of the prison government in the Macon convict camp. By the time Alex was nineteen years of age he had been before the courts a half dozen times for petty larceny; once he was sentenced to the convict camp for ninety days. He served his time; soon thereafter he was back in the courtroom, accused of having stolen a pair of shoes. Alex pleaded guilty. When he was being sentenced to the convict camp, he asked if someone would give him a dollar; when no one did he was noticeably disturbed. Inquiry brought from him the information that the prisoners at the convict camp had a court—judge, prosecutor, and all—of their own. Every first offender must pay an entrance fee of fifty cents, or submit to fifty stripes administered by the convicts who desired the fee. Worse yet, the fee was one dollar for second offenders, and if no money was available the victim was liable to one dollar's worth of stripes. It developed that Alex had had no money when he began his first sentence, and as a consequence the lash was laid on heavily. When his entreaties were responded to with the necessary dollar, Alex went to the convict camp quite at ease.

THE BLACK BELT'S PETTY COURTS

Numerous petty criminal and civil cases are disposed of by the justices of the peace and notaries public, one of each in every militia district. The justice of the peace is elected by the people and commissioned by the governor; the notary public is recommended by the grand jury, appointed by the superior court, and commissioned by the governor. Either of these officers can dispose of misdemeanors, can commit cases to the county court or the superior court, and can dispose of civil cases involving less than $100 without fine or sentence. The justice of the peace and the notary public have the services of the local bailiff.

Courts Supported by Fees.—These justice courts are self-supporting through a fee system provided by state law: a justice court has power to assess a fee for serving a warrant, a fee for hearing the case, a fee for the bailiff, and so on. These fees, each of which is fixed by law and is small, readily add up to a figure which often makes the justice court expensive for the type of service rendered.

Justices of the peace have much or nothing to do, depending upon their location and their ability to inspire the confidence of the people who have minor grievances to settle. In the rural militia districts of both counties they have next to nothing to do. Now and then some couple comes to them to be married, and occasionally some landowner and his tenant or other persons in the community get into a controversy which they cannot settle among themselves; then, too, there are intermittent "rows" at local crossroads' stores, lodge halls, schools, and sometimes even at churches.

The justice courts in the largest towns dispose of many cases during the year. At Montezuma, Macon County, a larger number of cases were handled than at any other militia district in either county. Between January 1 and June 13, 1928, seventy-nine cases were brought before this court: thirty-four were criminal and forty-five were civil. The racial distribution of the defendants by offenses charged is noted in Table LVII.

TABLE LVII

NUMBER OF CRIMINAL AND CIVIL CASES, BY RACE AND OFFENSE, COMING BEFORE THE JUSTICE COURT OF MONTEZUMA, MACON COUNTY, FROM JANUARY 1 TO JUNE 13, 1928

CRIMINAL CASES			CIVIL CASES		
OFFENSE	WHITE	NEGRO	OFFENSE	WHITE	NEGRO
Prohibition Violation.....	3	3	Account Garnishment..	14	5
Larceny.................	1	6	Collect Note.........	2	14
Assault and Battery......	..	5	Rent................	1	1
Worthless Checks........	3	2	Collect Auto Repair		
Reckless Driving.........	..	2	Bill...............	..	4
Bastardy................	..	1	All Others...........	2	2
Trespass................	..	1			
Forgery.................	..	1			
Carrying Concealed					
Weapons............	..	1			
All Others..............	..	5			
Totals...........	7	27	Totals...........	19	26

Settling a Quarrel Before the "Law."—The solicitor of Macon's county court commented upon the function of the justice of the peace courts in settling quarrels. Several cases were mentioned somewhat similar to this one: At a leading rural Negro church two factions contended for control. Each contributed to the general expenses. A rule had been in operation for some years which dropped from church membership any person who failed to make a financial contribution for four consecutive Sundays. Each faction tried to get the preacher committed; he managed to remain neutral until early in 1928, when one group got him under its control. The outcome was that the opposition leader just didn't contribute to the current expenses of the church, and on the fifth Sunday the leader of the faction in power made a motion that the delinquent be dropped from the roll. The delinquent laughed at him until he saw a possibility of the motion being carried, when he went after him in no uncertain manner. There was a fight in the midst of the service.

Early Monday morning the faction in good standing was in

the county seat town wanting the officers to arrest the opposing faction for "disturbing divine worship," while the latter was there trying to get the other arrested for the same offense. The case was of great moment; the whole Negro community was aroused; everybody was aligned with one or the other faction; all the people in the church were ready witnesses. One faction employed the solicitor of the superior court, the other the solicitor of the county court. After looking into the case, they decided that it should be tried before the justice of the peace court, because it was cheaper and sufficient time could be given for all witnesses to testify. The case was called; each side put up witness after witness.

The evidence presented suggested that there were persons in each faction liable to a road sentence from a higher court; however, since each group seemed to be equally guilty, the justice of the peace, following the advice of the legal experts, advised that each faction agree to let the case drop. It was so decided. Papers were filed withdrawing the case, with the understanding that the defendants, that is, the ones not in good standing at the church, would pay the court costs which amounted to something like $16, the justice of the peace getting half for his fee, while the other half went as fees to constables for issuing warrants, and so on. Thus the affair was settled; the justice court afforded the Negroes a chance to have their say and settle the matter before the "law."

CHAPTER XVI

WHITE AND NEGRO SCHOOLS

THE ONLY institutions which serve both races in Greene and Macon counties are commercial or governmental in nature; the institutions operated to improve, enlighten, and enrich the body, mind, and spirit serve the races separately. The teacher as well as the preacher deals with but one racial element within the community, while the business man usually has daily contacts with both races. Herein lies the chief reason why the Negro's efforts to own property and educate his children are often looked upon with more understanding and favor by the white business man than by the local white teacher or preacher.

The principal intraracial institutions in these counties are the the schools, churches, lodges, hotels, and cafes. First, we consider the schools, which, according to the Georgia Constitution shall be separate and equal.

Schools by Size and Race.—In 1934 there were 100 schools in Greene and Macon counties. During the last fifteen years the one-teacher white schools have been gradually consolidated into larger units. In 1928 the two counties had fourteen one-teacher white schools, in 1934 only six, and two of these—the last two one-teacher schools in Macon—were discontinued in the fall of 1934 and the children transported to centrally located schools. There is high probability that the one remaining small school in the county—the two-teacher school at Garden Valley—will be discontinued in the near future, completing the consolidation of the county's white school system into the four schools at Ideal, Oglethorpe, Marshallville, and Montezuma, each of which has seven or more teachers, and conducts an accredited high school department.

There are still thirteen white schools in Greene; three high schools; two of which—Greensboro and Union Point—are on

THE WHITE SCHOOL AT MONTEZUMA

THE WHITE SCHOOL AT IDEAL

THE MACON COUNTY TRAINING SCHOOL AT MONTEZUMA

THE ROSENWALD SCHOOL AT OGLETHORPE

TABLE LVIII

NUMBER OF WHITE AND NEGRO SCHOOLS BY NUMBER OF TEACHERS PER
SCHOOL IN GREENE AND MACON COUNTIES IN 1928
AND IN 1934[1]

| | WHITE | | | | NEGRO | | | | | |
| | Greene | | Macon | | Greene | | Macon | | TOTAL | |
	1928	1934	1928	1934	1928	1934	1928	1934	1928	1934
One-teacher schools.....	5	4	9	2	36	34	32	28	82	68
Two-teacher schools.....	8	4	2	1	4	7	4	5	18	17
Three-teacher schools....	2	..	..	..	1	..	..	1	3	1
Four-teacher schools....	1	2	..	..	1	1	..	1	2	4
Five-teacher schools.....	2	2	..	..	..	..	1	..	3	2
Six-teacher schools......	..	1	1	..	..	..	1	..	2	1
Seven or more teacher-schools............	2	2	3	4	..	..	..	1	5	7
Total schools..........	20	15	15	7	42	42	38	36	115	100
Total teachers.........	64	60	49	44	51	52	51	52	215	208

the accredited list; four 2-year high schools, two of which—
Siloam and Union Point—are accredited, and from all of which
tenth and eleventh grade pupils are publicly transported to the
high schools at Greensboro and Union Point; six 7-grade schools,
three with two teachers each and three with one teacher each and
transportation from them provided for high school students.

The Negro schools tell a different story. There were sixty-
two one-teacher schools in both counties in 1934, in 1928 there
were sixty-eight. These are not just small and old-fashioned,
but are ill-housed and almost without equipment.

The Macon County Training School for Negroes at Montezuma has seven teachers and will perchance be put on the list of
accredited high schools shortly; two years of high school work
are given in the Negro school at Marshallville. All the other
schools in the county offer just seven grades. In Greene County
only one Negro school, the Junior High School at Greensboro,
with four teachers, gives even ninth grade work;[2] five presume
to offer the eighth grade; the remaining thirty-six offer seventh
grade.

[1] Data compiled from the annual reports of the Department of Education
to the General Assembly of the State of Georgia.

[2] This school now offers four years of high school work.

NEGRO PRIVATE SCHOOLS

The five schools operated in whole or part by private funds in 1928 included two of the best and two of the poorest Negro schools in the counties.

Lampson-Richardson School.—The Lampson-Richardson School at Marshallville is housed in a brick building and equipped with modern patent desks and built-in blackboards which extend across two sides of each of the five correctly lighted class rooms. It was established by Edward Richardson, a local Negro politician and educator, highly respected by both races in Marshallville. The plant was built in the main by gifts which he secured from his acquaintances and friends, chiefly the Reverend J. C. Massie of the Tremont Baptist Church of Boston, Massachusetts, who was born and reared near Marshallville.

The founder of the school died a few years ago; and the Reverend Massie is now in the South, a traveling evangelist. Outside income has dwindled to the vanishing point. The county board of education now furnishes most of the money and the school is headed by the founder's daughter.

The Union Point Normal.—The other Negro private school of importance was the Union Point Normal School at Union Point, Greene County, established in 1911 by the Presbyterian Church in the United States of America for the purpose of training workers for rural churches and schools. A two-story frame building was erected with a hall, an auditorium, and two classrooms on the first floor and eight dormitory rooms for teachers and boarding students on the second. It has built-in blackboards, patent desks, comfortable and well-lighted rooms.

From 1911 until the death in 1925 of its founder, Italia Leconte, the school did very creditable work. Since his death it has declined rapidly. In 1925-1926 there were sufficient funds for five teachers for eight months; in 1926-1927, three teachers for seven months; in 1927-1928, after three teachers had taught for four months, the principal who was also the local preacher, continued the school until May by means of subscriptions which were to be paid in money, if possible, but coal, wood, peas, and even rabbits were accepted. Not one of the pupils who attended the Presbyterian school was a Presbyterian. In fact, with the exception of the imported teachers and the teacher-preacher, who was receiving an income as a missionary, there were no Presbyterians among the Negroes of Union Point. The local Presbyterian church was without membership—it was entirely a missionary effort.

By 1934, there were no funds provided by the denomination's educational board for this school; though an aged missionary preacher was still located in the school property and was pretending to have a "private missionary" school with "two or three teachers," offering work through the eighth grade. Actually, there was but one teacher, and her salary has been so tardy that she has repeatedly tried to get on relief; of the total enrollment of forty-six, twenty were in the "ABC Class," and only three were above the third grade.

The building is in urgent need of repairs, and it would seem the part of wisdom for the denomination to transfer it to the public school authorities, in accordance with their agreement to renovate the building, raise the salaries of Union Point's two public teachers twenty per cent, hire a third teacher as principal, and offer second year high school work. This proposal, however, does not meet the wishes of the missionary preacher for he has recently secured a few members in his church and looks upon the school property as a distinct personal asset, which indeed it is, for he secures the service of the school's one teacher by giving rooms in the building to her and her parents, the leading members of his church.

There are reasons for believing that while this school rendered a very valuable service from 1911 to 1925, its presence has afforded the Greene County Board of Education an excuse for doing little for Negro education at Union Point where two teachers in one schoolroom together receive $45.00 per month for six months.

Private Schools—Church Rivalry.—The other private school

in Greene for Negroes, located at Greensboro, has one teacher
and is supported by tuition. It convenes in a Negro Presbyterian
church and is conducted by a leading elder. Though losing
ground each year, it continues to operate upon an impetus gained
prior to the combining of two or three other denominational
schools to establish the local public school, the present junior
high school.

The Browns Chapel Independent School, about eight miles
east of Montezuma, is conducted in a small church. The building is painted outside and inside, and well lighted by large
windows; in fact, it is, though small, one of the best Negro
church buildings in rural Macon County. It was built when a
part of the membership at Williams Chapel, a mile away, became disgruntled with conditions at the old church. No sooner
was Browns Chapel organized than a successful effort was made
to move the school from the old church to the new one. The
next year the school was back at the lodge hall near the old
church. For years each church tried to get the public school,
one being successful and then the other.

At length, the two churches decided to compromise. A one-
teacher schoolhouse, midway between them, was well-nigh finished when the members of the old church refused to give up
the public school. The outcome is that the new schoolhouse has
never been used, the public school meets in the lodge hall at
the old church, and an independent school is conducted at the
new church. The four families who send their children to the
independent school are related by blood and marriage to the
Negro who is in charge of the plantation on which they live.
Each family contributes $5 each month; with this $20 they hire
a teacher from their "own folks," that is, a relative who belongs
to their church.

Lumpkin Academy—in Story.—In 1928, the principal of
Lumpkin Academy, for Negroes, described his school as follows:
The students begin at the first grade and pass through eight
grades to the Normal Course, which includes ancient history,
Latin, and algebra in the first year, and geometry, Caesar, and

GREENE COUNTY—UNTIL RECENTLY, A NEGRO HIGH SCHOOL WAS CONDUCTED HERE
BY THE PRESBYTERIAN CHURCH IN THE UNITED STATES OF AMERICA

MACON COUNTY—THE INDEPENDENT NEGRO SCHOOL AT BROWNS CHAPEL

THE RICHARDSON-LAMPSON NEGRO SCHOOL AT MARSHALLVILLE, BUILT IN PA
WITH GIFTS FROM BOSTON, MASSACHUSETTS

LUMPKIN ACADEMY, AT OGLETHORPE, COLLAPSED IN 1930

botany in the second and the third years; and in the fourth the theory of teaching, actual practice being offered. An Agricultural Department provides the theory of agriculture and an opportunity to plant, cultivate, and harvest a crop. The Music Department offers courses in piano and vocal training and instruction in the playing of brass and reed instruments. There was a regular monthly tuition of sixty cents per pupil; piano pupils paid $2.00 a month in addition.

Lumpkin Academy—in Life.—But what was the Academy really like in 1928 when the above description was given? The two-story frame building, erected in 1886, was a trap—the pupils were not permitted to go upstairs for fear it might collapse; weather-boards were falling off the framework, window sashes were rotten and most of the window-panes out; there was no inside ceiling, and dogs crawled into the schoolroom from under the stage.

The enrollment of the Academy was but thirty-one, and the average attendance was less than twenty. The principal taught everything except piano, which was left to his wife. He owned twenty-three acres of land near by, but as the Academy had no work stock, twenty acres had been rented to a farmer on condition that the agricultural pupils, if any, be permitted to use his mule to cultivate the three acres reserved for that purpose or for a baseball diamond, as the needs of the school demanded. The only "Normal Graduate" in 1928, a lad of fourteen years, was in the fourth grade three years before when he entered the school.

Lumpkin Academy may have served a real need decades ago, but in 1928 it was worse than a farce, for it retarded the public support of Negro education and subjected its pupils daily to a risk of their very lives. The building collapsed shortly after the writer's visit. The Lumpkin Academy is no more. The principal had been able to continue his "Academy" only because of gifts from one of Atlanta's leading families. It is a sad comment upon citizenship when such worthless Negro institutions can get money from well-intentioned but poorly informed white people, while Negro public education is so poorly financed and supervised.

PUBLIC SCHOOL EXPENDITURES BY RACE

The public schools of Greene and Macon counties had less money spent upon them in 1934 than in 1928, and in each county the shrinkage of expenditures was greater for Negro than for white schools.

Twelve and Eighteen to One.—In 1928, the white child of school age in Greene had $36.53 of public money spent upon his education, the Negro child, $3.11—a ratio of twelve to one. In Macon, the white child received $58.38 and the Negro $2.85— a ratio of eighteen to one.

In Greene, where 43.3 per cent of the school population was white and 56.7 was Negro, 90 per cent of all public school funds was used to maintain and operate white schools and only 10 per cent for Negro schools; in Macon, where 29.9 per cent of the school population was white and 70.1 per cent was Negro, 88.9 per cent of all public school funds was used to maintain and operate the white schools, leaving 11.1 per cent for the Negroes.

Seventeen and Twenty-five to One—Between 1928 and 1934, the amount spent in Greene upon the white child had decreased by 16 per cent, upon the Negro child by 40 per cent; in Macon, the white child's decrease was 12 per cent, the Negro's 36 per cent. Thus the racial differentials were even greater than in 1928, seventeen to one in Greene and twenty-five to one in Macon. The table below shows the exact amounts. For the state as a whole, the public money spent on the white educable in 1934 was 12 per cent less than in 1928, for the Negro child 32 per cent more. Even after this gain, however, the average Negro child in Georgia had but $6.73 spent upon his education while the white child had an average public expenditure of $32.46.

The Diversion of State Funds from Negro to White Schools.—In 1928 the General Assembly of Georgia appropri-

TABLE LIX

Total Current Expenditures and Average Expenditures by Race per School Census Child and per Pupil in Average Daily Attendance in Georgia, and in Greene and Macon Counties in 1928, and in 1934[3]

POLITICAL UNIT BY RACE	TOTAL CURRENT EXPENDITURES		Per School Census Child		Per Pupil in Average Daily Attendance	
	1928	1934	1928	1934	1928	1934
WHITE:						
Georgia...........	$19,402,217	$17,425,785	$36.88	$32.46	$54.60	$46.01
Greene County.....	72,879	56,285	36.53	30.87	55.89	48.27
Macon County.....	83,120	68,201	53.38	47.10	70.86	51.87
NEGRO:						
Georgia...........	1,732,756	2,241,470	5.07	6.73	9.90	10.99
Greene County.....	8,131	4,268	3.11	1.84	5.81	3.32
Macon County.....	10,420	5,565	2.85	1.82	5.89	3.00

ated to the Greene County Board of Education $11,874.63 for 1,995 white children of school age and $15,549.45 for 2,617 Negro educables. The total public expenditure for Negro education in 1928 was $8,131; the remainder, $7,418, was diverted by the County Board of Education to the funds used for white schools. This same year the General Assembly appropriated to the Macon County Board of Education $7,627.55 for 1,557 white educables and $17,882.65 for 3,651 Negro children of school age. Of the amount appropriated for Negro education, $10,420 was spent for Negro schools and $7,462 was diverted to white schools.

In 1933, according to figures secured from the Georgia Department of Education, an even larger proportion of the state's allotments for Negro education was diverted to the whites. In Greene, Negro schools received $5,001 of the $21,235 appropriation; in Macon, $5,964 of the $24,339 state allotment for Negro schools.

The boards of education in these two counties are not alone

[3] Compiled from the Annual Reports of the Department of Education to the General Assembly of Georgia, and from corrected data obtained from the Department of Education for 1934 subsequent to the publication of the annual report.

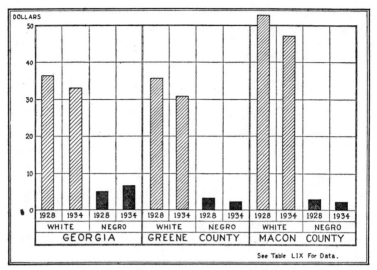

EXPENDITURES FOR PUBLIC SCHOOLS PER SCHOOL CENSUS CHILD
BY RACE IN GEORGIA, AND IN GREENE AND MACON COUNTIES
IN 1928 AND 1934

in this practice of diverting state funds from Negro to white schools, for the total amount spent for Negro education in each of nearly 120 of Georgia's 159 counties was less than the General Assembly's appropriations to these counties on the basis of its Negro school population. The total amount diverted from Negro to white schools throughout the state in 1933, according to figures from the Georgia Department of Education, was more than $1,150,000.

County and District Taxes for White Schools Only.—While the Negro schools had spent upon them only a part of the state appropriation to the county for Negro education, the white schools had spent upon them an amount equal to 100 per cent of the state appropriation to the county board of education for white educables plus the money diverted from Negro to white schools, plus all funds received from county taxes, municipal taxes, district taxes, bonds, loans, sale of property, endowments, or other sources.

Theoretically, certain Negro schools in Greene and Macon

receive from the county board of education "their part" of the funds secured from the local district school taxes. The Negro's "part" is usually determined by the taxes actually paid in the district by Negroes. Really, however, the Negro schools do not share at all in any of the funds from local taxes, for the total amount spent upon Negro education is equal to only a portion of the money appropriated to these counties for Negro education by the General Assembly.

School Expenditures by CWA and FERA.[4]—Through the middle of November, 1934, the CWA and FERA, exclusive of the FERA expenditures to maintain school terms, had spent $24,425.07 on educational projects in Greene County, of which amount $1,720.63, or seven per cent, was spent upon Negroes. The Greensboro Junior High School for Negroes was repaired and painted at an estimated cost of $1,305.13, and one unemployed teacher was employed for $415.50.

The $22,704.94 expenditures by the CWA and FERA for white education included the improvement of buildings and grounds at Greensboro, Union Point, White Plains, Penfield, and Woodville; the employment of six teachers to relieve congestion in rural schools, and three teachers to give instruction to adult classes; the erection of a basket-ball shell and the employment of a playground supervisor at Union Point; the construction of an athletic field at White Plains and of equipment for nursery schools; the remodeling of Mercer College's old Ciceronian Hall at Penfield, and the cleaning of fifteen white schoolhouses before the opening day of school in the fall of 1934.

During this same period, the CWA and FERA, exclusive of maintenance of school terms, had spent in Macon County for educational projects a total of $8,186.37, of which $544.23, or 6.6 per cent, had been devoted to Negro education and $7,642.14, or 93.4 per cent, to white education. The total Negro expenditure was devoted to the employment of unem-

[4] The data presented in this discussion of the expenditures of federal funds for educational purposes in Greene and Macon counties and in Georgia were secured from the offices of the state and county FERA administrators.

ployed teachers. The white expenditures were for the employment of unemployed teachers, schoolhouse plumbing at Marshallville, schoolground improvement at Ideal, and enlarging the school at Oglethorpe.

The average of these expenditures in Greene County for each white child of school age was $12.45, for the Negro child $0.75—nearly seventeen to one; between September 1934 and April 1, 1935, the FERA spent $1,371.00 for the improvement of white school property in Greene and none for the improvement of Negro school property. In Macon, the averages were $5.28 and $0.18—a little over twenty-eight to one. In the expenditures of these federal funds, the racial differential has been no less than in the use of state and local funds by the county boards of education.

As shown in Chapter XIV, beginning with February, 1934, the Federal Emergency Relief maintained rural school terms until their normal closing time. Of the $15,865.95 which was spent from this particular federal fund in Greene, $12,692.70 was spent for white schools and $3,173.25 for Negro schools. In Macon, $10,573.18 was spent, $8,534.68 for whites and $2,202.50 for Negroes. The allocation of this fund within Greene and Macon, as in other Georgia counties, was on the basis of salary scales already in effect and for school terms of duration equal to the ones which the county board of education had planned to maintain with their own resources. The figures on the employment of unemployed teachers in Greene and Macon counties under the Six Point Emergency Program were presented in the same chapter.

Expenditure of Federal Funds for Educational Purposes in Georgia.—The total federal expenditure for educational purposes in Georgia through the summer of 1934 was nearly five million dollars; of this the Negro received $643,733.34, one-eighth of the total. It will be observed in the accompanying table that the Negro received 16.8 per cent of the Six-Point Program (the smallest expenditure), 13.2 per cent of the school term maintenance (the second largest expenditure), and 12.4

TABLE LX

EXPENDITURES OF FEDERAL FUNDS FOR EDUCATIONAL PURPOSES IN GEORGIA
BY RACE, THROUGH THE SUMMER OF 1934[5]

PURPOSE OF EXPENDITURE	VOLUME			PER CENT	
	White	Negro	Total	White	Negro
1. Improvement of school property by CWA and FERA through September 1934..............	$2,686,684.87	$ 379,677.44	$3,066,362.31	87.6	12.4
2. Maintenance of school terms, spring 1934.................	1,390,611.85	211,383.94	1,601,995.79	86.8	13.2
3. Six-Point Emergency Program, Nov. 1933 through Aug. 1934..	260,851.63	52,671.96*	313,523.59	83.2	16.8*
GRAND TOTAL...............	$4,338,148.35	$ 643,733.34	$4,981,881.69	87.3	12.7

*The figures for 1935 show a larger relative expenditure for Negroes.

per cent of the CWA and FERA outlay for improvement of school property (the largest expenditure). Between September 1934 and April 1935, the FERA spent $634,957.83 in Georgia for the improvement of school property; $614,696.67, or 96.8 per cent for white; $20,261.16, or 3.2 per cent for Negro.

The further analysis of the expenditures by CWA and FERA for the improvement of school property, presented in the table below, demonstrates that the Negro in rural Georgia, where the need for improved educational conditions is greatest, shared least in this use of federal funds. It will be observed that the Negro schools received 8.0 per cent, or less, of the total in cash of the FERA's three expenditures and two of the CWA's three expenditures. In brief, only in CWA's expenditures for additions to schoolhouses did the Negro share as well in these federal funds as in 1933-1934 from the state funds, when he received 11.3 per cent of the state's total expenditures of $16,078,502.44 for public education. This one large expenditure by the CWA of $263,974.39 for additions to school buildings is of little concern to rural Georgia, because $240,851.27, or 90.0 per cent of the total, was used in Atlanta and Fulton County which already had the best Negro schoolhouses and school grounds in the state.

[5] These figures were received from the offices of the Georgia FERA.

TABLE LXI

EXPENDITURES BY CWA AND FERA FOR THE IMPROVEMENT OF WHITE AND
NEGRO SCHOOL PROPERTY IN GEORGIA, THROUGH SEPTEMBER, 1934[6]

RACE	CWA		FERA		TOTAL	
	Expenditure	Per Cent	Expenditure	Per Cent	Expenditure	Per Cent
WHITE						
Repairs.........	$ 610,691.03	92.3	$ 139,450.76	93.3	$ 750,141.79	93.4
Additions........	525,775.50	66.6	288,146.88	95.8	813,922.38	74.6
Grounds.........	1,048,562.33	96.6	74,058.37	93.4	1,122,620.70	96.4
Total........	$2,185,028.86	86.1	$ 501,656.01	94.7	$2,686,684.87	87.6
NEGRO						
Repairs.........	51,109.75	7.7	10,015.30	6.7	61,125.05	7.5
Additions.......	263,974.39*	33.4	12,655.83	4.2	276,630.22*	25.4
Grounds........	36,660.73	3.4	5,261.44	6.6	41,922.17	3.6
Total........	$ 351,744.87	13.9	$ 27,932.57	5.3	$ 379,677.44	12.4
WHITE............	2,185,028.86	86.1	501,656.01	94.7	2,686,684.87	87.6
NEGRO............	351,744.87	13.9	27,932.57	5.3	379,677.44	12.4
GRAND TOTAL...	$2,536,773.73	100.0	$ 529,588.58	100.0	$3,066,362.31	100.0

*Of this amount $240,821.27 was spent in Fulton County alone.

As a matter of fact, the urban counties received a large proportion of all federal expenditures in Georgia for educational purposes, white and Negro. To be specific, Fulton County whites, constituting scarcely one-eighth of Georgia's white population, received $1,042,690.93, nearly one-fourth of all expenditures for whites in the state, as shown in Table LX; Fulton County Negroes, constituting less than one-tenth of Georgia's Negro population, received $320,098.36, nearly one-half of the expenditures for Negroes in the entire state.

SOME SPECIFIC CONTRASTS—1928 AND 1934

The sum total of the meaning of the greater racial differentials in 1934 than in 1928 is that the vast majority of Negro teachers still have large teaching loads, receive very low salaries, and are poorly trained; that many Negro schoolrooms are still privately owned and nearly all are inadequately equipped; that Negro school terms are still short, and few or no Negro pupils are publicly transported.

[6] These figures were obtained from the offices of the Georgia FERA.

E WHITE SCHOOL AT PENFIELD, GREENE COUNTY, CONVENES IN ONE OF THE OLD
MERCER UNIVERSITY BUILDINGS

MERCER'S CICERONIAN HALL, RENOVATED BY FEDERAL RELIEF FUNDS, IS NOW
USED BY THE PENFIELD WHITE SCHOOL

THE NEGRO SCHOOL AT PENFIELD

Differentials and Their Sequels.—There are many conspicuous differences between the white and Negro schools. One
acquainted with Black Belt communities can pick out the Negro
schools by the appearance of their exterior while riding along the
road at fifty miles an hour. There are differences within quite
as great.

In 1928, the average enrollment of the one-teacher Negro
schools in these counties was more than twice that of the white:
37.2 as compared with 18.8 in Greene and 52.9 as compared
with 24.3 in Macon. In the two counties twenty-seven one-
teacher Negro schools had an enrollment of more than forty—
the twelve largest were: 60, 61, 62, 63, 64, 65, 68, 73, 75, 78,
80, and 112; nine of the twelve, including the last five, were
in Macon County. By 1935, most of the one-teacher white
schools had been consolidated. The Negro schools were even
poorer than six years earlier.

There are further sequels of poorly supported Negro schools
in these counties. The county school superintendents do not
exercise the same supervision over them as over the white
schools; they often do not begin on time, and the work is not
standardized. The common attitude of the county school superintendent and the members of the county board of education
was pretty well expressed by one of their number when he said:
"Well, since we give the colored people so little it seems a
shame to require much of them." The real meaning of these
racial differentials can best be appreciated by citations of specific
cases.

Red Oak Negro School and Lutheran White School.—In
1928 the largest one-teacher Negro school in Macon County was
Red Oak, with an enrollment of 112; the smallest one-teacher
white public school in this county was Lutheran, with an enrollment of twelve. The Negro teacher, with nine times as many
pupils as the white teacher, received $35 per month, $10 of
which was subscribed by the patrons of the school, while the
white teacher received $75 per month from the public school
funds. The public school authorities thus paid for teacher's

salary twenty-two cents each month per Negro child and $5.83 per white child. The Negro teacher had taught eleven years, was a graduate of the Fort Valley High and Industrial School and subsequently had attended three summer schools there; the white teacher had never taught before, was a recent graduate of the high school at Montezuma, and had never attended a summer school.

There were still other differences: the 112 Negro children sat upon rough, straight-backed benches and wrote on their knees; the schoolroom was the lower floor of a Negro lodge; it was unceiled, with board shutters at the windows to keep out the wind and the rain. The Negro lodge was used because the county did not provide a schoolhouse; the stove belonged to a near-by Negro church and had to be carried to the schoolroom each Monday morning and back to the church again at the end of the week; in case of a funeral or other church service during the week, the school had to be dismissed. The twelve white children at the Lutheran schoolhouse met in a county-owned schoolroom which was ceiled inside; they sat upon county-owned patent desks, in a room warmed by a county-owned stove, and looked through glass windows provided by the county.

Since 1928 the Lutheran school has closed: the children are now provided free transportation to the accredited four-year high school at Oglethorpe, five miles away, where the CWA spent nearly three thousand dollars to enlarge the modern brick building. The lodge hall at Red Oak collapsed during a storm in 1930; since then the school has been conducted in the Negro church close by; the Negro teacher now receives $15.00 per month.

Penfield Schools—White and Negro.—In 1928 the little town of Penfield in Greene County, former site of Mercer University, had fewer people than in 1860. In the town and within a radius of one mile a score of unoccupied palatial old homes, and numerous vacant farm tenant cabins, were falling into decay.

The enrollment at the local white school had fallen off from year to year, though some high school work had been maintained. One of the buildings of old Mercer was used. Repeated unsuccessful efforts had been made by the county school superintendent and the board of education to consolidate the school with the larger one at Woodville, four miles away. When consolidation was found to be impossible because of the town-consciousness of the Penfield patrons, an effort was made to discontinue the high school department. This, too, failed and in 1928 there were three teachers, receiving an aggregate of more than $200 a month for eight months from public funds to teach a total enrollment of thirty-six pupils.

At the local Negro one-teacher public school there was an enrollment of forty-six pupils. In explaining why the small building had a partition in the middle, the Negro teacher said: "You see, we have another room, and just as soon as our enrollment gets high enough the county school superintendent has promised us another teacher." The teacher received a monthly salary of $25 for six months, $5 of which came from the patrons. The schoolroom was ceiled inside and had glass windows; it had been recently deeded to the county by the Negro church society which built it.

In the latter part of 1934 the school convened in the same room as in 1928; the teacher received $25.00 per month for six months. There were only rough pine benches, the stove was without a grate or door and several window panes were out— the teacher expressed the hope that the superintendent would arrange for these repairs before another month.

The white school at Penfield now has four teachers and an enrollment of eighty-nine pupils, nearly half of whom ride to school in public buses; the term is still eight months, and the ninth grade is offered. This school's equipment and grounds have been greatly improved through CWA and FERA expenditures aggregating nearly $5,000, two-fifths to improve the school grounds, the remainder to renovate Mercer College's old Ciceronian Hall for a school auditorium.

The East Over Schoolhouse is Condemned.—East Over is a

Negro community in Greene County about midway between Siloam and White Plains, both of which have accredited two-year high schools for whites, and a public bus takes tenth and eleventh grade pupils to an accredited four-year high school. The new brick schools at Siloam and White Plains were erected by district bonds, and since the road through the East Over community is the dividing line, East Over's half dozen Negro landowners are helping pay for the white school at Siloam or at White Plains.

For more than a score of years the Negro school at East Over had convened in the same building. It was erected by the local Negroes, used by them for general purposes—preaching, school, lodge hall, community gatherings. About a decade ago the county board of education furnished some lumber and the local Negroes ceiled the leaning building to make it stronger and warmer. Encouraged by a few Negro landowners and a resident teacher, the school had become the best attended in rural Greene County; the eighth grade was added, the teacher's salary was raised to $30.00 per month, and his wife was hired to assist him at $20.00 per month. Such were the facts in the spring of 1934 when the county superintendent visited the schoolhouse, leaning dangerously despite its pole props, and condemned it for further school use.

The local Negroes, who had been trying to get a new school for a half dozen years, renewed their efforts to secure help from the county school board, from the state school fund, from the Rosenwald Fund, and from the county and state relief administrators. They could get no assistance from the FERA, because the local people were not on relief, and were asking for building materials rather than wages; the Rosenwald Fund and the state had no money for a school building, was the word which came back from the State Department of Education; the County Board of Education needed all the money it then had to take care of current expenditures for teachers' salaries, maintenance of school plants, reduction of bonds, and transportation of pupils. Thus passed the summer months.

A New Schoolhouse at East Over.—Unable to secure any assistance the Negroes went to the county superintendent in early fall to know what to do. He advised them to get together all the money and material they could and start the building at once—the county could help later. The Negroes had in hand $60.00, raised toward a "Rosenwald School" which they had hoped to secure.

The old building was torn down, and all boards carefully saved; the new building was begun on the same site, an experienced Negro carpenter in charge and the local people donating the labor. The specifications were copied from a Rosenwald School plan, with two large rooms, a smaller room, two closets, and two small porches.

By Thanksgiving the building was ready for rafters. To secure the money needed for additional materials, the Negroes had a rally and raised $81.22, $16.85 of which was secured from white people by a committee of four Negroes who made a list of the white people who might help, divided the names, and called upon each personally. The committeemen secured $1.75, $2.35, $3.75, and $4.00 respectively; the other $5.00 was contributed by the county school superintendent.

East Over's Roof and Ceiling from Teachers' Salaries.— Presently the building was ready for the roof, but no money was available, and the Negro patrons had done all they could. Would the county superintendent now help? Yes, he would divert the unpaid salaries of East Over's two teachers for two months (November and December) to pay for the roof. The roof was ordered, and was placed on the building at once. On the first Sunday in December the Negroes had a meeting and raised $26.25, which was used to put in window sash and panes. Then they went back to the superintendent—surely the county would buy the ceiling. No, the county had no money, but the superintendent would divert the salaries of East Over's two teachers for January to purchase the ceiling. Able to get no other assistance from the county, the Negroes accepted this and the building was ceiled. Except for the high school at Greensboro, the East Over schoolhouse is by far the best Negro school in the county, which has no Rosenwald School. Though the Fund has put nothing into the East Over schoolhouse, the local Negroes are tending to call it a Rosenwald School, a reflection of their appreciation of the standards set by the Rosenwald Fund in the construction of rural Negro schools.

The teachers, a man and his wife, have been doubly drained of their resources, for they made substantial contributions of money and labor to the erection of the building, and have been divested of $168.00, one-half of their combined annual income from teaching. In the meantime, the East Over children had been without a school. Early in 1935, school opened in the new schoolhouse; almost no schoolroom equipment was available. Desks, blackboards, folding doors, teachers' tables, and chairs can wait a year, even longer if necessary.

Up to this time, it will be observed, no public money had gone into this building, except the diverted teachers' salaries; and only $21.85 has been subscribed by white people, the sum mentioned above, and five dollars from a white man of another county. The county superintendent stated that he would recommend to the county board of education that about $20.00 be allocated to the East Over school building.[7] He explained that he was going out of office in two years and that he planned to improve the Negro schools, that he would like to do more for the East Over school, but he had to handle the matter in such a way as not to lose his leadership among the whites in the community; that this depression was a bad time to show partiality to Negroes; and furthermore, that if he began helping build Negro schoolhouses he would be overrun with requests, and might even disturb the harmonious race relations in this county. He had been county school superintendent for a quarter of a century (except two years) without providing an adequate high school for Negroes and without building a single decent schoolroom for them.

[7] According to a recent report, the county school superintendent has put about $70 of public money in the East Over schoolhouse.

GREENE COUNTY—THE WHITE SCHOOL AT WHITE PLAINS WAS BUILT BY TAXES
FROM WHITES AND NEGROES IN THE DISTRICT

THE WHITE SCHOOL AT SILOAM WAS BUILT BY TAXES FROM WHITES AND
NEGROES IN THE DISTRICT

THE NEGRO SCHOOL AT EAST OVER, LYING WHOLLY WITHIN THE WHITE PLAINS AND
DISTRICTS, WAS BUILT ALMOST WHOLLY BY DONATIONS FROM THE LOCAL NEGRO

TRANSPORTATION OF PUPILS—CONSOLIDATION OF SCHOOLS

Another reason why 1934 shows a greater racial differential in these counties than 1928 is the further consolidation of white schools and the greater expense of transporting white pupils.

More Public Money to Transport 500 White Children than to Educate 5,000 Negro Children.—In 1934 Greene County spent more to transport 510 white pupils to their consolidated schools than both counties spent on the education of their 5,368 Negro children. The exact figures for transportation in 1928 and in 1934 appear in the accompanying table. It will be observed

TABLE LXII

PUPILS TRANSPORTED AND EXPENDITURES FOR SAME BY RACE IN GEORGIA, AND IN GREENE AND MACON COUNTIES IN 1928 AND IN 1934[8]

	WHITE		NEGRO	
	1928	1934	1928	1934
PUPILS TRANSPORTED:				
Georgia.................	69,526	117,085	234	569
Greene County.............	171	510	...	...
Macon County.............	505	752	...	...
TRANSPORTATION EXPENDITURES:				
Georgia.................	$853,130.59	$1,270,859.83	$1,598.75	$7,189.20
Greene County.............	4,368.25	11,200.00	....	........*
Macon County.............	9,275.00	8,932.00	....	....

*$100 was spent in 1934-35, see text.

that Greene transported three times as many whites in 1934 as in 1928, that Macon spent more on the transportation of 505 in 1928 than on 782 in 1934, that the number of white pupils transported in Georgia increased from 69,526 in 1928 to 117,085 in 1934, that the number of Negroes in Georgia transported increased from 234 to 569, that the total amount spent for the transportation of Negroes in the entire state was much less than the sum utilized for the transportation of white pupils in either Greene or Macon counties, and that no public money was used in either county to transport Negro pupils. In the scholastic

[8] Data compiled from the Annual Reports of the Department of Education to the General Assembly of Georgia.

year 1933-1934 only five counties in the state—Camden, Chatham, Chatooga, Ben Hill, and Wilkinson—transported Negro children.

Greene's Negro Transportation.—In the fall of 1934 a half dozen Negro junior high school children were being transported from the Spring Creek Community to the Junior High School at Greensboro, a distance of about fifteen miles. The bus was bought by a Negro and the transportation launched when the county school superintendent had agreed to put $100 into this service for the year. Each of the seventeen white owners and operators of school buses in this county receive nearly as much each month as is devoted to Negro transportation for the year. This small beginning may be significant if it leads to the further consideration of Negro educational needs by the county board of education.

Public Transportation a Prerequisite to Consolidation.— When Georgia spends one dollar and seventy-five cents for the transportation of white children every time it spends one cent for the transportation of Negro children, as in 1934, it means that consolidation is limited almost solely to the white schools.

The fact that the two races live side by side in almost every section of Greene and Macon, as in other Black Belt counties, further necessitates the continuance of one-teacher schools where no transportation is provided, for it is difficult to find enough rural children of one race within walking distance of a common point to establish a school of two or more teachers.

Supersensitive Little Communities.—Provincialism in its purest form is found in the self-conscious and jealous one-teacher white school community. Some of the one-teacher white schools in Greene and Macon counties in 1928 were monuments to the stubborn pride of the local people who felt that it would be a real tragedy for their children to be "carted out of the community as if the home school were not good enough for a man's own children." Many schools were small and therefore ex-

pensive per pupil. Of the nine one-teacher white schools in
Macon in 1927-1928, five had an enrollment of twenty or less.
The enrollment of the five in Greene was from fourteen to
twenty-two.

Every effort is made by the residents in some communities
to maintain their own little school. News items in the county
weekly reflect the activities carried on at the schoolhouse to
demonstrate its significance in the life of the local community:

> Our children's day program [at the Oakland Schoolhouse] was
> very much enjoyed by all present. We appreciated the help our
> visitors gave with the afternoon program.
>
> A splendid sermon was rendered by Rev. Harry V. Smith. In-
> teresting talks were made by Dr. J. A. Stapler, and Mr. T. H.
> McGibony. Several songs were rendered by Mr. T. C. Sanders
> and Mr. Jack Alford.
>
> Mrs. G. C. Torbert visited Mrs. Paul Boswell Saturday after-
> noon.
>
> Mrs. P. B. Davis, of Shiloh, spent the week-end with relatives
> here. . . .
>
> Mrs. E. T. Gresham gave her Sunday School class a rook party
> at her home Wednesday night. . . .
>
> Mr. and Mrs. Will Bryant, of Walkers, were among the vis-
> itors of Oakland Sunday.[9]

The recitation of who visited whom is read by local people, not
so much to learn about the visits as to see their names in print
and whether they are correctly reported. The local correspond-
ent is not infrequently a married woman who lives in the community and realizes that with the removal of the school she may
be out of a place to teach, either because she cannot leave home
or because she could not qualify for a standardized school.

Politics and School Consolidations.—Shortly after 1928 the
Oakland School was put in a bus—and another one-teacher school
disappeared. The same thing happened to seven of these schools
in Macon County between 1928 and 1934. But the county
school superintendent is elected by the voters of the county and

[9] Quoted from *Herald-Journal* (Greensboro), 1927.

so often finds himself between two fires: if he insists too much upon consolidation he will be defeated by the reactionary element within the county, and if he does nothing he will be defeated by those favoring consolidation. The outcome is that practically all school consolidations take place midway between election years and are limited to the white schools. In 1928 there were nine one-teacher white schools in Macon, and the superintendent was reëlected; there were five in Greene, and the superintendent was defeated—largely by those who felt that he had consolidated too many schools. So at the end of his first term the consolidationist was replaced by the nonconsolidationist, who, except for this one term, has been the county superintendent for more than a quarter of a century.

The consolidation of the white schools in Macon was first completed in the eastern half of the county, in the big plantation belt where the white people are most prosperous, are in most constant touch with the outside world. Taking into consideration economic, social and political factors, it is by no means surprising that the white schools in the eastern half of Macon were consolidated before those in the west, or that consolidation even in the western half of Macon has gone ahead of Greene which still has fifteen schools.

Is Macon's consolidation the only wise course? Or is there something to be said for the Greene County plan? Is it better to have one school and transport all pupils there, or to have local schools for the lower grades and transport only the higher grades to the central school? Will the parents take as much interest in the far-away big unit school as in the smaller one near home? Can it be that the consolidated school is rural education's expression of America's mad rush for the big and efficient, even at the risk of losing the vital participation of the group which is to be served? It is just possible that the one- and two-teacher schools may hold for many pupils some advantages over the standardized grade work, where all are in the same grade and the teacher spends most of her time getting the backward pupils to pass their work rather than in stimulating the alert ones to advance as rapidly as they can. Be the answers to these questions what they may, it is obvious that the large expenditures for the transportation of white pupils in both counties are possible only because the county boards of education allocate to the white schools the lion's share of all funds for public education.

CHAPTER XVII

SCHOOLS—ESPECIALLY FOR NEGROES

Though some references have been made to schoolhouses and their equipment, to teachers and their salaries, and to the enrollment and attendance of pupils in Greene and Macon counties, the rural schools, and especially those for Negroes, warrant further treatment.

Rural Negro Schoolhouses and Their Equipment

Each of the four consolidated white schools in Macon County, as stated already, is housed in a brick building, with modern equipment throughout. In Greene the white schools at Greensboro, Union Point, Woodville, Siloam, and White Plains have brick plants, and are equipped with built-in blackboards, patent desks, and central heating plants or large stoves. The remaining white schools in this county are conducted in county-owned buildings with inside ceiling, blackboards, window-panes, patent desks, and tables and chairs for the teachers.

The Macon County Training School for Negroes at Montezuma is housed in a modern brick building with an auditorium, science laboratory, built-in blackboards, patent desks, and a small library; it will doubtless get on the state accredited list in the near future. Mention, too, has already been made of the Negro brick school building at Marshallville, and of the two-room Rosenwald School at Oglethorpe. The best Negro school buildings in Greene are the Greensboro Junior High School, the abandoned Presbyterian school property at Union Point and the new schoolhouse at East Over. The next pages are devoted to a description of the other rural Negro schoolhouses in these two counties.

The Ownership of Negro "Public" Schoolhouses.—In the table below it will be observed that forty-three of the fifty-eight rural Negro schools in these counties convene in buildings not

ON COUNTY—RED OAK ONE-TEACHER SCHOOL CONVENED IN A LODGE HALL IN
; IT COLLAPSED IN 1931. THE SCHOOL NOW CONVENES IN THE NEAR-BY CHURCH

ON COUNTY—SHADY DELL WHITE SCHOOL IN 1928. THE CHILDREN FROM THIS
OL ARE NOW BEING TRANSPORTED TO A FOUR-YEAR ACCREDITED HIGH SCHOOL

GREENE COUNTY—TO RE-ROOF THE NEGRO SCHOOL AT VEAZEY, THE COUNTY PAID [
OF THE BOARDS; THE PATRONS PAID FOR THE OTHER HALF AND PUT THEM O[

MACON COUNTY—TO RE-ROOF THE ANTIOCH CHURCH WHICH HOUSES THE LOCAL
SCHOOL, THE COUNTY CONTRIBUTED NOTHING FOR MATERIAL OR LABOR

owned by the county. Twenty-four are conducted in lodge halls, sixteen in churches, and three in abandoned tenant houses.

TABLE LXIII

THE SCHOOLHOUSE AND SCHOOLROOM EQUIPMENT OF 58 RURAL NEGRO PUBLIC SCHOOLS IN GREENE AND MACON COUNTIES, GEORGIA

	NEGRO RURAL SCHOOLS		
	Greene	Macon	Total
TOTAL RURAL NEGRO SCHOOLS.....................	33	25	58
SCHOOLS CONVENING IN:			
County-owned schoolhouses.....................	8	7	15
Lodge halls...................................	16	8	24
Churches.....................................	6	10	16
Vacant tenant houses..........................	3	..	3
INSIDE FINISH OF SCHOOLROOMS:			
Ceiled or plastered...........................	11	10	21
Part ceiled...................................	10	2	12
Unceiled.....................................	12	13	25
SCHOOLROOM SEATING FACILITIES:			
Patent desks.................................	1	3	4
Other desks..................................	3	2	5
Church pews..................................	8	9	17
Benches......................................	21	11	32
SCHOOLROOMS WITHOUT:			
Window sash and panes........................	6	6	12
A chair for the teacher.......................	11	13	24
A table for the teacher.......................	3	6	9

In both counties, the majority of the rural Negro schoolrooms owned by the county have been deeded to it by Negro lodges and churches.

Unceiled and Glassless Schoolrooms.—An unceiled room is really just a half-finished room. If a single weatherboard gets knocked off, the rain and wind come directly into the schoolroom; even when the weatherboards remain fastened to the upright two-by-fours they often fit so poorly that a stiff wind blows the rain between them. Thirty-seven of the fifty-eight schools convened in rooms partially or wholly unceiled.

Those which are listed as ceiled need to be described, for in many cases the "ceiling" is nothing more than rough pine boards from the sawmill, nailed one against the other with cracks between. It is not unusual to see through the walls.

Several of the Negro churches used for schoolrooms are finished inside with planed and matched boards, and some few are
painted inside and outside; but not one of the Negro lodge
halls used for schoolrooms is finished inside with planed and
matched boards, and not one of them is painted.

Twelve of the schoolrooms were without window sash and
panes. Wooden shutters where glass windows should be mean
that cold days, whether fair or rainy, will be dark days. To
keep warm the pupils are forced to sit in close circles around
the stove. In cold, cloudy weather it is scarcely possible to see
well enough to read; on a fair but windy March day, when one
first steps into a board-shutter schoolroom he can hardly see
whether the attendance is nearer five or fifty; after some minutes
his eyes become accustomed to the darkened room and he can
discern with some certainty between boys and girls. Inadequate
lighting is by no means limited to these twelve schoolrooms
without any sash, for many of the others have sash at only part
of the windows, with cardboards replacing broken panes.

Patent Desks, Church Pews, Straight-Backed Benches.—
Nine schoolrooms had desks, and four of these had patent
desks—in every instance the patent desks had been transferred
from a rural white schoolhouse which had been abandoned because of consolidation with some larger white school where new
desks were installed. In' the western half of Macon and in
Greene the scarcity of funds required transference of most or
all of the smaller school's equipment to the larger one, and so
patent desks appear less frequently in Negro schools there.

Either church pews or benches are the seating facilities in
87.9 per cent of the rural Negro schoolrooms in Greene and 80
per cent in Macon. Usually the pews or benches can be moved,
and the appointment of the schoolroom is often nothing more
than each pupil's attempting to find a comfortable place, not too
hot or too cold. Quite uniformly, the teachers insist that the
larger pupils allow the smaller ones to sit nearest the stove—
so all day long, and all winter long the larger students, trying
to get near enough to the stove to keep warm, push the smaller

ones so close to the stove that they have to move back. The darkness of the room intensifies the primitive quality of the scene, the pushing-up of the larger pupils and the pushing-back of the smaller ones.

Writing on Their Knees.—All the children who sit upon church pews and straight-backed benches write upon their knees. They keep their books in their laps, under the bench, or piled up on the floor around the edge of the schoolroom. Though inconvenient and awkward for the older pupils, this enforced writing upon the knees is very hard on the smaller children, whose feet do not reach the floor, and who in trying to write often lose their balance and slide off the bench.

Particularly convincing was a little seven-year-old girl who, when she wanted to write, got down on the floor on her knees and used the seat of the bench for a desk.

Miscellaneous Schoolroom Equipment.—Another handicap is the inadequate heating. Seven schoolrooms are served by fireplaces. The stoves are usually too small, and frequently in need of such essential repairs as grates, doors, and sound flues. Fuel is secured by the larger boys from near-by woods in nearly all instances, and it is not unusual to find wood sticking out of the top of the stove on rainy days when the correct lengths have all been used. That Negro schoolhouses seldom catch fire is due to the great care exercised by the teacher who always puts out the fire before leaving.

With seven exceptions, a blackboard of some type was found in each school; many, however, were nothing more than a wide unplaned pine board which had been stained black. Some few were satisfactory. Library books were altogether lacking; maps were seen only occasionally; pictures were plentiful in some schoolrooms, while in a larger number there were none—there is almost no place to hang a picture in an unceiled room, for it is hidden by the upright joists if hung between them and continuously swinging if hung upon them.

In twelve rural Negro schoolrooms, three in Greene and nine in Macon, there was no table for the teacher; in twenty-four instances, twelve in each county, there was no chair. In most cases, the pupils drink water from a common bucket and a common cup, though in a few schools each pupil brings a drinking cup—a tumbler, a tin cup, a salmon can, a baking powder box. This innovation, often dubbed a "new-fangled idea" by the parents, is strikingly evident when found in schoolrooms such as these.

Repairs on Rural Negro Schoolrooms.—The patrons of the rural Negro school not only build their own schoolrooms in nearly all instances; they take care of all repairs, the county board of education assisting a little in some cases. The following are representative of what was occurring in the fall of 1934: the school at Veazey, Greene County, had to be reroofed; the county board paid for one-half of the split-pine shingles, while the patrons paid for the other half and donated all the labor. The school at Antioch, Macon County, convenes in an old church; when it had to have a new roof the school board contributed nothing toward material or labor.

The amounts allocated by the county boards of education in these two counties for the maintenance and improvement of rural Negro schoolhouses and equipment are negligible; in 1928, Greene spent $60 while Macon spent nothing. The expenditures since that time in Greene have been limited to the purchase of a few stove repairs, some window panes, a little assistance for new roofs, and other smaller expenditures. In the fall of 1934, the county superintendent of Greene stated that the Negro schools should be improved and that he was going to try to find $200 for that purpose. The expenditures in Macon County were even smaller.

Some of the best rural Negro schools are the products of community coöperation. What happened at the Rock Hill school in Greene is a fine example. In 1928, the patrons decided to improve their school. They submitted their plans to the county school authorities and received a little assistance. The schoolhouse was recovered with tin; the room was ceiled inside; flower beds were made in the rocky yard; and the straight-back benches were nailed to the floor and to the top of the back of each bench a plank was fastened at such an angle that it afforded a crude writing shelf for the pupils sitting on the bench immediately back of it. The teacher and pupils and patrons are proud of their school.

Fertile Field for Federal Funds.—Rural Negroes in these two counties, as in most Black Belt counties, have need for schoolhouses, and schoolroom equipment. Here is a fertile field for federal funds—the construction of schoolhouses would utilize workers, skilled and unskilled, in all parts of the county; local building materials could be used; and the completed buildings would be the property of the county school board.

Despite the sordid condition of rural Negro schoolrooms, not one cent of the $32,000 spent through March, 1935, by the CWA and FERA for the improvement of school property in Greene and Macon counties had been devoted to rural Negro schools—in fact, as mentioned already, only one Negro school in either county shared at all in these expenditures, and it was in a town.

There is need for a special federal project adapted to the particular conditions of the service to be rendered—some arrangements will need to be made, whether with or without the financial coöperation of the state and county, for the purchase of building materials; the procedure will need to be flexible enough to transport skilled and unskilled labor into any community which needs a schoolhouse but does not have the needed labor on the local relief roll.

TEACHERS, THEIR TRAINING AND SALARIES

The majority of the teachers are women; more than half the male teachers of each race are in high school work. The ages vary widely but the Negro teachers are on the average older. They are older because their smaller salaries are attractive only to live-at-home persons and because the greater community responsibility of the Negro teacher makes teaching attractive to the public-spirited or ambitious Negro. The rural Negro teacher is often a community leader who supplements the family's farm income by teaching.

Teachers' Certificates and Salaries by Race.—The training of teachers can be measured, though not accurately, by their certificates. Since 1928, the number of higher certificates have uniformly increased while the lower certificates have decreased —the shift of Negro teachers in Greene from provisional elementary to no certificate means only that the county superintendent cared little whether his rural teachers had the lowest certificate or none.

With the exception of white teachers in Macon County, the annual salaries were uniformly lower in 1934 than in 1928, as will be observed in Table LXV. The largest decreases occurred in Greensboro—both races—and in Macon County for Negroes, the latter, according to the Annual Reports of the Georgia Department of Education, dropping from $230.40 in 1928 to

TABLE LXIV

NUMERICAL DISTRIBUTION OF TEACHERS BY RACE AND BY TYPE OF CERTIFI-
CATE IN GEORGIA, AND IN GREENE AND MACON COUNTIES
IN 1928 AND 1934[1]

CERTIFICATE HELD	WHITE TEACHERS						NEGRO TEACHERS					
	Georgia		Greene		Macon		Georgia		Greene		Macon	
	1928	1934	1928	1934	1928	1934	1928	1934	1928	1934	1928	1934
Professional College........	1,261	2,542	5	14	8	11	60	194	1	1	1	2
Professional Normal.......	2,134	3,581	8	10	7	13	296	443	..	3	2	2
Professional Elementary....	1,503	1,321	3	1	5	..	267	792	..	..	1	2
Provisonal College.........	870	1,722	5	13	1	9	43	210	..	..	1	1
Provisional Normal........	1,429	1,050	3	9	2	3	120	170	1	3	1	1
Prov. H. S. or Jr. College...	868	779	8	5	3	..	78	130	1	3	..	1
Provisional Elementary.....	4,157	2,527	32	8	12	7	1,448	981	46	5	44	38
Without Certificate........	1,312	856	..	..	11	1	2,884	2,789	2	37	1	5
Total..................	13,534	14,378	64	60	49	44	5,196	5,709	51	52	51	52

$106.93 in 1934. This figure, however, obviously referred only to the rural Negro teachers, and did not include the fourteen teachers in the towns of Montezuma, Marshallville, and Oglethorpe, which raises the average to $141.74, still a large drop

[1] Data from the Annual Reports of the Department of Education to the General Assembly of the State of Georgia.

TABLE LXV

AVERAGE ANNUAL SALARIES OF PUBLIC SCHOOL TEACHERS BY RACE IN
GEORGIA AND IN GREENE AND MACON COUNTIES
IN 1928 AND IN 1934[2]

POLITICAL UNIT	WHITE		NEGRO	
	1928	1934	1928	1934
GEORGIA............................	$792.32	$665.25	$303.76	$264.51
GREENE COUNTY:				
Greensboro........................	977.14	647.31	446.66	301.67
Rest of County....................	600.70	599.86	141.13	121.50
MACON COUNTY......................	905.53	993.75	230.40	141.74*

*Computed: The figure $106.93, as reported in the Annual Report of the Georgia Department of Education, is for rural teachers only. The fourteen urban Negro teachers raise the average to $141.74

and especially noticeable in view of the increase of white salaries from $905.53 in 1928 to $993.75 in 1934.

The Training and Salaries of Urban Negro Teachers.—The Negro teachers at Montezuma, Oglethorpe, and Marshallville in Macon County and at Greensboro in Greene have much better training and secure higher salaries than those in the rural areas.

The six teachers at the Macon County Training School for Negroes at Montezuma in 1928 were: principal, graduate of Tuskegee Institute, nine years' experience, $133.33 per month; normal graduate from Hampton Institute, forty years' experience, $50 per month; junior at Spelman College, three years' experience, $40 per month; graduate of Morris-Brown College, one year's experience, $40 per month; A.B., Morris-Brown College, two years' experience, $40 per month; and normal graduate of the State College of Alabama, nine years' experience, $40 per month. In 1934, the eight teachers of this school had training and teaching experience similar to the 1928 staff and received the following salaries: principal, $75.00 per month for twelve months; three, $50.00 each, and four, $40.00 each for nine months.

The four teachers at the Greensboro Junior High School for Negroes in 1928 were: principal, A.B. from Atlanta University, with some graduate work at Columbia University and six years'

[2] Data from the Annual Reports of the Department of Education to the General Assembly of the State of Georgia.

experience, who received $100 per month; an Atlanta University student, thirty-five years' experience, $22.77 per month; a graduate of Morris-Brown normal course, three years' experience, $40 per month; and another graduate of the normal course at Morris-Brown, two years' experience, $30 per month. In the fall of 1934 this school still had four well-trained teachers, but their salaries had been reduced to $50 per month for the principal, and $25 for each of his three assistants.

Training of Seventy-two Rural Negro Teachers in 1928.— In 1928 the training of the seventy-two rural Negro teachers ranged from the twelve who finished the seventh grade or less to sixteen who had attended some department of a college. In Greene over half of the teachers had had ninth grade work or less, in Macon over two-fifths. That there are more high school graduates teaching in Macon than in Greene is apparently the

TABLE LXVI

TRAINING OF SEVENTY-TWO TEACHERS IN THE RURAL NEGRO SCHOOLS OF GREENE AND MACON COUNTIES IN 1928

TRAINING	GREENE		MACON	
	Number	Per Cent	Number	Per Cent
Less than seventh grade..............	..	....	2	6.4
Seventh grade......................	7	17.1	3	9.7
Eighth and ninth grades..............	15	36.6	8	25.8
High grade graduate.................	3	7.3	14	45.2
Attended college*..................	13	31.7	3	9.7
Unknown.........................	3	7.3	1	3.2
Total.......................	41	100.0	31	100.0
Summer School work.................	12	29.3	15	48.4

*See explanation in text.

result of Macon's four-year high school, and its proximity to the Fort Valley High and Industrial School. After the decline of the Presbyterian School at Union Point, Greene had no senior high school for Negroes until very recently.

High School Graduates and "College Trained" Persons.— The training as reported requires interpretation, for some of the high school graduates claim to have finished their work in schools having no full high school course, while many of the "college-trained" persons are among the older teachers; and it must be remembered that practically all the Negro colleges in the South of two decades or more ago were little more than grammar and high schools with very poorly defined and inadequately supported college departments. After having ascertained from practically all the so-called college-trained persons what grade they were in when they entered "college" and the length of time they remained in "college," it was clear that the majority of them had merely studied for a year or so in a grammar school or high school of some institution which maintained a college department.

Even so, these high school graduates and "college-trained" persons are by far the best teachers in the rural schools. This was obvious to the writer, not only from his observations of the schools in progress, but from the fact that their pupils could answer quicker and with more certainty a series of questions asked in filling in a blank for each family represented. Almost without exception, these teachers possessed a poise which carried over into the behavior of their pupils—they could express themselves; they knew how to ask a visitor into the schoolroom, how to assure him that he was welcome, and how to make their pupils feel at ease. Several of these teachers had attended the Negro colleges of Atlanta, the Fort Valley Normal and Industrial School, Paine College, Tuskegee Institute or some other Negro boarding school.

Summer Schools for Negro Teachers.—It will be observed from the table above that over one-fourth of Greene's and nearly one-half of Macon's rural teachers in 1928 had attended summer schools. In 1934, a much larger proportion of the teachers in both counties, noticeably Macon, had studied in summer schools. Fort Valley is near Macon County, and the county board of education has provided free transportation daily to the Negro teachers who will attend the summer session there.

But small salaries make it difficult for the rural Negro teachers to care for the expenditures of tuition, of clothes and food during the summer school; when no transportation is provided, as in Greene, these expenses can be met only by those who are not dependent upon their earnings as teachers.

Uninformed Teachers and Uninspired Pupils.—The following incident indicates how poorly informed are many of the rural Negro teachers: When in a one-teacher Negro school west of the river in Macon County the writer asked a child by the name of Booker T. Washington Williams for whom he was named, he did not know. Not one of the thirty-eight pupils knew. The teacher had heard the name, but could not be certain whether he was a lawyer, preacher, farmer, doctor, or something else; whether he was living or dead; whether he was a native of America or Europe; whether he was a white man or a Negro. No one at this school that day, including the teacher, knew anything about R. R. Moton, Benjamin F. Hubert or H. A. Hunt, C. C. Spaulding or Maggie Lena Walker, Paul Lawrence Dunbar or James Weldon Johnson, John Hope or Isaac Fisher, W. E. B. DuBois or Walter White, Mary McLeod Bethune or Phyllis Wheatley, Matthew A. Henson or DeHart Hubbard, Jack Johnson or Tiger Flowers. The Baptist and Methodist denominational leaders in Georgia could not be placed, but were not altogether unknown.

Similar inquiries were then made at other schools in both counties. Many of the teachers were acquainted with two or three of the names mentioned above; several more were found, however, who knew no one of them. Now and then all the older pupils in a school knew something about John Hope or R. R. Moton or H. A. Hunt or some other Negro educator, and in practically every case their teacher had attended one of the educational institutions with which these men are associated. The majority of the rural Negro teachers are not acquainted personally or through reading with the leaders of their own race, and consequently the rural Negro children remain unaware that men and women of their own group have made outstanding contributions in education, literature, art, music, science, athletics, and business.

A Negro school teacher in the rural community who can

GREENE COUNTY—THE GRIFFIN SCHOOL IN 1928; IT COLLAPSED IN 1930. THE CHILDREN NOW WALK TO ANOTHER ONE-TEACHER SCHOOL TWO MILES AWAY

GREENE COUNTY—THE RANDOLPH SCHOOL IN 1928; IT BURNED IN 1931. THE SCHOOL NOW CONVENES IN A NEAR-BY LODGE HALL

BUT THEY CAN STILL LAUGH

instill a feeling of self-respect and confidence into Negro children is doing a work of first importance, for the local white mass mind and the local Negro mass mind can escape the deadening impasse of predestined racial determinism only by the production of Negroes in these rural areas whose personality gives the lie to the theory which the whites profess and which the Negroes nominally accept. Any leavening influence which permeates the Black Belt community points in the direction of resolving the interracial maze which engulfs the races of the South, no less than of the world at large. The Negro college, through its pupil who occasionally returns to the Black Belt, is affecting racial attitudes at their base, but the salaries for rural Negro teachers are so low that only a few well-trained persons teach in rural schools.

Salaries of Rural Negro Teachers—1928 and 1934.—The salaries of rural Negro teachers were quite low in 1928; they were still lower in 1934—less, in fact, than the typical Negro domestic receives in Georgia's larger cities. In 1928 the average monthly salary in Greene was $24.75; in Macon, $24.45. In the fall of 1934 Greene's average was less than $21.00; Macon's was $19.14. These figures do not include the salaries of four assistant teachers who received $10.00 a month.

TABLE LXVII

SALARIES OF RURAL NEGRO TEACHERS IN GREENE AND MACON COUNTIES
IN 1928 AND 1934

	GREENE		MACON	
SALARY FROM COUNTY	1928	1934	1928	1934
Under $12.00 per month................	..	..	..	4*
$12.00 – $16.00 per month.............	..	..	..	4**
16.00 – 20.00 per month.............	1	1	3	7
20.00 – 24.00 per month.............	16	30	14	17
24.00 – 28.00 per month.............	19	4	8	1
28.00 – 32.00 per month.............	3	5	4	..
32.00 – 36.00 per month.............	1	..	..	..
36.00 – 40.00 per month.............	..	..	1	..

*All these are assistant teachers @ $10.00 a month.
**One of these is an assistant teacher @ $15.00 a month.

No white teacher in either county received less than $60.00 in 1928; none in Greene and only two in Macon received less than $60.00 in the fall of 1934. These salaries ran for eight and nine months, while all rural Negro schools had only six-month terms. The Macon County superintendent stated that he hoped to raise the salaries of all teachers, white and Negro, about 25 per cent during the year. The superintendent in Greene hoped to increase all salaries 10 per cent or more.

It will be observed that the salaries of rural Negro teachers are somewhat higher in Greene, five of them receiving $30.00 and teaching the eighth grade. Also, from figures presented above, it will be recalled that Greene received about 50 per cent more federal money than Macon to maintain rural school terms in the spring of 1934. "To get over into 1935" with all bills paid, the county superintendent closed all but seven of Greene County's Negro schools on December 7, two weeks before the beginning of the Christmas holiday for the white schools. He explained that the Negroes would get their other four months after Christmas. Approximately an equal saving, however, would have been effected by keeping all Negro and white schools open and beginning the Christmas vacation a day or two earlier. On the tenth of December the writer stopped at St. Mary's, a rural Negro school in north Greene County, to find it cold and bare; these words, well written, were on the small blackboard:

Opened School October 15, 1934,
Closed School December 7, 1934;
Lord Teach Us to Pray.

What Twenty Dollars Will Buy.—What will the rural Negro teacher's salary buy these days? It will buy three meals a day, provided each meal costs less than twenty-six cents; or if the average cost of meals is reduced to eighteen cents, a room for five dollars a month can be secured. Of course it does not, but just suppose this eighteen-cents-per-meal board and five-dollars-per-month room included laundry, doctor's bills and medical supplies, periodicals and newspapers and books, tooth brushes and cosmetics, and contributions to church and societies—there would even then be left not one cent with which the teacher could buy a hat or dress or pair of shoes, not one cent left to take a trip to a near-by town or to pay her expenses at the next summer school. She may, indeed, not be able to pay her board and transportation, and so abandon teaching to enter domestic service.

Negroes who have incurred personal indebtedness by attending high schools or colleges can afford to teach in these rural schools only when they can live at home. Indebtedness can be reduced but one hundred and twenty dollars a year, even if every cent of the salary be applied to this end. Such salaries render the Negro colleges impotent to make their contribution to the improvement of rural Negro education.

No More Supplementing of the Teacher's Salary.—Though already on the decline in 1928, particularly in Greene, the long-established custom of patrons supplementing the meager public salary of the rural Negro teacher was then increasing the average monthly salary in Greene by $3.25, in Macon by $5.65. Each child who could was supposed to bring a dime or quarter each month; collection was irregular. Approximately two-thirds of the teachers in Greene and nine-tenths in Macon received a supplement ranging from one to ten dollars per month.

Although the Macon County superintendent in 1928 advised the Negro trustees of each school to supplement the teacher's salary ten dollars or more per month, this amount was raised in only five schools. The Greene County superintendent was not opposed to the supplement, but did not request the patrons to raise any particular amount.

The tuition fees in the Negro schools at Montezuma, Oglethorpe, and Greensboro in 1928 were mandatory: $2.00 per year, $3.00 per year. Approximately one-fourth of the salaries paid the Negro teachers by the school authorities of these towns was secured from these required fees.

By the fall of 1934 the supplement to the rural teacher's salary had been discontinued in practically every school, because the low price of cotton made collecting difficult after 1930. The compulsory tuition fees in the city schools had likewise been discontinued because of the inability of the patrons to pay. And so the Negro teachers' salaries have shrunk doubly; they now receive smaller amounts from the county and almost nothing from the parents.

Federal Relief for Unemployed Teachers.—Since the applications of unemployed teachers for teacher-relief employment passed through the hands of the county school superintendents, who were then paying Negro teachers around $20 per month, it is not surprising that the unemployed white teachers were the first to secure these "white-teacher" relief salaries. Though the number of such Negro teachers has increased, as noted in an earlier chapter, they have not yet received proportionate placement in either of these counties or in the state. One of the explanations has been that there were so few Negro teachers asking for relief in the rural counties who could meet the qualifications. It is unwise for the children of a particular race in a particular county to get little or no consideration from a federal educational expenditure merely because the county has provided no adequate opportunity for training teachers within its borders and has paid such low wages as to attract few who were trained elsewhere.

Enrollment, Attendance, and Advancement by Race

The enrollment and attendance of white children is much better than that of Negro children, but not so much better as might be expected from the facts about public school expenditures, schoolrooms and equipment, and the training and salaries of teachers.

Enrollment, and Attendance in Rural Schools—1928.—The total enrollment, enrollment per teacher, and percentage of enrollment in attendance in eighty-six rural schools—twenty-two white and sixty-four Negro—in Greene and Macon counties are presented in the following table. These schools were visited between January 1 and April 15, 1928. In every instance the enrollment entered was of the month when the visit was made, and the attendance as of the day of the visit. Since no teacher knew when her school would be visited and since the investigation continued regularly for three and one-half months regard-

TABLE LXVIII

TOTAL SCHOOL ENROLLMENT, ENROLLMENT PER TEACHER, AND ATTENDANCE
BY RACE IN 86 RURAL SCHOOLS IN GREENE AND MACON
COUNTIES, JANUARY-APRIL, 1928

	WHITE		NEGRO	
	Greene	Macon	Greene	Macon
Number of rural Schools................	12	10	36	28
Total enrollment......................	627	274	1,627	1,688
Number of teachers....................	20	11	41	31
Enrollment per teacher.................	31.4	24.9	39.7	54.4
Attendance...........................	506	214	910	875
Per cent of enrollment in attendance......	80.7	78.1	55.9	51.8

less of weather conditions, there is reason to believe that the average daily attendance in the eighty-six schools was no better throughout the year than on the day the school was visited. In Greene, 80.7 per cent of the white and 55.9 per cent of the Negro children enrolled were in attendance; in Macon 78.1 per cent of the white and 51.8 per cent of the Negro.

Age-Grade Relation by Race, Sex, and Tenure Class.—In 1928, of 1,477 white and Negro pupils, from as many rural families, only twenty—seventeen of which were white—had made advancement in excess of one grade per year. The distribution of pupils in age-grade relation by race, by sex, and by tenure class appears in Table LXIX.

Comparing all white pupils with all Negro pupils in both counties: 50.9 per cent of the white children and 18.4 per cent of the Negro children were making normal advancement; 24.7 per cent of the white children and 67.2 per cent of the Negro children were retarded two or more years, and 3.8 per cent of the white and 31.9 per cent of the Negro pupils were retarded four or more years.

Within each race the advancement of children from owner families was better than from tenant families. The difference, however, between the children of white owners and tenants was less than between white owners and Negro owners. The exact figures for male pupils retarded two or more years in Macon were: white owner 27.6 per cent, white tenant 36.7 per cent, Negro owner 55.2 per cent, Negro tenants 62.3 per cent; in

Greene, white owner 24.5 per cent, white tenant 35.5 per cent, Negro owner 44.4 per cent, Negro tenant 72.5 per cent.

In tenant families female pupils uniformly show larger enrollment than the males. Girls constituted nearly two-thirds of the enrollment from Negro tenant families. In Greene where 55.0 per cent of the attendance from white tenant families were girls, 21.3 per cent of the girls as contrasted with 35.5 per cent of the boys were retarded two or more years; in Macon County, where 60 per cent of the attendance were girls, 29.7 per cent of the girls and 36.7 per cent of the boys were retarded two or more years.

Unlike the attendance from tenant families, about half of the children from the owner families of each race were boys, but Negro owners are relatively few and the better attendance of their boys modifies but slightly the figures.

The greater attendance of Negro girls than of Negro boys is evident in the table, and is further shown by these figures from the 1934 report of the state department of education: Greene County 837 boys and 928 girls, Macon 1,319 boys and 1,403 girls, Georgia 125,639 boys and 135,104 girls. The superior advancement of the Negro girls is shown by high school enrollment: Greene 16 boys and 49 girls, Macon 32 boys and 69 girls, Georgia 4,438 boys and 8,155 girls.

School and the Tenant Farmer's Son.—To increase the attendance of Negroes in the rural schools some approach must be employed to keep the sons of tenant farmers in school. This is no easy thing to do! In the first place, "trading time is moving time," and the families in the lower tenure classes move often—the families with the poorest background for an appreciation of an education, the smallest amount of property, the shabbiest clothes, and the poorest food supply. The moving occurs during the winter, and the children may be taken out of school several days or weeks before, or they may not be enrolled because they plan to move. One day their belongings are piled in a wagon bed or Ford truck, and they are off to another farm

TABLE LXIX

NUMERICAL AND PERCENTAGE DISTRIBUTION OF WHITE AND NEGRO PUPILS, AS TO GRADE ADVANCEMENT BY SEX AND TENURE CLASS OF PARENTS, IN RURAL SCHOOLS IN GREENE AND MACON COUNTIES, GEORGIA, 1927-1928

AGE–GRADE RELATION OF PUPILS	WHITE								TOTAL
	OWNERS				TENANTS				
	GREENE		MACON		GREENE		MACON		
	M	F	M	F	M	F	M	F	
NUMBER:									
Superior Advancement	5	3	..	1	..	3	3	2	17
Normal Advancement	39	50	29	42	32	48	19	36	295
Retarded: One Year	21	7	13	22	17	23	9	14	126
Two Years	11	5	11	6	13	11	13	13	83
Three Years	6	2	3	2	8	6	3	7	37
Four Years	3	2	..	..	4	3	1	1	14
Five Years	..	1	2	..	1	..	1	1	6
Six Years	1	..	..	..	1	..	..	..	2
Seven and More	..	..	..	..	..	..	..	..	..
Total Number of Children	86	70	58	73	76	94	49	74	580
PER CENT:									
Superior Advancement	5.8	4.3	....	1.4	....	3.2	6.1	2.7	2.9
Normal Advancement	45.3	71.4	50.0	57.6	42.1	51.1	38.8	48.7	50.9
Retarded: One Year	24.4	10.0	22.4	30.1	22.4	24.4	18.4	18.9	21.7
Two Years	12.8	7.1	19.0	8.2	17.1	11.7	26.5	17.6	14.3
Three Years	7.0	2.9	5.2	2.7	10.5	6.4	6.1	9.5	6.4
Four Years	3.5	2.9	....	....	5.3	3.2	2.1	1.3	2.4
Five Years	....	1.4	3.4	....	1.3	....	2.0	1.3	1.0
Six Years	1.2	....	....	....	1.3	....	....	....	0.4
Seven and More	....	....	....	....	....	....	....	....	....
Total	100.0	100.0	100.0	100.0	100.0	100.0	100.0	100.0	100.0
Retarded Two or more Years	24.5	14.3	27.6	10.7	35.5	21.3	36.7	29.7	24.7
Retarded Four or more Years	4.7	4.3	3.4	....	7.9	3.2	4.1	1.6	3.8

AGE–GRADE RELATION OF PUPILS	NEGRO								TOTAL
	OWNERS				TENANTS				
	GREENE		MACON		GREENE		MACON		
	M	F	M	F	M	F	M	F	
NUMBER:									
Superior Advancement	..	1	..	..	1	1	..	..	3
Normal Advancement	7	8	8	6	21	57	23	35	165
Retarded: One Year	3	2	3	6	16	33	32	29	126
Two Years	1	9	3	2	20	34	23	48	140
Three Years	3	4	5	4	30	46	19	66	177
Four Years	1	2	2	4	25	36	16	52	138
Five Years	3	..	3	1	15	23	21	25	91
Six Years	..	2	3	..	7	9	10	12	43
Seven and More	..	..	..	..	3	6	2	3	14
Total Number of Children	18	28	29	23	138	245	146	270	897
PER CENT:									
Superior Advancement	....	3.6	....	....	0.7	0.4	....	....	0.3
Normal Advancement	38.9	28.6	27.6	26.1	15.2	23.3	15.8	13.0	18.4
Retarded: One Year	16.7	7.1	17.2	26.1	11.6	13.5	21.9	10.7	14.1
Two Years	5.6	32.1	10.4	8.7	14.5	13.9	15.7	17.8	15.6
Three Years	16.6	14.3	17.2	17.4	21.7	18.8	13.0	24.4	19.7
Four Years	5.6	7.2	6.9	17.4	18.1	14.6	10.9	19.3	15.4
Five Years	16.6	....	10.4	4.3	10.9	9.4	14.4	9.3	10.1
Six Years	....	7.1	10.3	....	5.1	3.7	6.9	4.4	4.8
Seven and More	....	....	....	....	2.2	2.4	1.4	1.1	1.6
Total	100.0	100.0	100.0	100.0	100.0	100.0	100.0	100.0	100.0
Retarded Two or more Years	44.4	60.6	55.2	47.8	72.5	62.8	62.3	76.3	67.2
Retarded Four or more Years	22.2	14.3	27.6	21.7	36.2	30.1	33.6	34.1	31.9

cabin. But it is usually some time before the children get into school.

In the spring the landlord may "put those lazy boys to work." There is evidence too that many Negro tenants, while hearing their white landlords and white people in general repeat daily, "Education has ruined many a good 'nigger'," are themselves largely without any positive determination to help their children get an education. Motivation seems to be lacking. The better enrollment, attendance, and advancement of owners' children suggest that an increase of landownership would be of some value in improving the educational attainment of rural Negro children.

The low educational attainment of Negro children studied agrees with these facts from the 1934 Annual Report of the Georgia Department of Education: 44.4 per cent of Greene County's total Negro enrollment was in the first and second grades, with more than twice as many in the first as in the second; in Macon, 57.4 per cent was in these two grades, with nearly three-fourths of them in the first grade. By way of contrast, only 23.1 per cent of the white children in Greene and 24.2 per cent in Macon were in these grades, the number nearly equally divided between the two. In the entire state, 50.8 per cent of the Negro school children in contrast with 29.7 per cent of the white were in the first two grades.

The Negro's situation is even worse than these figures indicate, for frequently the grades in the Negro schools are not up to the level of those in the white schools.

The Flexible Meaning of Grade.—Age-grade relations are useful in establishing comparative advancement of groups when schools are similar, but worth little where they are as unequal as are the white and Negro schools in these counties. The fifth grade, for instance, means one thing in the white school and another thing in the Negro school a half mile down the road. Only in the larger urban communities—Montezuma, Oglethorpe, Marshallville, and Greensboro—do the grades in the Negro schools correspond to those of the white schools. In the

rural Negro schools the meaning of grade may be almost anything, depending upon the standards of the unsupervised teacher
who, in nearly one-half of the instances, knows nothing more
about the meaning of grade than she had learned when a student
at one of these same one-teacher schools with its poorly trained
and inadequately supervised teacher. It is not unusual to find
so-called sixth and seventh grade pupils with but two or three
books.

The personal school equipment of the typical Negro student
is as inadequate as the schoolroom in which he sits. In 1928
several children throughout both counties were observed to have
no book. With the shift to new books in the fall of 1934, a
considerably larger proportion of the students had none; the
teachers were arranging as best they could, hoping that before
the year was gone some of their children would have all their
books and all their children would have at least some. There
is equally as great a need for tablets, pencils, lunch boxes, and
other student accessories.

The grade in the typical Negro school is flexible, and is, in
practically every instance, far inferior to that of the standardized
school. From observation, it appears that the fifth grade in the
typical rural Negro school in Greene and Macon counties would
be about equivalent to the standardized third grade, with the
other grades of corresponding value.

School Attainment by Race.—The average anticipated school
attainment for the Georgia Negro now in enrollment is slightly
above fifth grade, for the white slightly above eighth grade. It
is perchance about right for the state as a whole to count the
Negro fifth grade as equivalent to the standardized fourth grade,
reducing the average school attainment for the Georgia Negro
pupil from the fifth to the fourth grade. When the 163,237
Negro illiterates, 19.9 per cent of the total, are taken into account, the average for the Negro population falls approximately
to third grade. The white remains around the eighth grade, for
most white schools are standardized, and but 3.3 per cent were
illiterate in 1930.

Because of the larger percentages of Negro illiteracy in Greene and Macon counties, 22.3 per cent and 29.3 per cent, respectively, and of the larger proportion of Negroes in rural schools, the Negro's attainment is low third in Greene and high second in Macon, while the white's average is a good eighth grade in Greene and a high eighth in Macon. In educational attainment, as in expenditures and literacy, the whites in these two counties are above the state average for whites, while the Negroes are below the state average for Negroes.

The Denouement.—Realizing that they put little money and thought into the Negro schools, the county authorities encourage each Negro school district to maintain a school board, usually referred to as the trustees. They assume responsibility for the occasional repairs; within the expressed desires of the county school superintendent, they select the teacher; they supervise her work by visiting the schoolroom from time to time and making their wishes known; they officiate at the closing exercises. This practice is generally harmful, not because local leadership is relied upon but because that leadership is too often characterized by near or sheer illiteracy.

The architecture of the schoolhouses and lodge halls built by rural Negroes for school purposes bespeaks their ignorance of school needs. More than two-thirds of the rural Negro schoolrooms have stages, that is, a platform across one side or end of the room. Classes are called to this eminence to recite, and at the closing exercise at the end of the year all the dignitaries are seated upon this inside stage or upon an outdoor stage erected immediately in front of the building. This school closing is called an "exhibition." Orations, marches and pantomines, long rhyming speeches, gay clothes, string bands, pink lemonade, barbecue, liquor, and general rowdiness often make the closing exercises of the largest rural schools a real occasion. For this affair there must be a stage whether there are glass windows or not. It is not unknown for a schoolroom to be built with a second story so that the girls participating in the marches and pantomines can change their costumes.

EIGHT- AND TEN-YEAR-OLD PLOWERS

AT SCHOOL, THERE ARE MORE GIRLS THAN BOYS

THE FORT VALLEY NORMAL AND INDUSTRIAL SCHOOL AT FORT VALLEY; MOST
MACON COUNTY'S NEGRO TEACHERS ATTEND THE SUMMER SESSION OF THIS SCH(

The small amount of money which Negroes can devote to building their schoolhouses accounts for the shabby architecture but not for windowpanes darkened by dust and cobwebs, coats hung on nails in the window-facing, or blackboards placed before the windows, or cardboards used to replace broken panes extending over unbroken ones. Some of the Negro schoolrooms are kept as light as possible, but many are not lighted even so well as their sordid equipment would permit.

It is unusual to find a rural Negro school in Greene or Macon counties beginning on time; the children usually reach school within an hour of opening time on fair days, and later on rainy mornings, or not at all. Excuses: the teacher says the children always come late on rainy mornings, and the pupils say the teacher comes late. Truly enough, the children of most Negro families have no rubber overshoes and raincoats to wear on wet days and never a school bus to ride in. The weather, however, is the explanation for poor attendance on both foul and fair days —when it is rainy and windy the schoolroom is dark and cold; when the weather is good the older children must stay home and work. Quite aside from the landlord's instructions, Negro children, particularly boys, are needlessly kept out of school by their parents—any work, be it ever so little, means too frequently no school.

Looking at such facts as these the county school officials, along with the general white public, dismiss the whole matter by a shrug of the shoulders and the observation that there is no need to provide better schools for Negroes when they do not use the ones they have. Such are the rationalizations of the whites. The Negroes' excuses are inadequate schoolrooms, low-paid and poorly-trained teachers, absence of public transportation, and demands of the landlords for their children's labor.

Where the Responsibility Lies.—In view of the whole theory of public education, the public school authorities have the responsibility of breaking the impasse by providing equitable school facilities for the Negroes. If the county board will not do this, there is need for state or federal assistance and supervision. Al-

though additional funds are needed for the poorer counties, as
for the poorer states, an increase of funds alone will not solve
the problem so long as any and all funds which come into the
county are allocated by the county board. In 1928, for example,
Macon County received $10,000 equalization fund, and it was
used to raise all white teachers' salaries to $75.00 a month and to
transport additional white pupils, thus increasing rather than
decreasing the racial differential. Similar results, it has been
noted, have come from most of the expenditures of federal relief funds in Greene and Macon counties for educational
purposes.

All funds, whether county or state or federal, which are
meant for the Negroes should be ear-marked and their expenditure accounted for. This procedure would make it possible for
the officials of the state department of education and of the federal relief and other contributing governmental agencies to do
more than express regret that funds are being administered
unfairly. With ear-marked money for each race, too, the county
school authorities can vastly improve Negro schools without
being repudiated by the voters. With improved educational
facilities, there is every reason to believe that in enrollment,
attendance, and advancement the Negro pupils will approximate the white.

*Racial Differentials Are Smallest Where White Schools Are
Best.*—It is interesting, perhaps significant, that the differences
between the white and Negro schools are least where the white
schools are best. In 1934, the Greensboro white school term
was 180 days, the Negro term 180; in the remainder of Greene
County the white term was 161 days, the Negro term 121 days.
The average annual salary of white teachers in Greensboro was
$647.31, of the Negroes $301.67; in the rest of the county the
white teachers averaged $599.86, the Negroes $121.50. The
annual expenditures per pupil in average daily attendance were:
Greensboro white $47.57, Greensboro Negro $11.03; county
white $31.60, county Negro $2.71. The data on school prop-
erties, training of teachers, proportion of census children en-

rolled, proportion of enrolled pupils in attendance, and grade work done also demonstrate that the differences between the white and Negro schools of Greensboro, though great, are noticeably less than in the remainder of the county where the white schools are decidedly inferior to the white school in Greensboro.

The same is true in Montezuma and Marshallville, in contrast with the schools in the remainder of the county where white schools were last to be consolidated and standardized. As late as 1928 a one-teacher white school west of the river in Macon County convened in a schoolhouse propped with three big poles to keep it from falling over. In the communities with the poorest white schools were found the Negro schoolhouses without window sash, without table and chair for teacher, and with fireplaces instead of stoves.

Public Schools or "Public Schools."—The thesis that the *difference between the white and Negro schools is smallest where the white schools are best and greatest where the white schools are poorest* is demonstrated by a comparison of the racial differentials throughout the state. Statesboro: white $39.74, Negro $20.78; remainder of Bullock County: white $31.92, Negro $2.40; Douglas (town): white $43.89, Negro $10.62; remainder of Coffee County: white $33.94, Negro $2.53; Bainbridge: white $48.78, Negro $8.01; remainder of Decatur County: white $25.50, Negro $1.85; Covington: white $37.02, Negro $8.01; remainder of Newton County: white $21.07, Negro $1.81; Newnan: white $45.56, Negro $8.16; remainder of Coweta County: white $24.14, Negro $2.27; Rome: white $33.80, Negro $10.78; remainder of Floyd County: white $19.82, Negro $2.42; Thomasville: white $94.50, Negro $10.76; remainder of Thomas County: white $38.26, Negro $3.52; Madison (town): white $61.54, Negro $10.46; remainder of Morgan County: white $50.75, Negro $2.63.[3]

Differentials such as these between urban and rural communities, particularly between whites and Negroes, are so great

---

[3] These data were compiled from the 1929-1930 report of the Department of Education to the General Assembly of Georgia.

and so contradictory to the whole theory of public education as to leave one with the feeling that it is incorrect usage of language to write public education without quotation marks. Nevertheless, there is perchance greater consideration shown the Negro here than in other fields.

Significance of Public Education.—In the field of education the presence of the Negro is at least not wholly ignored by local white people—not so in the realms of politics and religion: the politician ignores the very presence of the Negro, except to use him as the subject of jokes and to capitalize race prejudice; the typical white preacher and churchman, as we shall see in the next chapter, ignores the presence of the Negro by preaching and professing theories of the Fatherhood-of-God and the Brotherhood-of-Man which do not include him. The Negro's status in the economic field, too, is even more precarious than in the field of public education.

The writer found the white people in these counties more aware of the injustices against the Negro in school matters than in any other phase of life. The chairman of the board of education in Greene County, 1928, freely acknowledged that the rural Negro schools of the county were a farce, that but little could be expected from them on the basis of their equipment, salaries, and supervision. The superintendents of both counties have stated to the writer recently that the rural Negro schoolrooms and salaries are far from satisfactory and that the county would have to spend more money for Negro schools. Like sentiments have been expressed by several members—not all—of the county boards of education. There is greater possibility of a more equitable allocation of public funds with the officials acknowledging the inadequacy of the present situation than if they defended it as right and inevitable—as do most local white leaders in political, religious, and economic matters.

Promises about educational matters are made to Negroes in these counties, and though often small and unfulfilled, they demonstrate that the Negro is not wholly restricted in this field from participating in the community and even from expressing himself. He is allowed to vote in school bond elections in communities where he cannot vote in political elections. It is only in the field of public education—even after the coming of the AAA, CWA, FERA, HOLC, Federal Land Bank, Land Bank Commission, and other federal services—that Negroes receive salaries from public funds for nonmenial public services. The best school in Macon County represents a promise made and kept. The chairman of the Montezuma school board promised the Negroes a brick building when a bond issue was voted. All the bonds were needed to complete the fifteen-teacher white school, but other public funds in the amount promised were devoted to the building of the Macon County Training School, with six rooms and an auditorium.

Some few of the rural Negro schools and those at Montezuma, Marshallville, and Greensboro are doing very creditable work. They are demonstrating to those rural Negroes who know about them what a school should be, and in the interim some of the more intelligent white people are being disabused of their long-time belief that the Negro cannot get or use an education.

Even though the Negroes are making some constructive use of their present inadequate educational facilities, it must be clear that the situation is in need of real improvement, which can come only in proportion as public funds and supervision are equitably allocated. Such a program can utilize the services only of those school officials who understand and will serve the educational needs of rural children as well as urban children, of Negro children as well as white children.

CHAPTER XVIII

CHURCHES—WHITE AND NEGRO

In GREENE AND MACON COUNTIES most of the rural church members, white and Negro, are either Methodist or Baptist. Each race maintains separate and distinct religious organizations: white Baptists and Negro Baptists or white Methodists and Negro Methodists have no more in common than the local white and Negro nonchurch members.

WHITE CHURCHES

Except for small numbers of Lutherans, Presbyterians, and Episcopalians, the white people of both counties are Southern Methodists and Baptists, with a few Primitive Baptists in Macon County. Jews are few in number and Catholics are almost unknown.

Many of the rural white churches were established near the one-teacher schoolhouse, a group of parents and children having organized a little community Sunday school there. The schoolhouse thus became the regular meeting place and there the occasional preaching services were conducted; later a church was built and a plot of ground set aside for the graveyard. Some of the churches, however, were established long before the coming of the public schools, seventy years ago; in these cases the schools were usually built near them.

Small Rural Churches Tend to Remain Intact.—The community consciousness which is developed around the neighborhood church is one of the strongest barriers to be dealt with in the consolidation of rural schools. It is significant to note that east of the river in Macon, where there are practically no white churches except at Marshallville and Montezuma, as early as 1927 all the white children were carried by public buses to the schools in these two towns; while west of the river, where there are many small churches, there were in 1928 nine one-teacher and two two-teacher white schools, in addition to the larger schools at Oglethorpe and Ideal. Only recently have the one-teacher schools in this area been consolidated.

It is no simple matter to consolidate rural churches: they are of different denominations—a small Baptist Church is more likely to be near a small Methodist Church than another Baptist Church; they have graveyards—the parents and friends of the members lie buried there, and the graves receive their personal attention; they have church buildings—the preaching services, revival meetings, and funerals with their emotional content make the meeting house a sacred object.

Buildings and Equipment.—In both counties the buildings and equipment of rural white churches are very inadequate when contrasted with town and city churches. The typical building is a box-like auditorium, with a platform and pulpit at one end. There are no Sunday school rooms, no kitchen, no balcony, no cloakroom, no toolhouse. Grave-digging tools, along with decorations for the Christmas Tree and large gilt letters for Children's Day, are stored away behind the benches against the wall at the back of the church and behind the two benches in either of the "amen corners." Not all but most of the church buildings are painted outside and ceiled and painted inside. Now and then one will have a Sunday school room or two, a cabinet stove, or carbide lights.

The typical furnishings, however, consist of painted and varnished pews, strip carpets in the aisles and in the open floor space about the altar, a pulpit and two or three throne chairs, a reed organ or piano, a stove or two, and more or less pretentious oil lamp chandeliers. In the largest towns the leading churches are brick structures, with a large auditorium, Sunday school rooms, central heating plant, and a small pipe organ.

Sunday School and Preaching Services.—Sunday schools are conducted each Sunday morning or afternoon at practically all the rural white churches. Before and after the class period, which takes thirty minutes, the whole Sunday school worships together by singing, reading psalms, and praying. The enrollment is not large, and is usually divided into three classes: the married people gather around one stove, the smaller children around the other stove, the larger children and young people retire to the back of the auditorium. In some of the larger Sunday schools there are as many as six or eight classes in the auditorium.

In these one-room Sunday schools, many people are speaking reverently at the same time. Their voices, though usually subdued, echo and reëcho throughout the high ceiled auditorium, producing a kind of meterless chant. This arrangement, while very poor for factual instruction, may have an emotional value; at any rate some children who grew up in this kind of Sunday school atmosphere have found the departmentalized organization with its separate classroom and projects peculiarly incomplete—they miss not only the meterless chant but the opportunity to listen in on some other teacher's discourse if uninterested in that of their own.

Preaching services are conducted once or twice each month. The sermons are confined largely to exhortations to personal morality, to theological dissertations, and startling statements about wanton conditions in the large and distant cities. There is little emphasis placed on the social aspect of Biblical teachings, and almost no mention of local economic and social conditions. As a general rule, the minister serves several churches and lives near the largest one, which may be in a town. To most of his churches he is an absentee or, at best, a quasi-absentee pastor.

The Annual "Big Meeting."—Each church has a series of revival services during the slack-work season in July or August, after the cotton and corn have been "laid by" and before harvesting begins. The "big meeting," an adaptation of the camp meetings of earlier days, is a series of services held at eleven o'clock in the morning and eight at night, continuing for a week or ten days. Here again the emphasis is placed upon personal salvation; the happiness of heaven and the horrors of hell are vividly portrayed. A visiting minister preaches the sermons and the regular pastor helps the "converts" become properly related to the church. In large measure, the success of the meeting is determined by the number of new members.

The local pastor takes care of the entertainment of the visiting minister, that is, he entertains him at night at his home, and accepts invitations to dinner and supper for each day of the meeting for the visiting minister and himself. Each leading family of a rural church has "the preachers" for one meal or for one afternoon, depending upon the number of well-established families taking part in the revival, and the number of days the meetings continue. Except in rare cases, only home-owning families entertain the "big meeting" leaders. While the local pastor must be certain that every one of these families has an opportunity to have them, he must be doubly sure that no family is expected to entertain them twice. In some of the larger churches an imported song leader is also used during the revival services.

Training and Salary of the Rural White Preachers.—Some of the rural white ministers are college graduates, but most of them have attended college little or none. Their only training has come through the denominational summer schools and the correspondence courses which rural ministers can take, and in some instances are required to take.

But, it takes money and time to go to college and rural churches pay small salaries to their ministers. College-trained ministers usually secure the churches which pay best; the more poorly trained ministers work at the lower salary posts, many of which are rural. Fifteen hundred dollars a year is an exceptionally large salary for a rural preacher in these counties; most of them receive less than a thousand dollars, some five hundred or less. Why are rural preachers poorly paid? Because cotton farmers have comparatively small incomes; because rural counties are sparsely populated; because half the people are Negroes, and hence are not contributors to the membership or financial support of the white churches; because half the white people are farm tenants and move often and contribute little to church budgets; and because there are competing denominations in almost every white community.

One must appreciate the social and economic significance of small incomes, of farm tenancy, of rival denominations, of two races set off by caste to evaluate correctly the present status of the white church in the rural Black Belt. Any program for its improvement must be evolved in the light of these facts. Rural church conditions could improve materially with an increase of landownership, with large incomes, and with less stifling race relations. In the meantime, the small rural churches need to work out some effective plan for unification or consolidation or federation.

The Townward Shift of White Church Membership.—The rural white churches are old churches, scarcely any of them established since 1890. Many are hardly maintaining their membership, and some are losing. In the largest towns in the counties, however, church membership is increasing. This occurs because the towns have grown and because individuals from the open country have joined the town church and not because the rural church as such has been consolidated with it. While at present it appears that relatively few of the rural churches will be consolidated or abandoned within this decade, practically all of them will be closed within the next twenty or thirty years by the personal-preference process described above. Churches located in communities where the children are transported elsewhere to school find it increasingly difficult to maintain themselves. Children who attend school together and parents with an interest in the same school have a natural inclination to meet together at church. Any road good enough and short enough for a school bus to travel regularly is good enough and short enough for the family automobile to travel every Sunday. When school consolidation has been realized, the track has been laid for larger church units, or at any rate for the disintegration of the smaller ones.

A concrete example of the relatively greater increase of church membership in the urban than in the rural churches is given in the table below. Negro slaves and their masters were members of the same churches until after Emancipation.[1] It will be noted that in 1866 over 40 per cent of all members were Negroes, and that Negro members were reported as late as 1886 for the church at Bairds. It will be observed, too, that the membership at Greensboro, county seat and largest town, was quite small during and after slave times, and that it was not until after 1866 that the other two town churches were established at Union Point and Woodville—both flag stations on the Georgia Railroad which was completed in 1841.

Bethesda Baptist Church.—A brief history of Bethesda Church, five miles north of Union Point and five miles east of Penfield, illustrates the important rôle played in former days by certain of these old rural churches, and acquaints us with the problems which they face today.

The present church, a stately brick structure, was built in 1818. There was a balcony on three sides for Negroes; seven Negro members were reported in 1846, sixty-seven in 1856, seventy-three in 1866, thirteen in 1876, and none in 1886. The Negro attendance, however, must have been much larger than the membership, and the Negro membership may have been larger before the slavery controversy developed. For as early as 1845, a group of Baptist laymen and ministers from several

---

[1] In 1846 a partition was built down the center of the Baptist Church at Travelers' Rest in Macon County. "The blacks occupied the west end and the whites the east end of the church." The master might be called into account for mistreatment of his slaves: "In the minutes of June, 1851, a committee appointed at a previous conference reported that they had investigated the charge of cruelty to his slaves against Brother Tillman, and found them true. Brother Tillman was present, and acknowledged his wrong, and promising not to do so any more, was forgiven."—Hays, *op. cit.*, p. 136.

Where the plantation church was without a balcony for the slaves, a partition across the auditorium, with whites seated in front of it and Negroes back of it, was common. Old Union Church was located in the Hick's District: of Macon County: "There was a balcony in this church where the Negroes used to sit before the War Between the States. After the Negroes were freed, they were told by the carpetbaggers to sit with the 'White Folks'—which they tried once; but when Mr. Carson shook his gold-headed cane at them and said, 'I give you one minute to get back where you belong, you black rascals,' they got."—*Ibid.*, p. 149.

TABLE LXX

CHURCH MEMBERSHIP FROM 1846 TO 1934 IN THREE OPEN COUNTRY AND
THREE SMALL TOWN BAPTIST CHURCHES IN THE NORTHEASTERN
PART OF GREENE COUNTY[2]

CHURCHES	1846		1866		1886*		1906	1926	1934
	White	Negro	White	Negro	White	Negro			
RURAL:									
Bethesda.................	106	67	183	73	129	..	126	202	94
Bairds..................	168	92	175	116	270	18	152	121	122
Shiloh..................	50	28	77	144	98	..	123	128	116
Total.................	324	187	435	333	497	18	401	451	332
SMALL TOWN:									
Greensboro...............	36	48	66	56	121	..	350	453	535
Union Point..............	..	..	..	..	65	..	124	589	582
Woodville................	..	..	..	..	120	..	105	201	212
Total.................	36	48	66	56	306	..	579	1243	1329
Grand Total...........	360	235	501	389	803	18	980	1694	1661
PER CENT OF MEMBERSHIP IN:									
Rural Churches...........	90.0	79.6	86.8	85.6	61.9	100.0	40.9	26.6	19.9
Urban churches...........	10.0	20.4	13.2	14.4	38.1	.....	59.1	73.4	80.1
Total.................	100.0	100.0	100.0	100.0	100.0	100.0	100.0	100.0	100.0

*No Negro membership was reported after 1886.

southern states, dissatisfied with the attitude of the Baptist General Convention of North America toward slavery, had met at the Augusta Baptist Church and set up the Southern Baptist Convention.

Although there were no Negro members officially reported at Bethesda after 1886, present members of the church recall that "Old Uncle Dad" continued to sit in the remaining gallery —the two side galleries having been removed—and retained his membership in the church until his death a few years ago.

Since Bethesda was the church home for the Mercer College community, leading preachers and teachers of the college filled its pulpit and took part in the life of the church. Jesse Mercer, the founder of Mercer Institute which later became Mercer College and still later Mercer University, was pastor from 1785 to 1796. The relative importance of Bethesda among the Bap-

[2] Compiled from Minutes of Annual Reports of Georgia Baptist Convention, 1846-1934.

OUNTY—BETHESDA BAPTIST CHURCH, BUILT IN 1818, BESPEAKS THE WEALTH AND
TY OF ITS SLAVE-OWNING MEMBERS WHO HAD NEARLY ONE THOUSAND SLAVES

THE OLD MERCER UNIVERSITY CHAPEL AT PENFIELD

GREENE COUNTY—THE WHITES ABANDONED THIS PRESBYTERIAN CHURCH AT SALEM.
WHITE DEAD ARE BURIED NEAR BY, THE NEGROES ARE NOT ALLOWED TO USE

MACON COUNTY—DAVIS CHAPEL NEGRO SCHOOL. HALF A MILE DOWN THE ROAD IS
TEACHER WHITE SCHOOLHOUSE, VACANT BECAUSE OF CONSOLIDATION; IT IS THE D
VOTING PLACE (FOR THE WHITES) AND THE NEGROES ARE NOT ALLOWED TO USE

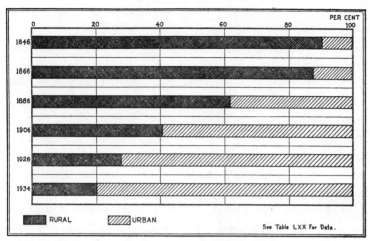

DISTRIBUTION OF MEMBERSHIP IN RURAL AND URBAN WHITE
BAPTIST CHURCHES IN NORTHEASTERN GREENE COUNTY
FROM 1846 TO 1934

tist Churches in Greene and surrounding counties has been on
the decline ever since the close of the Civil War; the wealthy
planters who supported the church were impoverished by the
War and by subsequent farm conditions, and in 1860 Mercer
College was moved to the city of Macon.

Bethesda is no longer one of the leading churches in the
Georgia Association of the Georgia Baptist Convention; it is,
however, still one of the best rural churches in Greene County.
It has a spacious auditorium, several classrooms made by the use
of curtains, preaching services twice a month by a college-trained
man. There is still a scattering of refined and cultured people
in the Bethesda community. But the church's membership has
dropped below one hundred, and it faces an uncertain future.

The Abandonment of Some Rural White Churches.—In
spite of the fact that once a rural church and graveyard come
into being they tend to remain intact, the number of rural
churches in these counties is decreasing from decade to decade.

The Salem Presbyterian Church, for example, in the hills
along the Oconee River in the southern part of Greene, for a
few decades after the Civil War was maintained by the planters

in that part of the county. With the passage of the years their fields became less productive, their children were educated and established in Athens, Augusta, Atlanta, Macon, and other prosperous, distant communities. Upon the death of the resident planters, their heirs, absentee landlords, leased the land to renters, many of them Negroes. Quite naturally these renters, using very little fertilizer and scarcely any forage crops, further impoverished the already depleted soil. As the depletion continued, and it is still going on, nearly all the white tenants moved away. There are hardly enough Negroes left to maintain their own local church and school.[3]

The Salem Presbyterian Church became weaker and weaker and was finally abandoned. The small but well-built one-room structure stands as a monument to the past, a memorial to the few wealthy planters whose acres have not been so attractive to their children. Rural churches have also been abandoned when the owners and tenants of one denomination have moved out and people of another denomination have taken their place.

"*Georgia—A Mission Field.*"—A pamphlet written in 1928 for Baptists contains a discussion which applies to all denominations. The author says authoritatively:

Rural churches are not made by human ingenuity after a particular plan, like a row of houses in a mill village, but are grown like the oaks of the forest . . . and no two are alike. . . .

(1) There are too many. . . . In many places we note that acute conditions prevail because the white people who constituted the church are gone . . . just a little handful has been left to carry on and because of the graveyard near by, this little few will "hang on." . . . The fact that the church has had a glorious history in the other years is not alone sufficient reason for its continuance. The sacred memories which cluster about the old building and the graveyard near by may be very precious and should be cherished, but these should not be allowed to hinder the ongoing of the kingdom of

---

[3] The Negro church and school at Pine Grove, near old Salem, are among the poorest in the county. The schoolroom is very small and old; the four small single-sash windows are without panes; the room is heated by a fireplace. The church, in 1928, was propped with poles to keep it from collapsing; it was unceiled, and one whole corner was without flooring; the pews were rickety slab benches.

Christ. As we study the situation in Georgia we are impressed that this is one of our problems: *We Have Too Many Churches,* and it would, we believe, work out for the glory of God if there should be many to disband, *provided* their membership would go to work in some other church and so render a better service.

(2) Let it be said just here, however, that we have *Too Few Churches* . . . but when we remember that in some sections ten or more are located within a few miles we realize that there are many large areas without a church. What a pity there could not be a more equitable distribution.

(3) Another problem, and a serious one, is the *Lack of Equipment and Insufficient Buildings.* With but few exceptions our rural churches have but one-room buildings with uncomfortable pews and but poor facilities for carrying on the Lord's work. . . .

(4) *Financial Problem.* . . .

(5) But the one great problem, underlying all other problems, is the problem of the *Pastor.* He is the preëminent force and factor for good—or for ill—in all our rural churches. If properly equipped, . . . there is no limit to his power and leadership . . . if incapable, then the church he serves drifts lower in its service to the community and to the work and to God. . . . The *Pastor* is the supreme problem of the rural church. One phase of this problem is that so often the pastor is not a pastor at all, but just a preacher who comes once a month.[4]

NEGRO CHURCHES

The largest white churches in Greene and Macon counties are in the largest towns; the largest Negro churches are located in the open country and in the smaller towns. New Hope Baptist Church, five miles east of Montezuma, has a membership of 766, which is about double the membership of any town Negro church in the county. In Greene, the White Plains Negro Baptist Church has a larger membership than any Negro church in either Greensboro or Union Point; prior to the exodus of a decade ago, it had a membership of 715. The Negro membership, unlike the white, is not being concentrated into the largest town churches.

The Negro church preceded rather than followed the Negro schoolhouse; even now, as shown already, over half the Negro

[4] Spencer B. King, *Georgia—a Mission Field* (1928).

rural schools convene in churches for want of schoolhouses. The Black Belt county school officials have followed the general practice of providing a teacher at each of the older and larger rural Negro churches.

Numerous and Weak Negro Churches.—There are not less than 130 Negro churches in Greene and Macon counties: seventy-eight Missionary Baptist Churches alone, and at least twenty Primitive or "Hardshell" Baptist, between fifteen and twenty each of the Colored Methodist Episcopal and African Methodist Episcopal, and two or three small Presbyterian Churches. Roughly, there are twenty-five in the small towns, and 105 in the open country. There are nearly as many Missionary Baptist Churches in the rural sections as there are one-teacher schools. The inevitable weakness of the typical rural Negro church is obvious when one realizes that on an average each one-teacher school community has one Baptist Church and one of another denomination.

The large number is explained by the keen rivalry between the Methodists and Baptists, by the many dissensions which arise within the established churches and result in new ones,[5] and by the belief of many large planters, particularly in Macon, that a church on the plantation helps to stabilize labor conditions. There is scarcely a Negro church in the plantation areas, and not many even among Negro landowners, which some white man's donated lumber or money did not help make possible.

The rural Negro church buildings and their equipment are

[5] That schisms resulting in new churches are not limited to the Negroes is apparent from the following story of a white church that was cut in two: "Just across the line in Taylor, but drawing much of its membership from Macon County, was a Primitive Baptist Church called Prosperity Church. When Missions began to be a subject of discussion and disruption in the Baptist Churches, this church took the subject very seriously. Wiley Passmore, a loyal contributor to the church, was opposed to Missions and determined that his church should not accept such ideas. While the discussion was warmest, he called the roll of the members, causing the old believers to sit on the right and those accepting the new idea on the left. The next day, he took his slaves and sawed the church exactly half in two from the roof to the foundation and moved the half which clung to the old Faith, so that it would not become contaminated." Hays, *op. cit.,* p. 151.

as inadequate as the rural white churches, only more so. This is inevitable in areas where family incomes are small and where there are so few families in each church. The cash expenses for the building of a rural Negro church are surprisingly low; after securing lumber and whatever money they can get from white and Negro friends, the church members do practically all the work.

The Rural Negroes Design and Build Their Own Churches. —The rural Negro churches bear mute evidence that no money was spent for a designer, that they were built by the local people at spare times, and that poor lumber often went into their construction. Of all the oddly shaped and oddly placed steeples and spires in Christendom, the oddest to be seen are on the rural Negro churches in the Black Belt. In nearly every instance, the unsupported side and end walls of the church bulge in and out and lean this way and that as though the curious little steeple or spire were of tremendous weight. Negro rural churches have a scattered look—seem to be too big for the amount of lumber used.

The one structure which has been designed and erected by the Negroes themselves is their church. There are only a few rural Negro churches which look as if a master carpenter had been present when they were built. The two most notable exceptions in Macon are at New Hope, five miles east of Montezuma; they stand erect and painted. They are so unusual that a local white man, upon passing them, might well say to his visiting friend from another Black Belt county, "Believe it or not, those are colored churches." One often hears of the wonderful carpenters which every large slave plantation boasted. Where were the good carpenters when these warped and uncertain rural Negro churches were being built?

In the first place, the building materials which the white landlords have donated are ends and odds rather than choice lumber. Furthermore, the churches were built by voluntary labor, and in such democratic gatherings no one can be dictatorial; consequently, the church buildings may not be so good as the best carpenters in the group could have made them. Negro rural churches, poor as they are, stand as monuments to the voluntary coöperative self-directed efforts of a group of people who have had little opportunity to exercise personal responsibility.

Crude Furnishings.—When the church is finished it is a box-like, one-room building which may or may not have window sash, or side and overhead ceiling, and most likely will not be painted. The equipment within these warped and twisted buildings is of a very crude and uncomfortable type. In half of them the benches are made of rough pine boards and stand as uncertain as the church itself; now and then one is equipped with painted and varnished pews which stand erect. It is very unusual to see more than a scrap of carpet or rug.

There is a pulpit of some description in each church, perhaps nothing more than a wide board nailed across the top of two upright planks which are fastened to the floor; two pulpits were observed with props. Occasionally, however, one finds a very substantial and even beautiful pulpit.

A large proportion of the churches are without lighting fixtures, and for night meetings each of the leading families brings a lantern and hangs it on the wall. Except during the annual revival meeting period, there are scarcely any night services conducted in either the white or Negro one-room rural churches.

A few Negro churches in Greene have been disbanded since 1922 because of the virtual depopulation of certain areas in the western half of the county, and many of the churches still intact are so weakened that they do not have Sunday school services and now raise for their once-a-month preacher but a fraction of what they raised before the exodus. Except for the emigration, there are no indications of a reduction of Negro churches in either county.

Facts About Fifty Rural Negro Churches.—To give a better understanding of the condition of rural Negro churches the following pages will be devoted to the consideration of certain data secured from fifty churches, seventeen in Greene and thirty-three in Macon. We note in the accompanying table that three-fifths of them were Missionary Baptists, with Primitive Baptist and Colored Methodist Episcopal and African Methodist Episcopal denominations making up the remaining two-fifths.

In Greene there were four rural churches without a Sunday school; in Macon there were ten. The migration accounts for the four in Greene, and the Primitive Baptist Faith for the ten in Macon—six were of this sect which has religious scruples against Sunday schools and musical instruments and foreign missions, and the other four are dominated by its influence.

TABLE LXXI

FIFTY RURAL NEGRO CHURCHES IN GREENE AND MACON COUNTIES CLASSI-
FIED AS TO DENOMINATION, NUMBER OF SUNDAY SCHOOLS, PREACHING
SERVICES PER MONTH, NUMBER OF CHURCHES SERVED BY ONE
PREACHER, TOTAL RESIDENT MEMBERSHIP IN 1920 AND 1928,
AND AVERAGE RESIDENT MEMBERSHIP AND AVERAGE
ATTENDANCE IN 1928

	GREENE	MACON
Total Number of Churches	17	33
NUMBER OF CHURCHES BY DENOMINATION:		
Missionary Baptist	14	16
Primitive Baptist	..	6
Colored Methodist Episcopal	..	6
African Methodist Episcopal	3	5
NUMBER OF CHURCHES HAVING:		
Sunday school	13	23
No Sunday school	4	10
One preaching service per month	17	32
Two preaching services per month	..	1
PASTOR SERVING:		
One church	2	1
Two churches	5	8
Three churches	6	10
Four churches	2	8
Five churches	1	1
Not reported	1	5
TOTAL RESIDENT MEMBERSHIP:		
In 1920	3,290	3,037
In 1928	1,404	3,201
AVERAGE RESIDENT MEMBERSHIP PER CHURCH:		
In 1928	82.6	97.0
AVERAGE ATTENDANCE PER CHURCH:		
In 1928	89.4	101.8

In the rural Negro church, the monthly preaching service is the all-important activity. The Sunday school and the mid-week prayer meeting serve to keep the flock intact while the shepherd is away. In the urban and in many rural white churches the Sunday school is an institution of real importance within itself, in fact so much so that many ministers complain about people coming to Sunday school and leaving before the preaching service.

The rural Negro church has preaching once each month; in one of the fifty, twice a month. Three of the ministers, it will be observed, served but one church; thirteen served two each; sixteen, three each; ten, four each; and two, five each. The average Negro rural preacher conducts three regular services each month in churches which have an average of 82 resident members in Greene and 97 in Macon. The memberships vary widely; New Hope has 766 members and a score have over 200 members each, while an equal number have less than thirty-five each.

Churched and Unchurched Rural Negroes.—The resident membership in the seventeen Greene churches decreased from 3,290 in 1920 to 1,404 in 1928, a decrease of 57.3 per cent. The resident membership in the thirty-three Macon churches showed a slight increase. The great population movement from Greene since 1920 took out of the county many families, and left crippled institutions for those who remained.

Not all the adult Negroes are affiliated with the church and in some cases whole families are unchurched. Facts about the church membership of the parents of 323 rural families show that there are almost three times as many unchurched parents in Macon as in Greene. In both counties a greater proportion of the women than of the men were church members: in Greene, 93.1 per cent of the women and 75.7 per cent of the men; in Macon, 83.2 per cent of the women and 59.1 per cent of the men. A major problem of the rural Negro church is to secure the active coöperation of the male heads of the Negro families. In

TABLE LXXII

CHURCH MEMBERSHIP OF PARENTS IN 323 RURAL NEGRO FAMILIES
IN GREENE AND MACON COUNTIES, 1928

	NUMBER		PER CENT	
	Greene	Macon	Greene	Macon
Both parents members*.......	107	88	74.3	57.2
Father churched, mother not.....	2	3	1.4	1.9
Mother churched, father not....	27	40	18.8	26.0
Both parents unchurched*......	8	23	5.5	14.9
Total reported..........	144	154	100.0	100.0
Unknown.....................	4	21	....	....
Grand total.............	148	175	....	....

*When there was but one parent reported this parent was entered as if two had reported alike.

this matter, as in many others, much depends upon the rural Negro preacher.

Elderly Absentee Negro Ministers.—The younger and better trained Negro preachers are not serving in the rural churches. It will be noticed in the following table that only one of the fifty churches was served by a preacher under thirty years of age, and but thirteen by men under forty years; whereas, nineteen were served by men over fifty. The lower average age of the preachers in Greene is due to the fact that a few theological students from Morehouse and other Negro colleges in Atlanta are serving churches there.

The length of time the preacher has been serving the present church was mentioned in twenty-six cases. The turn-over, it will be noticed, is much higher in Macon than in Greene, only one-fifth of the Macon churches as contrasted with two-thirds in Greene having had their present preacher for more than four years. The fact that more of the Negroes are croppers and wage hands in Macon than in Greene and that these tenure classes move more often than the renters may account for the shorter service of Macon preachers; for, as will be explained below, Negro preachers do not live solely by preaching—certain owners, renters, and croppers merely supplement their farm incomes by serving a church.

TABLE LXXIII

FIFTY NEGRO CHURCHES IN GREENE AND MACON COUNTIES, CLASSIFIED AS
TO AGE OF MINISTER, YEARS HE HAS SERVED PRESENT CHURCH, THE
DISTANCE OF HIS HOME FROM THE CHURCH, HIS SCHOOL TRAINING,
AND THE AMOUNT PAID HIM PER CHURCH PER YEAR, 1928

	GREENE	MACON
AGE OF PREACHER		
Less than 20 years	..	..
20 – 30 years	1	..
30 – 40 years	6	6
40 – 50 years	2	13
50 – 60 years	4	9
60 – 70 years	2	3
70 years and over	1	..
Not reported	1	2
YEARS SERVING PRESENT CHURCH		
One year	3	6
2 – 4 years	3	2
4 – 8 years	4	1
8 – 16 years	3	1
16 years and over	3	..
Not reported	1	23
DISTANCE OF PREACHER FROM CHURCH		
At church	1	..
4 miles or less	2	5
5 – 10 miles	1	..
10 – 15 miles	1	6
15 – 20 miles	..	2
20 – 30 miles	5	10
30 – 40 miles	1	2
40 – 70 miles	2	4
70 miles and over	3	3
Not reported	1	1
TRAINING OF PREACHER		
5th grade and less	1	4
6th – 7th grade	3	3
8th – 11th grade	..	12
Regular college course	..	..
Special college course	1	1
Degrees	2	..
Not reported	10	13
AMOUNT PAID PREACHER PER YEAR PER CHURCH		
Less than $50	2	1
$ 50 – $100	4	4
100 – 150	2	4
150 – 200	4	6
200 – 300	4	2
300 – 400	1	7
Not reported	..	9
AVERAGE AMOUNT PAID PREACHER PER YEAR PER CHURCH	$156.18	$182.20

Of the forty-eight reported cases, but one minister lived at the church where he preached, and only seven within four miles. Thirty lived more than twenty miles away, and twelve of these had to travel more than forty miles, while three in each county lived more than seventy miles away.

Except during the particular week-end when he is in the community for the preaching service, the typical absentee minister cannot visit the sick, baptize the babies, marry the young folks, or bury the dead. Complained a Negro landowner in Greene, "The preacher is never here to comfort the sick and bury the dead unless he has been sent for, and then he expects his traveling expenses to be paid." Now that many of the more prosperous farmer-preachers have automobiles, churches usually see their preacher for shorter periods than when he came in the buggy or on horseback and visited about in the community Saturday and Sunday. The automobile makes it easy for the educated Negro leaders to reach the rural churches on Sunday, but they have little inducement to go there as long as the churches remain so small and weak.

Poorly Trained and Poorly Paid Preachers.—These rural Negro ministers have had little formal education. Five of them had never studied beyond the sixth and seventh grades; twelve had got past the eighth, but not through the eleventh; two had taken special college courses, and two had D.D. degrees. Not one had finished a regular four-year college course. Most of the preachers' education was completed at the one-teacher rural Negro schools twenty or more years ago.

Several farmer-preachers were found among the Negro landowners, renters, and croppers in both counties. It seems that the most prosperous and the poorest farmers are more likely to be preachers than the typical ones. Most of the better paid preachers are landowners or renters, while most of those more poorly paid are croppers or wage hands.

The average annual amount paid the preacher per church was $156.18 in Greene and $182.20 in Macon. Now, if the typical preacher in Greene has three churches, his entire salary from preaching is but $468.54; in Macon it is $546.60. Small as they are, the preachers' salaries are much greater than the average gross income of rural Negro families, much greater than the school teachers' salaries. It takes approximately one-sixth of the income of the average Negro preacher to pay his traveling expenses, for at five cents a mile, the cost of operating even a small car, the preacher going monthly to and from three churches twenty miles away covers 1,440 miles a year at a cost of $72.00. The Negro minister's opportunity for leadership in his racial group makes the position attractive aside from the extra income he secures.

Themes of Negro Sermons.—It is unique to find a rural Negro preacher who understands and talks about present day community and social needs. Two themes predominate. The first is personal right-living. They seem to have taken this over from "their Southern white folks," who, throughout the years, have upon invitation attended their meetings, sat at the front and, for want of something else to say, persistently pleaded with them to quit stealing, quit drinking and laying off work, and quit violating family vows. The theme, stressed by the Negro preacher and supported by vivid descriptions of a physical heaven and a burning hell, is fittingly emphasized and preserved in the Negro spiritual: "You better mind what you talk about, or the devil'll get you—you better mind."

The other favorite theme of the rural Negro preacher grows out of his adeptness in Biblical portraiture. He talks to his congregation about Moses and Daniel at midday as though he had eaten breakfast with them. Incidents which the more learned preacher spends time explaining, he merely relates and presently the "arousements" are in evidence; the whole congregation responds with a rhythmical, "Ye-es, Lawd! Uhm-m!", which gradually gets louder and deeper—like the waves of the incoming tide—until some quivering woman springs to her feet, head thrown back, arms and fingers rigid and outstretched, every muscle in a tremor, eyes wide open; she sways as she screams;

she moves by jerks; after a while she shuffles down into a seat or falls to the floor in a swoon; a pall of rumbling silence—like the spent breakers of the outgoing tide—falls over the responsive congregation. Again the preacher lines off short assuring phrases; again the "Ye-es, Lawd! Uhm-m!" becomes louder and stronger; two, three, four—maybe more—clamber into the aisles, sever the air with jubilant shrieks, cry for "King Jesus' Blessing," and shout forth in throbbing alleluias their assurance of personal salvation—singing psalms of the lamb that was slain! Safe in the arms of the lovin' Jesus! Saved from old snickerin' Satan! Yes, saved, saved, saved—done saved—all saved—and all tired out.

But all religion is not shouting; worldly matters, too, must be looked after. The minister must have some money.

Taking the Collection.—For the preacher's salary the average church member in Greene contributes annually $1.89, in Macon $1.80. Although each member is supposed to give a certain amount each month, 15 to 25 cents being common, the money is secured almost universally by table collections at the preaching service. A ceremony within itself: The need for money is presented and, while a song is sung or while the preacher or a leading layman continues to stress the importance of the collection, persons walk slowly to the front, one at a time, and place their offerings on the table. From time to time the amount put down is announced, with the special plea for enough to round out the dollar; in rounding out one dollar another is begun, and then a special plea to complete it. The same person may go to the table three or four times during a single collection, which may last half an hour or more. When no one else can be induced to come forward, a layman waits on the congregation with a long handled collection bag, which resembles a butterfly catcher, and secures a few additional small coins. Occasionally the desired amount is secured, but more often the congregation tires, a closing song is sung, a lengthy benediction is offered— the monthly preaching service is over.

Religious Organizations and Race Relations

Negro "Big Meetings" and Baptizings and White People.— During the annual "big meetings" each Negro congregation celebrates in festal fashion. The custom serves social as well as religious needs. Speaking about the Negroes and their religious gatherings, a Greene County white man, sitting on his porch one August evening, remarked: "The 'cuffies' are all going to meetings these nights; they'll keep on going until pickin' time. You know, those wagons rattling by remind me of olden times; there goes three in a row, loaded with people. After an hour or so you can hear them moaning—you can hear them bearing the cross. Philip, my cropper on the Baker place, is attending the meetings regularly. Soon he'll be a 'brother'—soon he'll have enough shields to be one of the brethren in the church. See, his wife is trying to 'come through'; if she does then Philip'll have another shield. Let's see, next Sunday is the baptizing.

"You know, it is hard to have a service in our churches when they are baptizing, singing their low deep tunes, wearing their white robes. Besides, they like for us to come down to their pool. They always usher us close on one side; it's a show to see the ushers getting the 'niggers' out of the way so we can get through.

"The next day after one of their shouting meetings," he continued, "you usually hear them talking about what happened: old black Jim will be telling how he held sister Susan, and so on. Yes, and don't you believe but that those hysterical sisters knew exactly who was holding them, too. Always will remember one night, when two stout women were sitting right in front of me, and as the 'arousements' got on one of them turned to the other and said: 'Here, sistuh Merry, hole my hat; I'se gwine to shout!' 'Hole your own hat, I'se gwiner shout myself!' was the quick reply. I snickered; they looked around, got sullen and stayed in their seats."

The Location of White and Negro Churches and Schools.— At no place in either county is there a white and a Negro school or a white and Negro church located across the road or street

GREENE COUNTY—CULTIVATION CEASES; SEDGE AND PINES GROW UP; CHURCH
MEMBERSHIP GOES DOWN

GREENE COUNTY—HONEYSUCKLE AND CREEPERS TAKE THE DESERTED COUNTRY
CHURCHES WHEN PLANTERS QUIT "FURNISHING" THEIR TENANTS

MACON COUNTY—THE WHITE BAPTIST CHURCH AT MARSHALLVILLE

MACON COUNTY—INSIDE VIEW OF THE PINE HILL NEGRO BAPTIST CHURCH

from each other. The Negro community center, with its church, lodge, and school is located about midway between the white community centers. The geographic distribution of racial institutions in these counties is the spatial aspect of cultural segregation along the color line.

The white child and the Negro child go their separate ways to school and church and graveyard long before they are old enough to wonder why. They already are separated by the assumption of innate difference, already accept the dogmas which underlie caste distinctions. That the white man and the Negro are fundamentally and inevitably and unalterably different will scarcely be questioned so long as the two races go in opposite directions to recite their arithmetic tables, their reading lessons, their creeds about a loving Heavenly Father, their intentions to emulate a Jesus who called no man common or unclean.

The White Church Ignores; the Negro Church Acquiesces.— In many southern cities the white and Negro ministers have learned to meet monthly, quarterly, or upon call to discuss the matters of interest to both races. In these counties there is no such organization, though a few of the white ministers in the largest towns are acquainted with certain local Negro ministers and may even cherish their friendship. The absentee preachers of the open country, white and Negro, do not even know each other by sight.

Now and then a rural white preacher or Sunday school teacher denounces a particular Negro, or Negroes in general. Usually, however, the white church just ignores the Negro. Nothing is said about him, no mention is made of his inadequate school facilities, of his political disfranchisement, of his enforced landlessness. Little is taught in the Sunday school or said from the pulpit which would lead the rural white child to think that the church's theory of brotherhood includes the Negro.

Some few whites have a deep concern for the Negro, but the number is small and in these counties the church's practice of ignoring the Negro prevails unchallenged. The rural Negro church appears to acquiesce in the white church's inherited definition of the racial situation, and so both churches are paralyzed in so far as any economic and cultural reconstruction is concerned. In the churches of both races the emphasis is placed upon personal salvation, and it gets but little further, for any statement or activity which assumes that every person is of worth—the basic philosophy of community welfare—is tabooed because it threatens the established relation between the races. Small as are the economic assets of the open country churches, low as are the salaries of the once-a-month preachers, inadequate as are the buildings and equipment, the churches of both races are doubtless no more materially handicapped by economic conditions than they are spiritually paralyzed by race dogmas which rest upon the premise that Negroes are something less than normal human beings.

Though they have adjusted their theology and philosophy to include their racial dogmas, the rural whites dislike to be faced with the Negro question, and but few of them can discuss local race conditions without some show of excitement, or resentment, or even rage. They appear to feel that the attitude which they maintain toward the Negro is, though not a worthy one, an inevitable one, forced upon them by circumstances over which they have no control. They seem to be in the awkward predicament of being unapologetic in defending a distasteful but inescapable position.

There is urgent need that the schools and churches of these counties concern themselves with an increase in family incomes, an increase of homeowners, an increase in community participation for persons who can attain responsible citizenship only as they are afforded the opportunity for a larger measure of self-direction. In proportion as the Black Belt school and church devote themselves to services which reach the landless farmer— even the landless Negro farmer—they will find a new vitality, a new sense of mission.

CHAPTER XIX
LODGES, NEGRO LEADERSHIP, HOTELS

LODGES, SOCIETIES, AND CLUBS

THE RURAL CHURCHES, in addition to providing indirectly for some of the social needs of their members, have countenanced and even promoted lodges, societies, and clubs. The Negro church has been especially active along this line. Lodges, societies, and clubs have come into being at the church—the Negro cultural center—and naturally enough any lodge building erected is close by.

The Relation of the Lodge and the Rural Church.—Whether it wishes to interest the whites or Negroes, the best approach of any organization to rural people is through the church. The Farmers Union, the Grange, the Ku Klux Klan, and many secret orders for the whites know and practice this approach. As a general rule, the organization which cannot make itself acceptable to the rural church fails to secure any considerable following. Negro organizations must also be sponsored by the official leadership of the Negro church.

The lodges, societies, and clubs provide death claims and sick benefits and afford for the elders the opportunity of selective membership, secret rites, and organized participation in the ambition or mission of their lodge. The lodges and societies play more than a nominal part in the life of many rural white communities, and they are especially important among rural Negro communities. Except for the Primitive Baptists, who religiously belong to nothing, hardly a single rural Negro church, regardless of how small its membership, is without an organization of some description which pays death claims and sick benefits. There is a lodge hall, sometimes two or three, close by practically every church.

Names, Age and Affiliation of Negro Lodges and Societies.—

Among the eighty-seven Negro lodges and societies studied—forty-eight in Macon and thirty-nine in Greene—appear thirteen Knights of Pythias, nine Masons, one Odd Fellows, twelve Courts of Calanthe, eight United Gospel Aid, and one or more of each of the following: Kings of Honor, Builders of the Walls of Jerusalem, Progressives, Brothers and Sisters Benevolent Society, Sons and Daughters of Esther, Daughters of Tabor, Devoted Brothers and Sisters, Independent Fraternal Union of America, Mutual Benefit and Aid Society, Travelers Home of Rest, International Benevolent Society, American Woodmen, Improved Good Samaritan, Good Samaritan of Golden Heart, Home Mission, Brothers and Sisters of Charity, Improved Charity, Brothers and Sisters of Love, Young Shepherd of Pleasant Home, and Sons and Daughters of Peace.

Since 1920 the lodges and societies of Greene have been affected by the migration. A smaller proportion of the lodges in Greene than in Macon are affiliated with a national order and they are on the average scarcely half as old. Many lodges and societies were disbanded in Greene, subsequently others

TABLE LXXIV

AFFILIATION AND AGE OF 87 NEGRO LODGES AND SOCIETIES IN GREENE AND MACON COUNTIES, 1928

	GREENE				MACON			
	K.P.	Masons	Other	Total	K.P.	Masons	Other	Total
AFFILIATED WITH:								
National Organization.........	3	5	10	18	10	4	13	27
State Organization............	....	....	18	18	....	....	15	15
Independent Organization......	....	....	3	3	....	....	6	6
AGE OF LOCAL ORGANIZATIONS:								
Less than 4 years.............	....	....	5	5	1	....	3	4
4 – 8 years................	....	....	5	5	....	....	6	6
8 – 12 years...............	2	4	13	19	2	....	1	3
12 – 16 years..............	1	1	6	8	1	1	3	5
16 – 20 years..............	....	....	1	1	1	1	5	7
20 years and over............	....	....	1	1	5	2	16	23
MEDIAN AGE IN YEARS OF LOCAL ORGANIZATIONS...............	11.0	10.5	9.6	10.0	20.0	20.0	19.2	19.4
TOTAL LODGES AND SOCIETIES REPORTED.....................	3	5	31	39	10	4	34	48

were organized. In both counties, the Knights of Pythias and the Masons are slightly older than the others.

Death Claims and Sick Benefits.—The professed purpose of each of the lodges and societies mentioned above is to "look after the sick and bury the dead," provide for widows and orphans, help distressed and needy brothers, upbuild the people, and so on. Most of them pay death claims ranging from $35 to $400, and sick benefits ranging from $0.75 to $3 per week. The detailed facts about the Knights of Pythias, Masons, other organizations for males, organizations for males and females, and for the Courts of Calanthe in Macon County, are presented in Table LXXV.

It will be observed that but five out of the forty-eight organizations paid as large a death claim for a new member as for an old member, and that these five were among those paying the smallest claims. The Knights of Pythias' mature death claim is $400, but a member must keep in good standing for a period of eight years to secure the full amount; the Masons have a mature claim of $300 at the end of the sixth year; the Courts of Calanthe's policy matures for $200 in six years.

All lodges and societies, except the Masons and one other, provide their members with a stipulated sum of money when ill. Although the amount provided is less than a dollar per week in some cases, and not more than $3 in any, this is a great boon, coming in times of sickness to families with an annual gross income of scarcely $400. Sick benefits are provided for six weeks or less in twelve instances, and the duration of the illness in fifteen, while in the remaining seventeen the societies decide the period for each case. Three organizations pay all doctor's bills.

Costly Insurance.—The regular dues range from twenty cents to $1.25 per month; with additional annual costs of thirty-five cents to $2.50. The average amount of death claim per dollar cost during the first ten years' membership varies widely. It is $12.40 if an Odd Fellow (national), $20 if a member of the Knights of Pythias (national), $20 if a Mason (national),

TABLE LXXV

DEATH CLAIMS, SICK BENEFITS, AND MONTHLY DUES AND YEARLY EXTRA
COSTS OF FORTY-EIGHT NEGRO LODGES AND SOCIETIES
IN MACON COUNTY, 1928

	Knights of Pythias	Masons	Other Organizations for Males	Organizations for Males and Females	Courts of Calanthe	Total
TOTAL ORGANIZATIONS............	10	4	4	20	10	48
RANGE AND MATURE DEATH CLAIM						
$ – 49....................	..	..	..	1	..	1
50 – 99....................	..	..	2	3	..	5
100 – 199....................	..	..	2	13	..	15
200 – 299....................	..	..	..	2	10	12
300 – 399....................	..	4	..	..	..	4
400 – 500....................	10	..	..	1	..	11
DEATH CLAIM MATURES						
Upon Joining	..	..	..	5	..	5
1 – 3 years................	..	..	2	1	..	3
3 – 5 years................	..	1	..	5	..	6
5 – 7 years................	..	3	..	8	10	21
7 – 9 years................	10	..	..	1	..	11
9 – 11 years................	..	..	2	..	..	2
SICK BENEFITS PER WEEK						
None......................	..	4	..	1	..	5
Less than $1................	..	..	..	2	..	2
$1 – 2.....................	..	..	2	2	10	14
2 – 3.....................	..	..	1	13	..	14
3 – 4.....................	10	..	..	..	..	10
Pay doctor bills.............	..	..	1	2	..	3
SICK BENEFITS—PERIOD						
4 – 6 weeks...............	2	..	..	..	10	12
Duration of illness...........	2	..	2	10	..	14
Indeterminate..............	6	..	2	9	..	17
MONTHLY DUES						
Less than 25¢..............	..	..	..	3	..	3
25 – 49....................	..	..	3	3	10	16
50 – 99....................	..	4	1	13	..	18
$1 – 1.49..................	10	..	..	..	..	10
1.50 – 1.99...............	..	..	..	1	..	1
YEARLY EXTRA COSTS						
Less than 49¢..............	..	..	2	1	1	4
50 – 99....................	..	4	..	3	9	16
$1 – 1.99..................	9	..	..	14	..	23
2 – 2.99..................	1	..	2	2	..	5

$23.15 if with the Brothers and Sisters Benevolent Society
(state), $25 if with the Kings of Honor (local), $26.50 if with
the International Benevolent Society (state), $27 if with the

Sons and Daughters of Moses (state), $27.08 if with the Courts of Calanthe (national), and $37.82 if with the Travelers Home of Rest (local).[1]

The national organizations promise smaller benefits for higher dues because their overhead is greater and they meet their obligations more promptly and in full. The local lodge's advantage of having little overhead expense is offset by its disadvantage of having only the local membership to fall back upon in hard times.

Some Lodges Fail to Meet Obligations.—Some of the Negro lodges and societies meet promptly their full obligations; others are slow in paying claims, and not infrequently the beneficiary compromises with the lodge in order to get an immediate cash payment. The county attorney in Macon, who has had considerable experience in aiding in the collection of death claims and sick benefits, is convinced that rural Negroes would be greatly benefited if some of the best life insurance companies would establish an insurance service adapted to their needs.

Because of the irregular organization of some lodges, particularly unaffiliated ones, a great deal depends upon the business ability and personal integrity of the official leadership; some have been disbanded, while others with equally severe handicaps have continued and have met part or all of their obligations. In some instances the members have been inspired by their lodge officials to make whatever sacrifices of money and labor were necessary to preserve the good name of their organization.

Some of the lodges own a little property for renting, many have local bank accounts, some own nothing but their dilapidated halls and have no resources except their poverty-stricken

---

[1] The average amount of death claim secured per dollar cost during the first ten years of membership in the various organizations has been arrived at by deducting one dollar a year for a sick benefit of $1 a week, two dollars for a sick benefit of $2 a week, and three dollars for a sick benefit of $3, amounts which just about cover the cost of the sick benefit feature; the remainder of the lodge or society expenses was then applied directly to that of paying for the death claims. Of course, this is an arbitrary measure and consequently cannot be considered accurate, for some of the lodges contribute more than others to purposes other than sick benefits and death claims.

members. H. A. Hunt, principal of the Fort Valley Normal and Industrial School, stated that the failure since 1920 of county seat and small town banks in the Georgia Black Belt counties had disbanded hundreds of Negro lodges and left hundreds of others unable to meet their obligations.

Lodge Membership and "Hard Times."—The total membership in the forty-eight lodges and societies in Macon County in 1928 was 1,926. Ten of these lodges, with 260 members, had been formed since 1920; thirty-eight with a membership of 1,914 in 1920, had only 1,666 members in 1928. Ten Knights of Pythias lodges had 163 fewer members in 1928 than nine lodges had had eight years earlier; four Masonic lodges had twenty-five fewer in 1928; twenty organizations for males and females in 1928 had twenty-six fewer members than fourteen had in 1920; the Courts of Calanthe had one more chapter and forty-five more members than in 1920; other organizations for males increased from one to three, with an increased membership of twenty-three to 214.

In commenting upon the decrease of lodge and society membership in Macon County, local lodge leaders mentioned the

TABLE LXXVI

Total Membership of Forty-Eight Negro Lodges and Societies in Macon County in 1928 and the Membership of Thirty-Eight of These Organizations in 1920; Meeting Places in 1928

	Knights of Pythias	Masons	Other Organizations for Males	Organizations for Males and Females	Courts of Calanthe	Total
TOTAL MEMBERSHIP*:						
In 1920...................	465	212	23	899	315	1,914
In 1928...................	302	187	214	873	350	1,926
FARMERS:						
Members in 1928............	185	131	201	656	118	1,291
Per Cent of Total..........	61.3	70.1	93.9	75.1	33.7	67.3
MEETING PLACE OF LODGE:						
Own Hall.................	7	3	2	6	8	26
Other lodge hall...........	2	1	1	9	1	14
Church..................	1	....	1	3	1	6
Abandoned tenant house......	....	....	....	2	....	2

*Care should be taken to note that the total membership for 1928 includes ten organizations established since 1920, whereas the membership for 1920 includes only those thirty-eight in existence in 1920 which were still functioning eight years later.

following causes: "No members have migrated, but several have died." "Losses due to deaths alone." "Migration and nonpayment of dues." "Decrease due to migration of members, most of whom went to city." "Principal decrease due to suspension of members for nonpayment of dues." "Decrease due to inability of lodge to pay death claims and sick benefits when due." "Membership on the increase due to fulfillment of obligations and popularity of officers." "Decreases due to stringent times and migrations." "All subordinate lodges of the Sons and Daughters of Esther have gone to the wall—only this, the mother lodge, remains." The decrease in cash incomes between 1928 and 1934 has resulted in the continued retrenchment of lodge activities even in Macon County, where the boll weevil depression and farm emigration have been at a minimum.

Since the early twenties scores of lodges have been completely abandoned in Greene. What happened at Flat Rock, in the southwestern part of the county, is typical of the Negro farm communities most affected by the exodus. In 1920 there were three lodges at Flat Rock; in 1928 there was none; in 1935 there was none. A white farmer in the vicinity said, "Well, you see, when nearly everybody left out of here the Builders of the Walls of Jerusalem quit the job, the United Gospel Aid failed, and Noah's Ark went down."

The farmers are members of the less expensive lodges. Of the 1,926 members in the forty-eight lodges and societies in Macon 1,291 were farmers, or 67.3 per cent of the total membership. The Knights of Pythias, the Masons, and the Courts of Calanthe—the organizations affiliated nationally—had the smallest percentage of farmers, and the independent and state affiliated organizations with lower monthly dues had the largest percentage of farmers among their membership. Clearly, the rural Negroes have the poorest lodges and societies just as they have the poorest schools.

Shacks, Secret Ritual, Coffins, Mutual Aid.—A little less than half the lodges and clubs owned their halls, in several other instances two or more owned a hall jointly; fourteen met in halls belonging to other lodges; six had their meetings in churches, two in abandoned tenant houses. It will be observed in the table above that three-fourths of the nationally affiliated organizations owned their meeting place in contrast with but one-third of the others.

Most of the lodge halls are two-story, unpainted structures which, like the rural Negro church near by, appear to have been built too big for the amount of lumber used. The typical hall is located on the second floor; the ground floor frequently serves as a schoolroom. The roughness of the hall's interior and the crudeness of its furnishings are emphasized by the gaudy frame of the gold-sealed charter which hangs on the wall.

The anteroom conceals the robes and standards, the coffins and swords used in the initiation. The lodge member mounts the squeaking stairs, whispers the password through the key hole, and enters the hall. The neophyte is brought in, is teased and threatened and tricked, the ritual is read, his blindfold is removed, he is sworn to secrecy, the password is repeated. He belongs.

The secrecy and ritual of the lodge, along with the opportunity it affords for participation and personal leadership, tend to produce group solidarity. Some few organizations approximate mutual aid societies. A sick lodge member may have his crop planted, cultivated, or harvested in part or in whole by neighborhood fellow members. The widow and children of a deceased lodge member are often rendered some aid by the lodge as such and by individual members of the lodge. The Sons and Daughters of Moses, for example, composed of thirteen men and women, pay a sick benefit of $2 a week and receive a mature death claim of $150 at the end of three years. These amounts, or the part of them which is paid, are secured by assessments and contributions. Moreover, each well member takes to the sick members ten cents weekly or one pound of provisions—sugar, molasses, potatoes, rice, flour, meat, anything.

Social and Cultural Functions of the Negro Lodge.—The lodge's death claim provides the cash with which to put on an impressive funeral while the lodge's gowned members add importance to the occasion.   The funeral of a lodge member furnishes the rural Negro his best chance to put himself and his organization upon exhibition.   The Black Belt lodge member in his flowing robes has his counterpart in the larger world outside—the politician rides in a flag-laden vehicle at the head of the Independence Day parade, the college professor on Founder's Day appears in academic robes and hoods, the Shriner struts to the music of an oriental band, the president of the United States on Inauguration Day rides down a decorated avenue to the Capitol; a short time ago millions of people, wherever electricity lights the night, covered electric bulbs with yellow paper cylinders to celebrate the fiftieth birthday of the incandescent lamp.

It is little wonder that the bright flowing robes manufactured by commercial lodge supply dealers are attractive to a group of people who do not have electric lights, who do not see even the pictures of the inauguration of the president of their country, who are not on the community's patriotic programs, who do not have academic degrees, and who do not participate in county or state or national politics.   There is also little wonder that lodge politics is peculiarly fascinating to them, for a people without recognition in the community at large quite naturally turn their attention to asserting themselves within their own group.   And finally, the rural Black Belt Negro, knowing that his white acquaintances consider him of little consequence, finds the ritual, mysteries, and secrets of the lodge which meets behind locked doors on the second floor a welcome escape from reality.   Here he can cast a vote; aye, here he can be sheriff and juror and judge and governor and president!

Negro Institutional Leadership

The official leadership of Negro institutions is in the hands of relatively few people, the same persons being officers in the schools, churches, and lodges.   Among Negroes, as among other groups, holding one official position makes a person all the more likely to become a leader in other institutions.

Institutional Leadership by Age and Tenure Class.—The bulk of official leadership comes from persons over forty years of age. Less than one-tenth of the leaders were under thirty years. The median age of the church officers, it will be observed in Table LXXVII, was more than fifty years in each county. The lodge officers were only a little younger, but they had been living at the same place for a longer time. The median residence of the official church leaders was over nine

TABLE LXXVII

AGE, LENGTH OF PRESENT RESIDENCE, AND TENURE OF 203 NEGRO CHURCH OFFICERS IN GREENE AND MACON COUNTIES, AND 158 NEGRO LODGE AND SOCIETY OFFICERS IN MACON COUNTY

| | CHURCH OFFICERS | | | | LODGE OFFICERS | |
| | Greene | | Macon | | Macon | |
	Number	Per Cent	Number	Per Cent	Number	Per Cent
AGE:						
Less than 20 years......	..	....	4	3.1	2	1.3
20–30 years............	..	....	9	6.9	10	6.6
30–40 years............	8	10.9	22	16.9	26	17.1
40–50 years............	22	30.1	28	21.5	55	36.2
50–60 years............	22	30.1	36	27.7	47	30.9
60–70 years............	14	19.3	23	17.7	11	7.2
70 years and over......	7	9.6	8	6.2	1	0.7
Total.............	73	100.0	130	100.0	152	100.0
PRESENT RESIDENCE:						
– 1 year............	3	4.1	14	10.8	7	4.4
1– 4 years............	15	20.6	14	10.8	32	20.7
4– 8 Years..........	15	20.6	20	15.4	20	12.6
8–15 years............	19	26.0	19	14.6	32	20.1
15–30 years............	9	12.3	33	25.4	48	30.2
30 years and over......	12	16.4	30	23.0	19	12.0
Total.............	73	100.0	130	100.0	158	100.0
Median Age..............	52.9	....	50.5	....	46.9	
Median Residence.........	9.3	....	9.1	....	12.3	
TENURE:						
Owner.................	25	34.2	22	16.9	60	44.1
Renter.................	35	47.9	26	20.0	34	25.0
Cropper...............	9	12.4	59	45.4	35	25.7
Other.................	4	5.5	23	17.7	7	5.2
Total.............	73	100.0	130	100.0	136	100.0

years, of the lodge officers more than twelve years—from three to four times longer than that of the average Negro family.

The owners and renters appear most often in church and lodge offices. The rural Negro families in the two counties with children in attendance at school in 1928, show, for example, that Greene County Negro owners, with 13.1 per cent of all families, held 34.2 per cent of the church offices; renters, with 36.6 per cent of the families, held 47.9 per cent of the offices; croppers, with 42.9 per cent of the families held 12.4 per cent of the offices. The facts were similar for lodge leaders in Greene, and for church and lodge officials in Macon except in the peach belt east of the river where most officers are croppers or wage hands of necessity, for there are almost no owners and but very few renters in the area.

Significant Rôle of Landowners.—The participation of 151 resident Negro landowners in the official leadership of the local institutions is presented in Table LXXVIII. In these counties four-fifths of the owners were church members and over half were members of one or more lodges; a third were church officers; nearly two-fifths were school trustees; and over one-fifth lodge officers. It will be noticed that nearly three-fourths of the Macon owners were church members, and more than nine-tenths of the Greene owners; about half of the Macon owners were lodge members, almost two-thirds of those in Greene.

The degree to which the official leadership of all Negro institutions was concentrated in the hands of a small group is further illustrated by the fact that of 118 lodge officers in Greene all but seven were church members; in Macon thirty out of 159 were unchurched. In both counties approximately two-thirds of the lodge officers were also church officers.

HOTELS AND CAFES

Other racial institutions in these counties include hotels, rooming houses, and eating establishments.

Hotels, Rooming Houses, Cafes, "Tin-Can" Lunches.—Greensboro and Union Point, in Greene, and Montezuma, Mar-

TABLE LXXVIII

Church, School, and Lodge Official Leadership Among 151 Negro
Landowners in Greene and Macon Counties in 1928

HEAD OF HOUSE	GREENE COUNTY		MACON COUNTY		TOTAL	
	Number	Per Cent	Number	Per Cent	Number	Per Cent
CHURCH:						
Not a member.........	7	9.6	21	26.9	28	18.5
Member only..........	40	54.8	32	41.0	72	47.7
Member and officer.....	26	35.6	25	32.1	51	33.8
Total...................	73	100.0	78	100.0	151	100.0
SCHOOL:						
School trustee.........	32	43.8	26	33.3	58	38.4
LODGE AND SOCIETIES:						
Not a member.........	25	34.2	46	59.0	71	47.0
Member only..........	30	41.1	17	21.8	47	31.1
Member and officer.....	18	24.7	15	19.2	33	21.9
Total...................	73	100.0	78	100.0	151	100.0

shallville, and Oglethorpe in Macon, have hotels for white people. Except the one at Montezuma, all are on the American Plan, and are little more than boarding houses. With the opening of small tearooms and private homes advertising for white tourist trade, the cafes, restaurants, and hotels are becoming less popular. There is no auto tourist camp of any consequence in either county. In the smaller places and in the open country white travelers may find homes in which they can get room and board.

There is no hotel for Negroes in either of these counties. They can usually find lodging in some home. Only in the largest towns is there an eating place operated for Negroes. They can get sandwiches and other "handy" food from white eating places and carry it elsewhere to eat.

It is doubtful, however, if the tearooms, cafes, hotel dining rooms, tourist houses, and accommodating families combined account for more than half the meals eaten by Black Belt transients. A great number of the local white people and Negroes who happen to be in town without lunch eat at the store, making their meal of soda crackers and sardines, potted ham, and Vienna sausage or cheese, along with a bottle or two of Coca-Cola or other carbonated drink. Candy is often used as dessert for a repast of this kind. White people and Negroes sit on opposite counters or on the same counter and talk freely while eating their "tin-can" lunches.

A Unique Eating Place.—In 1928 the only public eating place in Woodville was operated by an aged Negro couple. When a white traveler stopped at this small town at lunch time he was sent there by the local physician or merchant, the leading white citizens of the town, who explained to him that the Negroes had been living in Woodville for many years, that they were respected by everybody in town, that they served fresh foods, that they were excellent cooks, that they knew how to treat white people and were as "clean as pins"—having worked a long time for the best families in the community. The stranger was further assured: "Several of the traveling men who come by my store like the old Negro's place so well they make it a point to be here at lunch time."

The transient upon reaching this eating place for the first time knocked at the door, so little did this unpainted and leaning cabin resemble a cafe. As he entered he was received with many words of greeting and bows from the owner, while Negro loafers filed out of a back door. Across one end of the small room was a rickety serving counter, with a stove and some almost empty shelves behind it. The base of this counter was partly covered with gaudy cardboard signs of Camel cigarettes and Armour meats. The two tables were covered with patched oil cloth; the five chairs were made more secure by splices from drygoods boxes. The ceiling and side walls had been whitewashed months before, and recently several rough planks had been nailed over the largest cracks. From much handling the backs of the old chairs were slick and shiny, as was the wooden latch to the door of an adjoining room.

The owner, called "Brudder Deek" by the Negroes who left the room, busied himself finding and washing a plate, a knife, a fork, a spoon, a tumbler. After more than a dozen trips across the sagging, creaky floor, he had a plate ready. In the meantime, the elderly Negro woman was busy at the stove. Just as the customer was about to leave, having nearly lost his appetite because of the delay and the surroundings, she dropped a steak into the frying pan. Presently the aroma from the sizzling steak, boiling cabbage, and home-made corn bread filled the room. By this time the old man had placed two halves of grapefruit before the guest. Presently the woman commanded: "Heah, 'Brudder Deek,' serb 'er while hit's hot!" He served a meal that justified the merchant's praise. While the guest was eating, the owner sat across the table, talked about the weather, the migration, the ones who were "drappin' back" because conditions were not so good "up there," and about the people, three or four a week, whom the local white doctor and the merchant sent to him. The meal was over and to the departing traveler "Brudder Deek" boasted humbly that once a white man eats with him he is as apt as not to come back for another meal.

Things have changed some since 1928: the white merchant has died; the cabin has been torn away to make room for the accumulated lumber from a near-by sawmill.

CHAPTER XX
LEISURE TIME AND RECREATIONAL ACTIVITIES

HERE IS OFFERED only a sketchy picture of the leisure time and recreational activities in Greene and Macon counties. Many have been suggested already, such as the gathering of rural folk at the crossroads store on cold or rainy days, the regular church services and the annual "big meetings," the custom of spending part or all of court week in the county seat town, the public exercises and barbecue on school-closing day, the regular meetings and the occasional colorful affairs of the secret societies, and the habit of going here and there in the family automobile or buggy to visit with kinsmen and friends—or just to be going.

RECREATION AND AMUSEMENT

Baseball, marbles, cards, and other games offer some recreational opportunities, as do also swimming pools and dance halls, while for amusement there are the school and church entertainments, movies, traveling carnivals, fairs, and the occasional black-face minstrel shows.

Baseball Very Popular.—There is a baseball team or two in each of the larger and in many of the smaller Black Belt communities. Ball teams range from pickup groups to organized clubs with a regulation diamond. Often on Saturday afternoons farm boys of either or both races collect in some level pasture and after two of the best players have divided the group, they proceed, often without gloves and mits, to see which side can get the most runs. The rivalry is very keen and many of the decisions are close. Someone acceptable to both sides is asked to call the game, and no farm boy loses the respect of his fellows quicker than by refusing to accept the decisions of the democratically selected umpire.

Some kind of ball is played at practically every school, and most of the larger schools, whether white or colored, have teams. Scheduled games come during the spring months.   No instance is known of a game between white and colored teams.   Many of the more important Negro games are played on the town ballground, an admission is charged, and whites as well as Negroes cheer for the home team.

The rivalry between regularly organized small-town white teams is very keen.   When one county seat town plays another, everybody turns out, less to see the game, it seems, than to "razz" their opponents while cheering for their own players. Much of the rivalry developed between the towns by baseball has been carried over into the annual football and basketball games of the white high schools.   Members of both races attend the school games in the spring and the town team games in the summer.

Marbles, Checkers, Cards, and Other Games.—Of less excitement to the community as a whole, but providing recreation and pastime to a considerable number, are marbles, checkers, and card games—especially poker and bridge.   In Montezuma the leading citizens can be found not infrequently back of one of the stores rolling marbles.   Everybody in town knows of this popular rendezvous and when a stranger inquires on the street about the location of a leading lawyer's office, he may be answered in this wise: "His office is on the second floor of that corner building; if he is not there you may find him behind Brown's store playing marbles."   The game is played in smooth yards now and then throughout the rural areas of both counties. Twenty miles west of Montezuma, at Ellaville, the county seat of Schley, marbles hold the spotlight of the community on summer afternoons.   The smooth shady side of the courthouse grounds is used.   The county officials, two or three storekeepers, the leading physician, and the local banker enter into the game, with white people and Negroes watching.   The game is usually called about 4:30 or 5 o'clock and continues until supper time.

Checkers, too, is a very popular game among courthouse officials, and at stores and other places where people spend their leisure time. This game is no less popular with Negroes, who often play on crudely marked cardboards with Coca-Cola and Dr. Pepper tops for men. It is no unique picture to see a white man and a Negro at checkers, with white bystanders rooting for the colored "champeen," and vice versa.

Poker and bridge receive much attention. Poker is the favorite leisure time activity at the sawmill camps and other places where men spend their evenings together. In no few instances, the best card player accumulates the major portion of the weekly earnings of a whole crew of men.

Bridge parties account for a large proportion of the evening gatherings and afternoon teas in the small Black Belt towns. The game is limited largely to the upper class of white people in the towns, and to the high school and college folk in the open country, whose parents may have nothing to do with cards, feeling that they "are of the devil." There are scores of young and older men and women in the towns who play bridge practically every night of the week, except when they go to the motion picture show.

In almost any Black Belt town, the people generally know who is the best marble player, who is the champion at checkers, and who is best at cards. There are other games which provide some recreation to the small town and rural dwellers, such as dominoes, rook, and quoits—played with discarded horseshoes.

Pools and Swimming Holes.—There are two commercially operated swimming pools for white people in Macon County. At Montezuma a cement pool is well patronized by the teen-age children of the well-to-do families. Up the Flint River eight miles north of Oglethorpe is Minoa Springs, where a small pool of crystal clear, cool water attracts occasional swimming and dancing parties from Oglethorpe and Montezuma. Of a semi-commercial nature is the spring-fed pool at Marshallville, called the Outing Club.

There are at present no commercially operated pools in Greene County. Some years ago Watson Springs, on the Greensboro-Athens highway, and Daniel Springs in the northeastern part of the county attracted picnic and dancing parties from Greensboro, Union Point, and other near-by towns. The spring at Daniel Springs is no longer cared for and the dance hall and frame hotel are rotting down. Although the hotel at Watson Springs burned a few years ago and the swimming pool is no longer maintained, the dance hall is still popular. A short time ago the Watson Springs property, consisting of 600 acres, was donated to the University of Georgia.

Groups of men and boys from the farms and small towns take advantage of the opportunities to swim in the numerous streams in both counties. But, the "Ole Swimmin' 'Ole," though popular with both races, is not so generally frequented in these counties as in communities where the people are of one race and where most families of this one race are of the same cultural class.

Dances.—In addition to the dances at the swimming pool dance halls in Macon and at the resort centers in Greene, many dance parties are given in private homes, particularly among the wealthier white families of the larger towns. Though by no means a common week-end pastime, there are some dances among the rural white tenant families. A local "fiddler" and "banger player" who never saw a written musical note, or records of the "hottest type" played on a portable phonograph, furnish music for the dancers. Stimulating drinks and boisterous conversation are typical at these occasional nocturnal gatherings of the landless whites.

The Negroes, too, have dance parties, but as with the whites, the farther away from town and the farther down the tenure ladder the fewer the dances. At Negro dances, particularly of the barn variety in the open country, there is frequently much drinking, with white as well as Negro bootleggers and white as well as Negro rowdies flourishing guns and seeking the attention of the flashiest dancers. There will be no white women present at the Negro dances, and no Negro men or women at the dance of the landless whites.

In the small towns dancing is most popular among the leading families, including those who support the church; in the open country the leading church families do not dance, except in those instances where the young folks have gone "again' their rasin'." Dancing, like card playing, is generally condemned by the rural church. This difference in the type of town and rural people who dance helps throw into relief some of the differences in the general philosophy of the small town and open country Black Belter.

School and Church Entertainments and Parties.—The school and church, in addition to their regular functions, provide some entertainment and parties for the rural people. Box suppers, spelling bees, lawn parties, amateur dramatics, bazaars, chicken pie suppers, and the like are sponsored by church and school supporters to balance the budget and to raise money for new equipment.

Chicken pie suppers, especially popular in some places, are of social value to the rural community; but, when the same families that make and sell the pies buy and eat them, there is indeed little economic gain beyond the fact that it provides a pleasant surrounding for the contribution.

Missionary societies and parent-teacher associations, with bi-weekly or monthly gatherings, provide some avenue for community participation and outside interests. But one- and two-teacher schools and small churches seldom have parent-teacher associations and missionary societies. As a rule, the leaders of the rural church and school do not see any need for improving leisure time and recreational activities in their communities.

Movies, Traveling Carnivals, and Fairs.—There is a small motion picture theater in each county. The theater at Greensboro has no arrangements for seating Negroes; the one at Montezuma has a gallery, at least half of which is reserved for Negroes.

Traveling carnivals, with Ferris wheels, swings, animal and human freaks, big snakes, and red lemonade, stop now and then for a few days in the larger towns of each county. The carnival in the county-seat town is no less of a show for the Black Belt tenant than is the Century of Progress for his landlord. There is usually no racial segregation in the carnival grounds, for Negroes and whites go where they will, but there is always a considerable amount of congregation—most of the whites voluntarily grouping themselves around some attraction and most of the Negroes gathering elsewhere. Then some unusual act is started and in the rush the races are thoroughly mixed and stay so until their attention subsides.

For several years Greene County had a fair at Greensboro, sponsored by the County Farm Agent and the leading business men. In recent years the Negro school at Montezuma has conducted a fair in its building to exhibit its work to the community, and to put on display any canned fruit and sewing and farm crops and woodwork which farmers and other schools would bring. A good number of white people came to see the exhibits.

The Black-Faced Minstrel Show.—The black-faced minstrel show is perhaps the most interesting expression of race relations in these Black Belt communities. Why do white people and Negroes like to see acts by black-faced white people? Why do the whites enjoy the ridiculous rôles conceived by the black-faced actors? Do the Negroes laugh at the jokes of the black-face or at his attempts to act like a Negro?

But not all black-faced minstrel shows use whites, some use Negro actors. In the autumn of 1934 such a minstrel stopped at Oglethorpe, the county seat of Macon County. Many of the leading white people of the town went down, bought their tickets from one white woman, handed them to another at the tent's entrance, and sat on the benches in one half the tent while Negroes, across a narrow aisle, occupied the other half. They heard a white man announce the acts, and laughed just as heartily as the Negroes at the ridiculous and daring skits of the Negro performers.

As the curtain rose one saw eight Negroes dancing on the small stage, four dark men with painted mouths and four light women in ballet costumes. Presently the four horn blowers, Negroes too, stopped abruptly and one of the dancers stepping to the edge of the stage announced: "Ladie-es and gentlemen, this first little lady is Miss Irene Jones, next is Joe Gunn, Miss Johnstone, James Kellum, Mrs. Sellers, Sam Baugh, Miss Mc-Ginder and me, Joshua Jennings"—his last words hardly said before the whole troupe was doing a twisting, jiggling dance which was followed by dialogue in which a black boy pleaded for the attention of a mulatto girl, only to be refused with: "Who, me? Why you don't know who I am; my daddy's the largest planter in Georgia." Just then the next skit broke in with some safe subject.

Ten minutes later a Negro man was strolling across the stage singing, "I'll leave my gun at home," if this and that and the other is done, each time pointing out his man; and it seemed quite accidental that he was on the front edge of the stage on the white side of the audience and pointing straight at a white man when he came to the line, "I'll leave my gun at home, if you'll leave my wife alone." Everybody laughed and almost simultaneously the next dance step was under way with the biggest black man exhorting his associates in good Black Belt diction: "Shake it, black boy; now you darkies is dancin'."

The show rambled along with the attention of the audience quickly and thoroughly transferred after each subtle gibe at the whites. At length one of the Negro actors was preaching a ser-mon—until a colleague came up from back stage and said: "Man, you sho' can preach. Why you remind me of my old daddy. He was some preacher, lived in Mariana, Florida, and the Lord called him to preach in 'Mericus, Georgia; and we walked and we walked to 'Mericus, Georgia, and my daddy preached in the middle of the street at the 'Federate Monument and the people stopped to listen the first day, and the high sheriff come to see what it was; and the second day more people come to hear my daddy preach, and the high sheriff told my daddy to get off the street, but my daddy told him he had been called to preach in 'Mericus, Georgia, and the high sheriff looked mad and went on; and on the third day my daddy was preaching and the high sheriff come and got him and hit him on the head and put him in the lock-up, and hit him some more, and my daddy was sick, bad sick, and the sheriff told him he'd let him out if he'd get right back to Mariana, Florida, and so my daddy was turned out and we started walkin', and we walked and we walked and I said, 'Do you 'spose the Lord knows how the white folks at 'Mericus, Georgia, treat us niggers?' And he didn't say nothin', and we walked and I said, 'Daddy, do you 'spose the Lord knows how the white folks at 'Mericus, Georgia, treat us niggers?' And he didn't say nothin', he was thinkin' other thoughts, and we walked on and I said, 'Daddy! daddy, do you 'spose the Lord knows how the white folks at 'Mericus, Georgia, treat us niggers?' And my daddy kept a walkin' and he said, 'Yes, son, he knows, but just don't give a damn!' And we walked on and. . . ." Suddenly a terrific din arose from back stage, the footlights went out, the actors screamed for help; then a woman struck a match and peered about the stage to find it empty and deathly silent, "Now, that's a good one on them niggers; they must a thought I had my razor wid me!" The people laughed and went out of the tent's single exit.

Within a few weeks, most likely, another black-faced show put up a tent at Oglethorpe.

LEISURE TIME ACTIVITIES

Montezuma has a Carnegie Library with over 6,000 volumes, and boasts one of the highest circulations of any library of its size in the state. In both counties there are people who cherish private libraries, read the best magazines, and take pride in their acquaintance with current literature. They are few in number and, except for an occasional small owner, belong to the planter and professional groups. But here as elsewhere many of the leading families prefer bridge to books.

When the typical dwellers of these counties find themselves with leisure, they ramble off to the store, go hunting or fishing, visit with kinsmen and neighbors and friends, or just sit and sit.

At the Trading Center on Saturday Afternoon.—Almost nobody in the Black Belt works on Saturday afternoon, except the storekeeper and the extra clerk he hires. The landlords give ration allowances, in rare instances checks, to their cropper families by Saturday noon; wage hands and casual laborers on farms and at sawmills and public works are paid off Saturday at noon. The landlord goes to town on Saturday to settle with his tenants or to secure new ones, to buy mules, or to deposit or withdraw money from the bank; the small owners, too, along with the renters and croppers and wage hands move townward. Except in severe weather, a great part of the white population and most of the able-bodied Negroes get into some trading center.

For miles in all directions by early afternoon the roads leading into the county seat and other trading centers are astir with automobiles, buggies and wagons, men astride horses and mules, and men, women, and children afoot. In the street or road about the store or stores, new automobiles and old ones, well-dressed and poorly dressed people, raw-boned mules, rickety wagons and buggies, and dogs of all sizes and colors go here and there. Everybody and everything is slowly moving about.

The crowd centers first at one store, then in front of another where a Negro is playing a banjo while one of his buddies from the sawmill is doing a clog dance. Later the largest crowd is circled around a radio which is tuned on the baseball returns. During the afternoon people of both races buy food and tobacco and sometimes clothing.

When sundown comes most of the women, all the children, and many of the men are on their way home with their packages. Some who are walking carry sacks of flour on their shoulders; some have overall pockets bulging with tobacco or baking powder. Others swing in their hands small buckets of lard or chunks of "sow belly." By late dusk only the people who live near by, and the younger men are about the store; the former go home to their supper, the latter have the store keeper cut cheese and open cans of sardines and potted ham, and pull the tops off bottled drinks until they have all they want to pay for. Some then go to parties, others remain.

Saturday night at the crossroads store is reserved for men.

Jokes are told; experiences are related. A couple of Negroes with fiddles and banjos provide additional entertainment for the few pennies and nickels flipped their way. When some "regular fellow" starts to go home he is called back to hear another "good one." After a time the whole crowd gets tired and stale; everybody yawns and goes home to bed.

Hunting and Fishing.—Other major leisure time activities for a great number of the rural folk are hunting and fishing. 'Possum dinners, fish fries, and mullet stews occur among the whites and among the Negroes. The sport-loving type spends much time in the fields and woods by day and night with shotgun, rifle, and dogs. In early fall from dusk until after midnight, the woods and swamps are combed for o'possum and coon; a little later squirrels and quail are brought down and occasionally a fox or wild turkey. Throughout the winter months many of the older people hunt with dogs almost continuously, and parents encourage the boys to set rabbit traps. Many a farm boy gets his first money by selling trapped rabbits; and sometimes an o'possum is found in the trap, which after a period of sweet milk feeding becomes a "possum dinner."

Fishing is a chief pastime for many of the farm women and children of both races as well as for the men. There is a network of foot paths along the larger streams by which they reach their favorite bank, to while away the hours in the hope of fresh fish for supper.

Along the Oconee River in Greene County and the Flint in Macon, hunting and fishing lodges are maintained by the wealthier white families of the larger towns. These retreats are usually very simple, but for those who can afford it, they provide the relaxation of hunting and fishing with a Negro servant to prepare and serve the meat. These lodges are located in unpopulated areas—the back side of a big plantation, or in an area where farming has been discontinued. They are used in much the same way as the wealthy city dweller uses his mountain lodge or an island hunting preserve.

Except for the acreage around some of the lodges and other

"DECORATIN' OFF" THE GRAVES OF THEIR DEAD—THE GRAVEYARD AT
ANTIOCH CHURCH, MACON COUNTY

OR THE LEADER, A LARGER WOODEN SLAB AND A LARGER PIECE OF PORCELAIN

PATHS ARE TO THE PLANTATION WORKERS WHAT ROADS ARE TO PLANTATION OWNE

GRAYLAND COMMUNITY HOUSE, GREENE COUNTY—PINE LOGS AND SPLIT BOARDS FRO
HILL, RELIEF LABOR FROM THE COMMUNITY, AND $2,000 FROM THE FEDERAL GOVER

"posted" land, the whole countryside is theoretically open for anyone who wishes to hunt or fish. Landless farmers, and especially Negroes, are expected to hunt in areas where their identities are readily known when the landowner comes across them.

The two races sometimes hunt together, more often they do not. But they are constantly meeting by day and night in the open fields and in the woods and swamps. It is a custom, seldom violated, that the game, no matter who kills it, goes in good spirit to the one whose dog was first on the chase. Any white hunter who would make a practice of killing and keeping the game which a Negro hunter's dog was chasing would be teased and laughed at unmercifully by his fellow white hunters. Some fishing places, it seems, are reserved by mutual agreement for the whites. But, along most streams, he who gets there first is ceded the rights of the bank. Most sportsmen readily give a choice place to the owner of the land if he comes upon the scene.

Visiting, the Chief Leisure Time Activity.—Congregating at the home of some kinsman or friend on Saturday evenings and Sunday afternoons is a popular pastime. During the summer months, watermelon cuttings are common; those who have them may serve peaches, grapes, figs, or pecans. The men sit under one tree and talk; the women gather about the porch; the small children busy themselves with a game; those of teen-age get into the family automobile and ride over the countryside, returning in time to take their parents home.

Families without cars either walk or ride in wagons to the home of some near-by family, or stay at home and talk with the neighbors who come to see them. Paths radiate across the fields and woods from one tenant house to another, and the smaller the houses the more distinct the paths. To all practical purposes, paths are to plantation workers what roads are to plantation owners. Paths lead from the tenant's house to the commissary, to the crossroads store, to the school and church and lodge, to the plantation quarters, to the neighbor's cabin, and to the midwife's house. Roads lead from the plantation owner's house to the cotton warehouse close by the railroad station, to the department store, to the high school and college, to the county seat, to the church, to the state convention of his lodge, to the hospital, to the home of his distant friends, to the rest of the world.

Visiting is an escape for the rural family from the loneliness of the solitary lives which they live; it is a very important part of the social life of the rural community. A considerable part of the inch-column news of each number of the *Herald-Journal*, Greene County weekly, is devoted to long lists of visits made in rural communities during the previous week. Some facts gleaned from the issue of September 7, 1928, are presented: The eleven communities sending in news were Bethesda, Centennial, Bairdstown, Bethany, Wesley Chapel, Harmony Grove, Grayland, Woodville, Greshamville, Siloam, and Liberty. From the first seven, the news was limited to the visits of the week. In the latter six, in addition to individual visits, mention was made of family reunions and birthday parties, births, illnesses, deaths, church and school activities, the weather, and the crops.

Who Visited Whom.—The total space taken by the news items from these eleven rural communities amounted to a little more than ninety-five column-inches of the *Herald-Journal*, or four and one-half full page columns, sixty-five of them being devoted solely to telling about the individual visits of the week. The typical community news runs like this:

Miss Rosabel Andrews returned home Sunday from a visit to her sister, Mrs. Guy Wagnon, of Madison.

Mrs. James T. King and Daughter, Corabel, spent a couple of days with Mrs. King's parents, Mr. and Mrs. J. Y. Rhodes of Crawfordsville last week.

Messers. A. L. Davis and J. A. Crawford were in our community awhile Thursday morning.

Mr. and Mrs. Bob Bramlett returned from a visit to Commerce last Wednesday.

Mr. and Mrs. James T. King and Corabel and Hugh King went down to view the destruction of Jordans Mill and milldam Sunday.

Mr. and Mrs. Cecil Taylor attended church at Margarets Grove Sunday and were the guests of Mr. and Mrs. C. A. Taylor.

Misses Elizabeth Monk, of Robinson, and Lillianbel Hancock, of South Carolina, were day guests of Miss Veazey Mae Andrews Monday.

Mr. and Mrs. C. B. King attended church at Margarets Grove Sunday and Sunday night and were the guests of their daughter, Mrs. Omer Taylor.

The news from each of the communities was filled with names, more than seven hundred appearing in this one issue of the paper.

The weekly social contacts of the rural Black Belt community are suggested by the area over which these visits extended. Of 95 visits by local people 44 were to the homes of rural neighbors, 8 to Greensboro and Union Point, 23 to small towns outside Greene County, 14 to Atlanta, Macon, Augusta, and other large cities in Georgia, and 6 outside the state. There were 38 instances in which families or individuals from outside visited in these eleven communities during the week: 13 were from small towns in adjoining counties, 19 from Atlanta, Macon, and other larger Georgia cities, and 6 from outside the state. The number of visitors from outside the county was doubtless larger than usual because of the time of year, for early September is within vacation time.

Community Happenings.—The following unrelated items, gathered from the eleven clippings, indicate other leisure time and recreational activities of these rural communities: "Several of the young people enjoyed a fox hunt Monday night." "The Smith reunion was held Sunday, August 26th, at the home of Mr. and Mrs. Foster Smith at Godfrey. Barbecue and all good things that go with it composed the dinner. Such dinners and family reunions are always enjoyed by the families connected, but always have to come to a separation, so when night fell, the families departed." "The community barbecue on last Thursday was enjoyed by a large crowd." "A delightful social event of August 20th was the party given by Mrs. Brown Caldwell and her sister, Miss Claude Caldwell. The reception rooms thrown ensuite were beautifully and artistically decorated in summer flowers. A delicious salad course and fruit punch frosted with sherbet was served. Twenty guests enjoyed this happy occasion." "Mr. Clifton Bonds, of Swords, and Miss Milidia Phelps attended the movies in Greensboro Thursday evening." "Miss Clara Thurmond and Mr. Claud Thurmond, of Cedar Grove, spent Sunday night with their grandmother, Mrs. H. D. Thurmond." "We are beginning to see a few bolls of cotton opening which means that it won't be long before the gins will be humming." "Mr. and Mrs. J. P. Wagnon spent Sunday at the home of Mr. Oscar Rainwater at Mosquito Crossing." "Sibley School opened last Monday with Mrs. Archer principal and Miss Myrtle Stevens assistant. There were twenty-five pupils with more to enter later." "Our school opens here next Monday. Let every child in the school district be enrolled the first day as it is very important in making up the classes. . . . Let's everyone pull together as this is the first year of consolidation and it needs the coöperation of every patron in the school district to make it a success." "Mr. Mitchell Bryan of Putnam County has moved into the home of Mrs. Ann Bryan." "Mr. F. B. Freeman is doing some improvements on his home which will add very much to its appearance." "Masters Carey Kelly, William Durham, Samuel Huff, Eugene Cardell, and Misses Elizabeth Wilson and Julia Lowe Durham, will be baptized here Sunday morning." "Rev. P. D. Doty a returned missionary from India delivered a very interesting lecture at Wesley Chapel last Wednesday night." "Services closed here at the Baptist Church Wednesday morning after the five candidates were baptized. Several from here are attending preaching services at Woodville this week." "Rev. A. C. Hall, of Social Circle, conducted the services at the Methodist Church. He brought the people some wonderful messages that we trust will bear fruit in the coming years." "Quite a number attended the services at Centennial last week."

In noting the mention of church services it is well to remember that early September is in the latter part of "big meeting" season. The weekly newspaper in Macon County does not feature community news items to the extent that the Greene County paper does, but there is little indication that visiting is less popular there.

Even in the eleven communities where reported visits involved more than 700 people, mention is made only of persons belonging to a few leading white families. The majority of the whites, and all the Negroes, are completely ignored. Class demarcations within the white race appear nowhere more marked than in the matter of family visits. The families of white owners visit white owners, and further than that, the most prosperous white owner families usually visit only with other prosperous families; the landless families visit with other landless families. Oh, yes, "blood is thicker than water," but when the wealthy brother does not share his wealth with his unwealthy brother, it is not "thick" enough to produce many visits between their families. Similar distinctions, perhaps a little less marked, appear within the Negro group.

Scant Recreational Activities for Rural Masses.—The majority of both races find nothing to do but to sit idly around, tramp off to their neighbors, or while away the time at the store. Their houses are unattractive and empty and their minds are unstimulated. Scores of farm boys and girls seldom hear the birds which sing in the trees over their houses at early morning and at the ends of their cotton rows during the day; they do not know there are flowers in every nook and corner of the fields and woods. Many a farm boy and girl can recognize only three or four birds; they do not know the names of more than a half-dozen insects.

In these homes there is very little stimulation for the growing child. The tired and fatalistic parents are interested in only a few things; too often, the few books they have are pictureless and dull, antiquated theories about philosophy or theology sold by transient peddlers. The child who begins a hobby is soon discouraged, for a hobby is certain to require either money or time, or both. Money is always scarce; during the busy seasons even small hands are put to hoes and cotton picking.

Some Suggestions.—Church, school, and community house can make important contributions, even within present conditions, toward a more wholesome use of leisure time. The rural church, with the leadership of the pastor, could readily sponsor for the boys and girls study groups, ball games, picnics, candy pullings, and parlor games. Within each racial group, the greatest handicaps to this development are the paucity of resident rural pastors and the general feeling that the church should not interest itself in helping the young people have a good time.

The rural school perhaps has the best opportunity of providing wholesome leisure time activities. A well-conceived schedule of ball games, dramatics, and debating clubs for the younger people, and parent-teacher associations, farmers' meetings, and mothers' clubs for the grown-ups would make of it a real community center. Movies, too, of educational and recreational value could be brought to the school. The school buses, however, will need to be used at times to transport to the meetings parents as well as children who live a great distance from the school and have no automobile. Otherwise, the community program of the consolidated school will be affording additional opportunities to the families with transportation of their own, while robbing the other families of even the occasional spelling bee or box supper which would have been held at the one-teacher school.

What possibility is there of building a community program around a rural Negro school with its poorly-paid and often poorly-trained teacher, its shabby and inadequately equipped house? Or, what possibility is there for the public transportation of Negro pupils to a central consolidated school? Even under present handicaps, a few of the one-teacher Negro schools are affording some little opportunity for the constructive use of leisure time through dramatics, spelling bees, farm and home clubs, and handicraft work.

The Federal Emergency Relief Administration is now completing a log cabin community house for whites at Grayland, four miles west of Siloam. Though smaller, this building is patterned after the one in the Springfield Negro community in Hancock County, twelve miles away. The cost of the Grayland building, made of pine logs taken from the site, was about $2,000. It is planned to have all types of community meetings, clubs, and group games here. The white home demonstration agent is especially interested in the project, and hopes to secure the cooperation of relief authorities in building a half dozen such community houses for whites in the county in the near future. A request by Negroes at Greensboro for assistance from the relief authorities in constructing a community house, also of logs, was turned back by the state administrator's office on some technicality.

The institution or agency interested in improving the recreational opportunities in the Black Belt must always remember that the rural family does not need more places to go so much as better places to go, particularly better schools and churches, and above all more interesting things to stay at home with—the crux of the rural situation.

CHAPTER XXI

FOR THE FUTURE

WE HAVE NOTED that the generally low incomes of rural families in Greene and Macon counties are related to farm tenure status and to race, and that the relationship of the average white farm family to the land has been lowered rather than raised by the assumption that the Negro must be kept servile, dependent, and landless. By the very nature of the plantation, the landless white family competes with the landless Negro family for a tenant farm. They have similar incomes, similar food, and at moving times may exchange houses. There seems little possibility that the landless white can rise without a corresponding rise for the landless Negro. Furthermore, the southern urban laborer cannot escape the low standards of the rural dwellers, for there is always the chance that if he takes part in any organized effort to increase his pay, he will be displaced by this cheaper rural laborer who will move into the city if he can get work there.

It seems evident that the ownership of land by Negroes under the present conditions of purchase can benefit but relatively few families, and these only in a restricted way: for landownership is limited almost solely to Negroes who keep themselves acceptable to the landed whites, to whom the preservation of the plantation system is paramount, and to the landless whites, to whom the maintenance of artificial distinctions between themselves and the Negroes with whom they compete is a cherished proof of their racial superiority.

It has been shown that the big plantations include the most fertile soil of both counties, while the poorer soil is the home of the small resident owner-operator. The fact that the rural dwellers on the poorest land have withstood the depression much better than those on the most fertile land forcibly suggests that the plantation economy, with its few privileged owners and many dependent workers, is ill-suited to the highest development of a region's physical and human resources. When rich land does not support its workers as well as poor land, the system employed on the rich land is in need of modification.[1]

The methods now employed in the production of crops in Greene and Macon counties utilize the labor of all the members of the farm family from sun to sun for a few months of each year. The rest of the time they have little opportunity for remunerative employment, and tire of idleness.

By continuous labor and enforced idleness, by low incomes and restricted outlook, everybody gets fagged out and seems to stay that way. Earning a living under a system which keeps the workers dependent and the owners ridden by debt leaves both planters and tenants without security or hope. Where the majority of the population chronically receive small incomes and maintain low planes of living, they come to expect nothing better. In truth, the fatalism which accompanies their low plane of living does to their minds what inadequate food, malaria, and hookworm do to their bodies.

To improve the living conditions of the rural people in these Black Belt counties involves not only an adaptation of institutional programs but an economic reorganization which will increase family incomes and foster the independence and self-direction of all the people. The present relation of man to land, of landlord to tenant, of white man to black man largely accounts for the crude agricultural practices, the resulting low planes of

[1] The location of the poorest people on the richest land in these counties has many striking parallels: the concentration of the relief load in the urban and wealthiest communities in Greene and Macon counties, the greater proportion of people on unemployment relief in the largest cities in the nation where the per capita wealth is the highest, the submerged lot of the agricultural workers in the fertile Yazoo-Mississippi Delta and in California's rich Imperial Valley, the low wages of the laborers in the Reynolds and American tobacco factories and in the textile mills owned by the wealthiest corporations, the low wages of the clerks in the five- and ten-cent stores and in many other chain-stores, and the small salaries of the rank and file of the employees of most giant corporations.

living, and the restricted outlooks of the Black Belt dwellers, particularly the landless.

For the rank and file of plantation workers there is little hope either in the rejuvenation of the present Black Belt plantation or in its collapse. The cotton plantation can be revitalized only by mechanizing it, which, without a change in the prevailing philosophy, will result in the employment of fewer people without materially raising the level of the majority of those still employed. On the other hand, as the plantation system disintegrates it disinherits its owners and enforces many of its workers to emigrate without materially improving the lot of those who remain behind. Dependent and fatalistic people, exhausted soil, and crippled institutions are the natural remnants of the collapsing plantation economy.

The independent renters and small owners which emerge in these impoverished and decadent areas constitute a new type of American farmer, almost as poor as the share croppers, but, within their limited sphere, almost as independent as the plantation owners. Here are the beginnings of peasantry in America. Indeed, the collapse of the Black Belt plantation is a preface to peasantry.

With no reasonable hope that an adequate civilization for the majority of the rural dwellers will come either with the rejuvenation or with the collapse of the cotton plantation system, the reclamation of Greene and Macon counties and of much of the cotton South awaits a constructive land policy—a use of the land which will serve the people who live on it and the larger economy, national and international, of which it is a part. Here is an enormous undertaking, but it can succeed where the plantation system has failed if it enables the poorest farmers to build up the soil, to own livestock, to raise vegetables and fruits for their own tables, to coöperate with their fellows making their purchases and in producing and marketing crops—in short, if it enables the landless farmers to attain ownership and self-direction on an adequate plane. Comfortable homes, more doctors, better schools, and wholesome human relations can be maintained only through such basic economic advances. These are not simple matters, and their accomplishment will require the investment of large sums of public money and an administrative personnel with scientific training and a bold faith in the common man.

INDEX